Longman Resources for Instructors

D0779644

Teaching in Progress: Theories, Practices, and Scenarios

Josephine Koster Tarvers
Winthrop University

An imprint of Addison Wesley Longman, Inc.

New York • Reading, Massachusetts • Menlo Park, California • Harlow, England
Don Mills, Ontario • Sydney • Mexico City • Madrid • Amsterdam

Editor-in-Chief: Patricia Rossi
Development Editor: Mark Gerrard
Supplements Editor: Donna Campion
Electronic Production Manager: David Munger/DTC
Electronic Page Makeup: Karen Milholland/DTC

Longman Resources for Instructors: Teaching in Progress: Theories, Practices, and Scenarios

ISBN: 0-321-02386-2

1 2 3 4 5 6 7 8 9 10 - 00 99 98 97

In Memoriam

Glendin A. Koster

what we have loved
Others will love, and we will teach them how.
The Prelude *XIV. 446-447*

Contents

Preface

> Let us try again. A direct hit is not likely here. The best one can do is try different approaches toward the same center, whenever the opportunity arises.
>
> —KENNETH BURKE

You should *see* my study. It's about 15' by 20', with an alcove for my computer, and every available surface is covered with paper and books. Revising a book *once* is hard work; revising it for the fourth time has been agonizing. But I think it's been well worth the effort. Chris Anson, Bob Schwegler, and I agree about many things on the teaching of writing, but we disagree in some places too, and it's been very profitable for me to revise my work in the light of our conversations. Writers need audiences, and they've been a great one.

When I wrote the first edition of this book it was virtually the only one of its kind. Both the sheer numbers of people who have relied on it and the number of imitations of it which have appeared in the last few years have served to emphasize to me both how impossible a notion it is that I—or anyone—can tell a reader *everything* needed to teach writing, and the responsibility I have to try to do the impossible. And having spent some years working with teachers and with writers beyond the academy, I realize even more what this book *should* do—and can't possibly. Rhetorical and composition scholarship have exploded in the last four decades, and it has proven impossible for me to read everything produced on the subject, let alone digest it all here. (Bob Schwegler sent me a list compiled by his graduate students of *books* published in composition in the last five years: it's unbelievably long!) So my first compromise in this book has been to focus very sharply: I'll discuss, sometimes not in very great detail, what I think someone with a literary studies background should know to start teaching academic writing. The bibliography has been focused in the same way: I've picked a few comprehensive articles to be included here, and included from the rest of the scholarship some of the works I've found most useful over the years. Where I could, I've included practical tips called "Teaching in Progress," as well as examples, references, and strategies for you to use. Inspired by Chris Anson and his colleagues, I've also added "Scenarios"—descriptions of real-world situations that I and my friends have encountered in the teaching of writing—for you to reflect on and possibly prepare for. I hope that what's helped me can in some ways help you.

I've kept the things from previous editions that you've told me you needed the most: the sample handouts, the syllabi, the full discussion of grading (which has been expanded even further), the essential articles. Frequent references throughout the text tie it to specific sections of the *Longman Handbook*, to help you make connections. This revision, like the three preceding it, has benefited greatly from the suggestions of people like you—offered both formally and informally. I would be delighted to have your suggestions about works, topics, or articles you'd like to see included in later editions of this book. Send them to me at the English Department, Winthrop University, Rock Hill, SC 29733-0001, or e-mail me at tarversj@winthrop.edu. If you or your classes want to write to me, I promise to answer.

This book doesn't embrace any one particular "camp" of writing theory, unlike the *Longman Handbook* itself. I've tried, instead, to do justice to as many as I can. It pleased me no end when a reader of the third edition wrote that "I thought that you belonged to [a particular camp of theorists], but when I reread this I realized you didn't." Good. That's what I intended. To paraphrase Ann McCaffrey, my hair is auburn, my eyes are brown, and the rest is subject to change without notice. What suits me may not suit you, and vice versa. So look to see a number of theoretical positions reflected here. My opinions are clearly marked, so that you can tell whose position is being expressed.

Part I reviews some of the most important theoretical bases for the teaching of writing, and explains the theory that underlies the *Longman Handbook* (If you are rushed for time, you may want to jump ahead to Part II, but for your own sake, come back and read the parts you've skipped; they'll explain things in Part II more clearly.) I've emphasized the relationship between scrutiny of language already produced (literary criticism) and scrutiny of the ways in which language is produced (writing process theory) so that you can connect what you may have learned in your studies of literature to what you'll be doing as a teacher of writing; where possible, I've attempted to show how the two theoretical schools have made parallel discoveries.

Part II covers the more practical aspects of writing instruction, from course inception to evaluation. Writing programs vary widely: some emphasize self-discovery; some writing about the writings of others, nonfictional and fictional; some the mastery of various modes and genres; and some writing in a variety of disciplines. The information in Part II is designed to be applied in any of these situations, and does not endorse any particular type of curriculum. This section begins with basic information about the design of courses and the selection of course materials. It moves on to conducting classes, designing writing assignments, and helping students understand and improve their abilities in all stages of the writing process. Two chapters are devoted to evaluation: the first deals with evaluating students' writing, including portfolios, and the second with evaluating whole courses and the performances of students and teachers in them. You'll find material on basic writing, critical reading, teaching in diverse classrooms, writing centers, portfolio grading, and gender issues; the material on computers, community, and collaboration has been expanded at reader request.

Part III provides a small reference section for your information. It includes an anthology of articles on the teaching of writing. The authors represented are all experienced classroom teachers, and their articles are characterized by a keen sense of translating theory into practice and by the provision of useful bibliographic references. The section concludes with a longer bibliography of secondary references.

One of the nicest things about belonging to the community of composition and rhetoric scholars is that, whether we agree or disagree on our theories and practices, we almost always talk to each other, share ideas, hone our thinking on the wits of others, spend hours over a beer sharpening our appreciation of each other's work. One of my chief professional (as well as personal) pleasures comes from participating in this ongoing conversation. George Kane and Erika Lindemann have taught me more about writing, teaching, and professionalism than I can ever acknowledge. Debra Boyd, Gloria Jones, Jane Bowman Smith, Bill Sullivan and Phebe Davidson have offered friendship and critical ears as well as helped me track down obscure references in the wilds of South Carolina. *Gratia ago.* And just as I was completing this book, word came that Robert Bain, my first teaching mentor, had passed away. It's impossible for me to list all the things he taught me, or to express my gratitude properly, but he was one of the kindest, most intelligent, and most dedicated teachers I have ever known, and I will miss him dearly.

To Maxine Hairston and John Ruszkiewicz for getting me into this in the first place; to my former colleagues Kathleen Kelly, Randy Woodland, Emily Seelbinder, Bob Barton, and Barry Qualls, and to too many others to name here—I extend my thanks for many provocative comments and suggestions, and lots of encouragement. Special thanks to my students in the Winthrop Executive MBA program, my employees at In*Scribe, my clients, Bob Yeager and the members of the Effective Writing Seminars at the BOC Group, Murray Hill, NJ, who keep reminding me of the value writing has in communities outside the academy, and who have taught me the truth and falsehood of many of my beliefs about teaching writing. I particularly thank my colleagues here at Winthrop, especially Evelyne Weeks, Bill Naufftus, Kelly Richardson, Dottie Graham, Gabriella Davis, Scott Gilbert, Marguerite Neary, and Susan Lancaster, for contributing ideas and making me go to lunch.

Several friends teaching at other institutions contributed scenarios anonymously because of the political situations at their schools; you know who you are, and I thank you. Finally, a special thanks to the friends I've never seen face to face, but to whom I "talk" regularly on the WCENTER electronic list, especially Bobbie Silk, Jon Olson, Neal Lerner, Mickey Harris, Jeanne Simpson, Eric Crump, Beth Rapp Young, Latisha LaRue [a.k.a. Katie Fischer] and all the others. The sounding board you've given me has been invaluable. The number of teachers who have taken the time to give me their comments, suggestions, and criticisms of the four editions of *Teaching Writing: Theories and Practice*, has astonished, delighted, and inspired me: I am immensely grateful. Needless to say, any weaknesses left in this book are not your fault!

My husband Rich is my strength and support—as always. And the four furrorists—B. B., Mishka, Morris, and Sable—have reminded me that texts, like the rights to use desk and couch space, are communally negotiated; and that one should not leave a teacup unattended on a pile of papers. Thanks for being there.

—ROCK HILL, S.C.
JULY 1996

PART

1

THEORIES

Introduction
Literature, Composition, Rhetoric

If you don't yet recognize the power of freshman composition teachers, know this: one of us is responsible for getting Jesse Helms elected. In the late sixties, Helms was the "After the News Editorial Reader" on a television station in North Carolina when he heard about a freshman writing assignment that had been given at UNC-Chapel Hill. The teaching assistant had asked students to read Andrew Marvell's "To His Coy Mistress," then asked them to write their own modern-day version as an assignment. Helms was outraged. "Those composition teachers are forcing our young folks to commit seductions," he thundered. The resulting firestorm of publicity led to Helms' first successful run for office; you know the rest. If you're reading this book, you either are or are contemplating teaching writing, probably for the first time. It's a high-stakes game. Welcome!

All of us who are in this business have at least one thing in common: we love well-chosen words. Most of us love—and have been trained *how* to love—the words selected and arranged by "great" writers, the professional authors of past and present, to see writing through the lens of literature. A growing number of us, too, have learned to prize words *about* well-chosen words, and theories about them; Derrida, Eagleton, Kristeva, Culler, Fish, Kolodny, and Vygotsky are among the names we value. It's safe to love these words; they're printed in anthologies, shelved in libraries, and discussed in scholarly journals. Slowly but steadily, many more of us come to the classroom with formal preparation in rhetoric and composition; the names of Elbow and Berlin and Rorty and Bizzell are among those whose approaches to language we value.

That love of language, however, doesn't make us immune to a number of disputes over the territory we are covering. Take the name of our subject, for instance. Is it freshman writing, composition, first-year writing, introduction to academic discourse, or what? (I'll use at least the first three interchangeably in this book.) Does what we teach belong in departments of English, of Rhetoric, of Writing, of General Studies, or of Discourse? Wayne Booth laments in "The Common Aims That Divide Us" that

> Of all our current fake polarities, perhaps the one that would surprise our ancestors most is that between "composition" and "literature." It would have surprised them because they could never have dreamed that one might try to teach scholars to write well without at the same time trying to teach them to read and enjoy what is well-written. (1)

Yet this "fake" polarity exists and continues to have a serious effect on the teaching of writing; it may well constrain what you teach, what you may *not* teach, and why you teach it. In most schools (the term that I will use generically to embrace universities, four-year colleges, and two-year colleges), the faculty is clearly divided into the elite, which teaches "interpretation," and the underclass, which teaches "composition." Since we like to pretend that manners still count for *something*, our Mandarin wars have so far been confined to traditional academic battlefields: the journal article, the conference panel, and, in their most bloody form, the tenure committee. (Recent MLA suggestions to the contrary, many schools still count scholarship in rhetoric and composition as "teaching," not "scholarship," in evaluating candidates for tenure; see Sledd's essay in Lindemann & Tate [1991] for a devastating picture of how the world works, and Holbrook [1991] for the depressing statistical profile of what writing teaching can be like.) But the wars continue.

There is a second polarity that, disturbingly, has begun to arise in the past few years: that between "rhetoric" and "composition." Perhaps it is a growing pain of the discipline, but in some cases (and some departments) rhetoric, perceived as a theoretical discipline, has come to be privileged over composition, which is marginalized as pedagogy. I don't make that distinction in this book. Instead, I see them as two sides of the same coin: rhetoric looks at the theoretical aspects of writing, while composition focuses more on praxis. Neither can exist without each other, for there must be writing for the theoreticians to analyze, and the practitioners must have theories to apply.

Moreover, those of us who have chosen rhetoric and composition as our areas of "English" usually have different interests and outlooks than our colleagues in literary analysis. In a significant recent essay, "Composition as a Social Science," John Bassett argues that

> Serious study of composition and nonliterary writing is usually grounded in rhetoric and allied less to the traditional humanities than to the social sciences, which through sociolinguistics, cognitive psychology, and ethnographic study have provided the field with a great deal of its methodological and substantive foundation. (323)

And at times it seems he's right; in some of the scholarship that dominates our field, it's hard to tell whether we're reading anthropology, psychology, political science, or a hybrid of many disciplines. But the concern with language, and with the lives behind the language, permeates the discussion. To quote Charles Moran's "A Life in the Profession,"

> "We are distinguished . . . by an empirical bent. We'd rather be close to the place where, as those in the automobile culture would say, the rubber meets the road. We are, moreover, a social crew: not for us monastic years in the library carrel. We need to be working with others, implicated in society. We also want to help people. We want to make things go better, in our classes and beyond. (Lindemann & Tate 160)

This is the fifth edition of a book that wants to help *you* "make things go better," in [y]our classes and beyond. I talk about theoretical approaches to writing from both the literature and composition perspectives, because each of us comes to our classroom from a different background and what resonates with one teacher may not help another make the connections he needs to make. You'll also find information about learning styles, pragmatics, and a number of scenarios to consider as you prepare for teaching. All of these are meant to help you position yourself in the large and lively community of writing teachers. It's a community with its differences, but also a community with considerable strength and cohesion. The Roman rhetoricians who established the paradigms of our field two millennia ago may have claimed *Non convivium est,*° but it's a wonderful, challenging, rewarding profession. What follows, I hope, will prepare you to enter it with eyes open.

° "It's no party out there."

2

Approaching Writing
from Literary Studies:
Products, Processes, and the
Problem of Language

Jacques Derrida speaks for writing instructors as well as literary critics when he opens *Of Grammatology* with the observation that "However the topic is considered, *the problem of language* has never been simply one problem among others." Because language is our chief way of making and expressing meaning, the complex difficulties it poses must occupy the chief part of our attention in writing instruction. Derrida's "problem of language," of course, is the chief province of literary criticism, and it has governed the development of many competing—and many complementary—views of discourse in this century. Likewise it is the concern of those who teach rhetoric and composition. Language controls and constrains the schemas we produce, inherit, and modify to interpret texts, so the problems it poses must be addressed in the writing classroom. What follows is an attempt to sketch briefly, and without the complexity each of these theories provides, some major critical responses to language as problem, and to suggest the relations of these theories to the major composition theories which will be elaborated in this book. If you aren't yet familiar with these theorists, don't worry: first of all, you'll be hearing about them often in your career, and second, the bibliography contains a number of sources that will help you learn about them. This discussion, of necessity, can't delve into the deepest intricacies of the subject; it's intended instead to suggest affinities between literary and composition theory, to bridge the gaps we sometimes perceive between the two. Seeing how literary product and composition process intersect may help you "find your feet" in writing theory.

The New Critics and Formalists

Probably the first major critical theorists to influence writing instruction in this century were the New Critics and Formalists, who considerably influenced the schools of composition which examined the end-products of writing, the kinds of products students produce. These product-oriented schools of composition, like those of literature, emphasized the essential identity of form and content and consequently privileged the study of form as inviolable and unassailable. Context and historical considerations became irrelevancies. Terry Eagleton, no admirer of such theories, sarcastically describes the New Critics' procedures in this way:

> The New Critics ... [insisted] that the author's intentions in writing, even if they could be recovered, were of no relevance to the interpretation of his or her text. Neither were the emotional responses of particular readers to be confused with a poem's meaning. ... Rescuing the text from author and reader went hand in hand with disentangling it from any social or historical context. ... Literature was a solution to social problems, not part of them; the poem must be plucked free of the wreckage of history and hoisted into a sublime space above it.(48)

The text, not its effects, then, lies at the heart of New Criticism. Coherence, shapeliness, and appropriate language (especially metaphor) are the proper objects of scrutiny. Such theories are still prevalent in composition textbooks. Traditionally these include descriptions of various modes or forms of discourse (narration, description, exposition, argumentation, "creative" writing); the shapes such forms take ("keyhole" introductions, the five-paragraph theme, the sentence outline, the resume); and the language for coherent, appropriate discourse (figurative language, logical fallacies, transitions), and may also contribute to some of your colleagues' concerns with "standards" in writing courses.

Because form was so effectively linked with content, texts influenced by the New Critics tended to omit exercises encouraging students to imitate models or to experiment with different ways of treating a particular subject. Likewise, because they de-emphasized context, they tended to present only parts of large discourses—usually paragraphs pulled from longer works—without identifying the original source, audience, or context. They were also (historically) weak on invention or prewriting exercises; idea and shape were expected to come into existence together, embodying Eliot's famous criteria of "wholeness, harmony, and brilliance." In student writing, these criteria are reflected in an emphasis on the modes of discourse and on mechanical correctness.

Cleanth Brooks and Robert Penn Warren's *Modern Rhetoric* (1949) was the first textbook adaptation of New Critical principles to the teaching of writing; still in print, it testifies to the generations of scholars believing in this approach. Other New Critics who have influenced modern composition theory and practice are Kenneth Burke, whose "dramatistic" theory of discourse between a sender and receiver and "pentad" of questions for finding material to write about are incorporated in many texts, and I. A. Richards, whose emphasis on "coherence" and the text's ability to confound our expectations is still reflected in many sets of grading standards.

In response to the New Critics, the so-called "Chicago School" argued for the restoration of classical rhetoric with a neo-Aristotelian emphasis on invention, classification, and imitation of professional models. The work of the Chicago formalists led to the reintroduction of heuristic *topoi*, to the use of literary examples to teach style, and, through ways too complex to describe here, to the development of sentence-combining strategies. Wayne Booth's essay "The Rhetorical Stance" introduced the study of audience and voice. Francis Christensen's generative rhetoric of the sentence and paragraph came from a reapplication of Aristotelian principles. And the impulse to classify forms of discourse led to the work of Kinneavy, Britton, and Moffett, among others (see Chapter 3). Structuralism's chief legacy has been in our emphasis on forms, and possibly formats; it presents standards for what texts should look like, and by implication, *be* like.

Speech-Act and Reader-Response Theory

Both speech-act and reader-response theories have also contributed to our understanding of writing instruction. Speech-act theory at its core assumes discourse is action; we use language to obtain some tangible or intangible result. Textbooks incorporating this assumption focus on both the writer's purpose (the desired result) and very pragmatic forms of transactional discourse (hence the ubiquitous sections on business writing, résumés, report writing, and documentation in most "composition" texts). Reader-response theory argues, in its simplest terms, that reading is as much a compositional act as is writing, because meaning exists in the *transactions between* writers and readers (Jacoby 1989/90). Reader-response and allied theories stressing reading as the construction of meaning currently play an important role in composition theory; as G. Douglas Atkins has wryly noted,

> as reading as an activity has declined, the Age of the Reader has arrived. . . . In what amounts to a virtual paradigm shift, emphasis on the reader seems to have replaced focus on "The text itself." (49)

A great deal of beneficial work in audience analysis done recently is based on reader-response methods and ideas.

One of the earliest versions of reader-response criticism was Louise Rosenblatt's *Literature as Exploration* (1938), which emphasized the reader's affective responses to the text, especially as that response was conditioned by the reader's past experiences. Although eclipsed for many years by the work of the New Critics, Rosenblatt's position has been resurrected in recent years, and her 1978 book *The Reader, the Text, the Poem* is now required reading in many graduate seminars in composition and rhetoric. Likewise Stanley Fish's earlier essays (many collected in *Is There a Text in This Class?* [1980]) discuss how readers construct hypotheses which are either confirmed or refuted as they progress through a text, and have led to his theory of interpretative communities, the notion that readers construct texts from the cues provided by the author based on communally-held assumptions. Wolfgang Iser, especially in *The Implied Reader* (1974), also focuses on this concept of cues the readers interpret.

Reading and writing as fundamental ways of knowing, for both writers and readers, are currently very popular in composition theory. Ann Berthoff's important work on reading and writing as ways of making meaning draws strongly upon reader-response; so do the discourse systems of Britton and Moffett, which hold that all writing starts from what writers know and move toward what they must discover. Cue recognition by readers forms the heart of David Bartholomae and Anthony Petrosky's, Patricia Bizzell's, and James Reither's expansions of the writing process into academic and institutional discourse situations. (These are described in Chapter 3, below.)

Much of this work draws from Michel Foucault's explorations in *The Archaeology of Knowledge* (1969). Foucault's complex theory of language and knowing explores in detail the conventions that various disciplines and "discourse communities" use, their reasonableness and applicability, and communally agreed-upon standards for the constructions of texts. Knowing, to Foucault, comes not just from observing things, but by observing how things work in systems, and how those systems are constructed and supported. The *tagmemic* system of Young, Becker, and Pike (described in Chapter 3) works in a similar way, determining the place of an item within a socially-constructed framework.

Closely allied to the reader-response school is the work of Mikhail Bakhtin. He argues for using dialogue as a way of understanding not only language and literature, but psychology and ideology as well. For him, dialogue involves both the actual transactions in language between speakers and hearers or readers and writers, and the negotiations they make "between the lines" of a text. To discover these often-hidden messages, both writers and readers must be aware of the historical context for the piece of writing, the social position of its readers and writer, and the very complex—"heteroglossic"—relationships between them.

Structuralism

Roland Barthes, who in his early work bridges the gap between semiotics and structuralism, also points us to the structuralist influence on composition theory. Structuralism assumes the multiplicity of meanings inherent in any text; connotation provides the possibility for a number of reader responses, all of which may be substantiated from the text. Composition theorists have incorporated this work into a number of studies of audience. We have come to assume that, just as a writer can assume many personae in writing a text, so readers can assume many different characters in accepting and construing a text. As Lisa Ede and Andrea Lunsford have argued, this theory also allow us to see that writers both address and invoke audiences simultaneously (1984, 1996). Michael Polyani's work on articulation is related to the structuralists to some extent. In *Personal Knowledge* (1958), he argues that there are two kinds of knowing, tacit and articulate, and that language study most properly should consist of explorations of the borders between the two, in systematic, "scientific," yet personal ways.

The work of Ferdinand de Saussure gave structuralism three key concepts that have broad applications for writing instruction: *langue*, the system and convention of language; *parole*, an individual communicative act conditioned by *langue*; and *ecriture*, the combination of personal and cultural codes as writing. *Langue/parole* has obvious similarities with both transformational-generative grammar's *competence/performance* opposition and many modern theories of error analysis (e.g. Bartholomae [1980]). We admit, for instance, that just because students may write a comma splice in one paper or a speaker commit a Spoonerism (problems with *parole*), that doesn't mean that their written or spoken abilities in language (*langue*) are necessarily deficient—these may just be mistakes in production on a particular occasion.

Likewise Young, Becker, and Pike's tagmemic theory (described below, p. 19) is based on the structural concept of the sign and how it differs from other signs in its discourse system. While they draw their analogies from physics, they are wrestling with semiotic problems: how do we teach students to know what belongs and what doesn't belong in a piece of writing? How can we describe this kind of writing? How can we characterize what the audience needs to know about it? The study of social constructions of discourse communities, including the work of Bruffee (1984), also draws on the concept of *ecriture* in its requirement for differing, and sometimes conflicting, implicit and explicit "codes" in writing (see chapter 3 for more elaboration of "social construction").

Post-Structuralism

Two forms of post-structuralist literary theory, deconstruction and intertextuality, have made themselves felt in composition theory and writing classrooms. As practiced by some critics, deconstruction, the critical exploitation of ambiguities and illogic often inherent in a text, looks like the traditional teacher's method of marking student papers. Vincent B. Leitch describes this kind of deconstructive reading thus:

> The deconstructer does not simply enter a work with an attentive eye for the loose thread or the alogical element that will decenter the text; he or she intends *beforehand* to reverse the traditional hierarchies that constitute the grounds for the text. (81)

In other words, the deconstructer presupposes that any text can be decentered, that gaps can be found. Such a prejudice may lead some readers to misinterpret or devalue the texts they encounter, even when those texts are meritorious. Yet deconstructive reading, by posing a conflict between ideal structure and actual construct, between competing hierarchies of meaning, between binary oppositions, seems to offer great resources for the teacher of writing. Teaching students a sense of linguistic "play"—perhaps loosely paraphrased as "flexibility" and more politically expressed by expressivist composition theorists such as Ken Macrorie as "subversion"—might open them up to other choices, other structures, other strategies, and other ways of communicating. As Jane Tompkins points out, post-structuralism can't really be *applied* to texts, because

> If you self-consciously apply [the deconstructive] method to a literary text, both the text and the method have already been constituted by you, by the systems of difference that allowed you to be aware of them in the first place. They are already the product of interpretation before you have even begun to apply the one to the other. So is the "you" who does the applying, insofar as you are the object of your own thought. (747)

Even with so strong a caveat in mind, it's quite possible to imagine the uses of deconstructive readings in discussing texts with students, in making them aware of the multiplicities of interpretive solutions to a text, and in helping them understand the constraints of language. Pam Gilbert (1991) has pointed out that deconstruction helps us understand how readers react to "lacks" they perceive in texts, for instance, and both Sharon Crowley (1989) and Gary Layne Hatch (1992) have pointed out that telling students to write or say "what they mean" overlooks the problems inherent in separating form from content, thought from language, or meaning from expression—more of the binary oppositions that deconstruction can help us tackle.

Intertextuality, like deconstruction, is another attempt to move beyond the binary oppositions of structuralism. Robert Scholes, its chief proponent, sees reading and writing not just as parts of discourse communities, couched in and created *by* the codes and constraints of communal interpretation, but also as crucial ways in which writers *create* those communities:

> . . . reading and writing are important because we read and write our world as well as our texts, and are read and written by them in turn. Texts are places where power and weakness become visible and discussable, where learning and ignorance manifest themselves, where the structures that enable and constrain our thoughts become palpable. (xi)

In teaching students to question texts, and to question the authority of texts, we teach them to question the codes underlying authority. As Scholes again observes, "Most acts that justify the term 'interpretation' at all involve the use of several codes, and most interpretative disputes can be usefully seen as disputes over ... whether a particular code is relevant at all, whether one code is more or less relevant than another, and so on" (162). This questioning the authority of codes currently enjoys widespread support under the labels "social-epistemic rhetoric," "critical thinking," and "critical inquiry," though it is doubtful if many who so complacently endorse it as such would do so if they thought it through to its revolutionary conclusion. In a sense, intertextuality is the logical conclusion to Bakhtin's and Foucault's theories of discourse that emphasize the contexts and historical circumstances that produce certain linguistic codes, and the communities which produce these interpretive schemas. Manifested as feminist criticism and new historicism, among others, it has penetrated the boundaries of composition studies, and is influencing more and more of our praxis.

This survey of literary theories, by necessity superficial, should at least begin to suggest to you how the theories you study (or studied) in your literature classes connect with the theories which can govern your writing classrooms. Again, it's chiefly a difference of focus: literary criticism taught you to look at *where* writers ended up, at the works they produced. Composition and rhetorical theory wants you to examine *how* writers arrive at those processes. So they begin their examination not with readers *receiving* (or, in the critical jargon, *writing*) a text, but with writers *producing* or writing texts. (As Linda Brodkey jokes, "Writers who write texts get royalties; *readers* who write texts don't.") In the next chapter, we'll shift our focus to the ways in which compositionists view writing, how it is produced, and where it fits into communities, to understand the complementary perspectives of approaching student writing.

3

How Compositionists
View Writing:
Product, Process, and Power

Compositionists approach writing with a formidable history behind them; almost three millennia have passed since Isocrates began coaching Greek farmers on ways to make their tax appeals more effective in the public forum. Yet as a discipline, composition (as opposed to rhetoric in the disciplinary sense) is a relatively young field. Youth, however, does not equate with lack of sophistication; the theories described in this chapter provide models of great depth and breadth for looking at writing. To help you make connections with current scholarship in rhetoric and composition, I've adopted the terminology of James Britton (1988) in this chapter, since it has become widely accepted in the field. *Current-traditional* rhetoric represents the schooling most of us received, with its heavy emphasis on mechanical correctness and the final product of writing. *Cognitive* rhetoric attempts to understand how writers think while they are writing. *Expressivist* rhetoric puts the individual writer and her or his actions at the center of attention, and *social-epistemic* rhetoric sees writing as socially constrained, involved in and implicated by the communities and power structures to which and in which it belongs.

The compositionist approach to writing represents a virtual paradigm shift from that of the literary approach—a radical revisioning of how we might view writing and its roles in the world. The term "paradigm shift" is borrowed from Thomas S. Kuhn's *The Structure of Scientific Revolutions* [2nd ed., 1970], and was made widely known to rhetoricians through a 1982 article by Maxine Hairston. It refers to the displacement felt by thinkers when a particular system of explaining the world, such as the notion of the sun rotating the earth, is perceived to be inadequate, and must be replaced with a new explanation, which takes some getting used to.

These new views of writing see it as whole discourse which results from a process—or many processes—of cognition, composition, and contextualization. No longer is it *only* a product to be dissected; now, to paraphrase Topsy, it's something that "jest grew." It is now a given in composition scholarship that writing is an organic process, and that attention must be paid to all of its stages of growth.

Current-Traditionalist Theories

In the classical world, one form of discourse received the majority of rhetoricians' attention—persuasion. It was studied as it applied to three separate audiences: the forum, the law courts, and ceremonial gatherings. These three kinds of rhetoric, called, respectively, deliberative, forensic, and epideictic, had individual functions, styles, and structural characteristics. This distinction of kinds by audience and the roles they played in shaping the opinions of various segments of society has had an enduring influence in discourse theory.

Over the centuries, other modes of composing came to be valued as rhetoric became firmly allied with education and the inculcation of morals and mores. (This sweeping change is best explained by George Kennedy; it's too involved to retail here.) The Scots in the eighteenth and nineteenth centuries were particularly important in forging this alliance, arguing that those who spoke and wrote correctly achieved a moral excellence. One of the last great Scotttish rhetoricians, Alexander Bain, in his influential 1866 textbook *English Composition and Rhetoric: A Manual,* divided the products, or forms, rhetoric took into the five modes most of us still recognize: narration, description, exposition, argumentation, and poetry (what we would now call "expressive" or "creative" writing). Bain's division shows how the social function of rhetoric had deteriorated over time; his system emphasized formal correctness rather than the use of particular forms to move audiences to correct actions. This "product-oriented" approach to writing, with its formalistic focus on shape and correctness, became institutionalized as the "proper" method for writing instruction in the late nineteenth century; its influence still remains strong today.

The energies of current traditionalists are usually directed into attention to style and form. Templates and rubrics, such as the five-paragraph theme or the journalistic "lead," are used to guide students in the shaping of discourse. Careful notice is taken of the writer's choices at the word and sentence level; current traditionalists care deeply about correct grammar and word choice, realizing how much writers are judged on these issues. A current traditionalist's syllabus often asks students to write in different modes or formal arrangements, such as narration, description, and the like; and there is often a heavy emphasis on "teacher as audience" in such classrooms.

"Current-traditional" as a label has become almost as pejorative as "liberal" is in American politics. Few scholars want to admit to being current-traditionalists, lest they sound curmudgeonly, as in this recent example referring to the two-decades-long decline in average scores on the verbal section of the Scholastic Aptitude Test:

> The most salient effect of [this malaise] is to encourage an atmosphere of indifference to expressive correctness (to coin a phrase). (Fleishman 81)

In fact, it's a common exaggeration to equate current traditionalists with other conservatives of language, such as those who espouse an English-only constitutional amendment or those who write language advice columns in prestigious newspapers. In some cases, this criticism is justified. Some current traditionalists *are* addicted to red pen, and try to impose their own view of a subject on every student text. Some have become obsessed with form; in their classrooms, today *is* the day students will write a comparison-contrast, whether they want to or not, and so on.

But current traditionalists haven't survived for so long by being dumb and bullheaded. Rather, they reflect a very important way our society thinks about language, one that descends from the Puritans through Bain: that "proper" language, language that meets certain arbitrary standards of correctness and arrangement, is valued in our world. The ability to write this language, as Ross Winterowd observed two decades ago, "is money in your pocket and power in your hand" (1979). I teach corporate communications in my school's Executive MBA program, and the people I meet there—all of whom have at least ten years' management experience in a number of fields—continually tell me of the demand for correct, organized, stylish writing in their communities. When I told them, for instance, that our undergraduate business writers can't get better than a "C" grade on an assignment that contains grammatical or mechanical errors, more than 90% told me that was too lenient, that such an assignment should be given an "F" because it *wouldn't* be acceptable in their communities. "I'd rather hire a kid with no business training but good writing skills than hire the best business school graduate who can't spell or edit," a vice-president of a major bank told me. "I can teach the kid the business; I can't teach him not to embarrass the bank through his language." Current traditionalists understand that these skills, mechanical, narrow and closed as they may be, are valued outside of academe. They try to teach them to their students. (Of course, there are other ways of teaching these skills than just swamping a paper with red ink.) As I'll discuss later in Chapter 9, current traditionalists are associated with directive response; that is, they tend to tell students exactly what to do in revision or correcting. This notion of teacher control is explored by Richard Straub in an article in the following anthology, as well as in Robert Schwegler's article there.

Expressivist or Romantic Theories

Early theories of the writing process focused on its expressive content, the attempts of writers to use language to mold and tell truth as they perceived it. For instance, D. Gordon Rohman and Albert O. Wlecke argued that techniques such as meditative exercises, journal-keeping, and the composition of analogies (called "existential sentences") helped writers find truth in even the most abstract of subjects. They argued that such "prewriting" techniques led in a smooth and linear fashion to drafting and revision as writers refine the expression of the truth they told. This privileging of self-discovery, what is now called the *expressivist* or "romantic" view of composing, is also held by Peter Elbow, Ken Macrorie, William Coles, Donald Murray, and Ann Berthoff, to name a few of its most influential proponents. Elbow argues for the primacy of prewriting in helping writers explore ideas; Macrorie prizes it because it forces students to go beyond the obvious cliches, which he calls "Engfish" (because they stink of insincerity). Coles values prewriting because it allows students to explore multiple relationships to readers and subjects (what he calls "plural I's"); Murray likes it because it cultivates surprise, new ideas, and combinations of old ideas which lead to personal growth; and Berthoff feels it enables students to reclaim the imagination which is their birthright. Activities such as prewriting, journaling, and collaboration in the classroom originally arose out of expressivist practice, though other theories have now claimed these ideas for their own. The expressivists have tremendous faith in student creativity and capability;

they firmly believe that, given the right environment, students can draw great writing from within themselves. Their classrooms are laboratories where they try to create such environments.

The expressivist theory gives discovery of ideas primacy in the writing process, lets drafting simply happen, and sees revision (when it gets discussed explicitly) as further discovery. Expressivist theories also see the writer as somewhat isolated from conventions and codes; they in fact encourage writers to flaunt or exploit conventions and expectations. These beliefs have thus attracted criticism from those who feel that the teacher's responsibility is to show writers how to become part of a community, not how to put themselves outside it. Theorists are generally suspicious of expressivists' ongoing refusal to articulate clear theories of how people make knowledge and construct subjects; and expressivist scholars as a whole have avoided the theoretical jargon that has swamped so many other schools of composition. It is nearly impossible to imagine, for instance, an expressionist using language like "The poststructural commitment to textuality results in a strong tendency toward epistemological antifoundationalism, an intellectual skepticism characterized by thoroughgoing relativism" (Blum 93). As Donald Murray once said in response to a conference participant's question, "I don't spend my time theorizing my writing because I am busy spending my time writing."

The expressionists' insistence that revising and editing are two radically different, and necessarily separate processes, has gained wide acceptance. Revision means getting the ideas right; editing means adjusting the etiquette of presentation (spelling, punctuation, and the like). In separating revising from editing, they began the undermining of current-traditional practice that has liberated so many classrooms; we owe these adventurers a debt of thanks for their efforts.

Cognitive Theories

One theory of the writing process roots it deeply in psychology, particularly in studies of cognition. For such *cognitive* theorists, "protocols" (detailed descriptions of how a document is produced) and draft analyses play a key role. One of the earliest and most influential of such theories is Janet Emig's. In *The Composing Process of Twelfth Graders* (1971), she studied writing behaviors: how student writers found and developed their ideas. She found that these processes differed with audience: if students wrote for themselves (expressively), they were concerned with the presentation of ideas, but if students wrote for teachers (transactionally), they were concerned (even obsessed) with mechanical correctness. Emig concluded that most writers develop some kinds of implicit knowledge about adjusting their writing for different readers. Nancy Sommer's comparisons of student and experienced adult writers (1980) show that experienced writers come to value development of ideas far more than mechanical correctness, whereas to students, correctness remains all.

Richard Young, Alton Becker, and Kenneth Pike also developed a cognitive theory of the writing process; however, theirs depends not on the writer's knowledge of the audience but of the subject. Their "tagmemics" theory models cognitive efforts to know a subject; it focuses on how writers perceive a subject's individuality, variability, and place in a larger system. This viewpoint has become increasingly important to people who see writing as a political act; tagmemics lets writers see where they fit into a power structure, and how the system might be changed. These cognitive efforts should help writers find and develop new combinations of ideas. Like expressivist theories, tagmemics emphasizes prewriting and only thinly discusses drafting or revision.

The cognitivist position has been most fully expanded by Linda Flower, John Hayes, and their graduate students and colleagues at Carnegie-Mellon University. Their complex position views the composing process as a series of decision-making strategies: planning texts, translating those plans into sentences, and revising the texts produced to bring them in line with the original (or reshaped) plans. Although Emig first suggested it, Flower and Hayes *et al.* have done most to demonstrate the recursive and hierarchical levels of writing processes, especially in the planning and revising stages of writing activities.

Cognitivists find Rohman and Wlecke's linear model too simplistic; they argue that writers continually move back and forth between stages to adjust their plans. Like the expressivists, the cognitivists value personal expression highly, claiming it represents most validly an individual's way of thinking. Cognitivists spend little time discussing the forms writing produces; it's rare to see an entire piece of discourse reproduced in the course of their discussions. More recently, they have been giving slightly more emphasis to the audience's role in the cognitive workings of writers. But for cognitivists, the writer's "brain work"—and reflections on it—remain paramount. This position, as you might expect, has inspired perceptive challenges. Most protocol studies are based on a few (three, seven, twelve) writers, and we are asked to accept that most, or even all, writers think like the subjects of the empirical studies do. Protocols ask writers to behave in ways they don't normally do—to "think aloud" or "write aloud" while a tape (or possibly video) recorder captures their words for later analysis. Students who normally work silently, but then know they are being asked to narrate their work for a teacher, may not react characteristically for a number of reasons. Since cognitive research is based on these small studies of protocols, despite our knowledge that individuals think and act differently, it is vulnerable to such critiques. At the same time, cognitivists point out that no matter how collaboratively a student works, no matter how decisively and directively a teacher intervenes, in the end, the writing is created by one individual agent who cannot be subsumed entirely in the notion of community.

Social-Epistimic Theories

Most recently, as theorists have once again come to admit the social functions of, and constraints on, writing that were the bases of classical rhetoric, studies of the writing process have broadened to examine the contexts in which writing occurs, to define the discourse communities in which particular writing processes exist, and to examine the power relationships inscribed in the acts of writing and reading. This broadening has also been influenced by the changing demographics of college populations. As more and more non-traditional—that is to say, more and more non-young, non-white, non-upper/middle class, non-Anglophilically educated—students have entered the academy, teachers have been forced to change their expectations about the kinds of knowledge students bring with them. No longer can a teacher take for granted that students know what an essay looks like, or what "thesis and support" are, or how academics think. (Indeed, research conducted by Robert Connors and Lisa Ede [1988] suggest that an unfamiliarity with the look of the printed page may be responsible for many student "errors.")

The traditional response to this situation has been to teach these students the kinds of discourse that our forebears, trained in literature and its criticism, privilege; thus the expressionists' emphasis on journals, poetry, writing fiction, and the current-traditionalists' emphasis on analyzing others' writing. Implicitly, we want students to recognize what constitutes discourse and literacy in English departments (see Robinson [1985]). But the *social-epistemic* theorists now argue that we should be doing more: "Rather than teaching them how to write in only one institutional role for only one type of institutional audience, we should help our students discover the basic strategies by which they can determine and fulfill the requirements of various types of discourse" (Perelman 476).

The social-epistemic position, also known as social construction, currently dominates scholarship in rhetoric and composition. It regards knowledge as a function of language (in linguistic terms, it accepts the "weak" version of the Sapir-Whorf hypothesis). This knowledge is produced through dialogue and discourse within a community; what we know is shaped by who we know and where we are. Understanding how this knowledge is created, examining unstated assumptions, and determining how and why power is exercised, are all parts of the social-constructionist project. (A fair bit of Marxist economic and political theory underlies social constructionism, as does ethnology, anthropology, and group psychology; this theory is the most social-scientific of all the compositionist positions on writing.)

In a social-constructionist classroom, authority may well be an issue. Unlike math or science classrooms, where the teacher demonstrates authority by showing her expertise ("I can solve this equation; can you?"), in a writing classroom, the authority is *de-centered*. The teacher gives up some of his authority to the students, who are encouraged to take active roles in their learning, teaching each other, responding to each other's ideas and work, making judgments and setting standards. This attitude makes many teachers nervous; after all, we've suffered all our lives to get on the right side of the desk, haven't we? And it may well be misunderstood by colleagues or departments, having serious consequences for decisions on hiring and tenure. Finally, because this decentering is so overtly a political act, the teacher who gives up that authority may be subject to criticism on political (or political correctness) grounds, especially in these days of increasing conservatism. These critiques may come from colleagues, from the community, and not infrequently from students: "Look, I'm paying for you to teach me. Don't tell me to teach myself, or to learn from these other bozos!" The social constructionist classroom is usually filled with energy (often with tension) as a result of this shift in power structures.

Adopting a social-constructionist position allows for different kinds of teaching to take place. For instance, take a grammatical rule like the comma splice. A traditional textbook would say something like "Never join two or more independent clauses with only a comma." As you'll see in many handbooks, current traditionalists can cast this ukase into a statement that connects the problem to the needs of the community:

> You can easily confuse and annoy readers if you inappropriately join two or more sentences using either a comma only (comma splice) or no punctuation at all (fused sentence). Because a comma splice does not clearly specify the relationship between main clauses, readers may have to look over a sentence several times to be sure of its meaning.

Such an approach makes the rules of formal English if not logical, at least rational: the problem with comma splices is that it annoys or confuses readers, and makes them work harder, not that it violates a commandment graven in stone and handed down on Mount Ararat. On larger issues like topic selection, voice, audience analysis, and development, the collaborative negotiation of meaning that underlies social construction also cast a writer's choices in terms of the needs of and effects on readers. Moreover the political and social emphasis on the ways in which communities function and communicate encourages students to see outside the narrow confines of the classroom, to develop the broad and open competencies they need to participate successfully in democracy.

Such social-epistemic theories of the writing process have two current focuses. The political focus, represented by David Bartholomae and Anthony Petrosky, Patricia Bizzell, and others influenced to some extent by the Brazilian theorist Paolo Freire, sees awareness of the constraints of a discourse community as politically liberating, as potentially enabling and revolutionary. The article by Robert Schwegler included in the anthology that follows builds on this impulse by looking at the loci of power and control in the writing classroom. If students can understand the constraints of their communities and master them, they can come to control and change the community through their own discourse. For theorists who believe this, discovery of the contexts in which students write and the constraints which govern those contexts comes before any other part of the writing process. The context is as important, if not more so, than finding and developing ideas and presenting them in a form the discourse community approves. A number of contemporary writing texts now employ this multi-cultural and overtly political approach to collegiate writing, but the increasing conservatism of American society does make it risky at times; for instance, when the University of Texas tried to structure its composition program around a social construction project, the resulting public opposition (which included eloquent voices from within the program) led to so much controversy that the plan had to be abandoned.

The second focus (which I called the pedagogical focus in earlier editions of this book) is a "conversational" focus. It sees writing as a fundamental tool for learning in all communities and attempts to foster the teaching of writing in departments besides English. Among its noted proponents are Kenneth Bruffee, Toby Fulwiler, and Elaine Maimon, who have all contributed to both scholarly and pedagogical attempts to put their beliefs into practice. This conversational focus is reflected in many "writing across the curriculum" and "writing across the disciplines" movements, and is an underlying principle of many handbooks: writers in all disciplines can use writing as a means of learning. Discussion of discourse expectations in other fields such as literary and business writing are good ways to integrate this idea into a composition class.

The theory, however, is neater than the practice. Beyond the concerns voiced above, there are others. One tenet of social construction, for instance, is that the teacher must not be directive, imposing his or her viewpoint on the text. Responses to student writing should be phrased as questions and choices, for example, rather than commands of what to do ("What kinds of examples would prove this case?" for instance, rather than "You need to give examples supporting your thesis here"). As I'll explain later in Chapter 9, some students may *need* directive criticism; the social constructionist fails the needs of this community unless she provides it. Moreover, the social constructionists' smugness in attacking other theorists, particularly the expressivists, is beginning to draw fire. As Thomas O'Donnell recently wrote, "When accusations take the form of 'here's what you think you're doing, but here's what you're *really* doing' . . . I feel justified in placing the burden of proof for such claims on the accusers" (1996: 426). (For instance, of the many articles about composition theory and practice that I considered for inclusion in this book, two were rejected because they could not bear that burden of proof.) Finally, social constructionists sometimes project the belief that theirs is the only theory that takes into account the community, and how the community constructs meaning through language. As the preceding discussions have shown, most theories take into account how people interpret language, assign value through it, use it to shape their work and their worlds. What social construction does differently is to use this "big picture" as the controlling metaphor for writing, not as an outgrowth of other activities and principles.

Theories of Discourse

Scholars in rhetoric and composition have also found it difficult to describe all the kinds of writing that can be produced in student classrooms, largely because we continue to disagree so strongly on what constitutes academic writing—in other words, on what kinds of writing *belong*. In the last two decades, though, several major scholars have made significant strides towards constructing models of discourse production which incorporate most of the factors which influence the writing of texts. Four have gained considerable status: James Moffett's in *Teaching the Universe of Discourse* (1968); James Britton's in *The Development of Writing Abilities ([Ages] 11-18)* (1975); James Kinneavy's in *A Theory of Discourse* (1971); and Frank D'Angelo's in *A Conceptual Theory of Rhetoric* (1975). While vastly different, all four share some basic principles; for instance, they all work with full pieces of discourse (as opposed to isolated paragraphs or passages, as in Bain); they all attempt to be comprehensive; they all locate the origin of composition in thinking skills; and they all view the relationship between writer, reader, and subject (the "communications triangle" in Roman Jakobson's term) as a social one, constrained by overt and implicit codes.

James Moffett's Universe of Discourse

Modern literary criticism has focused on how the reader "constructs" one or many texts and subjects through her or his methods of making meaning. James Moffett, on the other hand, locates his cognitive hypotheses in the relationships of writer and reader, and writer and subject. His writer/reader relationship is based largely on Jean Piaget's theory of developmental decentering (see Beard [1969] for a synopsis of Piaget), suggesting that this authorly conversation can move from egocentrism (inner dialogue) to increasingly wider audiences (dialogue, correspondence, public narrative, inference). Likewise, his writer/subject relationship is shaped by Piaget's notion of abstraction. Moffett separates fictive from nonfictive discourse; fictive discourse moves from the personal expression of poetry and plays through fiction to the abstract level of the essay. Nonfictive discourse begins with the writer's perception of what happens (description or drama) and gradually becomes less personal; next come narration (what happened), exposition (what happens), and finally argumentation (what might happen). In *Student-Centered Language Arts and Reading K-12* (4th ed. 1991), Moffett and his colleague Betty Jane Wagner create an entire curriculum that ties these kinds of writer-reader and writer-subject relationships to the appropriate stages of the students' cognitive development, and a later series of texts under the group title *Active Voices* explores them further. His theory is widely respected in schools of education and has had considerable influence on elementary and secondary education.

James Britton's Spectrum of Writing

In 1966, James Britton and his colleagues at the University of London began one of the most ambitious studies of writing ever; over nine years they collected and fully analyzed over 2,000 "scripts," pieces of writing done by British schoolchildren between the ages of 11 and 18. Britton, like Moffett, concentrates on the writer/reader and writer/subject connections in analyzing these texts. The writer/reader relationship begins with the self as audience, moves to teachers as readers, then to a "wider" audience, and finally an indeterminate audience (what our students like to call "the general public"). The writer/subject relationship is defined by the writer's purposes in tackling a particular subject: those using language to express the self ("expressive"), those using language in recognized patterns for artistic purposes ("poetic"); those using language to influence actions and behavior ("persuasive"); and finally, those using language to gain or impart knowledge ("informative"). Britton's conclusions were sharply critical of the product-oriented approach used to teach writing in schools; his work showed that students were most often forced to compose transactional (informative or persuasive) writing tasks for an audience of teachers, even if these students were cognitively before or past the stage at which such writing was developmentally appropriate. Britton's criticisms have influenced many secondary and college educators and has slowly been adopted in textbooks, but have had less effect on curricular practice: Arthur Applebee's study (1986) revealed that most American high-school students spent only about three percent of their school time writing scripts of a paragraph or longer.

James Kinneavy's Theory of Discourse

Although James Kinneavy's *A Theory of Discourse* does not include a cognitive element as do Moffett's and Britton's, his is perhaps the most elaborate theory of discourse yet articulated. He expands the triad of writer, reader, and subject into a pyramid, adding a fourth point, language; and he argues that theorists must consider not two-dimensional but three-dimensional relationships. Since language must always be one of the dimensions under consideration, Kinneavy's social-epistemic theory is pragmatic and essentially semiotic; it involves the use of meaningful signals or codes. (Kinneavy's theory in this respect has been heavily influenced by Kenneth Burke's literary theory of language as symbolic action.) Most of Kinneavy's book discusses aims, the reasons why writers create discourse. In this respect, his theory harks back to the notion of rhetoric as social function derived from the classical world, ties in with Stanley Fish's notion of interpretative communities, and prefigures both the "social construction" of Kenneth Bruffee and others, and the cognitive studies of Flower and Hayes. Kinneavy's work has been very influential in graduate training in rhetoric and composition; teachers with this training now exert a noticeable influence on college composition curricula.

Frank D'angelo's Theory of Topoi

Finally, Frank D'Angelo has developed a current-traditional discourse theory based on the classical *topoi* or sources for arguments. He identifies two large categories of discourse, dividing them by what kind of product the writer produces, and applies to them the classical labels of "logical" and "nonlogical." However, his groupings of products are not very like the classical proofs. His nonlogical topics are drawn from cognitive research into creativity, and include condensation, displacement, and transformation. His logical topics, those which can be rationally perceived, are distinguished by the changes they describe over time or space. Static topics (which include most of the traditional expository modes) do not change over time or space. Dynamic topics, which change over time or space, either show progression (narration, process analysis, cause/effect, syllogisms) or repetition (iteration, narration, alternation).

D'Angelo provides elaborate heuristics and structural outlines for readers and writers that attempt to describe the cognitive structures that underlie each category; these are invaluable for teaching "organization" in an expository writing class. They may well remind you of the lessons you had in literature classes on "how to structure a five-act play" or "how a sonnet gets built," for good reason; D'Angelo's theory is drawn from analyzing a body of examples already produced. Like Kinneavy's theory, however, his model fails to provide a developmental component and has had more influence on teachers than on curricula so far.

Each of these theories has its enthusiastic proponents and each its perceptive critics. Kinneavy's has probably received the most attention in published scholarship; the others have been very influential in classrooms. All emphasize the notion that "product-oriented" rhetoric had lost sight of: as the relationships between writer, reader, subject and language shift, so does rhetoric. Each relationship requires a different kind of attention, and each writer will have different writing processes for the different circumstances he or she faces and the different products she or he is expected to produce. There is no universal "right way" to write. So situational or purposive theories have come, rightly, to dominate our thinking about written products. The journal, the literary criticism essay, the résumé, the lab report, and the documentation of software each require a different application of rhetorical strategies. It's important to remember that writing processes must be just that—plural.

Most effective teachers find themselves synthesizing bits and pieces from a number of larger theories. Such eclectic constructions are very characteristic of most rhetoricians and compositionists, who realize that any given class of students presents far greater variety than most single theories can encompass. A certain philosophical flexibility, in fact, is one of the hallmarks of successful writing teachers.

We have gradually evolved models of the writing process that approximate what goes on when a writer sits down to compose a work. But we have only begun to scratch the surface of this immensely complex activity. The theories discussed in this chapter generally accept division of the writing process into prewriting, drafting, and editing, but emphasize the three components differently. Please keep in mind, too, that many textbooks move in linear and usually chronological fashion, beginning to end, making the process seem seamless and smooth: here's the beginning, the middle, and the end of the process. But in reality, as you've doubtless discovered yourself, we often draft the body before we write the introduction and conclusion; we go back and do more research long after we start drafting; and so forth. Writing is messy. For the sake of introducing you to the complexities of the theories explained in this chapter, I've tried to clean it up a little. Don't worry if the practice you find in your classrooms and on your desks is a lot less tidy. That's the way this game works.

In summary, then, the writing process is complex, and any effort to characterize it (or them) must necessarily be reductive and simplistic. What we can say about it is this: It has a great deal to do with how writers

- are able to perceive and explore themselves and their worlds through the medium of language.
- think about their subjects and audiences, and adjust their hypotheses accordingly.
- understand their writing situations, and how they use or circumvent the constraints their purposes and situations impose.
- understand, and to some degree invent their audiences.

The strategies for teaching elements of the writing process (below) focus on the mechanics we can isolate from a complex activity. For now, we must content ourselves with James Reither's summation: "Writing is clearly a more multidimensioned process than current theory and practice would have us believe, and one that begins long before it is appropriate to commence working with strategies for invention" (623). Writing—and teaching writing—is messy. If you want right and wrong answers, stick to algebra. If you like kaleidoscopic views, always changing, read on.

Theory in the Classroom

In such a Babel of theories, you may wonder (and rightly so), can any of them be carried into the classroom? If so, which ones? The answers vary. Charlyce and Arn Tibbetts, arguing from their experience in writing textbooks, say no; teachers want mechanics and correctness, not innovation. Hayes and Flower, on the other hand, say writing instruction is one area in which research has actually had a large and visible impact on teaching (1986). The disparity in answers shouldn't surprise you. It is, however, safe to say that classroom practices in writing are still far more conservative than the theory would like to see—but this is also the case in many literature classrooms, where we teach students to explicate texts before they learn to deconstruct artifacts.

The trends in composition and rhetorical theory explained in the this chapter mirror the trends in critical theory explained in chapter two: we're coming to terms with the necessity of multiplicity. Just as no two writers produce identical products, or no two readers construe identical meanings, so no two teachers will produce the same class—and no two classes will be alike. Establishing a theoretical base—finding people who talk like we talk and see the world of writing instruction like we do—helps us anchor ourselves in the shifting tides around us. In turn, our theoretical stability enables us to help students "find their feet" in our writing classrooms. I've never been in Chris Anson or Bob Schwegler's classroom, for instance, although based on what we've talked about and written, we can probably describe each other's classrooms pretty well. Chris's classes will spend a lot of time with journals and peer work, developing their portfolios. Bob's will spend a lot of time tackling big social issues, arguing about the politics and giving as good as they get. My classes end up talking a lot about gender, conducting their own research projects and surveys, and critiquing the results. I sometimes have part of the class working in groups while others work on their own. In all three of our classrooms good writing is produced, and students learn. They are living our theoretical decisions.

When you get right down to it, anything you do in class—even taking attendance (i.e. imposing your authority on the community) has a theoretical basis and theoretical implications. So probably the question shouldn't be "Can I use theory in my classroom?" but rather "What theories will I *consciously* bring to the teaching of writing?" You needn't use fancy labels unless you want to; labels can confuse or intimidate students. But if you consciously think about the theories you bring in, you stand a much better chance of organizing and articulating a writing course which will benefit your students.

Actually, you can incorporate as much theory into your course as you like and are comfortable with; theory, as Frank D'Angelo properly reminds us, helps us "see our field of inquiry and see it whole" (1976: 143). In particular, the theories outlined above will explicitly help you answer five of the most perplexing questions you'll face in determining your classroom practice:

- What community's notion of discourse will I teach?
- Who are my students?
- What models for good writing will I use?
- What will my role be in the classroom?
- What kinds of competencies will I try to teach?

Each question requires a separate kind of consideration.

What Community's Notion of Discourse Will You Teach?

If your theory of writing accords it a social function, you will have to identify the community or communities your students need to know about and in which they participate. If you are teaching writing in college, the academic community will be one you select. Your school, in fact, may publish (or have a test for) the standards of writing that community demands. You and your students will need to discuss those standards and set clear goals for meeting them.

But which segment of the community? Just the English department? Or the humanities? Or will you include both arts and sciences? If so, what kinds of writing occasions will you construct to help students learn about and write for these varying communities? Will you also ask students to write for more personal communities—themselves, their classmates, friends? Or less personal communities—the world of work, other forms of professional discourse? Again, what occasions will students have to learn about and write for these communities? You and your students will again need to decide; outside pressures at your school (for instance, the insistence of the sociology department that students can write abstracts) may also influence your decisions. You may need to discuss with colleagues in other disciplines just what constitutes "good writing" in economics or physics or pharmacology, so that you can help your students succeed in their chosen disciplines.

And in all cases, how will you judge that writing? Students implicitly know a great deal about the constraints of communities. Asked to describe a campus protest that got a bit overenthusiastic, they'll choose one strategy for writing to a friend at home, another for writing to grandma, a third for writing an excuse for the Dean, another for writing an account for the local newspaper or *Ne* *on Campus.* They have been, since early childhood, able to switch "codes" for discourse when they need to. How can you help them tap that implicit knowledge? Your decisions about the authority of discourse communities and the role of that community in the writing process will help you decide.

Who Are Your Students?

Typically, textbooks have addressed a narrow range of students: middle-class, late adolescent, mainstream, implicitly white. But when you look at the faces in your classroom, you are likely to see a very different group: some minority, some older, some very inexperienced, some professional. (In New Jersey, for instance, the Commissioner of Education estimates that by the year 2000, over 40% of college freshmen won't speak English at home.) America is "browning" as well as "greying"; our classrooms will continue to provide more variety semester by semester. You won't see *just* students, either; according to the American Council on Education, in 1989 almost half the full-time college students were employed. Almost forty percent of all college students work between fifteen and twenty-nine hours a week, and close to fourteen percent work thirty-five hours a week or more. No longer do students *just* go to school. They have jobs, families, competing agendas, lives; writing class may not be the most important activity in their worlds.

How do you mold this group into a coherent class? Again, theory can help you decide. Since many will be at different developmental stages, you'll want to include a variety of kinds of and purposes for writing and a variety of audiences, to stretch all your students. At times, you may have to arrange students in groups according to their backgrounds, so that each group can work on particular problems; on the other hand, you'll often want to mix students within groups so that they experience many perspectives. Differing student populations make it possible for you to talk with students about different discourse communities and their expectations (writing, for instance, looks different to students who never write at all outside school than it does to students who write forty or fifty sales letters a week). Sometimes you may have to juggle the balance between introverts and extroverts. And no two classes will be the same, so you will have to make these decisions individually, every semester, for every class you teach.

What Models for Good Writing Will You Use?

Again, your notion of what kinds of discourse "count" will give you your answer. Because many novice writing teachers are trained in the analysis of *belles lettres*, that's where we turn first. The anthologies we use in expository writing classes include fiction, poetry and belletristic essays from *Harper's*, *The New Yorker*, *The Atlantic* and *The New Republic*. We're comfortable with these models; they represent the kinds of writing prized in our discourse community, English departments. As Edward P. J. Corbett sympathetically remarks,

> I always understood why the young, eager instructors succumbed to the temptation to sneak literature into that writing class. Literature was what those instructors loved most and what their formal training had best qualified them to talk about. They yearned for an opportunity to introduce their students to the delights of literature. They were not deliberately ignoring the directives for the course; they just could not resist the siren call of literature. (1983, 181).

Such models work, though, if we believe the discourse that counts is that of the English department. If we believe that other communities have valid discourses that students should learn, then we introduce other examples as well: scientific articles, political speeches, and the like. If we believe that students should know that not all good writers are white males, we try to include women writers and minority writers. Sometimes we even include writers from non-Western cultures—if we know how to locate them. It speaks sadly of our own tunnel vision that most of the "non-literary" examples we put in our texts come from fairly "literary" non-literature people: John F. Kennedy, Martin Luther King, Stephen J. Gould, Lewis Thomas. Most of us haven't taken the time to learn what constitutes the principles of "excellent writing" in other discourse communities—and those standards can be very different than those of the literary community.

This theory of models, though, may convey a pernicious message to students: professionals write well; students don't. After all, professionals get published; their work is typeset; people pay to buy it. Somebody put it in a textbook, so of course it's good. The only other kind of writing most students see is their own, and that is rarely praised. It's covered with corrections and comments. It's rarely typeset. If it is included in textbooks, it's always a weak example—"see what this student did wrong." Students draw the inevitable conclusion: all professional writing is good and strong; all student writing is bad and weak. Yet we ask them to produce good, strong student writing. Is this a contradiction?

There are ways to show students this isn't the case. Teachers can use student examples in class, including drafts; this helps students see that they, too, can learn to revise and produce good work. Student writing can be circulated; more and more anthologies include some sample student essays, and a few are devoted almost wholly to student writing. We can encourage students to bring pieces of their writing that have been successful: an essay exam from political science that got full credit, a chemistry lab report that received an A, a sales letter that won a big contract, or a letter home that got money from Mom. We can encourage students to talk about these successes, to analyze what they did well, and to consider how those strategies might transfer to other writing situations. We can even publish our students' writing; the advent of "desktop publishing" and laser printers makes it possible for nearly anyone with a word processor and access to a photocopier to put student writing in print. If you decide that student writing is important, you can do a lot to implement that theory in your class.

What Will Your Role Be in the Classroom?

One of the hardest decisions for new teachers to make is the choice of a classroom persona; inexperience leads them to believe that their lack of years or title or practice somehow disqualifies them as teachers. They want to sound like "professors" (see below, Chapter 9). The compensating disguises they adapt could be amusing, if they weren't so potentially dangerous for teacher and student alike. The late Robert Bain, my first mentor in teaching, told me, "Just put on your best teacher like a jacket. Wear that teacher's style—how he talked, how he moved, what he did, how he worked—until you find your own under it. Then you can take that jacket off." I've always found this good advice; even now, I wear a bit of Bob Bain's "jacket" in the classroom with gratitude. Most of us can remember specific likes and dislikes about our teachers: this one really listened, that one popped her knuckles, this one made lectures lively, that one droned on and on. These memories can help you decide what to do and what not to do as a teacher. Experience, then, can be your first determiner.

But theory can also help. If you don't believe in what Paolo Freire (1970; transl. 1986) calls "banking education"—the notion that a teacher deposits information in a passive student and gets it back with interest on exams and papers—then you can design your classes so that students take a more active role in their own learning, through topic selection, discussion, standard-setting, and collaborative work, for example. If you believe that writing should help students learn, then you can design activities that help them explore new subjects and ideas and let them write about their discoveries. If you agree with Robert Scholes that "in an age of manipulation, when our students are in dire need of critical strength to resist the continuing assaults of all the media, the worst thing we can do is to foster in them an attitude of reverence before texts" (16), then you can employ strategies to help them question the authority of texts, the constraints of code, their own work, and the work of "great authors."

Likewise, the small decisions you make about theory can greatly affect your role in the classroom. As Erika Lindemann has observed (1985), teaching is a rhetorical act, conditioned by constraints of writer, reader, subject, and language. For instance, will you use lots of exotic terminology to demonstrate your expertise to the classroom ("Oh, that's a hypothetical subjunctive, Billy")? Or will you seek a common language? ("Those adverbs which can move from place to place in a sentence are called 'conjunctive adverbs'") Will you help students find out about the work they're reading and doing, or will you set yourself up as the Great Answer-Giver? Will there only be two ways in your class—your way and the wrong way? Will you exert your authority by your own example—showing them your work as a writer and the ways you've solved writing problems you've faced? Or will you wield your power through the grade book and red pen? Will you, or textbooks, or your students, do the teaching? Where will the center of the class lie, with students and their writing or with you and your brilliant *explications de texte*? Bob Scholes again has the appropriate remark:

> The more culturally at home in a text our students become, the less dependent they will be on guidance from the instructor.... [O]ne of the reasons we teachers favor the big anthology is that it keeps our students dependent on us, justifying our existence. We must get beyond this. There are better ways to make ourselves seem useful. One of them is to *be* useful. (27)

What Competencies Will You Try to Teach?

One of the most useful books I've ever read on teaching is John Passmore's *The Philosophy of Teaching*. In it he defines the competencies involved in any learning act as *closed, narrow, open*, and *broad*. *Closed* competencies are those that can be mastered with practice by nearly everyone of normal intelligence; in composition, these would include spelling, punctuation, grammar, construction of a topic sentence, and the like. In literary study they might be scanning a poem, or pronouncing Middle English, or identifying the kind of sonnet being used; in other disciplines they might be titrating a solution or determining the validity of a statistical measure. They are the building blocks: essential, but not complete in themselves; but they *are* the kinds of competencies that can be tested by standardized exams. Test scores in almost all cases represent students' mastery of closed competencies and nothing else. Current-traditional theories are heavily rooted in closed competencies, as discussed above.

Narrow competencies are those that apply only to selected situations: writing a goal statement for a résumé, for instance, or writing the materials and methods section for a scientific paper, or explicating a short story or poem. Their focus is restricted. Again, they are essential skills, stepping stones to master on the way to bigger and better things. Given time and guided practice most people can master them. Essay tests often measure narrow competencies, giving you and the students tested an accurate snapshot of mastery at a particular point in time. However, like closed competencies, they are tightly focused on one world, one situation, and do not always transfer well.

Open competencies—and writing and teaching are two of the best examples of these—require that persons apply closed competencies in ways they never have before, in ways they've never been taught to apply them. In other words, an open competency is the surprise discovery achieved through the application of closed skills. A student may know all the rules for writing an introductory paragraph or villanelle, for instance (closed skills), but only rarely achieve a lively and interesting introduction or a poem worth the name. When the student writes that surprising introduction or poem, she's shown an open competency. Teachers can provide guidance, constructive criticism, and feedback, but they can't "teach" open competencies. These have to be achieved; and not all students can achieve them with the same degrees of success. Some won't achieve them at all. (Bahktin discusses "surprise" in literature, and Donald Murray is one the leading proponents of the cultivation of surprise or open competencies in composition, though he does not use the "competency" terminology.)

A *broad* competency is the ability to generalize, to apply what one has learned from narrow competencies to different or more generalized situations. When students realize, for instance, that the skills required to explicate a poem (for instance the closed capacities of identifying metaphors and connotations) may be used to analyze advertisements or political speeches, or that the strategies used to write a persuasive essay may be employed in conducting successful fund-raising drives, they are transferring the narrow competencies they've learned into broader fields. This belief is a foundation of social-constructionist theory. Teachers can suggest how those competencies are achieved, but they can't make the students transfer the knowledge. Each writer must seize that power for herself. One of the beliefs underlying portfolio evaluation (see Chapter 9 below) is that portfolios, by encouraging revision and self-reflection, helps a student demonstrate mastery of broad and open competencies, and therefore stand as a better measure of learning.

As a teacher, then, you'll have to decide what competencies you feel it's important for your students to master—and what ones you don't want to hear your colleagues in other departments complaining about. For instance, you want students to acquire the open competency of writing, so you'll need to provide time to let them write. This means that while you may spend some of your class or conference time reviewing punctuation or paragraph development as isolated skills, most of your time will be better spent in having students write—and commenting on problems with closed skills in the context of student writing, usually through comments on student papers.

You want them, moreover, to acquire the broad competencies of generalization, so you'll need to provide opportunities for them to generalize. If students write only five-paragraph themes, for instance, how can they learn which strategies transfer to writing larger and different structures? If they examine only belletristic discourse, how can they determine which skills would work in other forms of discourse? Sometimes your school may require you to focus on narrow, closed competencies, perhaps by requiring that students pass a minimum competency test on spelling, vocabulary, reading comprehension, paragraph development and the like. In such cases, you will need to teach these capacities; however there's no law preventing you from teaching these in the context of acquiring broader, open competencies. Forster's maxim—"Only connect"—applies as much to deciding which competencies you will emphasize as it does to literary criticism.

But this, of course, is all theory. What follows is a discussion of how you can put theory into practice as a writing teacher. Good luck! And keep in mind Herman Melville's prayer for writers: "O Time, Strength, Cash, and Patience!"

Pragmatics in the Classroom:
Or, Caveat Instructor

> [L]imitations and difficulties are the native habitats of English depart-
> ments, and we must work within them.
> —ROBERT SCHOLES (1985:25)

Teaching writing is a complicated process, and it has its own complex
problems both within and outside your classroom. This section covers,
although not in great depth, some of the most common problems you
may face, especially as a new instructor. Each campus may have its
own ways of handling these issues; don't forget to consult your department's policy manual for its recommendations or to consult your program director if you have questions.

Student Attitudes

The students you'll find in your classroom may be very difficult from
what you expect. They probably won't be much like the students
who were in your own freshman composition classes, however long
ago those were. Differences in attitude and education will greatly
affect your classroom; these are some of the problems you might
anticipate.

Motivation

One of my campus' experts on student retention claims that the one
subject almost all high school students master is "Getting Away With
Things." What she means is that under the conditions found in most
American high schools, students learn just how much effort is
required to get by, and that's the effort they produce. They are wonderful at "figuring out" teachers: Mr. Medved wants this, Mrs. Holoka

wants that, Sister Rosarita can't stand something else. For some of them, writing classes have become a series of hoops to jump through, and they have become rather agile at doing so. Other students, those who are at most risk for retention, find the "figuring out" process to be demanding and intimidating; if they lose their confidence that they *can* figure college out, we're likely to lose them.

When these students come to college, their focus is on "figuring out" the professors again, rather than on learning and self-development. Since your composition class is likely to be the smallest one they have and the one with the highest ratio of student-teacher contact, this attitude is magnified. (If I had a nickel for every "What do you want on this paper?" I've heard in my career, I'd be driving a German luxury car right now.) It takes a conscious effort, on both your part and theirs, to shift the weight of the course from "figuring out what the teacher wants" to "becoming a better writer." I often talk about this attitude very early in the semester, just to get the subject in the open and to invite discussion and response.

Time Commitment

When I was in college, I worked forty hours a week (on an 11 P.M. to 7 A.M. shift) to pay my way through an Ivy League school. I was unusual then; most of my classmates had a combination of small part-time jobs and loans but were spending most of their time on school. Today's students are very different. Studies show that the average student may be working at least twelve hours a week, and a sizable percentage may be working as many as thirty hours a week. That means much less time to collaborate outside of class, use the library, reflect on a piece of writing, and so on. If the student is trying to juggle the demands of a family as well, the demands on his or her time increase dramatically. One of the questions I always ask students on the first day of class is "What are your time commitments outside of school?" I want to know so that I can plan my assignments and activities accordingly. If I tried now what I was able to do when I began teaching (assign a paper Friday, class discussion Monday, rough draft Wednesday, receive the paper Friday, repeat the cycle at least eight more times), my students would get out their Uzis, and, to use a current slang term, "postalize" my classroom. Just because we seem to spend all our time on composition classes doesn't mean that our students can do so.

Respect for Teachers

On my first day of college, when I went in to that 9 A.M. sociology class and saw a white-haired man in a tweed jacket put down his pipe and launch into a lecture, I remember thinking, "*This* is a professor." It took me eight or nine weeks to get enough courage to ask him a question (he, of course, never stooped from his lofty heights to ask any of *us* questions). Aside from my upbringing and the metal-edged rulers of the nuns who dominated my early education, I had a healthy respect for this professor just because of who he was. Some of our students still have that attitude (particularly if you happen to be a dignified, pipe-smoking, white-haired man who wears tweed in the classroom). However, today resistance is becoming more common in our class-rooms. Students, especially if they have had negative high school experiences, are more likely to challenge the credentials and authori-ty of their teachers. This isn't necessarily bad; many teachers, in fact, encourage such attitudes because they feel the tension engendered may produce better writing. But for a young TA or a part-time instruc-tor, being treated like a high-school substitute teacher can be unnerv-ing and demoralizing. Again, I try to address this issue in a low-key manner on the first day of class by telling students a little about myself as part of our icebreaker activities. This lets me establish my credentials without making an issue out of "who's in power here."

Consumerism

Education these days is driven by money. Our administrators make decisions based on it, and so do our students. Whether they are paying for their own education or letting someone else do so, they tend to view their schooling as a consumer experience: so much quality and content for so much money. Today it's not uncommon for a parent to call an instructor and complain that his or her child is not getting his or her "money's worth" out of a course. Those of us reared in a liberal arts tradition view such attitudes with horror, but our position doesn't make those attitudes go away. Students are faced with an increasingly competitive world and no guarantee of employment or a secure future, and their insecurities color their responses to our classrooms. (See the student paper "Who's To Blame For Generation X" in Chapter 9, below, for a powerful articulation of these fears.) Your own attitudes toward education will color your response; I tend to use a version of Ross Winterowd's old "The ability to write well is money in your pocket and power in your hand" and work from there.

Changing Literacies

Most writing teachers are text-based literates; we are used to getting our information by reading and writing, whether the texts be books, periodicals, other written texts, or, now, electronic media. Our students, however, are less text-based than we were. They have been raised in an environment of visual and auditory messages; they can recall an ad campaign that aired six or seven years ago, or a song that was popular when they were in middle school, but somehow seem unable to remember a chapter they read the night before. They're also used to getting their information in short bursts; thus, their attention spans for text-based literacy are shorter and they may find completing a long reading assignment or writing assignment much more difficult than handling a short one. They aren't used to processing text-based information, and when they come to college and confront a text-based system so intensely, their literate skills may well suffer, and you may have to coach them in the techniques needed to increase their text-based literacy. Reading for content is a skill you will probably want to cover with your students quite early in the semester.

Copyright

The most common need of writing teachers is a way to duplicate material: exercises, sample papers, student drafts, and outside readings. Whether it be by photocopying machine, duplicator, mimeograph, or printing station, we generate multiple copies of multiple pieces of writing for the educational benefit of our students. But we can't approach this process naively; many of these sources are protected either explicitly or implicitly by copyright, a legal right that must be respected. State and federal courts have consistently defended publishers in copyright suits, so you could be in trouble if you don't abide by the law. Most libraries and professional copying centers have their own policies about making copies available within the copyright law and are usually quite willing to help you stay within the law; never hesitate to ask.

The "Fair Use" section of the copyright law says that libraries may put on reserve a single copy of the following at a faculty member's request: a chapter, an article, a short story, a graph, a chart, a picture, a short poem, an essay, or a book owned by the library. (Workbooks, because of their "disposable" nature, *cannot* be handled in this manner.) The faculty member may arrange to provide up to four more copies of those reserve materials, under the following circumstances:

- the number of copies is reasonable with regard to the total enrollment in the course, to a maximum of four copies;
- the library stamps the materials with a notice of copyright;
- the amount of material is "reasonable" in relation to the total amount of material required for the course ("reasonable" varies according to the nature of the course and subject matter and the level of the students taking it, but I've found that one copy per seven or eight students is usually acceptable);
- the market (salability) of the work is not harmed by making it available in photocopies (i.e., the author's royalties are not affected; this is the rule governing duplication of workbooks); and
- the instructor decides to use the material "spontaneously," so that there is not enough time to receive an answer from the publisher to a request to duplicate the material.

In practice, you can make a small number of published sources available to the students through your library without violating copyright. If they choose to photocopy one copy of the material at the library for their own use, they are also abiding by the law. However, if you want students to buy or otherwise obtain a large number of articles (usually handled through a commercial photocopying service), you must "clear copyright" for those sources. You do this by writing to the copyright owner (usually the publisher), describing how you want to use the material, and asking for permission. This is usually granted, although sometimes you will have to pay a small royalty (again, often collected and forwarded by the photocopying service). A few journals—those published by the National Council of Teachers of English among them—provide a copyright release in each issue permitting you to make a limited number of copies for spontaneous use. But most journals need to protect their incomes by charging copyright fees; they, and the original writers, must earn a living, and we must respect this.

A sample letter asking for permission to reproduce material follows. Note that you must specify what you want to use, how much of it, how you will distribute it, when you want to use it, and what kind of use you will make of it (stress "educational purposes"). If your department permits you the use of letterhead stationery, by all means, use it!

[date]

Permissions Department
Addison Wesley Educational Publishers
10 East 53rd St.
New York, NY 10022

Dear Permissions Department:

I would like permission to copy the following material for continued use in my English Composition classes in future terms:

Text: Elizabeth Cowan Neeld, *Writing*, 2nd edition, 1986
Material to be copied: pages 43-48 ("Classical Invention")
Type of Reprint: Photocopy
Use: Supplementary teaching material for students' educational use
Distribution: 5 copies will be placed on reserve in the campus library; a typed summary will be distributed to students.

I have enclosed a self-addressed envelope for your convenience in replying to this request. If I do not hear from you by two months from the date of this letter, I will assume that I have your permission.

Sincerely,

J.K. Tarvers

Although there have been rather fewer legal challenges, it's clear that student papers are also covered to some extent by copyright. Papers produced by students in your current class do not need copyright clearance; the exchange of student materials is an accepted pedagogical method. However, if you want to keep a copy of a student's paper to use in subsequent terms (or someday, perhaps, in an article or book), it's best to obtain a simple copyright release from the student.

Most students are flattered to be asked and grant the permission willingly; but they have the right to refuse and should feel free to do so if they wish. Here's a sample of a student paper release:

Permission to Use Your Writing Again

Student Name

Course Number, Name, and Semester

Description of Material to Be Used:

    I would like to keep a copy of the work described above to use in subsequent terms and possibly in scholarly publication. If you are willing to let me use your work, please answer the questions below to tell me how you'd like it used. (Circle Yes or No).

1. Change the real names in the material.
    Yes   No
2. Correct minor errors before the material is used.
    Yes   No
3. Give my [student's] name as the author.
    Yes   No
4. Change confidential or identifying material before the material is used.
    Yes   No

Your signature

Your permanent (home) address

(Please print or write legibly)

Today's date

Thank you for your help!
J. K. Tarvers

Plagiarism

Instances of plagiarism, unfortunately, seem to be on the increase as students compete for higher grades and a better chance of success in the world (as they see it). Campus bulletin boards, the classified ads, and the Internet advertise a number of sources of papers to be purchased, usually for the specious reason of "letting a student know how another student handled this topic." Sadly, many recent studies indicate that a sizable majority of students don't think plagiarism is "wrong," in an ethical sense, because "it's just words." Plagiarism originally meant "kidnaping," and the plagiarizer steals words and ideas as precious to the original writers as their children might be (remind students how jealously proud they are of their own papers and how hard they find it to discard anything they've written, by comparison). Perhaps if you do so, students might see why, ethically, plagiarism cannot be tolerated in a university. You may have to remind them that the academic freedom they enjoy in a university—the kind of freedom students in Beijing died for in the summer of 1989—is based on respect for the free and honest exchange of ideas. If we fail to acknowledge the source of those ideas, we are not being honest; if we silence the voices of the people who first phrased them, we deny those people their academic freedom.

Four kinds of student are likely to commit plagiarism: the lazy student, the desperate student, the grade-hungry student, and the unknowing student. Each must be handled differently. Lazy students see a borrowed or purchased paper as a way of getting the grade without doing the work; you'll see this problem most often with literary criticism or research papers. The best remedy is prevention: require drafts, hold workshops and conferences, and have students submit their preliminary materials along with the finished paper. Be suspicious when students produce polished papers without the supporting materials. Few lazy students are willing to forge several sets of drafts for a paper, after all!

Desperate students are usually swamped by time, outside activities, personal circumstances, or a combination of the three. They may find it hard to submit a paper because two others are due that day, while they're working 25 hours a week to pay tuition. These students often turn to friends, school paper files, the Internet, or outside vendors. Prevent these situations by giving students adequate time to complete assignments, setting mini-deadlines (such as draft workshops) to help them manage their time, and encouraging honesty. Tell students who are swamped to talk to you before the due date; obviously you can't mark all 25 papers the night they're submitted, so you can allow a student a little leeway in submitting longer papers. Then encourage those students to uncomplicate their lives a bit. Burnout is not a good future!

Grade-hungry students see grades as the only value in education. They're convinced that one B- will keep them from medical school or a lucrative career in investment banking or a scholarship. Encourage these students to be realistic; after all, if they plagiarize and are caught, they'll receive a much lower grade (at some schools, an F for the course as well) than if they'd written the paper themselves. All students can benefit from a de-emphasis of grades and a refocusing on goals, but some students won't be able to get those red letters out of their heads. Again, requiring drafts and keeping a close eye on student progress is the best remedy for such a problem.

Finally, some students really don't understand what plagiarism is and are usually horrified at such an accusation. Typically such students learned to "do research papers" in high school in a system that encouraged them to copy passages from books and encyclopedias and rewarded them for presenting as much copied material as possible. Footnoting, paraphrase, the use of quotation marks, and attribution of sources may never have been raised as issues. Their papers may be filled with what some scholars call "patchwriting" (e.g. Howard 1995), where the students attempt to work sources into their own work but fail to complete the task skillfully. To remedy such problems, teach documentation; explain why a writer uses quotes (and when), why readers need to find attribution for sources, and how to write a correct note and bibliographic entry. Teach true paraphrasing (recasting both vocabulary and syntax) and summary as alternatives to quotation, again emphasizing the need for footnotes and attribution. Take time to explain where the quotation marks—double and single—go. This teaching can be handled inductively; use samples that allow students to infer how source material can be handled, then practice on examples to get the mechanics down. Check rough drafts for the handling of documentation and help students correct their errors. Most students are willing and quite able to handle sources correctly, and the recent simplifications of MLA documentation will help them be more accurate. Most handbooks have documentation sections that are quite useful in helping students correctly document sources.

Social constructionists in particular have begun to campaign to decriminalize patchwriting. As Rebecca Moore Howard says in the article referred to above, "patchwriting [is] a pedagogical opportunity, not a juridical problem. . . . Teachers [should] treat it as an important transitional strategy in the student's progress toward 'membership' in a discourse community. To treat it negatively, as a 'problem' to be 'cured' or punished, would be to undermine its positive intellectual value, thereby obstructing rather than facilitating the learning process" (788-89). Like all sweeping generalizations, this one holds some truth. If a student truly is trying to master the incorporation of sources, but hasn't succeeded yet, it *would* be cruel to subject that writer to a university's judicial code or to fail him or her for the course on this ground alone. On the other hand, harking back to the principle of Getting Away With Things, one can easily see how this concept can get out of hand. If you encourage a student who patchwrites, but that student still doesn't master the concept, what next? That student may go on to Professor Ramachandran's Economics 211 class, and patchwrite again. But Professor Ramachandran is a "hard-liner" on plagiarism, and flunks the student in his class. The student then appeals the grade to the Dean, claiming, "My writing teacher said that this was okay, that it was a sign of my intellectual growth." At the very least, you're in for an uncomfortable conversation with the Dean; one of my lawyer friends even speculated that a student under these circumstances might have grounds for legal action against you, for misrepresentation or malpractice.

Moreover, if you encourage or promote a positive attitude toward patchwriting in your classroom, the superior "Get Away With It" strategists may plagiarize intentionally, then claim patchwriting as their defense. Perhaps my experience has made me cynical, but I would be tremendously hesitant to recommend the acceptance of patchwriting in a classroom, particularly if you are an untenured writing instructor who has no institutional protection. I might discuss patchwriting in a conference with a student who is having trouble, but my theme would be "This is still plagiarism and there are people out there who will punish you badly for doing this, so let's work on overcoming this very serious flaw." And I would be very careful about any written comments I made about the subject, just in case. Those paper trails will eat you every time.

The best remedy against plagiarism, when all this is said and done, is still you; you know your students, how they write, and what they're writing about. If you see something that looks unfamiliar, ask your student about it (you may not want to actually use the word "plagiarism" unless you've found the source) in conference. (Some teachers like to have their office mates present at such a conference as an unobtrusive note-taker and witness.) A simple misunderstanding can be cleared up fairly easily. More serious cases should be handled according to your school's established policy. If you are not familiar with that policy, or your institution doesn't have a clearly articulated plagiarism policy, consult your program director or student judicial affairs officer before taking any action. An ounce of prevention, after all, has considerable worth.

Outside Help

In this age of consulting services, students can often find a number of outside aids to help them prepare their papers. These can range from formal tutoring services to "edit and type" agencies to the two-cents' worth of a student's roommate. You have to decide what you'll allow as outside help, based on the goals of your course. If students are expected to learn to edit and correct their own writing, you'll have to decide what kinds of editing help they can use: a tutor, a spell checker, a typist. If they are supposed to learn to present their own work, will you accept papers prepared by mom, daughter, boyfriend, or paid professionals? Make your decisions in advance and make them clear to students. Then abide by them.

Some students may have access to tutoring—through an athletic team, foreign students' office, minority services program, sorority development program, or whatever. If your students are getting tutoring, set limits on what kinds of help the tutor should be giving your student. (Writing Centers are places where these limits are already known, and they provide invaluable assistance; see Muriel Harris' excellent article on this subject in the anthology that follows.) For instance, tutors might help students with a number of paragraph development exercises, but shouldn't tell them exactly how to develop the second paragraph on p. 3 of their drafts. You might suggest particular areas the tutor could focus on to help the student achieve her goals, and ask for progress reports or mutual conferences so that you can coordinate your assistance. Some schools ask students, tutors, and teachers to write out a contract that covers the responsibilities of all three. Remember that not all students can get access to a tutor, so be sure your evaluation is not biased in favor of (or against) such students.

The Professional Environment

The biggest problem, unfortunately, that many writing teachers face comes not from the course or from the students. Rather, it comes from the institution in the form of nonrecognition of a teacher's professional status. Compositionists continually complain that they are marginalized or even "feminized," and to a considerable extent, these complaints have substance (see for instance Reichert 1996). Since some institutions still regard composition as a "service course," they feel justified in hiring part-time teachers but denying them faculty status (even library cards), benefits, and rights (such as offices, access to duplicating facilities, and even written contracts). Some members of literature faculties (and some whole departments) look down on, and snub outright, those who teach about creating written products instead of analyzing products already written. Since these faculty members are usually the powers-that-be in departmental politics, their attitudes carry weight and are often contagious. Alas, many teachers must endure such unpleasant situations, having no alternatives. And the economics of education don't seem to offer much hope for change. As James Sledd writes, "The debasement of 'writing' rationalizes the status of the faculty who teach it and the base salaries they receive" (Lindemann and Tate, 149).

In 1987, the Conference on College Composition and Communication (CCCC), the professional organization of college writing teachers, adopted the so-called "Wyoming Conference Resolution," which calls for establishment of grievance procedures for writing teachers and encourages better professional treatment of writing teachers by institutions. In 1988, the Modern Language Association (MLA) weighed in with a "Report of the Commission on Writing and Literature," which recommended that departments consider the different natures of research and publication in rhetoric and composition when it evaluated teachers for promotion, salary increases, and tenure. And schools everywhere have begun to realize that teaching must be given the same professional respect that publishing now receives; in some states, legislatures are planning to hold college teachers responsible for the quality of their undergraduate teaching. All of these are positive signs.

In the long run, these attempts may have some effect; in the short term, speaking realistically, things are not likely to get better quickly. Try, if you can, to act as a professional, even if your institution does not. Join the various professional organizations such as CCCC and NCTE;

go to professional meetings as often as you can afford to; present your work. Most reputable journals and conferences now have policies of blind submission, so you need not worry that the name of your institution will help or hurt your submission's chances of acceptance. There are hundreds of journals now publishing in rhetoric and composition (see the *CCC Bibliography*, Anson [1986], Anson and Miller [1988], Weimer [1992], and Kroll [1990] for ideas and places to send your submissions). If you have access to the Internet, get in touch with other scholars in rhetoric and composition; united, we are stronger than separate. Do the best teaching you can. If your institution continues to mistreat you, take your valuable skills somewhere else, even outside of academe. *Illegitimum non carborundum*° has long been the watchword of composition teachers; make it yours, too.

And if you are teaching in such a situation, don't forget to see the possibilities as well as the limitations. An electronic correspondent and friend, Neal Postman, who is an instructor at Boston University, recently posted this comment on one of the electronic mail lists read by compositionists. With his permission, let me conclude this chapter with his "spin" on the pragmatics of teaching writing:

> I've been thinking about how much real freedom I've had as an adjunct to do pretty much what I wanted in the classroom.... There's a certain freedom I've found within the instability of comp [sic]. In other words, in a course where outcomes are so inherently fuzzy, where curriculum is contested, where textbooks seem more responsive to publishers' needs to make money than to teachers' needs to teach effectively or students' needs for accurate and relevant information, where grades are antithetical to the "paradigm shift" and the "process revolution," there's room for tremendous creativity from those of us being poorly paid for what we do.... Anyway, I think there's a great deal of exciting things being done in the composition classrooms of our colleagues, particularly those who can't stay around very long after class because they have to hit the road in order to get to their other job(s). (via WCENTER, 5 July 1996)

With that energy and attitude in mind, let's look at the practices and scenarios that might govern *your* classrooms.

° Don't let the bastards grind you down

PART

2

PRACTICES AND SCENARIOS

Organizing a Writing Course

> A way of teaching is never innocent. Every pedagogy is imbricated in
> ideology, in a set of tacit assumptions about what is good, what is pos-
> sible, and how power ought to be distributed.
>
> —James Berlin (1988: 492)

Understanding the theories that underlie the teaching of writing is
one thing. Doing something with those theories, in a structured and
purposeful way, is quite another. How do the elements go together?
Can the theory somehow transfer into your classroom on some cloudy
Thursday in November? The answer, of course, is yes; but as in any
other structure, the success will depend more on the architect than on
architecture. Experienced teachers have learned, usually the hard
way, how to organize and pace a course and how to fit the material
into the eight or ten or thirteen or fifteen weeks available. It doesn't just
happen in a semester, either; after more than fifteen years of teaching
writing, I still find myself tinkering with my syllabi in midsemester,
as do most of my colleagues. What follows, then, is not a foolproof
recipe for constructing a writing course. It's common sense advice that
should save you from making some of the more painful mistakes in
putting your course together.

Goals, Time Management, and Flexibility

Even if you've never taught writing—or any other subject—before, you
can construct a course that is clear and coherent. First, you need to
consider the three chief elements in course design: goals, time management, and flexibility.

Goals

Goals for any class are set by asking three questions. At what level are
my students beginning? By the end of the course, what level should

they have attained? Along the way, what subordinate goals should they achieve? These three questions define the territory you must cover. Once you have these answers, you can begin to consider strategy.

Many departments will answer the first two questions for you. You'll be told that your class contains students whose test scores, for example, fell between 400 and 600 on the SAT, or students who got B's in high school English. (Remember that these scores mark mastery of closed and usually narrow competencies, and that most American high school students spent only about three percent of their high school years writing discourse of a paragraph or more in length. [Applebee, 1982]) More and more schools gather writing samples from students, either through the application process or during the school's orientation period. These samples are far better indicators of the actual level of your students' writing abilities and will give you a far clearer indication of their competence than mere numbers will. Usually, a majority of students show similar levels of skill in focusing, developing, and supporting topics, although their closed skills (including punctuation, grammar, and spelling) may vary widely, especially on timed writing samples. If a few students seem markedly advanced or behind in their skills, see if your department has a procedure for transferring such students to a course commensurate with their level. (If your school does not collect writing samples for you, elicit them on the first class day. Don't neglect this important diagnostic tool.)

Likewise, most departments have clear requirements for passing writing courses. These requirements take a number of forms: a minimum grade, submission of an acceptable writing portfolio, a passing score on a competency examination, or the like. The ideal situation, of course, is to have all students pass the writing course. But in reality, some won't. Resolve now to be firm; students who have not met the minimum requirements should not be sent on to other course work. If you pass a student who is not able to write according to your school's standards, you help no one—not yourself, your colleagues or school (who will have to cope with an unprepared student), and especially not the student. It's unpleasant to make a student repeat a course, but it's far less unpleasant than sending that student into a discourse community without adequate communications skills.

The goals you will most frequently set are the subordinate ones, the milestones along the way. Sometimes you'll be given guidelines for these: students must write in six or seven modes, or master five set forms, or submit 10 papers or 7,000 words, and so on. You may set conceptual goals for the whole class: everyone should be able to support an assertion with evidence and analysis, or incorporate sources without plagiarism, or create an inductive argument. Individual goals can be drawn from diagnostic essays and the students' own work: Jerry will solve those dialect interference problems, Casey will conquer the comma splice, Lynn will learn to write complex sentences. Some goals will be teacher-specific: I still expect my students to learn when and where to use an apostrophe, despite road signs for the Farmer's Market and newspaper articles on "buying Hornet's tickets." Many of these goals will be set in your writing assignments and in comments on student papers: they'll be discussed below.

Teaching Tip

This is a goal statement under discussion at a midwestern university. It has undergone several revisions already, as the faculty struggle to express themselves clearly not only to their students but to their colleagues and administration as well. Notice that it's trying to balance the concerns of the writing faculty with the demands of the larger university community, as well as to project the course forward into the students' futures. See if your program has a similar statement. If not, take the time to write a goals statement for your own class. The clarifying power it has for organizing your course is well worthwhile, and it would make an excellent addition to a Teaching Portfolio (see below, Chapter 10).

> The Freshman Writing Seminars are designed to help you write better through experiencing writing as a way of learning and as a recursive, multi-step process in which you explore, analyze, and refine your ideas. They will also acquaint you with the expectations readers have of college-educated writers, both in content and correctness. When you have finished your seminar, you should have sufficient confidence to adapt easily to any writing project you may encounter at the university or in your future careers.

Time Management

A ruthless sense of realism must go into planning your course schedule. Start by laying out on a calendar or class planner the actual boundaries of your class: how many class meetings will you have? Be sure to figure in both academic and personal events; legal or religious holidays may reduce the number of class meetings, as may a professional meeting or your own academic and personal commitments. (Your department will probably require you to find a substitute for personal absences; if so, try to make the arrangements well in advance.) If in-class midterm and/or final examinations are required at your school, reserve those class meetings as well.

Next, schedule in the due dates for submitting assignments. Assignments in the beginning of the semester usually take longer to complete than those later in the term; space out the due dates accordingly. You may need an extra class period for more discussion or draft work, for example, early in the semester; later on, this may be dispensed with. If you plan to hold conferences during the semester, you may have to cancel a class meeting for these as well. Some creative scheduling may be needed to prevent assignments from backing up on desks. The last thing you want is a stack of papers due the weekend the *Job List* arrives or the week of your doctoral examinations.

Some papers, particularly the longer ones, take more time to assess, and so do portfolios. They'll need to be turned in several weeks before the end of the term if you're to report class grades promptly. Likewise, students will need longer to complete some papers than others. To use time efficiently, you may have students complete several shorter papers, for instance, while work on the research paper is in progress. And despite good intentions, very few students will work on an assignment over a break period. It's best to schedule an assignment to come in the last class before a vacation; then at least the students can go on holiday with a clear desk.

Flexibility

The best laid plans, of course, still go awry. No course schedule can be carved in granite. Sometimes students will master material more rapidly than you anticipated; at other times, they may need extra time to complete an assignment. Be ready to give a little, in the interests of the sanity of all concerned. (Some experienced teachers try to leave a few open days in their schedules for catching up; if by some miracle the class is on schedule, this leaves time for conferences, practice, and public sharing of students' work. If your schedule permits, one such day in each month's schedule can be invaluable.)

And, too, events outside your control disrupt even the most careful planning. Flu epidemics, an earthquake, a candidate's visit to campus, the basketball team's unexpected success in the NCAA tournament— all of these may require class cancellations or rescheduling. A few years ago my spring semester began with a strike by the secretarial and maintenance staffs, accompanied by three major snowstorms in seven class days. With no staff to conduct registration and process course changes, or plow sidewalks and parking lots, and picket lines around unheated buildings, it took us until Spring Break to really get things back to normal. While you should still have a clear idea of pace for your class, leave yourself space to react to changing circumstances.

By establishing major and subordinate goals for yourself, working out a reasonable time schedule, and allowing for flexibility, you can establish a clear and effective skeleton for your course. Now it's time to put some flesh on that structure.

Choosing Course Materials

Most departments simplify matters for both themselves and their new instructors by prescribing which texts will be used in each writing course offered. These texts could include a complete rhetoric, a reader, a handbook, a departmental policy guide, a research paper guide, a dictionary, software, or combinations thereof. Obviously the real "texts" in any writing course are those produced by the students; the other materials are supplementary. It's up to you to decide what materials you'll use and when and how you'll use them.

There are thousands of composition texts on the market today. How do you choose from this bewildering variety? In some departments, the director of composition chooses the texts from the many examination copies submitted each year. Sometimes departments have a committee that makes these decisions. Sometimes the staff participates in such decisions through an election or book fair. Textbook company sales "reps" are always willing to supply teachers with information and sample copies. But if you're starting cold, what do you do?

First, decide what sort of theory you want in your textbook. If you like the traditional "product-oriented" approach, you'll have a number of choices. But many textbooks now are partially or wholly process-oriented. A few include cognitive research, and many recent ones address the concerns of social construction and discourse communities. The book(s) you pick should reflect your view of writing; you don't want to contradict the text for the entire semester. The journal *Writing Program Administration* each year publishes an annotated guide to texts published in that year; this can help you choose a group of texts to examine more carefully. Ask the publishers' representatives who call at your school for texts that use your approach; ask like-minded colleagues at your school (and at others) what texts they're examining. And don't neglect the book exhibits at professional meetings; there's a great deal more available there than free pens and coffee.

Next, you have to decide what sorts of texts you want to use. Most programs require their students to have a handbook for reference, and students find it reassuring to have that book to hang on to. (Guess which one we recommend?) A good college-level dictionary with some information on usage, such as the *American Heritage* or *Webster's New Collegiate*, is absolutely essential. (Remember that most high school students rent or borrow their books from the school; they don't have these books to fall back on.) If your course is going to focus intensively on critical reading, you may choose to use an anthology for examples (many anthologies now include published student writing). You may wish to find your own models for students or to have them bring in models to discuss; if so, remember the restrictions of the new copyright law (discussed above, Chapter 4). If you will need to demonstrate a number of rhetorical modes or forms to students, a full rhetoric text may be useful. If there is to be a great deal of documented writing, a research paper guide may come in handy. If your school requires or encourages computer use, a certain kind of software may be prescribed.

Once you have decided what categories of books to examine and have narrowed down the field to a handful of choices, you need to examine the books themselves closely. You want a text that supports you, of course: it should cover the topics you want to cover, with examples, exercises, discussion questions, and activities that will help you present material to your students. But remember that you know this material; students don't. So look at the texts from their point of view as well. Do the examples and exercises really help students master these competencies? Are the explanations clear and to the point? (Once, a student justifiably complained on an evaluation that the text

took twelve pages to say "Be concise.") Is the book designed and produced well, with a good index, readable type, wide margins for notes,
and a strong spine to avoid lost pages? Is the author's tone condescending? Does the preface intimidate or invite students? If a question
arises at 2 A.M., can the student find the answer in the text? And how
much does the text cost? (Teachers get free desk copies, but students in
a course with rhetoric, reader, handbook, research guide, and dictionary may spend more than $75. Add software and writing tools and
the cost becomes prohibitive.) Spend the time to pick a book both you
and the students can live with. Good texts are invaluable; unsuitable
ones waste time, money, paper, and goodwill.

The Syllabus

Once you have created a skeleton for your course and chosen the materials you'll use to teach it, you are ready to put a syllabus on paper. The
syllabus establishes a contract between you and your students; it
explains what both parties can expect from the course. Insecure students need syllabi for confidence; employed or academically burdened
students need them for survival planning. Some teachers prefer to
hand out only the simplest of syllabi and modify from week to week;
others (and I fall into this group) like to lay out matters clearly at the
beginning of the term to avoid the protest of "You never told us" later
on. The following checklist, adopted from Erika Lindemann's *A
Rhetoric for Writing Teachers*, 3rd ed. (1995), includes eight key points
for syllabus information:

1. Descriptive Information. The name and number of the course, its prereq-
   uisites and other requirements, and the instructor's name, office location
   and hours, and phone number(s).
2. Specifications of Course Goals and Content. The goals—short- and long-
   term—of the course and of the individual course parts.
3. Reading Materials. Names of texts, where to acquire them, a list of reading assignments, and the dates by which these should be completed.
4. Writing Assignments. The number and description of writing assignments, with due dates, policies on late and revised papers, group work,
   and presentation requirements.
5. Description of Instructional Procedures. Time devoted to lectures, group
   work, writing workshops, etc.
6. Course Requirements. When and how work is due, how it will be evaluated,
   attendance and participation, missing and late assignment policies.

7. Course Schedule. A meeting-by-meeting calendar of events.
8. Evaluation and Grading of Students. Required assignments, how they will be graded, and how final grades will be assessed.

Teaching in Practice

Below is the syllabus for my freshman writing course at Winthrop. It's not as detailed as some of yours may be, because I can allow students a considerable voice in choosing reading assignments from a collection they all read in the collective first-year seminar. However, you can see how the eight elements are included and how easy it would be for me to include specific reading assignments in the course schedule.

ENGLISH 101: FALL 1996

TTh 2:00-3:15   Dr. Tarvers
Kinard 204   Bancroft 214A
X-4557 (office); x-2171 (messages); 555-1212 (home)   In office M-Th 9-11
e-mail: tarversj@winthrop.edu   and by appt.

Texts (all at The Bookworm on Cherry Road):
The Longman Handbook for Writers and Readers [LH]
American Heritage Dictionary or equivalent
First-Year Student's Information Guide [FIG]
We will also use your *Critical Issues* coursepack for outside readings.

Other materials:
    A folder to keep all your papers and drafts
    Writing materials (bring these to class every time)
    2 3.5" computer disks and something to keep them in

<u>Goals</u> English 101 is a course in critical reading, writing, and thinking. Winthrop believes it is important that you be able not only to read material, but also to understand it: its assumptions, biases, hidden agendas, messages. This course, we hope, will help you develop your critical skills and learn to present your ideas and viewpoints to differing audiences. The course will be conducted partially in lecture/discussion form, and partly in workshop form, to give you maximum practice in developing these skills. Be prepared to write frequently—often for every class, and to prepare about 30-40 pages of reading material for each class.

<u>Attendance and Behavior Expectations</u> Attendance for this course is mandatory; please be familiar with the material in on page 4-6 of the FIG, since this explains the policy I must follow. Certainly, if you miss four or more classes,

you can expect your grade to be lowered significantly. Education is not like banking; I can't simply "deposit" information in your brains and expect to get it back with interest. If you want to learn to write well, you have to work at it, to make it important to you. This means you have responsibilities to yourself, to your classmates, and to me.

Be on time; do your preparation; bring your materials to class; be awake! On days when we hold writing group sessions, you are expected to bring a readable draft to class (and copies, if it is your turn to read a draft aloud); if you aren't prepared for these sessions, or miss a scheduled conference, I will count you absent. You can take one 24-hour extension on a due date this semester, provided you notify me a class in advance. Otherwise I don't accept late papers.

Grading Grades for the class will be based on your portfolio of revised papers, with consideration given to your attendance and the quality of your participation in class discussion and writing group sessions. This system is explained in pages 5-8 of the FIG. Basically, you will submit a sample portfolio of two revised papers for my comments at midterm, and a final portfolio of four revised papers and some supporting material on December 10. There will be six papers assigned in the term, each with revision opportunities, so you will have plenty of work to choose from when it comes time to put together your portfolios, and you control what material goes in the portfolio. The paper "due" dates in the syllabus indicate when we will complete class work on each paper and you give me a copy for my response.

Reading Reading assignments will be given out in chunks for each unit, at the beginning of each unit; I will make some required assignments from your CISM packet and poll you to decide on others. If you find a reading you'd like to share with the class, bring it to me in advance and I'll have it duplicated. (Please include a correct MLA bibliographic reference; consult Part IV of LH.) Each unit will have a critical goal and a stylistic goal, and these will move from basic to more sophisticated techniques so that by the end of the semester you will be writing (we hope) with intelligence and verve.

SCHEDULE

Unit 1	Sept. 3-Sept. 19
Goals:	Mastering strategies for effective critical reading
	Discovering your writing strengths and weaknesses
Dates:	Writing group day Sept. 17
	Paper 1 due Sept. 19
Unit 2	Sept. 24-Oct. 3
Goals:	Writing to an audience
	Understanding the differences between student and
	professional writing
Dates:	Writing group days Sept. 26 & Oct. 1

	Paper 2 due Oct. 3
	Conferences will be scheduled individually in this unit.
Unit 3	Oct. 8-Oct. 17
Goals:	Writing logically
	Cutting the fat from your prose
Dates:	Writing group day Oct. 15
	Paper 3 (HOURLY) written in class Oct. 17.
Unit 4	Oct. 22-Nov. 5
Goals:	Writing persuasively
	Polishing your style
Dates:	Preliminary portfolio due Oct. 25
	Writing group days Oct. 31 & Nov. 3
	Paper 4 due Nov. 5
	Conferences for the portfolio reviews will be
	scheduled individually in this unit.
Unit 5	Nov. 7-Nov. 28
Goals:	Writing synthetically
	Expanding your options; writing under time pressure
Dates:	Writing group days Nov. 19 & 24
	Nov. 21; NO CLASS. Work on revisions.
	Paper 5 due Nov. 26
	Thanksgiving (and my mom's birthday) Nov. 28; NO CLASS
Unit 6	Dec. 3-12
Goals:	Review and Evaluation
	Preparing to write your way out of the course
Dates:	Writing group days Dec. 3 & Dec. 5
	Paper 6 (FINAL) Dec. 7 at 8 AM in our classroom; pick up
	copy for revisions at noon December 8.
	Portfolios due December 10.
	Exit conferences will be scheduled individually.

Paper Preparation Papers should be printed out or typed with a legible ribbon, double spaced, on decent computer paper or nonerasable bond (correction tape and fluid exist for a reason). Legible word-processor printouts (with dark ribbons and on white paper) are also quite acceptable. Amateurish typing that has been neatly corrected is perfectly acceptable. (Use correction fluid or tape, not a dirty eraser!) Any sort of uncorrected paper is unacceptable. Follow the guidelines in the FIG and your handbook for writing, documenting, and presenting your paper. If you do not do so, I'll return the paper to you ungraded for you to prepare correctly. There is no need to put your papers in fancy binders or covers; one reliable staple in the upper left hand corner is all that is required. There is a need for your name and student number, a title, page numbers, and very careful proofreading and correction. If you wish to bring outlines or drafts of your papers to my office, I'll be glad to discuss them with you.

It's important to have the syllabus typed and ready to hand out on the first day of class and to have extras for the students who will join your class in the first few weeks of the term. It's helpful to have the syllabus duplicated on colored paper; students are less likely to lose pink or green sheets in the welter of paper they accumulate at the beginning of the semester. (If you don't want to overwhelm them with the complete syllabus on the first day, at least have the minimum information ready: how to contact you, what the requirements and texts are, what the due dates are.) A few students may be intimidated by all this information, but most are grateful to know what to expect; to them it is evidence of your professionalism. College is new to them and they usually have no idea what to expect. Your department, too, will appreciate having your policies laid out in case of a later grade appeal or problem. Now, with syllabus in hand, we can consider how you'll teach your course.

6

What Goes on in the Classroom

If one new maxim has entered the composition classroom as a result of all the research in the last thirty years, it's this: we learn to write by writing. Not by talking about writing, not by filling in blanks in workbooks, not by admiring set pieces of good writing—but by taking pen or pencil or keyboard in hand and actually making meaning in language. Most experienced writing teachers set aside regular class time for writing—in journals, on drafts, as reactions to readings, in freewritings, and so forth. My classes begin—except on workshop days—with five to ten minutes of some writing activity every day. (I write with my class to reinforce my identity as a member of this community of writers.) For me, this is an absolute necessity; if we don't start by focusing on writing, I end up talking too much about writing. A writing start helps me and protects my students.

The sections that follow describe a number of techniques you can use in conducting classes, beginning with the first day of class. These are tips based on my experience and the experiences of a number of other writing teachers. If you want further suggestions for classroom practices, ask your colleagues. Almost every teacher has one "surefire" discussion starter or idea of how to get students engaged with some tough essay. Collegiality is one of the most important reference sources for the teaching of writing. Moreover, talking to other teachers will help you anticipate problems and obstacles that may arise, as well as giving you some points of reference against which you can compare your own performance. If your office mates are assigning their third papers, and you haven't yet graded your first set, you'll know you need to ask questions about the pace you are setting. And collegiality is essential when you need to react to someone—but not the student— about papers you're reading. One of the most reassuring exchanges for college writing teachers is the one that begins, "You've got to listen to this." Even veteran teachers still need to share their students' successes and failures with their colleagues; it's part of the tradition of our profession.

The First Day of Class

Almost every teacher, no matter how wizened a veteran, has had nightmares about the first day of class. We walk down endless corridors unable to find our classroom, or find ourselves naked facing a room full of students, or suddenly in a foreign country unable to speak the language. These attacks of nerves are understandable. After all, teaching is a performance; every actor gets butterflies. And there's a lot of pressure on us: we have to teach these students to write, to succeed at our school, to become effective communicators. Studies show that one of the most important environmental factors in the writing classroom is the relation between teacher and student; we want that relationship to start well. With all this pressure, opening the classroom door becomes an act of supreme courage!

But relax. There are no documented cases of students eating a teacher on the first day of class, just as there are no cases that prove a bad first day of class ever killed a student, either. The first day is a time for both students and teachers to find out a little about each other, to establish a tone for the course, and to exchange some basic information. Once you conquer the sweaty palms and stomach gymnastics, in fact, you're likely to discover that the first class isn't long enough for everything you want to do.

Nuts and Bolts

Some elements of the first class are pretty basic. You'll want to introduce yourself, trying to give a sense of your personal and professional qualifications for teaching the course. This is sometimes a problem for new teachers, because they think students will not respect a TA or part-time faculty member. I tell them I've been a writer for more than twenty years (this goes back to my high school days, but they don't need to know that). Students are very nervous on that first day, too; they want to know that you have experience with writing. So tell them. You can let them know a little about your writing subjects; I tell them I study English written before Shakespeare's time, especially writing by women, but I also mention that I work with engineers and scientists in editing technical manuscripts. I usually tell them that I have a Ph.D. (they love titles), collect classic detective novels and lousy jokes (which I sometimes inflict on my students), am married, and raise cats and tomatoes. I'm a person, just like they are; most students have no idea what an academic does outside the classroom. My openness invites them to tell me things as well; it begins the process of establishing a writing community in our classroom. I also tell students what I'd like to be called in the classroom (usually "Dr. T.," but some of my older students eventually adopt "Jo") so that they'll be a little less nervous in asking me questions.

But I cover a lot of business too. I hand out the syllabus, explain it, and answer questions on it paragraph by paragraph (even drawing a map on the chalkboard for finding the bookstore, if necessary). I ask them to read it again after class and to bring in three written questions about it for the next class; this establishes some good habits of reviewing class material for the semester. Then I get some information from them by having them fill out a brief information sheet (illustrated below). This gets them writing quickly and provides me information about their schedules, possible time conflicts, and attitudes toward the course. Then I make the assignment for the second class meeting: besides constructing three questions about the syllabus and buying the books, I ask them to write down as full a list as they can of everything they do when they have a paper to write—from the day it's assigned to the day turned in. This will provide an opening for discussion of the writing process in the second class.

Teaching in Practice

One of the most useful things you can do on the first day of class is to elicit a brief writing sample from students. If you have not received a copy of their placement sample or portfolio, I'd go so far as to say that this is a "must" for the first day. The writing you get won't be very fancy or well-developed, and it will probably have a lot of editing problems, but you can begin to see how your students engage with a topic, what kinds of skills they already have, and what kinds of instruction you will have to make sure they get. Here's the sample I used last fall, along with a student response and my notes about it.

One of the common concerns of American universities these days is that they need to teach people about a much wider range of cultures, values, and ideas in our democratic society; previously, college courses had emphasized Western, predominantly white male culture and downplayed the contributions of the rest of the world. Here's what Professor Paula Rothenberg says about the old curriculum that colleges are replacing:

> The traditional curriculum teaches all of us to see the world through the eyes of privileged, white, European males and to adopt their interests and perspectives as our own. It calls books by middle-class, white, male writers "literature" and honors them as timeless and universal, while treating the literature produced by everyone else as idiosyncratic and transitory. The traditional curriculum introduces the (mythical) white, middle-class, patriarchal, heterosexual family and its values and calls it "Introduction to Psychology." It teaches the values of white men of property and position and calls it "Introduction to Ethics." It reduces the true *majority* of people in this society to "women and minorities" and calls it "political science." It teaches the art produced by privileged white men in the West and calls it "art history."
>
> The traditional curriculum is too narrow. It leaves out too much. Its narrow approach to defining knowledge implies that people who look different, talk differently, embrace different cultural practices are not studied because they have nothing to teach "us." . . . The perspectives and contributions of [white males] are valid and valuable; there is much to be learned from them. The difficulty is not with their inclusion but with the exclusion of everyone else. ("Critics of Attempts to Democratize the Curriculum Are Waging a Campaign to Misrepresent the Work of Responsible Professors," *Chronicle of Higher Education*, 10 April 1991.)

Some critics of changing the curriculum would call Professor Rothenberg's pointed argument a case of "political correctness" and claim that her curriculum would confuse people and diminish some of humanity's greatest achievements. You're just starting your college career: what kind of curriculum do *you* think you should study? Would you put yourself on one extreme or the other, or would you chart some middle path? In two or three paragraphs, describe the *ideal* college curriculum that will prepare you for democracy in the 21st century. Describe as specifically as you can the kinds of subjects, ideas, and courses that will give you that preparation. Are there areas not mentioned here that should be included?

Latisha's response:

At my high school graduation, the speaker told us that we were going to have to expand our minds and our hearts if we wanted to succeed in the world. I guess I just thought that meant to keep going to school, I didn't think about it as a controversial issue. But when I read the story you gave us, I started to think about what we learned at Lancaster High School, and most of it was from the white perspective. A good example is that we had a one hour assembly for Kwanzaa, the African American holiday celebrating personal responsibility, however, we did tons of things for Christmas, in all our classes. Mrs. Stevens, our English teacher in 12th grade, let us read stories by Toni Morrison and James Baldwin, but she always told us how to interpret them, from her white viewpoint. That is what we got tested on, we had to tell her what she wanted to hear so that we could get good grades. I guess that's what I think a curriculum was about.

This story made me think that I should ask about what I am being taught at college, and about what courses they are making me take. Like writing, ha ha. I know Winthrop has about 20% black students, what about the faculty. Will I be exposed to multiple viewpoints, or just one. I guess since you are asking us this, maybe you are asking the same questions too. Maybe an ideal cirriculum is one where you ask lots of questions like these. In my college career, I hope to endeavor to explore these matters.

My response:

Latisha has some very good ideas here, even if they are only in the 'emerging' stage. She has drawn some correct inferences not only from the article, but about me as well, and she has come up with two very good examples of the kind of curriculum Rothenberg is criticizing. OK, she can read critically. That's crucial. And she has the confidence to talk to me; I love that "ha ha" and her asking me questions. What I think she'll need to focus on is focus; this takes a long time to get going, and she hasn't really begun to address the task yet. She can probably prewrite but won't like organizing. Her language control isn't bad, though at some time I bet we'll end up talking about comma splices. WRIT 101 is the right course for her; she may be one of my better students.

Student Information Sheet

Name   Student ID#
Campus Mailbox   Local Phone
Local Address   College Advisor
E-mail Address (if you have one)

What other courses are you taking this semester?

What extracurricular time commitments do you have this semester (sports, activities, jobs, home responsibilities, whatever)?

What do you think your reading and writing strengths are?

What areas of reading and writing would you like to improve?

Do you like to work alone or in groups?

When you're writing, are you most comfortable writing from beginning to end, or starting anywhere in the paper that inspires you?

Aside from school assignments, what kinds of reading and writing do you do?

Tell me some distinguishing things about you to help me associate your name with you, the person.

The writing sample can set a tone for the writing course; it's never too early to ask students to read and think critically, to use their brains to prompt good writing.

Tailoring Your Classes to Your Students

Getting students to talk in class isn't difficult. Getting them to talk about what you want them to talk about, on the other hand, takes some careful planning. Many factors may influence students' willingness to talk: the weather is too cold, the World Series is in progress, it's midterm week, and so forth. The learning and personality styles of individual students will also affect class dynamics. Occasionally you'll have to throw your carefully planned discussion notes out and improvise. If the class wants to talk about baseball, have them argue the pros and cons of the designated hitter rule, or playing the World Series in daytime, or write columns imitating their favorite sportswriter. (If you don't think baseball is a literary subject, just poll writers and literary critics on the Cubs and Red Sox. You'll change your mind quickly!) Many handbooks provide a number of collaborative exercises to help keep class moving; as you're planning your classes, you can choose and adapt these suggestions to help your students focus on their tasks.

Lesson Plans

A short note here about lesson plans. Depending on your background, you'll either think these are essential or never have seen one. Most teachers use some kind of written notes for class, even if those notes wouldn't pass muster in an educational methods class. Too many things happen in class and too often discussion ranges in unexpected directions for you to rely on memory alone. At minimum, your notes should outline the day's goals, the topics you want to cover, and any announcements or reminders you have for the class. (I make announcements after we write, to avoid repetitions for latecomers.) If the goals for the day include discussion of readings (see below), some notes about the points you want to make, along with the appropriate page numbers, will save many wasted moments of thumbing madly through the text. Often you can lay out a week's class on one sheet (see the example included) to help organize discussion; then you only need tick off the topics you've covered to keep track of your goals. If you

Course Name/Number/Term

Week of: Goals:

	Meeting #1	Meeting #2	Meeting #3
Their assignment			
Announcements			
What they'll write			
Discussion			
Reinforcement Activities			
Next assignment			
Handed out			
Handed in			

NOTES

need more detailed notes, by all means make them. But try to avoid writing out full lectures which you read word-for-word to your students. Remember that flexibility as well as structure is needed in conducting classes.

Learning Styles

One of the biggest difficulties in running classes is in allowing for the different personality types and learning styles of the students in your class. Some will respond enthusiastically to class discussion, jumping into every conversation. Others will be more reticent, or even resistant, to committing themselves in public. Our colleagues in schools of education have talked about these differences in learning styles for many years; composition scholars are slowly catching up. A learning style is just that: a student's tendency to acquire and process information in a particular way. While there's a huge body of research on learning styles to take in, two of the most important differences in style for teachers of composition to know about affect the ways students take in and organize information.

Visual vs. Verbal Learning

Neuropsychologists and psycholinguists have spent years studying the ways the two hemispheres of the brain interact. We know that the left brain is associated with language, analysis, and sequences, while the right brain is associated with vision, recognizing images, and perceiving spatial relations. (To call the left side "scientific" or "logical" and the right side "artistic" or "creative" is a dangerous overgeneralization.) Students whose left hemisphere predominates may prefer written information and instructions, and favor outlines, sequence, and heuristics. Students whose right hemisphere predominates may prefer diagrams or drawing pictures, and may favor brainstorming, journaling, and following their instincts. Composition instructors need to vary the kinds of writing activities they choose to expose students to both kinds of learning, so that they can find the methods that best suit their learning styles.

Holist vs. Serialist Learning

Holists are students who see the big picture first—then they try to add the details and support. Many of them will jump to conclusions; it can be hard to get them to see that not all their readers can follow their intuitive leaps. Their natural method of proceeding is by deductive reasoning. Serialists, by contrast, start with the building blocks and gradually construct a big picture. They like to work inductively, start to finish, and being asked to jump around can be torture for them. These are the students who can develop the body of a paper but have trouble with writing conclusions; they often just don't "see" where their ideas are taking them.

These are only two of the dichotomies learning style theory can help you understand in your students. If you want to read further, I would recommend starting with a collection edited by Ronald Schemck called *Learning Strategies and Learning Styles: Perspectives on Individual Differences* (1988).

Another way of describing personality styles that many education professionals use is the Myers-Briggs Type Inventory (MBTI). This scale rates people on how they react to social interactions, work routines and schedules, and unexpected situations. (Sample question: In a large group, are you more likely to a) introduce others, or b) wait to be introduced?) Your university career placement center or someone in the psychology or education departments is likely to have a sample

MBTI testing sheet that you might consult. Three very good books that explain the MBTI and explore its implications for learning are Otto Kroeger's *Type Talk at Work* (1992), Isabel Myers' *Gifts Differing* (1980), and George Jensen and John DiTiberio's *Personality and the Teaching of Composition* (1989). I'll try to summarize what the MBTI can suggest to us about classroom practices, but please be aware this is only a preliminary sketch.

The MBTI categorizes people in four areas: Extrovert vs. Introvert, Feeling vs. Thinking, Intuitive vs. Sensing, and Perceiving vs. Judging. So someone might be described as an ENFJ, or an INFP, and so on, based on test results. (One of my colleagues is skilled enough in Myers Briggs evaluation that she can make these descriptions on very short acquaintance. She thinks I'm an ESFJ [I'm not], but I make her crazy by saying I'm a Spring.) Making rigid assumptions about a writer based on her MBTI can be dangerous in a writing class, I think, since most people have both kinds of tendencies even though one may predominate. Nonetheless, each of those four areas does affect a significant area of writing performance.

Extrovert vs. Introvert

This category describes how people direct their behaviors and energies. Extroverts like to talk, to be with others, and to be the center of attention. They use conversation and interaction to sharpen their ideas and develop their thoughts. They like to share and to take risks; they often prefer "trial and error" methods of proceeding. Extroverts are the hand-wavers, the interrupters, the dominators of classroom attention. Introverts, on the other hand, are the quiet ones. They prefer to think about things before talking about them (if they ever do talk about them); they work better alone, or quietly, and without interruption. Being forced to lead or participate actively in class discussions, or read journal entries aloud, may be agonizing for them. This is a kind of "shyness," true, but it's not something that they can easily overcome. Introverted students need to be handled differently than extroverts.

Feeling vs. Thinking

This category describes how people make judgments. Feelers go on their instincts; they like to make decisions based on their own values and how they would respond personally. They are very concerned about their audience, and don't like to "hurt someone's feelings." They'll write pages and pages in their journals. Following structured rules or rubrics is hard for feelers; so is giving substantive criticism. Thinkers, on the other hand, rely on those objective criteria. They like analysis and categories, and tend to go with "cut and dried" formulae. They are "letter of the law" students who will do exactly what is asked of them—and expect their classmates to do this, too. They can be pretty hard on their classmates in group and classroom discussions, and their journal entries tend to be succinct and impersonal.

Intuitive vs. Sensing

Sensers like to make use of their senses (sound, vision, touch, etc.) to compile large bodies of concrete detail. They are practical and pragmatic; they like to have templates, specific examples, or guidelines to follow, and they will follow these very well. These are the students who compile stacks of note cards three inches high while preparing a research paper. Most of them can collect and organize lots of concrete material; what gives them trouble is abstracting, generalizing, or seeing the big picture. They can find all the topic sentences, but may not be able to summarize a writer's chief concerns or come up with words to describe the tone of a piece of writing. Because they have such a fixed idea of what they want to do, they may have trouble revising on a global level. They may not be comfortable unless they start with the introduction and go serially to a conclusion when writing. Intuiters, on the other hand, are comfortable with synthesizing and seeing a big picture; but they'll go with the flow rather than follow a plan. (They'll be the ones who turn in papers with creative fonts and graphics.) They're more likely to start in the middle, jump around, modify ideas, or even totally change topics (usually the night before the paper is due). Revision comes more naturally to such students, who are comfortable with changing generalizations and abstractions. However, intuiters sometimes don't see the need for using concrete examples to support their ideas, and may have great difficulty coming up with such material.

Perceiving vs. Judging

This category measures how people assign values within their worlds. Perceivers like an unstructured world; unfinished tasks or missed deadlines don't really bother them. They can tolerate mess, either literal or metaphoric. They tend to assess performance by the amount of effort that was put in rather than the success achieved. They'll be the students who say "I deserve an A because I put so much time into this paper." They may well be multi-drafters. Judgers, on the other hand, like things to get done. They may limit their scope or narrow their focus in order to complete things tidily; they prefer a smaller, tight subject to a global, diffuse one. They will ask "How many points is this worth?" and expect clear definitions of grading standards and grammar rules. They may do so much of their prewriting in their heads that they only feel they need one draft, and they have trouble going back to revise and re-see their writing. Judgers can be hard on other students in groups, because they will point out every fault they find. Perceivers will say,"The paper is really interesting even if it wanders a little"; the judgers will say, "I don't think it's very good because it has four spelling errors and the thesis isn't clearly stated."

Make a direct effort to provied exercises for students of all learning styles, including verbal activities (freewriting, listing, detailing, questioning, dialoguing) and visual ones (clustering, tree diagrams, time sequences, grids, outlines). The solitary exercises should appeal more to introverted students, while the collaborative ones will engage the extroverts. Be aware, though, that there can be conflict in styles; an introvert who's a verbal learner may keep a journal but not feel comfortable sharing it, or participating in keeping a dialogue journal. Likewise, visual learners who are intuiters may not be comfortable generating detail lists or creating grids. You'll need to maintain your flexibility and resist pigeonholing students. You may have noticed that I got a little information on student learning styles from the information sheet shown above; that combined with the list they bring to the second day of class helps me start to figure them out. With some insight into your students' learning styles, you can better plan how to conduct your classes.

Running Class Discussions

There's no substitute when planning a discussion for knowing the material. If you're working with written materials, you have to read the texts thoroughly, mark passages for close examination, and highlight examples and techniques you want to point out. (It helps to know something about the author and original context of essays and other works; that's why there are instructor's manuals.) Try to anticipate the questions that will arise from a text; I write mine out, just as I ask my students to (they are asked to bring at least three written questions on the readings to class). Questioning the text is a very productive way of starting a discussion.

Of course, the questions have to be carefully worded. Nothing kills a budding discussion like a question that implies its own answer: "This was a pretty weak essay, don't you think?" Yes/no questions ("Does Rodriguez use good examples?") are also dampening. Some students worry that teachers in conducting class discussions are secretly checking that students have read the essay, or ensuring that they agree with the teacher, or are trying to embarrass the student. Starting from the text's perplexities fosters instead an attitude of exploration, of shared attempts to solve the problems a text poses. Don't be afraid to play devil's advocate in starting discussions; tell your students you'll do this. Sometimes offbeat questions can provoke lively engagement. (In the last few semesters I've taught a number of essays that present essentially selfish positions (we should end welfare, or foreign aid, or Medicaid-funded medical services to the poor or chronically ill) and begun discussions with questions like "What religion do you think this author practices?"   When students hesitantly answer, "Christian" or "Jewish," I ask, "What about the notion of 'I am my brother's keeper,'?") By playing devil's advocate in this way, I force students to turn the essays inside out, to start from the opposite tack and consider how the author has shaped her argument. Often with a provocative essay and some surprising opening questions, you won't have to say much in the class, just act as traffic cop for answers. If only all classes went this well!

Sometimes, though, you'll need to do more. If students come up with the seed of an idea, you'll need to encourage the students, and their classmates, to develop it, to think out loud. Extroverted students will dominate the early discussions, so you'll need to try to draw the others in. If a student's response seems off line, you may have to redirect it gently. Replies like "I didn't get that from the essay. Is there a particular passage in it that led you to led you to that conclusion?" or "That's a different approach. Do any of the rest of you want to react to that?" allow you to probe the student's response in a positive manner. Certainly you don't want to ridicule a student or intimidate her so that she won't speak out again.

Likewise, you want to encourage students to respect each other; try to keep them from showing their exasperation. If one or two extroverts habitually try to dominate class discussion, you'll have to intervene to permit other students to respond. One way is to appoint the dominators as temporary discussion emcees while you act as "scribe," recording responses on the board; give them the responsibility of calling on other students. (You won't want to do this all the time because it may lead to charges of favoritism, but the experience usually makes the dominators more willing to allow other students to speak.) A word or two privately after class may also be necessary; assure the student you know she's doing the work and need her help to encourage others, or tell an introverted student "Your fellow students would really benefit if you told them about X. Next class, will you bring it up?"

The most important role you can play in these discussions is that of facilitator; you're helping students reach understanding of the material. Often you'll be rephrasing what students have said or turning it into a new question. You can draw out quiet students ("Lisa, you're frowning back there; do you disagree with what we're saying?") or simply recognize those who want to join the discussion. (Obviously this works best if you know the students' names!) Sometimes you can draw a consensus ("OK, then, we agree Will's essay doesn't seem very appropriate for 1996") and use that to move on to a new topic or facet of the discussion. ("If you were going to revise this essay for *Newsweek* this year, what would you put in it?" or "If you were going to write about sexual harassment for a men's magazine, what would you put in and why?") These questions are particularly useful when you need to shift the focus from content to writing strategies.

Gradually you'll become more comfortable in conducting class discussions and will find that the "good days" happen far more often than the bad. Often, using writing to prompt discussion will help you find this comfort. Asking students to read and discuss their written responses to reading will often get a discussion off right. If discussion bogs down or hits an impasse, you can ask students to stop and write about it for a few minutes ("Okay, I want everybody to stop and make two lists—one of all the reasons to pass an English Language Amendment and one of all the reasons against it"). This kind of pause for controlled reflection often clears the air and allows discussions to proceed productively.

Teaching in Smaller Groups

Not all discussion has to involve the whole class. Sometimes you'll want to teach in smaller groups, through one-on-one conferences, small editing groups, or larger workshop sessions, perhaps using the collaborative suggestions in your handbook. These take a little practice to become used to, on the part of both teachers and students. Often these activities involve the critiquing of a piece of writing—sometimes published or completed essays, but most often drafts in progress. You'll need to teach your students what to do in such workshops, but once they feel confident with the process they often achieve remarkable results.

Each size of group activity is best suited to a different issue. Large workshops—the whole class—are best suited for global issues: support of a thesis, development of evaluation standards, and the like. You might duplicate one or two student papers and discuss them with the whole class. (An overhead projector or on-screen computer projector can be very useful for such discussions, because it makes students look up and make eye contact.) At the beginning of the semester you may wish to use papers from another section or from a text so that students don't feel self-conscious about criticizing them. If you're going to use papers from your own students, make sure that all students have one analyzed in the large group before the end of the semester; don't just single a few out.

Large group workshops teach students how to look globally at pieces of discourse, a technique that sensers and judgers often fail to use in revision. They also teach students to look at a piece of discourse as a teacher (evaluator) looks at it. Start with some basic questions: What's the point of this paper? Who are the readers supposed to be? What are some things this writer does well? Then you can move to slightly smaller issues—the assertions backing up the thesis, the examples supporting a definition, the descriptive details that create the mood. Finally you can move toward identifying problem areas: What points in this paper should the writer revise before turning it in? Are there other things she should bring up? Should she leave any of this out? If questions get asked frequently, you may wish to make up a list that students can consult as they revise their own work. (I use the *Framework for Judging*, discussed in Chapter 9.)

After large workshops, students are usually ready to begin in small groups. Here they can examine the local concerns caused by larger issues. If, for instance, the text seems choppy or disorganized, they can experiment with rearranged paragraphs. If the thesis is underdeveloped, they can suggest new examples or analysis. If the style is too wordy, they can help each other tighten the prose. In essence, they're coping with two questions for each draft they examine: "What works?" and "What needs work?"

The composition of small groups requires care on your part. Somehow you have to mix strong and weak students, aggressive and shy ones, in cells of three or four students who will work together and help each other. Some teachers try to put all the strong extroverts in one group, and all the strong introverts in another to control group dynamics. For the first few sessions, you may want to give out specific lists of questions to ask, so that the judgers don't impose their own agendas on the group. And you'll have to monitor discussion carefully to make sure it hasn't veered around to a sociology exam or an upcoming concert.

Besides discussing learning styles with the class and using them to set up groups, I find it very useful to give students a written description of writing groups and discuss it with them at an early class period. This gives them an idea of what to expect and helps them approach the strategy productively. Below is an example of the handout I provide.

Writing Groups

Working in a writing group will be a little different from the group work you have done before. First, you have different responsibilities: to give careful, thoughtful advice to your fellow group members. Second, you have different rights: to expect careful, thoughtful feedback from your fellow group members. This is serious business; you can only expect to get as much, and as useful help, as you contribute. So you must have a draft ready for group workdays, and come prepared to help others. Failure to do so not only deprives your partners of your help, but may also lower your grade on the final paper. You'll find out when you leave school for jobs that such "collaborative" partnerships are very common— here's a chance for you to develop a valuable professional skill!

For draft days, make sure you furnish a readable draft in advance. Put four legible copies of your draft (keep the original!) in the box by my office door by 3 p.m. the day before the workshop; make sure they go in the folder for your group. Pick up copies of the drafts from the other members of your group and read and annotate them before the draft workshop. This will prepare you to give and receive the most possible help.

When working in a group, first establish the day's priorities: what do you have to accomplish today (reading everyone's draft, proofreading everyone's final copy, planning everyone's next paper, or whatever)?

Estimate the amount of time needed, then divide it up equitably; each member is entitled to a fair share of the time. Let one group member be the timekeeper each session; he or she is responsible for keeping the discussion moving and making sure no one is denied fair time. Take turns being timekeeper.

After you divide up the time, pick a draft to start discussing. The writer of that paper should tell you what he/she is trying to accomplish in the paper, what areas he/she thinks are coming along well, and what areas he/she particularly wants help with. In response, the group should begin by telling the writer what is good/strong/well-done in the paper. Then offer advice on the matters for which the writer can strengthen the weak spots. The writer should ask you questions to get your suggestions clear in his/her mind and is free to accept only those suggestions he/she agrees with.

You will have time to review each other's papers at least once in each workshop session. If you finish early, start incorporating some of the suggested changes into your draft and ask the other members of your group what they think of them. The rest of the period can be spent finishing the other work on the agenda, proofing, working on individual problems, drafting/brainstorming/discussing other papers, conferring with me, or writing. When you need advice, call on another member of your group for help. As you learn to trust each other, you will be able to work more effectively as a group; you may choose to meet outside the class (perhaps on the night before a paper is due) to work or just to socialize. At any rate, working in a writing group should increase your confidence-and your skills-in writing and working together. If you are uncomfortable in your particular group, see me privately. I'll do what I can to adjust groups or group dynamics to provide the best writing environment for everyone.

Most group sessions work like this: One student reads his draft aloud, while other group members read along on copies. Then comes the response period. The group members first tell the writer what they think works in the draft. The writer then identifies two or three areas he wants help with, and the group responds with suggestions. The writer asks for clarification, if that's necessary. Finally, the group raises other questions it has about the draft and tries to help the writer answer them (often these come from the group's own experiences in previous papers). The writer is not bound to accept all the group's suggestions, but should be encouraged to think of them as the response of potential members of the audience for that piece of writing. Then another member of the group reads her draft, and the process begins again.

At the beginning of the semester you'll want to make these sessions short, to help students get the feel of the procedure. You may want to analyze one draft together as a class for ten minutes, then break up into small groups with five minutes or so for each draft. At first you may want to have each writer focus on the paper's introduction, or the paragraph in which she develops the most important point, or whatever. Then you can reassemble in the large group to talk about matters of general concern. If this is going to be the case, students should circulate their drafts in the previous class, so that they can be read in advance. Later in the semester you may wish to spend entire classes in group work, letting students spend more time reading and responding. Your job in these classes is to move from group to group, answering questions, serving as a member of the audience, and keeping attention focused on the task at hand. You also need to help groups find a balance between focusing on global concerns and on local ones; after all, if the paper doesn't make a point, do perfect punctuation and spelling really help? Or if an audience can't get past the mechanical distractions, does a good argument really work? Here's where your experience as a writer can help guide and direct student efforts.

Teaching in Practice

Here's a sample group revision checklist that you might use with groups early in the semester. Notice that it enables students of several different personality types to find a question to really "get into."

1. What are this paper's strengths right now?
2. As a reader, what about this paper gets your attention?
3. What big issues in the paper need work? Circle or read them, and try to give two suggestions for improvement.
4. Based on your own experience and instincts (and the successes and problems you've had), make three concrete suggestions that will help the author improve this paper.

One of the reasons I write the prompt this way (usually I give it to students on handouts so that they will write their responses) is to get students to provide concrete feedback. By challenging them to provide two or three suggestions, I'm reducing the chance of either one-word answers or impressionistic, "Gee, this is pretty good; I wouldn't change anything" responses. Having the reaction of real readers is invaluable to writers. Revision checklists like these give them something concrete to work with.

There are some inevitable problems involved in group teaching. Some students will forget to bring drafts. Your syllabus should make clear that this is a responsibility, just as turning in papers on time is. (Some teachers—and I'm one of them—lower grades on the final papers if no drafts appeared.) You need to make it clear to students that drafts are not optional. Some students talk too much, or too little, or offer destructive criticism, or no criticism at all. You may have to tinker with group makeup to alter the balance of learning styles and psychology types. Speak privately to students who are not cooperating, and be sure they've had the chance to have the whole class critique their work; this increases cooperation markedly. By virtue of your position you're the authority in the classroom; sometimes you will need to exert control.

It's typical for intuitive students to talk about the content of drafts, not the way they were written, or to get off subject and not talk about the drafts at all. Feelers may try to personalize every topic, while thinkers won't be comfortable with anything including the pronoun "I." You'll need to monitor their discussions and help students focus their attention on the writing. No two classes have the same dynamics and you'll always find yourself scrambling a

Scenario

Henry, the TA in the cubicle across from yours, peers over the top at you. "I don't understand it," he says. "I try everything to get groups to work in my classes. I've switched around who's in what groups, I give them really specific lists of questions to use, I keep time on the board for them, and they still don't seem to be getting anything out of them. I look in the door of your class and your groups are going fine. Why do groups work for you and not for me?" What would you say to Henry?

little. There are classes in which group activities just don't seem to work; they'll be dominated by introverts. If so, you may have to revise radically the kinds and numbers of collaborative activities you use. It happens; don't be discouraged. In the bibliography you will find a list of sources that will help you improve your group teaching techniques.

Conferencing

A variation on small group work is conference teaching; its leading exponent is Roger Garrison. This strategy works best when class members are at many different competency levels, since you can individualize instruction, or when you wish to establish (or have established) a strong rapport with your students. Introverted students can be more comfortable with this style of class than extroverts. Some teachers spend the entire semester in one-to-one teaching; most of those have the luxury of small classes and are strong extroverts themselves. Other instructors incorporate one-to-one techniques in small doses, usually combining them with larger group work and discussions.

In such situations, the teacher holds brief (1-5 minute) conferences with each writer at four or five stages in a paper's development. Each conference has a clear goal: information gathering, central plan, organization, sentences and grammar, and editing. This kind of intervention tends to raise grades and limit the number of papers submitted; most teachers balance it with papers written without help to control grade inflation. If you are using a portfolio system in your class, conferencing may be a productive activity, especially when students are working on different assignments at the same time.

Another kind of conference that has proven useful writing courses is the "progress report" conference. After every few papers, the instructor and student sit down for perhaps fifteen minutes to discuss the student's progress to date. They try to identify the competencies the student has already mastered and the goals the student wishes to achieve in the next few papers. Students can ask questions about the teacher's comments on papers, discuss problems with the editing or error log (about which, see Chapter 8), and review plans for subsequent papers. I try to hold these about three times a semester and usually cancel a class in the week I hold them. Some words of advice: when you make your conference appointments, schedule a break at least every two hours to "decompress." Make notes in advance so that you'll know what points you want to make with each student; I keep these in their file folders and check them off as we cover them. (See the example below.) Keeps fluids and throat lozenges on hand, because you'll do a lot of talking. And leave yourself some free time once the conferences end, because they will exhaust you.

Here's an example of a student progress record I keep, along with the student's information sheet and other work, in files in my office. (You might also keep all the progress records in a binder so that you can take them home when grading papers.)

Name
Diagnostic Comments:
Student's goals for the course:
My proposed goals for student:

Paper 1
Strengths:
Problems:
Goals set in comment:
Conference date:
Points I want to make:
Points students made:
Goals student set:

Paper 2
Strengths:
Problems:
Goals set in comment:
etc.

Paper 3
Strengths:
Problems:
Goals set in comment:
etc.

Conference 2 date
Points I want to make:
Points students made:
Goals student set:
etc.

Exit conference date
My assessment of student's performance:
Student's assessment of performance:
Recommendations:

After some experimenting you'll find the right mixture of writing, discussion, and group work for your own teaching style. But you must always keep flexibility in mind. Some classes will never be comfortable with group work; others will resist discussion but flourish in small groups. Don't be afraid to vary the types of techniques you use and to change the pace; nothing is more deadly in a course than monotony. For every writing goal there are probably twenty ways of conducting class to achieve it. The makeup of your class and your rapport with the students determine best what techniques you'll use and when. If you feel dissatisfied with a particular technique, you might consider inviting a colleague to observe one of your classes. Sometimes a neutral observer can see ways in which you can better use time, or move discussions along, or encourage small groups; when you're involved with your students, it's hard to develop an objective view alone. You can also poll students on what techniques most help them; some of these strategies are discussed in the chapters on evaluation, below.

"Messing Around With Texts"

There are many things you can ask students to do with their textbooks besides carry them to class. Donald Murray of the University of New Hampshire (now emeritus) calls the process of active reading "Messing Around With Texts" (1986). That's a great phrase, both because of what it encourages students to do, and because of the attitudes it inculcates in them. For too many students, the texts in printed books are somehow sacred: they're in print, they have no (all right, few) typos, a writing teacher chose them to use as examples in a writing class. They're something a writer doesn't "mess around with." Especially not when that writer's a student! Encouraging a healthy sense of skepticism towards texts is always helpful; discussing strategies for active reading may be something you want to discuss early in the semester. Students are notoriously hesitant to write in their books, either because of previous school training or because they're concerned it will affect the book's resale value. (I know: we want them to keep the book, but it's unrealistic to expect all financially-strapped students to do so. It's a class and vocational assumption to assume that writing texts are as valuable to our students as they are to us!) Here's a place where you may have to impose your authority, and make them try some of these activities.

My definition of a text, whether it be a whole book, the essay in question, a memo, an ad, a letter, or a check, is that it's the solution to a problem a writer, in a particular circumstance for particular readers at particular times, had to solve by a set deadline. Many problems have more than one useful solution; this happens to be the writer in question's solution at that time. (It might be different the next day, or week, or month, or year; such changes are called *revisions* and every writer makes them. I also use the joke that the only texts carved in stone have to do with dead people; they're on tombstones or monuments.) Some of these texts are written locally, by the students in that class or in other classes. Others are written and published in other formats, for other audiences; your program may ask students to buy a collection of essays, either bound or duplicated, or you may have students explore their outside readings and bring interesting pieces in for the class. (Chapter 4 explains the copyright laws covering such activities.) Readers are much less fashionable in composition courses than they used to be, as the focus of such classes has shifted away from other people's writing to the students' own writing. That's as it should be, I think, but don't discount the value of showing students how other writers have solved particular writing problems. Examples can really help, especially for some kinds of learners.

Teaching in Practice

Here are some strategies you can have students use to "mess around with texts." Some can be done in class, either individually or in groups, while others would make suitable journal or prewriting activities. All of them ask students to become active readers, and to *transfer* things from their reading to their writing. Most first-year college students have trouble with such transferral, so anything you can do to enhance their skills will probably benefit them.

Pick a passage you really like and imitate it in what you're writing now.

Have students select a passage (start short, with maybe 4-5 sentences or a 1-paragraph limit) they liked, and figure out why (both in content and technique) they liked it. Then they try to use that technique in their current writing assignment. After they've done so, they write a note to the teacher explaining their process.

Recreate the author's writing process.

Sometimes students can guess, from a particularly vivid anecdote, example, or punch line, where an author started from in writing a text. At other times, they can only guess what kinds of preliminary activities (interviews, writing questions, outlines, time in the library) an author went through. Ask them to "reconstruct the crime" and to imagine how the author went about creating this text. Such an activity not only makes them more aware of their own writing processes, but also helps them realize that published essays, like their own papers, are the results of a process and don't just appear in print like magic.

Think like an editor.

Take a passage (a paragraph, a page, a section of the text) and cut it by some arbitrary amount—a third, a half, seventy percent. Students should preserve the meaning, the structure, and the writer's voice, but make it conform to some fiercely-set reduction in length (and *a, an,* and *the* count!). Writers often have to do this; it's great practice.

Do just the opposite: Expand your text.

Assume your editor loved it so much she asked for twice as much text. "Don't change it," she says, "expand it. Tell me more!" Students aren't allowed to try to overwhelm the teacher with meaningless filler; they have to come up with additional information to enrich what they already have. As a group, they might start by brainstorming ways to enrich the text (i.e. interviews, research, more examples, metaphors) and deciding which of these ways is most appropriate for their audience.

Reorganize the text.

Move the points of an argument around, or start with the objections to a solution, or go from strengths to weakness, etc. I have an old student paper I use sometimes: it was slipped under my office door without a paper clip, and it's virtually impossible to tell which pages go in which order (even the writer couldn't figure it out). I copy it one paragraph per sheet, give the paragraphs to each team, and ask them to decide on the best order for the paper. Then we compare our solutions.

Play Siskel and Ebert and review the text.

Not only do students have to say what a text is about, they then have to say how well or how poorly the author fared in writing it, and to compare it to similar texts for their audience's information. I encourage humor and levity in this (usually getting responses like "Dr. T, you really fell out of the balcony on this one. Clarence Thomas wrote a wonderful essay, because . . ."). Giving students a persona like a movie or book reviewer helps them find a voice and get an "angle" on a reading.

Write a letter to the author.

Students can comment on ideas that interest them, or offer praise, blame, even constructive criticism; they can ask questions about the writer's decisions, or offer hypotheses as to why a writer included or excluded particular material (e.g. "Did you end with the sunflower metaphor because you wanted to imply the rootlessness of our culture as well?"). I often collect these letters and mail them off to the author or editor; to my students' great delight, some authors will write back! (As a text author and editor, I know I take great delight in getting such letters, and I do answer every one personally.)

Learn to see the bones beneath the flesh.

In other words, help students see the structures that underline essays. This can be done in terms of outlines (formal or informal) or strategy maps (such as problem-solution). If you have an overhead projector available, give teams of students transparencies and transparency pens and have them write out their "skeletons," then share them with the rest of the class.

Write Cliff's Notes *or a similar study aid for the class.*

Students know that such guides must not only summarize what is in a piece, but pick up the most important techniques and concerns as well. This is often a good way to get students to read more texts than those assigned in class; you can, for instance, divide the class up into teams of two or three students each and have each team write a guide to a reading that you don't plan to discuss in class. The guides can be collected, photocopied, and circulated to the entire class, and then be discussed; students can play Siskel and Ebert with each guide, and decide which teams have had the most success and why. This kind of activity helps students transfer their "classroom knowledge" into "outside knowledge," which should be useful to them in the future.

Recast the text.

If the author originally addressed a group of laypeople, students can rewrite the text (or parts of it) for a group of professionals. If she or he argued in favor of a policy, use the evidence to argue against that policy. If she or he used high-flown language, rewrite the essay in a colloquial style; if he or she waxed poetic, rewrite the essay in a plain and pragmatic voice. Discuss how the changes were made, and what the effects were on the readers.

Pair up the text

Pair up the text with something else you've read or discussed—not necessarily limited to something students have read or discussed in a writing class. Students have taken Orwell's "Politics and the English Language," for instance, and used it to "read" speeches by political candidates or television advertisements for dishwashing liquid, and so forth. Some have used essays to critique their curricula, or particular classes, or current campus arguments. Some have talked about how purpose in arguments can carry over into the "goals" statement of a résumé, and so forth. When you encourage students to connect their readings to other texts and actions, you are encouraging them to build a wealth of skills useful in areas far wider than the composition classroom.

"Film" the text.

That is, make it into a movie or TV documentary by writing a script, choosing what to leave out and include, "hiring" actors, and in essence "adapting the book for the screen." One recent success with this came using an essay opposing affirmative action, which students "dramatized" for a TV cable show. Filming the text lets students understand that texts are part of a dialogue, of an author speaking who wants (or expects) a response.

Take advantage of the writing center (if your campus has one).

Writing centers are much more than places to send students with punctuation and spelling problems; they can be a valuable resource for you and your students. Ask the writing center tutors to help your students "mess around" with texts; they will have a number of other suggestions beyond those listed here to help your students improve their textual facility.

Teaching Critical Reading

Closely allied to the question of "messing around with texts" is the whole notion of reading itself. This isn't a subject most English teachers are trained in, unless our paths have taken us through departments of education. But critical reading has become an important part of our job, since our students have so little experience with it. While a book of this nature can't tell you everything about teaching reading, here are some places to start; both the essay by Robert Schwegler in the anthology at the end of this book and the Bibliography contain a number of suggestions for further exploration.

Reading, to paraphrase Michael Polanyi in *Knowing and Being* (1969), is an ability to interiorize, to probe a subject and to become part of what is being probed. It is more than recall of content or vocabulary recognition (though these are what reading tests measure): it is an ability to absorb new material, correlate that material with what the reader already knows, and operate on this new knowledge. In George Kelly's term, what such active readers make are *constructs* (1963) or templates that they use to overlay, and organize, the realities they perceive. One way of teaching this more active reading is to use reading logs, in which students write after every reading session, to talk about their pleasures, confusions, agreements, disagreements, reactions to what is read. Teachers prompt further use by asking questions about the responses, helping students see what prompted their reactions to the text, and helping them use these discoveries as prompts for more writing and reading. Double-entry journals, reader-response exercises, and similar activities can also be used to help provoke better reading; to make students better readers, try to arouse their curiosity and make them eager to see what reading can show them.

As you teach reading, you are also teaching social construction: students need to become aware that they as readers are entering into a dialogue with writers, one in which they negotiate a meaning based on communally-agreed-upon beliefs. (This position is best articulated by Fish [1980] and Ede and Lunsford [1984].) As you ask students to question the assumptions behind texts and the processes by which they may have been created, you are encouraging them to see that reading is an active, critical process, and one that requires their full attention.

Finding Support on Campus

Even in these days of severely-pared budgets, most schools provide a network of support systems that you and your students can turn to for further assistance. A few moments of your time spent thumbing through the campus phone directory or school bulletin to find out about these are well spent, so that you can refer your students to them if needed. Your department may provide you with orientation materials that help you locate these resources; if not, your dean's or advising or student affairs offices may be able to direct you. Among these services may be:

Counseling

These services may run from full psychological support (often offered through the infirmary or office of student affairs) to advice for confused students to workshops for older or returning students to seminars on time-management and stress relief. At most schools, these services are free to students. By virtue of teaching the smallest classes most students are enrolled in, composition teachers often find themselves hearing confessions from students who really need counselors. Know where to send them for help.

Tutoring

Some students, by virtue of membership in a campus "special interest group," may have access to free or inexpensive tutoring. Often such services are offered for minority, foreign, nontraditional (sometimes called adult or returning), and handicapped students, as well as for athletes. Some other campus groups, such as Greek organizations, future teachers, and student government associations, may also provide outside help. If you refer a student to such a tutor, make sure you establish clearly the kinds of help the student may accept on graded assignments.

Skill Centers

Many schools offer professional help in reading, computer use, study skills, and cognitive development. The key is to find out what these centers are called and what services they offer. Computer skills are usually offered through the school's computer center; research paper skills through the library's reference department. Other skills—note taking, reading comprehension and cognitive development, for instance—could be housed in a number of departments. If you can't find them immediately, see if your school has an academic services, student services, educational skills, or like-titled office. Sometimes the counseling center may house these services; at some schools, they are under the aegis of the school of education. (Of course, some schools can't afford to offer them at all.) Ask your dean or director if your school can provide any of these services to students.

Writing Centers

One of the best resources many campuses offer is a writing center. Contrary to popular student belief, writing centers aren't places where someone will proofread the student's paper. Writing centers focus on metadiscourse—talking about, and writing about, student writing. They are there to help students become more aware of their own writing processes, to help students refine and improve their writing skills, and to teach them techniques for improving all facets of their writing (including proofreading). If your campus has a writing center, make sure you visit it and find out what services its staff can offer. Oftentimes you will find strong allies there, who can give you suggestions for working with particular students as well as making arrangements to see students who need the center's help. (Muriel Harris's article in the anthology that follows is an excellent overview of working with a center tutor.) Writing center theory is too complex to summarize here (the bibliography offers a start at doing so); don't neglect this vital resource or dismiss it as merely an editing service, or you will be shortchanging yourself and your students.

Okay. So now you know the nuts and bolts of putting your course together and running your classroom. But this isn't a talking and reading class, is it? It's a writing class. So let's talk about what's at the heart of such a class: the writing assignments.

7

Designing Writing Assignments

Only the actual pieces of writing that students complete provide them opportunities to practice the closed competencies they have studied and to incorporate those closed competencies into open structures. In short, writing assignments let students and teachers see how far they've come in achieving their goals. But if assignments are to serve this purpose, the instructor must design them with care. The writing assignment must create a purposeful rhetorical situation and invite students to use that situation to create meaning in language. This takes—like everything else in teaching composition—an understanding of the writing process *and* careful planning. This chapter covers the development of formal writing assignments that serve the purpose of both teacher and student.

The Principles of Good Writing Assignments

One of the most common things writing teachers tell their students is that writing always happens for a reason. So do writing assignments. They must form part of a sequence that helps students achieve the short- and long-term goals of the course. If the goal of a particular section of the course is to have students develop inductive arguments, then the writing assignment must create a situation where induction is appropriate. It should also ask students to use strategies or skills they have learned previously, to build on those achievements, to complicate their writing. If you identified your class goals clearly in the planning process and set up your syllabus to achieve those goals, then sequencing your writing assignments should come more easily; you already have a theoretical framework in place. If not, it's never too late to start!

Second, writing assignments must have a context. Too often students are given assignments whose constraints are not made clear. One of my students once showed me a paper assignment for his literature class: "Write a paper about the most interesting aspect of *Paradise Lost*." No wonder the student was bewildered! What kind of paper—critical analysis, explication, argument, personal interpretation? Who decides what the "most interesting" aspect is—the student, the teacher, some critic? Aspect in what context—structural, orthographical, poetic, literary critical, historical, theological? How long should the paper be? Can the student consult outside sources? What kind of documentation is required? When is it due? How will the teacher evaluate it? Is it too late to drop the course?

We've all seen assignments like this, of course; many of us had to complete them when we were students. Experience has taught *us* that the first thing we do with an assignment like that is bombard the teacher with questions like those in the previous paragraph. But inexperienced students may lack the courage or knowledge to do so; many will try to wrestle with the assignment as given, and many will despair. It's not their fault; they're not stupid, as they may believe when they fail with the assignment. No, the assignment is at fault. It is completely arhetorical; it omits totally the context needed for successful completion.

Third, assignments must be concrete. They should be written out and distributed to students well in advance of the due date. It's only fair to students to know exactly what is expected; and it will save you the phone calls on the night before the due date when students ask "What exactly did you want us to do in this paper?" If duplication is a problem in your teaching situation (budgets are tight everywhere), write the assignment clearly out on the board, and see that students copy it carefully. Review the key points (goals, physical constraints, procedures) to make sure all students know what is expected. And make sure the assignment is distributed far enough in advance of the due date for students to complete it successfully. Adjust your evaluation standards accordingly: your criteria should be different if students have one night to complete a writing task than if they have a month.

Composing Writing Assignments

The following list identifies four fields of information that a good assignment should cover. It also suggests places where less specificity, rather than more, may be helpful. If you cover these four fields, your students should have enough information to tackle the assignment successfully.

1. *Physical Constraints.* When is the assignment due? When are drafts due? What form is it to be in (essay, lab report, editorial, etc.)? What would be a reasonable length? Must it be typed? Should all scratchwork be submitted? What kind of documentation should be used?

2. *Discourse Context.* What is the topic, subject, or principle behind the assignment? Has the instructor specified an exact topic, or is the student supposed to find a topic by narrowing down the subject area? If so, what kinds of narrowing might be profitable? What kinds of skills are students expected to demonstrate? Who is the audience? For what purpose is the author writing? What questions or problems does the assignment raise?

3. *Resources.* Where in the text can the student seek help? What class discussions are relevant? Are there particular kinds of prewriting, drafting, and/or revising activities that will be helpful? May the student seek outside help from fellow students, authorities, and librarians? Is the student expected to consult secondary scholarship? If so, what kind(s)?

4. *Evaluation Criteria.* What will determine success or failure in completing this assignment? Will students have an opportunity to receive feedback before they submit the assignment for a grade?

Teaching in Practice

Here are perspectives from five teachers (three in subject areas, two in composition) that show the reasoning behind writing assignments they design. They've each included parts or all of assignments they have recently given.

Kelly: At the school where I teach, we're expected to give assignments out of the textbook so that "students get their money's worth." They have to show particular skills like narrative, analysis, and so on. Anyway, that means I adapt the assignments written by the textbook authors to the needs of my class. This, for example, is what I did with Exercise 4 in Chapter 6 of the our handbook. I typed up that exercise on a ditto, and added this paragraph:

"Make your analysis about four typed pages long, and assume that your classmates will be your primary audience. Bring your notes, outlines, grids, and preliminary materials to class on Wednesday, and bring a rough draft to class the following Monday (the 19th). Turn a completed version in for my response by noon on Friday (the 23rd)."

Joaquim: I have a lot more freedom in what I assign in Comp 101; our students have to produce a certain number of words each term, but we are expected to have them read other writers' work as well as student writing. So this is one of the kinds of assignments I have them write; like you, Kelly, I also include due dates and suggested length guidelines.

"You have been reading essays about discrimination and affirmative action this week. Now, I would like you to write about it in terms of your own experiences. I would like you to consult the *University Bulletin's* policy on affirmative action ('96-'98 *Bulletin*, p. 31), and write a letter to President Fretwell's Committee on Equal Opportunity (which is made up of four administrators, four professors, and four students). In your letter, I want you to either support, defend, or ask for some concrete change in a part of the University's AffAct policy. Please make sure that you tell the committee why you feel as you do, and give reasons to support the actions you want them to consider."

By suggesting they write a letter, I'm trying to get them to stretch beyond the typical "papers" they've written. Since we're using portfolios, I won't grade the letter at this stage, but I did include this statement in the assignment: "In evaluating your letter, I'll consider the clarity of your presentation, paragraph and sentence development, lack of wordiness, and your ability to select an appropriate tone of voice and style in explaining your criteria and presenting your conclusions to your audience." We've been working on these things for the past month, and I want to see how they're mastering these concepts.

Bob: In Political Science, I use writing as a way for students to stretch their skills and show me that they can use what we talk about as a class to conduct their own analyses. I do have requirements for form, documentation, and editing, but mostly I'm concerned with their development of ideas. So this is a typical assignment I use.

"We have used the Clarence Thomas confirmation hearings in class to discuss the Constitutional theory of separation of powers. For this paper, I would like you to choose a contemporary (since 1985) federal political issue other than this one that involved all three branches of government. Describe its development and resolution (if it's had one) to begin your paper, then use this issue to consider how well (or poorly) the separation of powers doctrine worked in this case. From your evaluation, conclude by recommending what changes (if any) you find necessary in the separation doctrine."

I also include how many sources I expect them to find and what kind of documentation (Turabian) I want them to use, as well as the usual due date stuff.

Anita: I use writing in my Earth Science classes to help students learn course concepts, and I offer them the option of working collaboratively on assignments like these. These short assignments help me check on their mastery of ideas, as well as to reinforce things they should be learning about form and documentation. I know it's not as fancy as what you do in writing courses, but my students seem to benefit from it.

"In our course notebook at the Reserve Desk you will find an article from *Scientific American,* May 1989, p. 22, entitled "Pinning Down Clouds." With one or two classmates, do the following:

· list the words you don't fully understand. Write their dictionary meaning on your paper. If there's more than one dictionary meaning, explain why you chose the one you did.

· write a summary of the article's main points, about a third the length of the original. Use your own words and sentence structure to avoid plagiarism.

· list several questions raised in your minds by this article. If two people work together there should be five questions; if three people work together there should be seven questions.

> · write out the complete, correct, MLA citation for this article.
>
> This assignment is due in class on Monday, Sept. 28."
>
> (Assignment contributed by Anita Rau of the Biology Department, Bucks County Community College)

John: My experience has been that students don't really learn something until they try to explain it to someone else. So I pick a principle we're working on in physics, and try to think of some "real world" application of it, then ask students to explain the concept in their own words and pictures. It's a challenge to them, but most of them think that doing these kinds of writing tasks helps them learn the concepts more thoroughly.

"As part of *Newsweek's* America's Cup coverage, you are assigned to write a short sidebar article explaining the physics of "tacking," that is, sailing into the wind. Your audience will be laypeople who have an interest in science and sport, but not much formal training in either. Your article of about 500 words should be accompanied by a clear diagram and written in a style suitable for this magazine. Your deadline is November 5, in class." (Assignment contributed by John Jewett of the Physics Department, California State Polytechnic University—Pomona)

These assignments succeed because they carefully place the writing task in a context; the students can tell what the instructor wants them to demonstrate, yet are allowed considerable freedom in choosing how to fulfill their requirements. Consider the possible alternatives: "Analyze the audience for a particular magazine"; "Critique the University's affirmative action policy;" "Use a contemporary federal political issue to show what aspects (if any) of the separation of powers doctrine should be changed"; "Summarize and provide vocabulary words for an essay"; "Explain tacking." Assignments like the ones shown challenge students to succeed rather than doom them to fail. They also encourage students to use narrow competencies to reach broader ones, to achieve growth in writing. Finally, they all make students specify a particular audience (either a community of known or unknown readers) or by imply information about what the teacher-as-audience expects. Goal-directed writing assignments like these, either individual or collaborative, are the true backbone of writing courses.

Scenario

As you come into the coffee room, you hear two of your colleagues, Dr. Leon Haroldson and Chris Mayagama, talking about the comp courses they are teaching. Dr. Haroldson, an older professor who specializes in James Joyce, is advocating very specific assignments. "In twenty-six years," he says, "I've learned that the less rope you give students to hang themselves on, the better. Give them a really specific topic, like 'How to Tie Your Shoes,' and see what they do with it. It's easier to give fair grades because all the students are trying to do the same thing and you can compare their achievements. When you don't give them specific direction, you're setting them up to fail."

"I don't know," Chris, a second-year TA, responds. "I like to give them more choice on assignments, so that they can find a subject or an angle that they have some stake in. Then they can't say 'I don't care about this topic'; they have no excuse not to get involved. I think a more open-ended topic lets them have more control, and use more of their writing skills, even if they do crash and burn once in a while."

Both teachers look up at you. What are you going to add to the conversation?

It takes time to design writing assignments that help students reach their writing goals, but it is time well spent. Not until you've seen an entire class misinterpret—and botch—a writing assignment can you really appreciate how worthwhile the time spent in working up a good assignment is. If it weren't for the harm done to the students involved, who almost always do their best to meet even the worst assignments and suffer the penalty for bad ones in grades, it might almost serve teachers right to have to read twenty-five or fifty papers on "The Definition of Friendship" or "My Interpretation of *Song of Solomon*" or "The Causes of the Civil War." Some teachers come away from such experiences blaming their students; most, though, will honestly wonder what went wrong. Usually the students were asked to write without context or an understanding of their goals. If your assignments cover the four fields outlined on page 94, you should be spared the agonies of grading papers you should never have assigned.

8

Intervening in the Writing Process:
When and Where to Teach What

The writing process is a complex matter; it varies for each writer, on each writing occasion. The differences in individual learning styles (delineated above in Chapter 6) make writing a very different task for each writer. So it's hard to generalize about teaching techniques that "improve" the writing process. Probably the best we can do is to help students develop a repertoire of strategies to use in writing and help them learn when and where the strategies work best for them. Though the process is recursive, it can be best discussed in a linear fashion, so that's how this section will proceed. You'll have to emphasize to your students, however, that it's never the wrong time to call on one of the stages; invention may be part of the revision techniques on a final draft. (Ask how many of them make changes in wording and sentences as they type their final papers; most do, an illustration of revision still in progress as they complete their editing and presentation.) This chapter presents what both Stephen North and Louise Wetherbee Phelps call the "lore" of composition study—the collective wisdom about praxis that a profession develops. The bibliography lists a number of works that will help you further explore and understand the lore I refer to here.

Teaching About Prewriting and Audience

Prewriting, or invention, has drawn a great deal of scholarly attention; in fact, it might be said to have been *the* rhetorical subject of composition scholarship in the early and mid-1970s. It's the equivalent of warming up before exercising, as well as the preliminaries of any event. Teaching invention strategies provides you many opportunities for groupwork, discussion, and one-on-one conference teaching. Be warned: prewriting can be seductive. Many classes get so involved with it that they neglect writing. You and the students must remember that prewriting is a way for finding things to say in writing; it's not a substitute for composing written texts.

Prewriting strategies full into two very large, ill-defined categories: unstructured and structured. Unstructured prewriting works best when students are trying to find a topic or form; it helps them find new material, to make new connections, to pursue (in John Passmore's and Donald Murray's term) surprise. Structured prewriting works best when the topic or form is known or has been assigned; it helps students discover what they know and need to know about their writing subject and to make sense of the material they've found. The techniques for both kinds of prewriting are closed competencies; most students can learn to use them. But when they use them to develop new knowledge, or to structure their knowledge in a different way, these strategies become gateways to open competencies and to better writing. As teachers, we want our students to know about as many of these gateways as possible; we have to be careful, however, not to swamp them with all the techniques. You may need to introduce the techniques in pairs or triads—perhaps mixing unstructured and structured kinds—by choosing those that seem best suited to the assignment students currently are completing. At the same time you'll want to encourage students to try other methods, so that they don't limit themselves and their chances of discovery.

There are few if any instances where prewriting should be graded; it's successful only insofar as it helps students find things to say in their larger papers. But you'll probably want to collect it along with the finished papers to see what kinds of prewriting the students are doing and to suggest alternate or more advanced strategies to help them develop their skills. As discussed in Chapter 6 above, students of different learning styles and personality types will find different methods more amenable than others. I always encourage my students, no matter what their initial preferences, to try the other methods at least once. They are often surprised at what methods stir their creative juices; often students who have "blocked" using their most comfortable methods can get around the block by trying some other strategy. Students having trouble beginning a revision for a piece of writing might go back to their prewritings to look for other entrees, or try a new technique to get restarted. Here are a few suggestions for prewriting that may help.

Perception Busters

Often, students forget how many ways there are to view a particular subject. Exercises in developing perceptual skills may help students break out of old patterns and find new ways of viewing their subjects, so they're particularly valuable both for judgers and for intuiters in MBTI terms. Ask students to draw something they're sure they know—such as the keypad on a telephone or the gauges on the dashboard of their cars. Then have them compare their sketches to the real thing; where are the differences? Have them describe some familiar setting—their room, the classroom, a local watering hole—as specifically as possible, then revise the description for someone who has been blind since birth. What does the classroom look like from the point of view of that bee banging against the light fixture? How does the cafeteria look from the server's side of the line? Encourage students, too, to play devil's advocate; if they're going to be arguing for a position, have them freewrite about the other side, about comparisons and contrasts and precedents for their positions; have them pick the celebrity endorser who will do commercials for their position ("Hi! This is Dennis Rodman for the American Tattoo Association!") When students break the barriers of habit, learn to use all of their senses, and see other perspectives, they take giant strides toward learning and applying their new knowledge.

Commonplace Books

Personal journals aren't the only kinds of writing notebooks students can keep. Often students will benefit from keeping old-fashioned commonplace books, where they not only record observations and summarize readings, but copy down words, phrases, and passages of writing they admire. Some sensing writers (as opposed to intuiters) can compile wonderful commonplace books even though journals are anathema to them. (I know; I'm one of them.) Like the journals, such commonplace books can become treasure houses for students in search of paper topics to plunder, as well as collections of models they might imitate. If students are to keep commonplace books, you can encourage them to expand their range. Students may want to include only items from *People* magazine or from rock lyrics; you can direct them, gently, to alternate sources as well. It's best to encourage students actually to copy out the model; this makes them more aware of the words they copy than if they cut and paste in entries. If you use this prewriting technique, you might want to leave some class time occasionally for students to share their most recent gems.

Range and Variation

In the late 1960s, three rhetoricians—Richard Young, Alton Becker, and Kenneth Pike—adapted the terminology and methods of modern physics to invention strategies. Their "tagmemic" method (from the Greek verb meaning "to arrange") encourages writers to see their subjects not just as static objects or entities but as processes and parts of larger systems. Writers using tagmemic invention look at the subject's identifying characteristics (called "contrast"), the amount of changes it will tolerate before it becomes something else (called "variation"), and its role in the larger systems in which it plays a part (called "distribution"), in order to discuss it fully.

For instance, an aluminum baseball bat has certain features of design, engineering, and equipment that make it unique. They give it its contrast. Some of these features and options can be varied or left off, but at a certain point, the bat becomes a different kind of bat—a wooden Louisville Slugger® or a WiffleBall® bat. The limits to which an aluminum bat can be modified and still remain a bat are its variation; at what point does it become a golf club or a cricket bat? Finally, the bat plays a part in a number of systems: all baseball equipment, products of sports technology, targets of baseball purists' criticism, reasons why "the game has changed." These systems represent the bat's distribution, the worlds in which it plays a part.

Many authors have tried to include tagmemics in texts, but the method has never been widely popular; nevertheless it does work in the classroom. I once had a class made up largely of engineering and computer science students, and this was their favorite prewriting exercise. Among textbook adaptations of it you might find useful are W. Ross Winterowd's in *Contemporary Rhetoric;* Janice Lauer, et al.'s in *Four Worlds of Writing;* and Dean Memering and Frank O'Hare's in *The Writer's Work.* Charles Kneupper's article "Revising the Tagmemic Heuristic" (1980) also provides a number of suggestions for using this multifaceted invention strategy in the classroom. Freewriting and journal keeping work well with tagmemics.

Research

Although we seldom think of research as an invention tactic outside of the research paper, reading and asking questions of a subject are often the most productive ways for students to find and organize material on their topics, and is certainly one of the most common prewriting methods used in business situations. Moreover, the different kinds of research encompass all kinds of personality types, so it's a technique the whole class may be able to use. For sensers, book research can provide facts, figures, authorities, and perspectives the student didn't know. Talking to experts can be even more rewarding, especially to intuitive learners who value narrative; an expert's interview can add eyewitness testimony and illustrative anecdotes to facts, figures, and printed sources. The student who is writing about the Nintendo craze, for instance, might talk to a games salesman, an computer programmer, an elementary school teacher, and both inexperienced and experienced players as she gathers material. The student writing about business school admissions can talk to an admissions counselor, students undergoing the process, and students who already are in business school. Ken Macrorie calls this process "I-search" rather than research, because there are live people involved, and therefore the subject becomes more real to the writer. Research encourages the student to provide her own answers as well as those she finds through reading and interviews; journals, freewriting, and discussion work well as preliminaries to research prewriting.

Audience Awareness

There is considerable controversy as to whether audience awareness is a prewriting, drafting, or revising technique; I personally find it's all three. Research into the nature of audience has boomed in the last decade (see bibliography), and a number of studies have shown that students will profit by writing for, and thinking about, audiences other than "the general public." That's why, as part of your prewriting exercises, you may want to encourage your students to experiment with audience choices. What kinds of questions will they ask for what kinds of readers? How does changing the audience affect what kinds of materials they will want to invent, what kinds of structure they will want to posit, what kinds of language and example they will include? Students often have not thought of these matters in any detail; they shrug and say, "The teacher is my audience" or "I'm writing for the general public." It's important to teach them that these statements are only partially true.

Some strategies beyond those suggested above for fine-tuning audience awareness include writing in forms other than academic essays (for instance, computer documentation, appliance users' manuals, letters, résumés, scientific documents, etc.); interviewing readers from other fields to discover what their expectations are; role-playing, and the like. Students should be encouraged to consider whether they are writing for an audience they are making up, or for a real audience (see Ede and Lunsford, 1984), and to consider the ramifications of such choices. Many handbooks include exercises that will help students make such considerations.

Caveats

Lots of advice students have received about prewriting in their previous schooling can confuse them. Some have been told, "Write to find out what you want to say; don't start out with a preconceived idea of what should go on." Others have been told, "Always start by writing down your thesis statement, so you won't lose track of what you want to say. Then develop a full outline so that you'll have a clear roadmap where to go." (Some unfortunate students have had eleventh-grade teachers who told them one of these truisms, then had a twelfth-grade teacher who insisted that the other truism was gospel.) It takes time, and trust, for students to believe that different starting strategies will work better for different writers in different situations. And then there are some students who do most if not all of their prewriting in their heads; they have incredible difficulty not starting right off into a draft. (Again I sympathize; I'm one of these, too.) Students, and many teachers, tend to believe that the way things are described in textbooks are the way they *ought* to be, and that there's something wrong with a writer who doesn't follow them. Furthermore, teachers tend to emphasize the activities and styles they're most comfortable with. I'm sure Chris Anson encourages journaling enthusiastically in his classes, based on what he's written in the *Longman Handbook* and in the article we've included in this anthology. On the other hand, since I hate to keep journals, I don't require them in my classes, though there are some students I encourage to keep them. We both tend to favor our own styles, but we have both learned to be flexible for students who respond better to other styles.

With all these techniques, students can quite easily spend an entire semester prewriting, simply generating material. But that's not the goal of a writing class. At some point, the student must do something with this wealth of material: sort it, thin it out (sometimes easier said than done), and start shaping it: "face the white bull of the page," as Hemingway would say. That's drafting—the next step in the writing process.

Teaching in Progress

One of the ways I use journals in classes (when I do) is to have students keep a "patent notebook." I explain to them how many of the writers in the workplace with whom I deal have to document everything they do on a particular project, so that if someone ever legally challenged their company's right to patent a product, they can get the numbered and signed notebooks out of the corporate vault and prove that on such-and-such a day, they got certain results. This fascinates most students, who have never thought of journaling as being something that might be part of a *job*, let alone something that would constitute proof in a court of law. It gives students who may not like to keep journals, or who have trouble keeping up the momentum, an incentive to stick with it.

I ask them to treat one of their writing tasks in the class (usually the third paper or so) as a "patent case," and to document everything they do on that task fully in their journal, with dated, signed entries. This means that drafts, ideas, outlines, reports on conversations with their groups or with me—everything—for that assignment go in the journal. Then, once they've completed the writing task, I ask them to conclude the patent case by writing about their documentation efforts in their journals. What was different about journaling when we changed the stakes? Did this change any of their attitudes about keeping a journal? If their learning style doesn't incline them to journaling, did creating this fictional situation help them use the technique?

One of the things I have learned from using this technique is that for some students, journaling is more effective when there's an imposed stake put on keeping it (one that doesn't include a grade). For others, this kind of imposition is paralyzing. It reinforces my belief that while writing to learn is important for all writers, journal keeping *per se* may not always be the best way. I've learned not to make sweeping generalizations about this or any other kind of prewriting, but to give my students more flexibility, more choices, more situations in which they can practice varying techniques.

Teaching About Drafting

"I love being a writer. What I can't stand is the paperwork." Whether we attribute this quote to the writer Peter DeVries or the imaginary poet Gowan McGland (from the film *Reuben, Reuben*), most of us share the sentiment: writing stops being fun when we have to do it. This is why drafting is such a lonely job. Before we can revise, reshape, rewrite, and retire, we have to put words on paper. Many students panic at this stage; they either slam material down on paper without much thought and refuse to change it ("It's there; it'll do") or avoid as long as possible the drafting of the paper ("It's not due until Friday and today's only Wednesday"). Some students do so much of their prewriting and early drafting in their heads that what they produce is more like a near-final copy than a draft; when such students are in groups with students who struggle to produce even a few paragraphs, homicide is a real possibility.

We can't really force students to draft, but we can provide them with some strategies and support while they do battle with language.

The Zero-Draft

First, we can reduce the intimidation factor by introducing students to what Donald Murray and others call a "zero-draft." This essentially is an extended freewriting: students write down their ideas hastily, without stopping to edit or revise, putting in squiggles or stars in areas they want to fill out later, and either skipping the introduction and conclusion if those are trouble spots (for many inexperienced writers, they are) or writing "semi-draft" intros like "In this paragraph I am going to start talking about computer pornography and I'm going to get my reader's attention by bringing in something shocking, etc." The goal is simply to get a couple of sheets of writing together, so that the writer can begin working; they're private, safe places to put down ideas. Both introverts and extroverts usually like this activity; moreover, serial learners can sometimes get past the intimidation of the introduction by using such strategies.

Sometimes students do better with zero drafts if they're not written on loose leaf paper; many like old sheets of computer printout if it's available since the wide margins will leave so much room to revise. Some students will want to put each "chunk" of their papers on a separate sheet so that the chunks can be shuffled to determine the best possible order of ideas. Encourage students to experiment; techniques that seemed far-fetched often prove most successful, and your perceivers in particular will really expand their ranges this way. On the other hand, one-drafters will almost always want to skip this stage, and many will simply not be able to recreate the zero-version of the completed draft they produce.

Examining Models

Second, we can make sure students know what it is they're trying to draft. If students are writing reviews, make sure they know what reviews look like, what sorts of elements go into them and what kinds of structures could be used. If students have discussed the assignment together and have looked at a few sample papers, they'll understand better "what the teacher is looking for"; this gives them more concrete goals to aim at and may help them draft more effectively. Both visual and verbal learners seem to benefit from examples, and intuiters are especially responsive to them.

Discouraging Premature Editing

Third, we can try to discourage premature editing. Many students paralyze their drafting by trying to edit each word and sentence as it moves onto paper; then they complain "Oh, I can't remember what I was going to say next" because they've totally destroyed their trains of thought. Try to get such students to stick to freewriting rules in their zero drafts; if they hit a spot that isn't right, suggest they put a star or check in the margin, circle the offending word or phrase, or just leave a blank, and go on recording their ideas first. Compulsive editors find this difficult and you'll have to encourage them, perhaps through your comments on papers or by intervening in groupwork, to try new ways to liberate their creativity.

Creating an Environment for Drafting

Fourth, we can provide a supportive environment for drafting. Discuss with the class how drafting methods differ; I draft some things sitting at the computer with at least two cats sitting on the desk, the radio playing classic rock, and a cup of tea at hand. Some routine things get composed orally into my tape recorder on my 90-minute drive into work. Other things—usually pieces of writing I'm not sure about—I draft in pencil, on yellow legal pads, alone, and in silence. I'd estimate that this book was composed about fifty percent each way, though part I was written more in silence at my keyboard in the workshop, and part II written with more distractions, especially the parts drafted in Terminal A of Logan Airport.

What sorts of environments do your students prefer to write in? What do they do when they hit a block? (The answers to this one will really surprise you.) Does anyone talk into a tape recorder? Talk to herself? Need a Garth Brooks or Itzhak Perelman album playing to be creative? Students feel better about drafting when they realize that everyone has difficulties some, if not all of the time. They've been indoctrinated by the "blithely outline and briskly draft" propaganda that older texts and previous teachers may have promoted. When they realize that there's nothing wrong with them for producing texts in different manners, often the barricades begin to crumble.

Allowing Students to Practice Drafting

Finally, we can provide practice in drafting. After all, in many situations students will have to draft quickly: on essay exams, during the LSAT, in the office. So short practice sessions, where students examine a drafting strategy and then apply it, or practice in the journal, will help students learn to "get on with it." Most freshman classes include in-class writing, so many composition programs require at least one graded in-class writing per semester to help students build these skills. In the ideal classrooms described in theoretical tomes, students have all the time in the world to find material and incubate it. In the real world, the test may be over in twenty minutes; that letter may have to be in the 2:30 mail. The more student resistance to drafting is lowered, the more likely they are to meet their deadlines.

Learning styles aside, a common student misunderstanding is that he or she need only write one draft, which can be tinkered with a bit and submitted "as is" to the teacher. After all, that got them by in high school. This is a notion you'll have to dispel. Some parts of a text do remain the same from incubation to final submission; the more of these, the easier the writer's task. Of course this requires that the writer produce suitable material the first time out; most writers aren't that good unless we've practiced a great deal. Students may need two, three, or four drafts—even more—to arrive at language that meets their goals. This is fine: Hemingway rewrote the last, painfully beautiful page of *A Farewell to Arms* thirty-nine times to get the words right. Most of us don't need that many drafts, but it's nice to know that we're not the only ones who struggle.

Over the last few years, I've really changed how I approach drafting. I used to require beginning writers to go through at least five drafts of a piece of writing: a zero draft; a shaping draft (where students work on structure, audience, and voice); a style draft (where they tinker with paragraphing, sentence structure, and word choice); an editing draft (where they work on mechanical and format problems); and the final draft they submit. Each draft encouraged them to focus on particular kinds of revising, which enabled them to revise more thoroughly; their grade reflected the efforts their drafting revealed. Now that I have switched to a portfolio system and am trying to be more responsive to different learning styles, I don't *require* as many drafts, but I do ask to see evidence of multiple drafting at some point to see how the student handles the process.

For group workshops I ask students to bring at least a style draft; if time permits, I schedule shorter group sessions on editing drafts. (These requirements have several practical ramifications. The student has to start the paper well in advance of the due date, so I get fewer hasty papers; and it cuts down on instances of plagiarism, since I require and examine multiple drafts.) Even students who claim to be "one drafters" need to produce a final clean copy, and I particularly check their two copies until I am sure that they are true one-drafters and not just trying to take shortcuts. (If you are interested in more distinctions between the kinds of writing processes used by one- and multi-draft writers, I suggest Mickey [Muriel] Harris' article, "Composing Behaviors of One- and Multi-draft Writers," *College English* 51 (1989): 174-191.)

Teaching About Revising

When writers move from the drafting to the revising stage of a piece of writing, they shift perspective radically. Heretofore they have been the creator, the parent, the controller of the words. Students who have difficulty producing texts in fact become protectors of their words; after all the effort spent in getting that language on paper, they're not about to omit or change the fruits of their labors. Thus, when we ask them to turn about, become members of their own audience, challenge, examine, and change the texts they've produced, it's no surprise that many become defensive, confused, and recalcitrant. Revision seems to them an attack on their own best efforts, not an attempt to refine and improve their performances. In teaching revision, then, we have to stress the necessity of re-seeing their work, of thinking as a member of the audience, of getting outside of their personal involvement with their compositions. For students with intensely sensing and/or judging personalities, this can almost seem to be a personal attack, so the process has to be undertaken with care. I like to give students a piece of advice attributed to Oscar Wilde: "Criticize your own writing as if your worst enemy had written it." Students might not need to be this hostile an audience to themselves, but Wilde's advice can be well taken.

Many students, in fact, misunderstand what revising is all about. They think of it as "fixing" or "correcting"; that is, finding what they've done "wrong" and remedying the problem before the teacher with his red pen comes along. Nancy Sommers has discovered that students often don't have the word "revision" in their writing vocabularies; it's a teacher's word. Students use terms such as "scratch out and do over," "review," "redo," "mark out," and "slash and throw out" (1980: 381). These indicate how limited a version of revision they understand.

So one of the first things to teach in revision is what the word means and what the process can involve. To use Sommers' definition, revision is "a sequence of changes in a composition—changes which are initiated by cues and occur continually throughout the writing of a work" (1980: 380). For students, Sommers argues, these changes are largely rewording, as if changing a word or two may guarantee success or failure on an assignment. But she also finds that experienced writers start from the other end; their key phrases include "finding a framework," "taking apart and putting back together," "reworking," "chiseling," and the like. They work with ideas, not just words, to ensure the success of their writings (1980: 383-384).

This means revising usually starts with the large concerns in the draft: what is the writer trying to do? How well have her efforts succeeded? What kind of audience is she trying to reach? and so forth. The smaller concerns, such as word choice, punctuation, and spelling, come at the very tail end of revision. They shouldn't be the only revising activity that goes on. Sometimes it helps students to see revision in process; show them some of your own drafts, other student examples, even literary manuscripts. Seeing can be believing. It will always help for students to see an example paper going through this process, and it would be very valuable for students to discuss together just what it is the author is doing, why she does it, and why they might need to do similar things.

Revising Major Issues

Questions of purpose, audience, and structure can be productively addressed in large group workshops first. Show students a paper that is weak in one or more of these areas (you might want to "sabotage" a paper for demonstration purposes) and ask them "What do you think this writer wanted to do in this paper? Who do you think he imagined as his readers? How can you tell? Is he talking to a different audience than he imagined?" From there, you can ask more specific questions. "How, would you describe the shape of this paper? What do you think about the order of his ideas? How would you tinker with them? Could you arrange them in a better way? Should there be a different form here?" (If you'll notice, these follow the order in the *Framework for Judging* below, Chapter 9.)

You may have to help sensing and judging students focus on these larger issues; show them that this is where revising begins. Then they can break into smaller groups of three to four students and share drafts; in such a system, each student will get two or three sets of responses to these questions, outside perspectives on her work. She should feel free to ask questions of her readers: "Why don't you think I'm talking to you? Where did you get lost on page 2?" These sessions help writers see their own texts as other readers—if not their worst enemies—see their work. You will probably also have to help all students see that judgments about their *work* are not judgments about *them*; learning not to take this criticism personally is a big part of the maturing process for first-year college students, and you can expect some bumps along the road.

Revising Structure and Organization

Sometimes structure can be a hard topic for students. If your department requires that students write in a number of modes or in several prescribed forms, students will generally struggle through; the mode or form is generally determined in the assignment, and like it or not, the student must deal with it. But what about open topics or when students find that their approach to a topic just won't "fit" into the assigned mode or form? Here you have several alternatives. For open topics, both prewriting and classical heuristics might come into play to help students decide what form their paper is going to take. They might also consider some "recipes" for paper structure, such as Frank D'Angelo's "paradigms." He argues that most paper structures represent patterns of thought, and that students can learn to use these patterns to arrange ideas according to the intentions they have. D'Angelo's paradigms are too long to list here; you can find them in his *Conceptual Theory of Rhetoric* (1975) or conveniently summarized in Lindemann. (1995: 135 ff.)

One structure you may want to discuss with your students is that old war-horse, the five-paragraph theme. Many students learned this generic writing structure (introduction, three paragraphs of development, conclusion) in secondary school. For some limited topics it works; it's quite useful on essay exams and the LSAT and for short pieces of exposition. But students need to know that there are many other ways to organize pieces of writing, and that they needn't try to confine all of their ideas to five cramped boxes.

When students want to write something that doesn't fit into the prescribed structure, you have some tough decisions to make. When students really show interest in a piece of writing, I want to encourage, not discourage them. So I temporize. If they want to write in a mode that's not appropriate at the moment, I tell them to get their ideas down in a zero draft and save it for a later paper or the portfolio, suggesting that they develop the ideas in journal entries and freewritings in the meantime. Then we try to find another topic that fits the current assignment. If they want to write in a form that doesn't really fit in the class—for instance, a science-fiction spoof in an argument class or the analysis of a novel in an exposition class— I will agree to read and comment on it, but not count it for a grade. I remind the student that she has to show competencies in a number of areas the school has defined; those are the minimum. But since I'm glad she's making meaning in language, I'd enjoy the chance to read what else she's written. (This has on one occasion landed me with the 400-page handwritten draft of an experimental novel, but for the most part I've enjoyed my students' other production.) These situations don't arise often, but when they do, try to stay as flexible as you can. You will have to exercise some authority here, and some rhetoricians may criticize you for doing so, but basically, you're getting paid to be the authority, and sometimes you just have to *be* directive.

Revising Paragraphs

The question of large structures inevitably leads to discussion of smaller ones, particularly paragraphs. Inductive teaching, letting students examine samples and learn some techniques from what they find, seems to work best here. For instance, take that old stalking horse, the topic sentence. Most of our students were taught, as we were, that "good" paragraphs have clear topic sentences supported by several sentences of development and ended with a firm recapitulation of the topic sentence. But only about half the paragraphs in published writing seem to work this way (the seminal article on the subject is Richard Braddock's "The Frequency and Placement of Topic Sentences in Expository Prose" (1974); his numbers can be duplicated roughly in the prose of doctors, lawyers, biochemists, and literary critics, according to examinations my students have conducted over the years).

Thus, students can become researchers and determine for themselves how topic sentences are used. Have students examine paragraphs from a number of sources—textbooks, novels, newspapers, magazines, instruction manuals, coffee table books, and so on. How many topic sentences do they find? When they start to wrestle with the "topic-less" paragraphs, how do they describe the structures they find? Do the paragraphs use statement and comment, question and answer, problem and solution, or other organizing principles? Can they paraphrase a topic sentence, even if one is not expressed? Here you can bring in the notion of the controlling idea: just about all good paragraphs have one of these (transitions may be an exception), even if it's not stated explicitly. This data will help students internalize the notions of focus, coherence, and linking, especially if they are sensing or visual learners.

These discoveries about topic sentences can lead to new strategies for paragraphing. For instance, students might try to pinpoint the relationship between writer and audience when topic sentences are used; usually they are found in situations where the audience knows less than the writer (such as in textbooks or instruction manuals). How might that affect students' decisions about their paragraphs?

And how long are good paragraphs? I once had a student who indented every seventh sentence; she explained it worked more often than it didn't (actually, she'd learned to cram her ideas into boxes of that size). Students are amazed to find one-sentence paragraphs or, if skimming periodicals like the *New Yorker*, paragraphs of a page and more. Students can also decide when one-sentence paragraphs work (as transitions, when making snide or summary remarks, in narrow-columned newspapers, etc.) and when they don't (when they provide an opinion without support, when they're the introduction to a paper, etc.). Likewise, they can decide what relationships between the writer and audience permit longer paragraphs (the writer trusts the audience's knowledge, interest, and/or intelligence) and can develop some intelligent rules of thumb for each piece of writing ("My readers won't have heard any of these terms before so I'm going to break things up into small chunks for them to handle"). Above all, encourage them to see that paragraphs are tools that writers use to shape information; they aren't mechanical recipes that constrain writers. You may want to use some example paragraphs both in full-class and group sessions on paragraph revision.

Encourage paragraph dissection and recombination by students; let them experiment with several different structures and lengths of paragraphs to get the feel of each. Let them see, too, that while the paragraph may present a "complete idea" (whatever that may be), they may need several paragraphs on that same idea, from different perspectives, to treat it thoroughly in the paper. I encourage students to think of the body of their paper in chunks of discourse rather than in paragraphs; a chunk can contain one or many paragraphs, depending on the complexity of the idea discussed. This allows students to keep a sense of form without feeling constrained by a five—or however many—paragraph structure.

Simply knowing how a paragraph may be shaped, however, doesn't always help students know what to put in their paragraphs or how to arrange this material. Here some strategies developed from transformational-generative grammar may prove very useful. For example, Francis Christensen's "generative rhetoric of the paragraph" (1967) suggests that most paragraphs work through subordination and coordination. That is, they start with a general statement, then paraphrase, elaborate on, or modify it. Christensen describes the directions his paragraphs take as "levels of generality." Sentences are numbered to show how specific the information they contain is; the most general information is level 1, and each subsequent level of given a higher number. Sentences that represent about the same level of generality (which are often rhetorically parallel or coordinate) have the same numbers.

Here's a paragraph from Allan Bloom's bestseller *The Closing of the American Mind*, arranged to show Christensen's levels:

1. What Aristophanes satirizes is the exterior of science, how the scientist appears to the nonscientist.
2. He can only hint at the dignity of what the scientist does.
   3. His Socrates is not individualized; he is not the Socrates we know.
   3. He is a member of the species philosopher, student of nature, particularly of astronomy.
      4. The first known member of this species was Thales.
         5. He was the first man to have seen the cause of, and to predict, an eclipse of the sun.
            6. This means that he figured out that the heavens move in regular ways that accord with mathematical reasoning.
            6. He was able to reason from visible effects to invisible causes and speculate about the intelligible order of nature as a whole.
               7. He at that moment became aware that his mind was in accord with the principles of nature, that he was the microcosm. (270)

Students can practice analyzing their own and other students' paragraphs to see what kinds of levels are reflected, and you can tie this analysis into exercises on adding depth to paragraphs. Many students, for example, will only attempt one or two levels of generality in a paragraph; they don't probe their ideas in great detail. These students might be encouraged to revise by adding more examples, details, and specific explanations to make their paragraphs more three-dimensional. Likewise, students might tie the levels of generality to D'Angelo's paradigms or other models of structure to create templates for paragraphs: A comparison-contrast paragraph arranges its levels so, or a narrative paragraph arranges its levels so. (Students must be warned to use such strategies as starting points and to vary them; otherwise the paragraphs will seem machine-produced and have very little appeal.) These strategies can lead to new paragraph-length hypotheses: a paragraph is long enough if it contains enough material and enough specifics for the particular readers. Encourage students to play with these and other structures to find out what paragraphs really can do.

Revising Sentences

Sentences, too, need attention in the revising process. Most students play it safe with their sentences; the shorter the better, they feel, because the possibility for error is less. Many students have done little reading aloud, so they haven't learned to perceive sentence rhythms and the effects of variation on those rhythms. They're used to spoken sentences—often short, snappy, and incomplete ("Less filling! Tastes great!"). They may have had exposure to loose, periodic, and cumulative sentences in the lower grades, but most simply don't know what those labels mean, or how to employ those strategies. Example sentences, as well as individual and collaborative exercises, will help students strengthen their own sentences and apply their knowledge to their own papers.

The revising stage can offer students the opportunity to experiment with their sentences, to take risks without fear of punishment. In the 1980s, "sentence combining," a set of strategies enabling students to generate longer, more complex sentences, was very popular with some teachers for this stage. I still use a fair bit of it, since I like the results my students have achieved. However, as with prewriting, some teachers and students got carried away with sentence combining. Doing the exercises (mostly using someone's else prose) can be fun, and students seem to enjoy the activities; but they are no substitute for the students writing their own sentences and applying the techniques to their own work as part of a larger writing assignment.

Sentence combining arose from applications of transformational-generative grammar principles to classroom practices. Researchers such as Kellogg Hunt and Frank O'Hare determined that encouraging students to expand sentences by coordinating (adding on), deleting (eliminating repeated words), and embedding (inserting new information into a main clause) enabled them to write complex, fluent sentences without having to master elaborate grammatical terminology. The practice they recommended was giving students a base sentence and several other sentences of information to incorporate in the base sentence; then students experiment with various ways to combine the information.

In most sentence-combining instruction, students learn various kinds of combinations, starting with relatively simple coordination and subordination using conjunctions. Then they progress to removing repeated elements, embedding information as adjectives and phrases, culminating in "advanced" strategies such as adverbials and absolutes. They're provided with the information to combine (in most cases) so that they will focus on the structures they are trying to produce. After they control the structures, they are introduced to the punctuation conventions the new sentences require. Students are rewarded for taking risks, for trying new combinations, and are generally not "punished" for punctuation faults until they have mastered the patterns structurally. Of course, the problem here is that they are operating on someone else's prose, not their own. You can remedy this by asking them to imitate sentences using their own ideas, or to "decombine" or practice combining on sentences from their own papers. (Reading notebooks and journals provides a great deal of material for them to operate upon.)

Many textbooks include sentence combining exercises; some are devoted entirely to the technique. If you're interested in learning more about it, you might wish to consult *Sentence Combining and the Teaching of Writing*, an anthology compiled by Donald Daiker, Andrew Kerek, and Max Morenberg; Steven Witte's review of this book (1980) makes some wise suggestions about how the method might be used more productively in classes. Francis Christensen has also applied similar principles to develop a "generative rhetoric of the sentence" (much like generative rhetoric of the paragraph); it's described in *CCC* 14 (1963): 155-161, an article that is frequently reprinted.

Students can incorporate sentence strategies in a number of ways. One of the best is to have them read passages aloud to groups; if the sentences sound choppy or get too tangled up to be followed, the group can suggest ways the writer might revise them. Students can be encouraged to pick two or three paragraphs in a draft and try to combine sentences in them; gradually this can be expanded to pages and to the whole draft. Group readings can also help uncomplicate overcombined sentences and to find faulty connections ("You said 'Because' here but you're talking about a contradiction. Wouldn't 'But' be better?" or "About every fifth word when you read that sounded like 'and.' Did I hear you right?") Students need to be reminded that sentence work is usually a revising, not a drafting activity; most of them shouldn't start tinkering with sentences until after they have the zero draft completed. With practice, sentences may start coming out in combined form; but it's not "wrong" to draft in choppy or incomplete sentences and refine them later.

Revising Words

Finally, in revision students need to consider words. Most of our students have fairly limited academic vocabularies; they've read little and have received little encouragement to expand their linguistic resources. But they actually know a great deal about words; one of your chief jobs is teaching them how to tap that knowledge productively. For instance, though students may not be familiar with the terms "connotation" and "denotation," they can tell you the difference between "drunk," "buzzed," "plastered," "wasted," and "toasted." You might give them a number of terms (usually neutral) and ask them to provide varieties of ways to express those terms (usually positive and negative) as a way of introducing connotations and denotation. They may have been introduced to the thesaurus but have few ideas how to use it; you can teach them to cross-check in the dictionary by "gussying up" plain statements with synonyms from the thesaurus, or let them try the process themselves (in such experiments, "Twinkle, twinkle, little star" becomes "Scintillate, scintillate, asteroidal nimific" and "Happy birthday to you" becomes "Permit me to express my best wishes for the felicitous celebration of your natal anniversary"). Different students will need to attack this stage at different times; some handbooks move this topic to the editing stage, although for most writers, it's right there on the seam between revising and editing.

Reconsidering language choices inevitably raises questions of purpose and audience: when and why would a writer want to use these strategies? What happens when "tax increase" becomes "revenue enhancement"? Are the terms "pro-life" and "pro-choice" mutually exclusive? What happens when they use the pronoun "he" to discuss doctors and the pronoun "she" to discuss nurses? What effects do different connotations or phrasings have on different readers? Students may wish to examine advertisements, published examples (the school bulletin is usually full of excellent examples), junk mail, and other kinds of written products to develop their sensitivity to language manipulation. (For instance, what are "light" potato chips? What is "diet" lasagna?)

Where you can, use good student examples to show students that they can manipulate language as effectively as the professionals. Dictionary work can also play a productive role in these discussions: has the word always meant what it does now? (For instance, the first instance of "freshman" in English refers to someone who has changed to a new religion.) Who decides what words get in dictionaries, and whether they are properly spelled and defined? Who puts those usage labels on words? Does the student's dictionary tell her when to use "nauseous" and when to use "nauseated," for instance? (I won't go into the question of dictionary authority here, but students may ask you about it—especially if they note that members of a dictionary's usage board have been dead for many years. I usually tell students that these experts were consulted by Ouija board.)

In revising words, students can apply the techniques used for sentence revision. Reading passages aloud and discussing the word choices with other students seem to have best effect ("It sounds weird when you say 'you could have barfed' when he said that"; or "I like calling those people 'parasitic' in the second paragraph"). Students might begin experiments with connotation a few paragraphs at a time, expanding gradually to the whole paper as they grow more confident. Encourage them to ransack their freewritings, journals, commonplace books, and reading notebooks for words or phrases that might give their meanings new force. They may overuse the thesaurus at first; teach them how to cross reference the synonyms in the dictionary to make sure the one they've chosen is appropriate. Botching a few word choices shouldn't make or break a paper; but finding good ones, as Mark Twain wrote, is like knowing "the difference between a lightning bug and the lightning," and deserves some reward.

All of these discussions about language can be conducted without much reference to elaborate grammatical terminology. Once the students have mastered the ideas, you might wish to introduce them to some of the terminology ("The name for these good and bad rephrasings of a word is 'connotation'; that's what you look under in the index of your book"; "The words which often cause you to fasten two sentences together with commas are movable adverbs, because you can move words like *however*, *thus*, and *therefore* around in a sentence. Your book describes them under the term for joining, 'conjunctive' adverbs"). It's far more important, however, that students learn to use their own language, to develop their own repertoires, than that they master a cluster of latinate labels. Likewise, they should be spending most of their time working with their own words, not filling out exercises in a book or running through someone else's drills. Remember: we learn to write by writing. If your students are to learn to use language effectively, they have to be creating language.

Teaching in Practice

It takes some courage to do this the first time, but letting your students watch *you* revise—and critique you as you do it—can be one of the most effective ways of teaching revision. When I do this, I bring in a chunk of something I'm working on. Usually it's some project I'm working on with a writer in the workplace—a corporate document, a speech, a professional newsletter—which gives it extra interest. (I have never been able to persuade students that there's not a difference between "student writing" and "real writing," and over the years I've decided that they're right—they're more honest about it than I am.)

I project it on an overhead projector, or if I'm lucky enough to be teaching in the computer classroom, on our computer projector. I explain to students who the audience will be and what the context is, and any constraints on me (for instance, a length limit, the requirements of patent or contract language, policy limitations, and so forth). Then I take a deep breath and start to revise it. But instead of doing it privately at my desk or on my couch—where I am comfortable revising—I do it out loud, in front of them. "Okay," I'll start, "I think the biggest problem here is X, because...." Then I start to describe what I want to do about it. I encourage them to interrupt me, challenge me, ask me questions about what I am doing. I get booed if I make a typo, sometimes (which has been a real goad to improving my keyboarding), and sometimes really lively disagreements break out. One group of students will like a passage, another will want me to change it, and they argue it out, with each other, and with me.

I only use this technique once or twice a semester, usually early on, and scheduled right before revision sessions for their writing tasks. It seems to goad a lot more global revision for students, and some of the comments they make in their portfolios tell me how much it has affected them. Last semester, Kwesi wrote, "I was really impacted by what you said in one class session, about how you would have to take out a particular paragraph, even though you thought it was the best thing in the article, because it just didn't fit the tone you wanted for the audience who would read it. I guess I always thought that if *I* really liked something, my readers would have to like it. When I was revising my abortion argument, I took out several sections in the middle, because I had come to believe that it's what my readers need and want, not just what I need and want, that counts. This is one of the most important things I have learned about revision, and I don't think I would have believed it from the textbook if I hadn't seen you do it too."

Scenario

Gabriella, one of your colleagues, wanders into your office in mid-semester with a perplexed look on her face. "Last week I spent about half an hour with one of my 101 students," she says. "I suggested areas where he needed expansion, areas that needed more examples, and areas that probably needed to go. I commended him on other areas so that I wouldn't discourage him too much. He seemed confident about revising the paper at that point.

"Well, he just came in with his revised paper a few minutes ago, and I started to ask him about some of his revisions, because some of the paper just wasn't clear. I pointed this out to him; he said, 'Well, I thought I was *done*. I don't want to work on this paper any more. I have done enough.' So I tried to explain to him about practice and about how it sometimes takes more work than we expect to make writing good but that it can be rewarding. I know he thinks I'm crazy. He listened very politely and kept nodding his head, but I can tell he wasn't buying it. I don't know what to tell students like this. What would you have said to him?"

Teaching About Editing and Presentation

It's a sad fact that most writing instruction gets focused on etiquette: the editing and presentation of ideas. Sometimes teachers concentrate on these areas to the exclusion of finding, developing, and organizing ideas entirely. The result can be described by a line from *My Fair Lady*: "[They] don't care what you do, actually, as long as you pronounce it properly." Of course, editing and presentation are important; they have a lot to do with the reader's reaction to a piece of writing. And in a state or institution where there may be a competency or an exit exam or portfolio for students, teaching good editing skills is essential. But their place is last; they involve the applications of a set of closed competencies that nearly all students can master with time.

Learning to edit is no substitute for learning to write. Unfortunately, that's not the message that most of our students have received over the course of their schooling, and if they have judging tendencies, they're really going to focus on editing as the most important part of their writing processes. After all, they've been rewarded for good editing all along in school—and consistently punished for misspellings and mistakes. Some have become obsessed with error hunting; others, convinced that they'll never learn *all* the rules, give up entirely. You'll have to do a fair bit of missionary work to help students develop a strategic plan for editing and see its place in helping readers comprehend meaning. But you won't be able to overcome their lifelong habits in a few months. You may also want to enlist some help; often the Writing Center will have materials available to help students improve their editing skills, as well as providing coaching for students who need help. (However, you'll have to remind your students that most Writing Centers are *not* proofreading services!)

Teaching Grammar and Punctuation

The most frequently-raised editing concern for most writers and readers is grammar; in fact, some people mean "learning standard grammar" when they say "learning to write." The two are not the same. "Grammar" can have a number of meanings; Patrick Hartwell identified at least five in his article "Grammar, Grammars, and the Teaching of Grammar" (1985). In most writing courses, grammar means "school grammar," the rules for punctuation, spelling, and syntax. These can be presented in a number of ways.

The most common way of presenting grammar for many years was to have students memorize rules and do exercises in workbooks. Somehow, the theory went, students would internalize these drills and their grammar, as manifested in the papers they wrote, would improve. But years of studies (summarized neatly by Hartwell) have failed to prove that this is the case, and experience reinforces our awareness of this. We've all known the students who were letter-perfect on the drills in the text, yet couldn't prevent comma splices or dangling modifiers in their own writing. Students apparently learn better by having their writing diagnosed, keeping an error log, and learning to predict the situations where errors may occur so that they can check them carefully. Usually they do this best working one-on-one with the teacher or in small groups; there are few instances where the teacher has to lecture on grammar to the whole group. Thus, you'll probably be assigning relevant parts of your handbook to individual students, not to the entire class.

Teachers may want to help students by providing some inductive exercises. If a number of students seem to be having problems with placing the comma in compound sentences joined by a subordinator, the instructor might duplicate a number of these from a set of papers and ask students to determine where the commas go. Then the teacher can provide another list of samples, some punctuated incorrectly, and ask the class to decide which need correction. (I make these lists up by taking sentences from student papers; I'll sabotage some and correct others if needed, to get sufficient examples. If you keep a ditto master in your typewriter or grade papers near your computer keyboard, you can make these exercises up as you grade—another time-saver.) Finally, the students can examine their error logs and current drafts to see if they've applied the rule properly. Induction—figuring the rule out either verbally or visually, practicing it, and applying it—seems to offer students of all learning styles a better chance of learning to correct their most common errors. (Such exercises also work for common problems such as faulty agreement, verb complications, and homonym detection. They're very versatile.) Each student can develop his personal "editing checklist" (often confirmed in conference with you) to identify his particular grammar demons. Not only does such a technique help students in the writing class, but often they carry it over into other courses.

Grammatical and punctuation problems, too, can be a sign of growth; often the etiquette falls by the wayside as students try new sentence patterns and rhythms. Since most students don't make these mistakes deliberately (although some make them carelessly), teachers shouldn't penalize them too severely—at least not the first time they occur. Some teachers in the past would give a student a failing grade if a paper contained more than a certain number of misspelled words or grammatical errors. This is certainly counterproductive; it tells the student that presentation, not content or skill, is what the teacher values. In fact, Maxine Hairston's research (1985) suggests that readers can dismiss some mistakes quite easily; only a few are regarded as serious offenses. While you want your students to observe the etiquette of academic discourse, it needn't be your first priority. You may want to reinforce to your students the idea that errors are regarded differently by different classes of readers.

Teaching Spelling

Spelling is another problem that gets some people very agitated. In fact, spelling is a closed skill that students learn with differing degrees of mastery; much has to do with the kinds and amount of instruction they received as young children and much with the amount of reading they've done. Students can learn to conquer spelling demons in the same way they master grammatical problems: learning to recognize the words and spelling situations that give them problems and developing strategies to correct them. And since audiences react with particular virulence to spelling errors (especially if a proper name is involved), it's worth the time understanding what causes spelling problems so that you can help students correct them.

Many students, for instance, spell "by ear"; they try to record how the word sounds, especially in our visual age where they get less and less information from printed texts. Unfortunately, the many pronunciation changes in English language history have left sound as an unreliable guide to spelling. Students who have this problem may be able to diagnose the sound or sounds they habitually misspell: the unstressed vowel [ə] and the consonant cluster [dʒ] are prime culprits here. Sometimes they overgeneralize a rule, doubling a consonant or changing a vowel where such is not required. The teacher can help the student use error logs to find such situations and to work out revising strategies (such as reading aloud and checking the spelling of all words with suspect sounds) that will help the student overcome the problems. Other students may not have learned (or have learned imperfectly) some basic spelling rules, such as those for vowel clusters or doubling consonants. Often a short review of the rule by the teacher, and some practice on the student's own writing, are enough to help the student conquer the problem.

Many students today rely on spell-checker computer programs. These are fine as far as they go, but since the student can't always take the computer along, it's far better for the student to master the rules and use the spell checker as a time saver. Nor is the computer fool-proof; mine keeps trying to substitute "anteater" for "intuiter" in this text, for instance. Be sure to remind students that shortcut editing has its pitfalls.

Teaching in Practice

Almost everyone has a few words she misspells consistently. I show students a medieval history paper I wrote as a college sophomore, in which I misspelled the word "privilege" twenty-four times in four pages. (I spelled it "priviledge," the same way the TA had on the assignment sheet, but that *still* didn't make it right.) That's a word I still look up, along with "judgment" and "occurred." These have become part of my personal editing strategies; I know I have to check.

I ask students to bring in a stack of papers they've written, including ones from back in high school, or things they have written at work or for other activities they're engaged in. They give their stack to a partner, and each partner hunts through the stack for misspellings, putting them on a list and eventually trying to break them into categories (common ones are "wrong spelling for this sound," "forgot the rule," and "stupid errors.") I do a fair bit of coaching as this goes on, but let them name the categories. The "analysts" may find similar spelling problems (such as "arguement" for "argument" or "develope" for "develop" or "alot" for "a lot"). Then they explain their analysis to their partners. Once students get their analysis back, they make up a personal spelling checklist on a 5" x 8" index card, which they tape to the cover of their handbook, so that their customized spell checker is right at hand when they compose.

Students get two kinds of benefits from this assignment. First, it's easier to find problems in someone else's work than in their own, so they seem to pick up errors more easily, which ties into what I teach them about short-term memory and proofreading. Second, they learn to analyze the causes of particular errors, so that when I ask them to keep an error log as they revise their own efforts, they have a better sense of how it feels to perform such analysis, which is usually totally foreign to their experience. A student I taught three years ago came to see me about her résumé recently, and to my surprise she brought her spelling list along. Some of the categories had gotten a little longer (she's a psychology major and the terminology she deals with is often daunting), but she was still analyzing her categories. And the résumé she showed me—unlike any document she'd ever turned in in my class—was letter perfect.

Teaching Format and Presentation

Format, the physical layout of a student's paper, can provide unusual problems for students. Not all will have access to typewriters, for example; those who do may not know much about using the typewriter. And when computers are introduced into the picture, the possibilities for foul-ups become immeasurable.

It's important that students understand what format you require for each assignment. Many schools will have a format guide or policy sheet that spells out the constraints on paper presentation. If your department doesn't have such a guide, you can usually find one in a class text. Basically, students should be required to produce legible, double spaced texts (skipping lines if handwritten), in dark ink on one side of a page. For some, this means investing a few dollars in a new typewriter ribbon for their family's 1957 Smith Corona; you're well within your rights to ask them to do so. Others may be using school-provided computing equipment; depending on the quality of maintenance, the printout may be easily readable or palimpsest (some students may have to photocopy their printouts to get readable print). Remind students that if you can't read their work, you can't give them a grade; they, not you, will suffer for it.

Students often don't know what an essay or review or memorandum or research paper should look like. When you review samples, then, it pays to spend a few minutes noting particular features of the layout ("The footnote number is a little above the line"; "Notice that paragraphs in business letters don't get indented"). If students are using computers, you can suggest they ask the computer lab attendants how to set up "macros" or "style sheets" that will automatically format their papers, putting page numbers, footnotes, and the like in the proper places. (Some computer centers maintain such style aids on a master disk and will allow students to copy them directly onto their own disks.)

Teaching Proofreading

Proofreading is one of the simplest closed competencies in writing, but one that few students have learned. When they reread their papers (usually just before class) they see what they intended to put on the page, not what's actually there. As a result, static from surface errors can end up detracting from good work. These days, students are less familiar with the visual appearance of text than they used to be, and proofing is a skill they aren't very comfortable with. So students generally appreciate some tips for proofreading. Here are a few that work well.

Proofreading Tips

1. Give it time. Once you've finished typing or copying your final draft, set it aside for a few hours (overnight is ideal) and go do something else. Let your short-term memory empty out. When you come back to the paper, you'll be more likely to see what is there than what you *intended* to put there.
2. Proofread in several directions. First start from the last word and read the paper backward to check for misspellings and typos. Then read the paper from first word to last to check for omitted words and punctuation problems. Hold a blank sheet over the paper so that you can only see one line at a time. This will keep your eyes from jumping ahead. Go slowly; skimming won't work. Refer to your error log to remind yourself of the special problems you're working on.
3. Correct carefully, using one line to cross out mistakes and printing in changes carefully in black ink (or matching ink, if the paper is handwritten). If you use correction fluid, make sure you're using the right kind. The alcohol in typewriter correction fluid dissolves most pen and felt-tip ink. There's correction fluid made especially for ink; use it instead. In a crisis, typewriter correction fluid can be thinned with nail-polish remover; ink correction fluid can be thinned with water. Brush the fluid on lightly and let it dry; you can add a second coat if needed.
4. Consider using a backup proofreader if proofreading is a real problem for you. You're still responsible for finding and correcting your own problems,

but if using a computer program or another set of eyes helps you catch more problems, you'll benefit in the long run. (Make sure you add problems your outside proofreaders find to your error log so that you can begin to handle those problems yourself.)

5. The more tired you are, the more mistakes you'll make. In such cases, it's particularly imperative you proofread carefully; you may have accidentally left out sentences or even whole paragraphs, and a spelling checker or other artificial aid won't catch such omissions. You might want to keep your draft handy as you proofread the final copy to make sure this isn't the case.

When students have put their papers through the cycles of the writing process as many times as they feel are needed, and have edited and proofed them, it's time for the most painful (to them) part of the writing situation: submitting the paper for evaluation. This is a complex step, one which takes most of the teacher's time and causes most of the anxiety. It's worth a closer look, which the next chapter provides.

9

Responding to Writers:
Evaluating Writing

No single activity in teaching writing can cause as much heart wrenching and anxiety as responding to student writing. Both you and your students are naturally apprehensive about this task; for you, what your students write and how they perform are in some way a measure of how well you teach them. For your students, your comments and grades on their papers are an indicator of how you see them (they don't just think you're critiquing their *writing*), of how they are doing in college, of where they stand. The goals you're all working toward, the kind of community you are trying to create—all of these are called into question by the tension and stress of dealing with what your students write.

In the last few years, composition scholars have begun to reflect on the ways in which teachers respond to student writing (although rather less on the ways the students respond to teachers, an equally important subject). A growing consensus in the field suggests that there is a great difference between *responding* to student writing and *evaluating* it. *Responding* involves all the things we do while the student is in the process of writing—giving feedback, asking questions, pointing out weak spots, teaching new strategies and approaches. Most theorists stress that this is a dialogue with a writer, not with an essay or other piece of writing. You, as audience and experienced writer, respond to the student writer's efforts with praise, assessment, and suggestions for improvement. *Evaluating* means letting the student know how well she has succeeded with that piece of writing. It is a judgment of a *product*, not a person, though that's the hardest distinction to convey to students. In this chapter I am going to be using these terms carefully to help you delineate between the two activities and to understand the implications of each. But first, let's look at the big picture.

Two dominant models of assessment dominate composition programs today. One, probably the most common, requires teachers to give students grades throughout the term, as well as assigning a final grade at the end of term. The other, which is quite popular with publishing scholars but hasn't really taken over the field yet, requires that the student pass some program-wide "gatekeeper" at the end of the course, such as a state-mandated proficiency exam, a departmental exam, or a portfolio review. Some hybrids of these theories exist; for instance, my own program requires that students pass both semesters of composition with a "C" or better and pass a final exam as well. That final is made up and graded by the section instructor, who also has the option of permitting students to submit a portfolio of work or grading individual papers.

The importance of beginning this section by looking at the model for your program may not be obvious at first, but experience will tell you how important it is. If you are required to evaluate a number of pieces of student writing, you and your students are put through a number of anxious times, but at all times students know where they stand in the course and (presumably) what they must do to improve. If you are preparing students to pass an end-of-term gatekeeper, often you may not grade all their individual efforts, and can concentrate the class's focus on the reviewers who will read their portfolios or the requirements of a proficiency examination. This may seem to cause less tension during the term, but does concentrate it (for you and for your students) at the end of the term, when they are under pressure in all their courses. Moreover, an "all or nothing" gatekeeper at term's end may make students less aware of the need to revise throughout the semester; they're convinced they can "cram" at the end and still escape. Thus, whether your students are evaluated on an on-going basis or at the end of the course will probably strongly affect what you tell them about their writing, how you'll convince them to improve, and how much antacid you and they will need to finish the term.

Responding to Student Writing

As I discussed above in Chapter 3, social constructionists have alerted us to the theoretical differences between the kinds of non-directive response we make as a reader and the kinds of directive response we make as teachers at the point of assessment. Both of these, too, are different from the coercive responses some teachers make as they try to force students to approximate some version of an "Ideal Text." (Again, I refer you to Bob Schwegler's article in the anthology for further discussion of this difference.) Responding takes place at many more points in the writing process than does evaluation: you respond when you go over the assignment with students as you give it; they respond to each other in peer sessions and get your response in conferences or through written comments on drafts; there may be conversations about the assignment in hallways or on e-mail. All of these are sites where you as teacher can help the student realize the potential of her writing.

When you are asked to respond to a paper, you have to be directive to some extent, because that assessment is based on what the writer has and hasn't done in this context. In your role as teacher, you must convey those strengths and weaknesses to the student in a way that helps her improve as a writer. The "direction" you give can vary widely, depending on the issues you feel are most important, the goals of your course, and the needs of your students. Recent articles, most notably those of Richard Straub (1996a, 1996b) critique the responding styles of some of composition's most respected figures (one of these articles is included in the anthology at the end of this text). Many of these analyses, however, don't make a clear distinction between responding to a draft in progress and evaluating a finished text, and that's a key difference to understand. *Responding* is usually characterized as reacting to a student's text as a reader, though the terms used to describe the teacher's role as responder vary: coach, collaborator, common reader, guide, nurturer, and so on. Since response is aimed at helping student writers develop their texts as fully as possible, this reaction has to help the student see where that development is needed. At the same time, the teacher must avoid trying to impose her or his own notion of what the text *should* be; this is called "taking over" the student's text by the theorists, and it's a real problem for some teachers. Rebecca Rule sums up the balancing act teachers must play in response quite neatly:

> I must be careful not to take over—because the minute I do, the success (if there is one) becomes mine, not his—and the learning is diminished. I can contribute, I can guide; I can brainstorm with him; I can suggest exercises; I can offer models; I can tell him where the comma goes; I can support him wholeheartedly. But I must not take over. (50)

Different students, especially those with different learning styles, need different kinds of response as well. Verbalists and serialists, and especially intuiters, may need a more directive kind of response to open the doors to revision; their learning styles sometimes won't *let* them see where revision is needed on their own. On the other hand, sensers and feelers particularly blossom with deliberately non-directive response, which gives them considerable freedom to choose the direction of their revisions. Students who are confident of themselves and their eventual success in college need much less direction than do at-risk students who may be struggling to understand and manage the demands academia makes of them. How to reconcile these needs with the theorists who insist, "Don't be directive! Don't take over!"?

Our colleagues in the school of business have the answer; it's called Situational Leadership Theory (SLT). This theory argues that a leader (you, the teacher) best inspires your dependents (the students) to reach leadership status (and therefore parity with you) by tailoring the nature of your leadership to the person and the situation. The first time a dependent is asked to do something, the leader provides a high level of instruction and guidance; as the dependent becomes more proficient, the leader steps back and allows her more freedom of choice and action. While some people would argue about calling the teacher-student relationship a leader-dependency relationship (and I grant their case), the analogy has value. At the beginning of a semester, when students are still learning to trust themselves, their peers, and you, you may need to provide more guidance. As the semester progresses and you all learn to trust each other, and to form a community, you can give up more of your control to the students, and settle into a more equitable relationship.

Some theorists say that the marks you put on a student's text, whether they be marginal comments or a comprehensive end note, are a means by which you impose your power on the student, and I can see how this is true. But I prefer to approach responses, especially written ones, as places where some of the most important learning can take place in your classroom, where you can let a student know just how far he or she has come toward reaching the goals of the course, rather than as opportunities to oppress some helpless student text-owner. And a great deal of what eventually happens in *evaluating*—a part that's very hard to quantify or describe—comes from the way *you* approach grading and convey that attitude to your students, long before you ever start grading papers.

If we are to teach in this manner, we have to suspend, a little, our natural tendencies to prejudge, to circle in red every error we can find. The most useful weapon we have in doing this is the question, since it keeps us from imposing ukases that the student is forced to accept. Students perceive a big difference between a comment that says "You need transitions here and here" and one that says, "It's hard to follow your train of thought on page two. Can you find some more obvious ways to show us how these ideas connect?" The first tells a student *what* to do; it imposes the teacher's will on the writer. The second identifies a problem, but leaves the *how* of solving it up to the writer.

Another useful response to students is the kind we make in our own books and journals, the comment reacting to *what* has been said. It can be an expression of praise or sympathy, a yoking of ideas, sometimes even an expression of disagreement, but it shows the students that their texts have engaged us, have caught *our* eyes. To them, such comments are a measure of their success, and eagerly anticipated. I've had students give me drafts and tell me, "I know there are three places in here where you're going to write 'Yes!' on the margins," and most of the time they're right. The message they're giving me is that they as writers are eager to know what I think as reader, rather than Lady With The Grade Book, and that's the attitude that can be fostered by thoughtful response.

Rather than turning our responses into error-hunting, that old bugaboo, we can also look for patterns in the the student's writing, and try to help her or him learn from what we recognize. This is particularly true of local issues. Is the student truly a "lousy speller," as he claims, or does he consistently misspell the sound [dʒ]? Can the student truly not support an assertion, or does she think that quoting some authority by itself constitutes support? Often you can begin to solve these problems in conference; ask the student about her hypothesis, then help her see how academic conventions require her to alter or refine it. Sometimes it's a matter of helping students appreciate fine distinctions in language: main clauses introduced by subordinate conjunctions are fragments; those introduced by "movable" (conjunctive) adverbs are not. One of the best things we can do in responding is help students learn to diagnose their own trouble spots and learn to solve them. An emphasis on what readers expect from writers will be helpful in such discussions.

Many times, in fact, errors and weaknesses signal growth, and that's also an important point to make in our responses. Often student papers submitted after sentence-combining practice are plagued with comma splices, as students struggle to master new syntactic patterns, and they get easily discouraged. The students are courageously trying new techniques; penalizing them for failing on the first try to master the punctuation etiquette required will defeat your attempts to help them grow. Sometimes, of course, there will be true errors: a word transposed or omitted in copying, the fingers one key off on the keyboard, an embarrassing or amusing typo (such as "Shakespeare's play of love and punishment, *Romeo and Joliet*"). These represent failures of editing skills, language performance rather than language competence, and can be treated as such.

Teaching in Practice

Here's an example of a student's draft with sample teacher responses in the margin. It's the first piece of writing in the semester, in which the students were asked to pick one incident out of the first two weeks of their university careers that crystallized the impact their new lives were having on them. Since it's the first time the teacher has responded to the student, you'll see some of the caution both are using.

How To Grow Up In A Week	Okay, so I'm anticipating a "how-to" strategy in your paper.
In choosing a topic to write on, I tried to locate an event that had the greatest impact on my	This sounds like you're warming up, talking to yourself. Where is the place where you imagine your readers coming in?
life and values. Such an event happened my first week after moving here to Aberdeen. Really, I suppose one could say that week as a whole was vastly important.	I'm a little confused here— are you going to focus on one event or the whole week?

The move from high school to college was certainly a maturing one. As an incoming freshman here at Northern, the first thing I noticed here was the enormous number of students. I came from a senior class of 26! I had not been here fifteen minutes and I felt like a number already.

This sounds like you're talking to me now—what would be the impact if you started from here and then developed the paper?

The next enlightening experience came at registration. I found out quickly that if you want anything done, you do it yourself. Such was the case at registration. I was not used to totally arranging my schedule. I entered registration not knowing where to go or what to do. After eight hours in the gym, I completed my task.

This is a great detail—it makes your generalization really come alive.

Eight hours! That may be a record. Can you tell me more of what went on, so that I see what you had to do for yourself? Would using the journalist's questions from the Handbook help you recall some of these?

It was at this point that I realized the extent of the new responsibilities this move placed upon me. I became, more or less, my own boss. There was no one to tell me what to do or when to do it. Why, I even had to wash my own clothes!

This "stepping back" for perspective is a nice change of pace. But the time sequence is a little fuzzy—were you washing clothes during registration?

I guess the point I came to understand was that one can mature and come to a new understanding with oneself if one is placed in the right situation. It has been a reassuring experience, and one that I will not soon forget. As for the remainder of college—who knows, I may even graduate some day.

It's okay to use "I" and "me"—you don't have to use "one" unless that's the tone you really want.

Stone, it's nice to have a writer in class who has a sense of humor, and that shows through in your paper, especially in the second paragraph and right at the end. Getting your readers to feel what you felt is a considerable achievement, and I hope we can build on that strength this semester. As you'll see from my marginal notes, what I want from you as a reader is to know more about what you were thinking, feeling, seeing, experiencing. Can you make the experience more concrete for me, create more word pictures to help me see things through your eyes? The detailing lists we started talking about last class might be a good place to start. Don't worry about squeezing everything into five paragraphs; you can use as many as you want.

One of the things you might want to think about is whether you want to talk about the whole week and all these incidents, or just pick one and see if you can make it representative of the whole week. Both approaches offer lots of possibilities, but you'll need a different strategy for each. Pick the one you think you can do the most with, and go with it; I'm looking forward to seeing your results.   CRC

As you'll notice, the teacher has identified focus and lack of details as the chief problems in this draft, but she never uses that kind of teacher language; instead, she reacts as a reader, and lets the student see the kind of questions this draft raises for her. Praise is provided for several very good moves the student has made, and the teacher has deftly addressed two high-school taboos, the use of "I" and the five-paragraph theme, without making them major issues. The response gives the student a firm direction for revision, but leaves him with considerable freedom of choice.

Evaluating Student Writing

At some time, of course, all the work that you and students put in has to be judged—and in the final analysis, you'll be the one who has to make the judgments and assign the grade. This is one of the hardest parts of your job as a writing teacher, but it's also one of the most essential. You do neither the student, yourself, nor your colleagues any good by certifying a student as able to write acceptably on the college level when he or she isn't. Grading firmly and fairly will occasionally mean flunking a student; it isn't easy or pleasant, but it is necessary, and both you and the student will survive. (I speak from experience: I flunked organic chemistry as a sophomore and still managed to graduate with honors from an Ivy League school.)

And you needn't go it alone; students can individually and collaboratively do a good deal of the preliminary work for you and set standards that enable you and students to agree upon grades. This can be done serially, with grades assigned to each individual assignment, or collectively, by means of a writing portfolio. Let's look at what is involved in each method.

Grading Each Individual Paper

When you assign a grade to each individual paper in a course, you are reinforcing for your students the importance of individual products in assessing their writing ability. A "paper," to use the generic term, is a snapshot of how some writer is performing at a particular moment in time. Such evaluation has advantages and disadvantages. It lets you and students know where they stand in the course, and alerts them to the kinds of improvement they will need to complete the course successfully. It breaks down the skills students are asked to demonstrate into smaller units that may be easier for them to manage. It convinces your institution's administration, and maybe even your state legislature, that you have clear and definable standards for your students. At the same time, there are disadvantages. First and foremost, they're subjective. Unlike mathematics or the sciences, there's no "right" answer to any writing problem, and thus no grade that is independent of the teacher who gives it. As Pat Belanoff so cogently puts it,

> I inevitably judge the paper in front of me in terms of all other papers I've read. I make no apologies for that. That's the only way any of us ever judge anything. ... I cannot know beauty, perfection, or loveliness

apart from specific examples. It is hardly to be expected that decisions on the quality of writing could be made any differently. Thus the model of an A I have in my head is a product of all the papers I have read as well as of my own individual way of reading. (1993: 183)

Subjectivity is not the only concern that scoring a paper raises. Individual grades may not mask overall growth (or decline) in skills; they put the emphasis on written products rather than writing processes, and they can mislead students into thinking the focus of the course is on grades, not on improving. Students may also be less likely to revise a graded paper. Some instructors will go so far as to argue that grades in general are detrimental and should be totally abolished; I have some sympathy for that position, but I also realize that in the late twentieth century, such proposals aren't likely to fly. Grading is a tough job; you are the one picked to do it.

Complicating the grading process is your knowledge that most students will give you an honest effort. They will use the strategies they know to complete an assignment well and—let's be frank—to win your approval in the form of a high grade. But effort notwithstanding, students will have differing degrees of success with an assignment. And your reactions will have to differ accordingly.

Here is the key area where *evaluating* differs from *responding*. Where responses try to take the power differential out of the equation, evaluations are by design judgmental. You, the teacher, as an experienced writer, reader, consumer of texts, and the person paid by your institution to measure the progress of this class, *are* exercising power—the power of the grade book. Moreover, in grading you are by design being directive, telling students clearly which standards they have met and which they have not. (If you don't explain the criteria, your students will be in your office constantly with the refrain of "But I don't understand why I got a C! I worked so hard!" or whatever.) Whereas responders try not to take over the writing situation, instead leaving writers free to make choices, evaluators must tell them what the results of those choices are. Many novice teachers, confused by all the current critiques of evaluation, find assessment incredibly difficult because they (and, to be frank, the authors of some of those critiques) don't make a distinction between a teacher's response and a teacher's evaluation.

Teachers trained as readers of literature may use intentionality as a touchstone for evaluation: we assume that features of a text are there on purpose and proceed to critique the text on that assumption. The late Mina Shaughnessy in her book *Errors and Expectations* did all of us a great service by reminding us that the intentionality of student texts is quite different than that of literary works. In a literary work the writer is in control; he or she adheres to or violates conventions based on deliberate decisions. Joyce and Faulkner and Walker violate many standards of "good English" just as Dickens and Hemingway and Woolf observe them; in each case we assume that the writer did so for a reason. But when students violate the etiquette of syntax or spelling or punctuation, Shaughnessy reminds us, we assume that they did so with the same kind of artistic control experienced writers wield. And this is usually not the case. Students rarely if ever make deliberate errors; they are trying to succeed. Often, however, they attempt syntactic structures or make linguistic choices over which they have imperfect control. They approximate control of discourse structures, narrow competencies, that they have not yet mastered fully. And so we must regard their errors and weaknesses not as intentions to fail; rather we must determine at what they were trying to succeed. We must not just identify and criticize their errors; we must analyze them and try to help students fulfill their true intentions.

David Bartholomae, applying some of Shaughnessy's observations to basic writers, argues that such error analysis can be a valuable diagnostic technique for instructors. "By investigating and interpreting the patterns of error in [students'] writing, we can help them begin to see those errors as evidence of hypotheses or strategies they have formed and, as a consequence, put them in a position to change, experiment, imagine other strategies. Studying their own writing puts students in a position to see themselves as language users, rather than as victims of a language that uses them" (1980, p. 258).

Bartholomae's summation is, of course, a good description of what teachers might do when they *respond* to student writing. However, it's also a good example of why some teachers get so confused about the difference between responding and evaluating. One of the things an evaluator does *is* to indicate where a writer falls short of standards, including those for editing their writing. Unfortunately, many overworked and overwhelmed teachers see error identification as the sole task in evaluation, which limits the benefits of evaluation to the student. In a mammoth survey (looking at over 3,000 marked papers), Robert J. Connors and Andrea Lunsford have discovered that teachers mark almost 47% of errors occurring in student writing—though what errors they mark when varies greatly (1988). In tabular form, here's part of what they found:

Error or error pattern	% of total errors	Rank by # of errors marked
No comma after intro. element	11.5%	2
Vague pronoun reference	9.8%	4
No comma in compound sent.	8.6%	7
Wrong word	7.8%	1
No comma in non-restrictive element	6.5%	10
Wrong/missing inflections	5.9%	5
Wrong or missing prepositions	5.5%	8
Comma splice	5.5%	6
Possessive apostrophe error	5.1%	3
Tense shift	5.1%	12
Unnecessary shift in person	4.7%	14
Fragment	4.2%	9

(While these instructor targets are disheartening, Connors and Lunsford do point out that the number of errors per hundred words (2.26) has not changed markedly since before 1917—so complaints that student writing is getting worse are really unfounded.)

In a follow-up to this study, Connors and Lunsford looked at teachers' end comments in another 3,000 papers. Their research determined that teachers seem "genuinely involved in trying to help their students with rhetorical issues in their writing," but that "many teachers seem still to be facing classroom situations, loads, and levels of training that keep them from communicating their rhetorical evaluations effectively. . . . The emphasis still seems to be on finding and pointing out problems and deficits in the individual paper, not on envisioning patterns in student writing habits or prompts that could go beyond such analysis" (1991). The message we can draw from this research is clear: If you're going to evaluate a student's writing fairly, you need to do more than just point out the errors.

Identifying Strengths

Any writing effort will have strengths, even if they are few and sometimes hard to find. It's essential to identify these; not only do they show what interim goals have been attained, but also help the students see which competencies they can apply to different situations and build their confidence as writers. Even if you praise a very basic feature ("Gerri, your tone here really sounds like *People!*") the positive encouragement may encourage the student: you liked *something* about her work. And, of course, the strengths often outweigh the weaknesses; then the problem is deciding what to praise. Those are the papers we're glad to receive; we don't begrudge the time spent commenting on them.

But what about the weaknesses? These, of course, are what most of us first see when we read a student paper. Nothing more encourages us to play deconstructive critic than a paper with ambiguities, gaps, and faultily-observed conventions. And part of our job is to alert our students to these problems so that their writing can improve; that's why our institutions hire us as instructors. But the method of identifying such weaknesses need not be *destructive*, even if our technique is essentially deconstructive. Once you've identified a particular text's strengths and weaknesses, you must convey this information to the student writer. This can be a touchy process; students may sometimes confuse criticism of their texts with personal criticism. (This is the grounds for most student grade protests; they claim you don't like them or have a "personality conflict" with them.) Handling these complaints requires patience and careful selection of language; you must point out that grading requires you judge the *product* being turned in on its own merits—not the writer, or the effort, or anything else. Again, if you have developed clear grading standards to which you can point, you'll be able to handle these largely personal attacks with some objectivity.

It's important to maintain an objective, supportive tone in your comments; the occasional snide remark or mild joke is likely to come back to haunt you in unexpected ways (as in a grade protest), as well as harm the rapport you've tried to build with the student. If you're tired, *stop* writing comments rather than let your fatigue and frustration come out in nasty comments like "I'm really disappointed with this paper; I know you can do better." Leave spanking to the parents. Instead, start by identifying what the student did well and can carry forward to subsequent papers. This encourages students to look back at the text, to reexamine it in terms of their own development.

Marginal comments

A recent e-mail message from one of my friends included this wonderful passage: "The margins are the best part of the text. That's where interactions occur as I react to the writer, then later react to what I wrote previously. Margins are where the action is! The only problem with them is that they are often too small. Perhaps we ought to work toward expanding and extending the margins." That's how I feel about marginal remarks, too, and I try to convey this to my students. Just as I ask them to write in the margins of their texts, so I write in the margins of their papers the same way, to summarize my understanding of what they are doing and to indicate points of perplexities and conflict. I always try (though I don't always succeed) to make as many comments in the margin as I do at the end, so that students can see how engaged I have been with their text.

Marginal comments generally identify the weaknesses and errors in student papers. You can write them in many ways; unfortunately, many intimidate students. If you circle or mark every mistake, the paper can sink in a sea of red (or green or whatever) ink; this tells the student "You'll never learn to write 'good English.'" Or you can use a number of cryptic symbols referring to sections of a handbook or to obscure proofreading rituals; this tells students "Only English teachers can learn all these rules." Or you can deliberately undermark, perhaps by putting checks in the margins of lines that contain errors, as Richard H. Haswell suggests (1983). This puts the responsibility of finding and correcting errors on the student, and the teacher can judge the success of the student's efforts by reviewing the paper in conference or in the portfolio. Probably the best method of identifying weaknesses is to mark only major concerns in detail and use minimal marking for questions of punctuation, grammar, spelling, and other mechanical etiquette. As Nancy Sommers reminds us (1982), marginal comments focus a student's attention on this particular draft, often causing the student to ignore the possibilities of revision and moving on in new drafts.

However, as in response, carefully-phrased marginal comments can also inspire students to revise. Often in such a system, the marginal comments that identify weaknesses are questions or statements that lead students to examine the text more carefully ("Look back at your detailing list and see if you can produce a more precise description of the hotel than 'nice' and 'spacious'?" "Does your reader know what a 'buydown mortgage' is?" "This is a big jump—what are the interim steps that led you to conclude this?") Or they can describe your reaction as a reader ("I can't see the connection between these two ideas. Did you leave a step out from your plan?") Occasionally you may want to refer the student to a particular reference source ("Your footnotes should be in MLA form; see sec. 46b in the handbook as you revise them"). Comments like these refer to the kinds of prewriting and drafting the student may already have done, or neglected to do, without being judgmental. For instance, the student who wrote the description of the hotel probably didn't make a detailing list originally; this marginal comment subtly prompts her to make one before she revises.

Checks in the margin can direct student attention to procedural or mechanical weaknesses. Such individual problems should be summed up as part of your end comment: "Often you provide a quote to support your assertions, but you rarely analyze the quotes to show how they fit into your argument. Where you do this, as on p. 3, it really strengthens your argument. Where you leave it out your argument is less persuasive—you make your readers guess the connections you see;" or "A lot of your checkmarks have to do with where commas go in complex sentences. Review section 31a when you're revising so that you can clear up these problems." Remarks like these remind students that readers expect writers to observe certain conventions of discourse, without making the entire focus of revision "getting the commas right."

End comments

Your end comments need to give focused rhetorical response and guidance to your students. This doesn't mean long-winded justifications, just that you describe clearly what has and hasn't been achieved. If you can also connect those descriptions to future writing, so much the better:

> Your explanation of the accident doesn't make clear which was your version and which was his—if you revise this for the portfolio, think about how you can make this clearer.

> Your careful examination of King's religious language gives your paper a great deal of credibility. In your subsequent papers you can use this sensitivity to language to support your own assertions.

Every writer likes to know she's succeeded; tell your students what competencies they show, and give them goals to strive for. Your end comment needs a context just like the student papers do; don't neglect it!

Of course, you have to pick the issues you address in your end comment carefully. Two, or at most three, weaknesses are enough for a student to focus on for the next paper. Try to address the largest issues first; if the writer can't address an audience or formulate a thesis, spelling and colon placement are trivial problems. And often, as in the cases discussed above, the weaknesses are signs of growth. Even if the student has not yet learned to analyze evidence, he's learned to provide it; even if the student continues to make comma splices, she's learning to write more complex sentences. Your comments can be phrased to reflect these tentative steps of growth:

> I'm glad you tried some of the sentence-combining we practiced. Now that you've learned the patterns, take a close look at where the punctuation goes so that you can use those elaborate sentences to their best effect.

> You've picked really sharp quotations to back up your points. Next time follow up each of those quotes with a sentence or two of comment to help your audience see how they fit into your argument.

Finally, your response needs to help the writer set and reach new goals. These will usually involve conquering competencies that were mastered incompletely in the current text or moving on to apply those competencies in new contexts. Here is where the critical teaching in comments takes place: you want the student to move to a new level of achievement. The goals should be clearly expressed.

> Now that you've mastered simple and compound sentences, it's time to move to complex ones;

> It's clear you can persuade an audience that basically agrees with you. Next time why don't you aim to persuade a mildly hostile audience?

And they should suggest clear strategies for achieving those goals:

> Try detail lists or using the journalist's questions to generate more specifics about your subject. Then you can pick and choose which ones you want to use;

> Make a list of all the arguments objecting to your position you can think of, and try to find reasonable answers to those objections.

You may even need to offer a small reward to encourage timorous students to take risks (*"Try to write some different kinds of sentence patterns; I won't 'mark off' if you don't quite master the punctuation next time."*) Your response can also encourage students to reconsider their writing processes (*"The drafts of this paper show you just changed a few words each time; you didn't revise much. Editing works best if it follows real revision. Next time try moving paragraphs around, change sentences, scratch out! Don't settle for the first thing you think of!"*)

In sum, your end comment should encourage the student not only to go back into this paper, but to move forward to the next. If you keep the tripartite structure—praise strengths, identify weaknesses, set goals—in mind, you'll find it relatively easy to write a coherent, goal-oriented end comment. Encourage students to discuss those comments with you before they submit their next paper; often a word or two of reinforcement or clarification can lead to quantum leaps in writing performance. No two teachers will ever make the same comments on a paper, and often we'll disagree about grades. These are context-dependent; they are controlled by you, your students, conditions at the schools where you teach, and a host of other outside factors. But your own good judgment can be a solid guide; learn to trust it.

Teaching in Practice

This is a paper written by a student midway through her first semester of composition. The assignment was to choose an editorial or a letter to the editor from a local newspaper, and to write a reaction that opposed it, explaining the reasoning for that stance. Jennifer chose a satiric letter written in response to a newspaper article that reported an increasing incidence of cheating episodes on college campuses. She submitted it for peer review and held an oral conference with her instructor on an interim draft. This is her final paper; the teacher's marginal comments are in italics to the right, and his endnote follows the paper. Note that he's trying to balance his judgments with more responses, since she has the option of revising this paper later in the semester. The checks in the margin indicate an editing error she needs to correct.

Response to an Editorial

Cheating on an examination is the focus of this letter. Mr. Harwood, the author, meditates on the possible justifications for Generation Xers to cheat and help others. He explores the idea that cheating is in fact a sign of a forward-looking mind, a sense of aiding a friend, a manifestation of a college professor's unrealistic expectations, and just another excusable social ill.

I believe that Mr. Harwood does *not* express an ethically or morally acceptable assessment of cheating. Call me a dweeb, but I believe cheating is *wrong*. For me, it cannot be excused or explained as a viable option for students. From my experience, I cannot accept cheating as beneficial for anyone.

While enrolled in an advanced mathematics course, two of my fellow students were caught and punished for cheating on a final examination. I watched closely after they were discovered and observed the teacher's response. He gave the students both Fs on the exam, but their choice to cheat also had other long-term consequences. Neither student was ever really trusted by the

Would this title "hook" you to read this in the paper?

Since we don't have the letter in front of us, give at least the title and the date it appeared.

I like the parallelism here—that's a big improvement.

Think about the word dweeb—how will 'Herald' readers react to it? You don't really explain to them why you think cheating is wrong, either.

I like how you use your experience here, but it's long-winded. You're substituting narration (the story) for explanation of how this supports your argument that cheating hurts everybody.

teacher, or by other teachers, again. Their cheating also haunted them when they applied for the next accelerated math course; admission was based on the recommendation of the teacher in the previous course. These two students were denied admission to the next level math course because they cheated, which in the case of one of the two led to his losing a competition for a full scholarship to Cornell University.

No matter what some lax people say, cheating is not an acceptable action because it ruins the trust and honesty in the relationship between students and teachers, between students and the community, and between students and themselves. *Trust* is a fundemental idea necessary to acheive knowledge and maturity, but it cannot prosper when a student cheats. Cheaters destroy the trust we have in our schools, in our neighbors, in all the members of our communities. Mr. Harwood, cheating cannot be tolerated.

OK, now here we have some analysis to work with.

✓

✓ *Why is trust so important?
Is this what he was saying? I thought you said he was being satirical.*

Jennifer, this paper has come a long way since the peer review. You did a good job of incorporating Nancy's suggestion about substituting a better example that really showed the readers the consequences of cheating—losing a scholarship to Cornell is a serious punishment. All of the energy of the paper goes into that story, so the rest—where you are trying to explain why cheating is wrong and why trust is so important—loses out by comparison. You assume your readers know exactly what you are thinking and will agree with you, so you don't explain yourself. As a result, your readers don't know what you're thinking, etc. When we had our conference, you talked about doing a grid to map out where the paper might go, but I don't see one with the drafts you turned in. I think that either gridding or outlining might help; it may help you see the balance between generalities and particulars more clearly. I also think there's a lot more you can say about this subject; you might want to consider it for your portfolio. This version is still an average paper, so your grade is the average grade: C.

Scenario

This paper was written by Brian late in the first semester of his college writing course. His assignment was to write a causal analysis of some situation that he felt was not well understood by people not of his generation. Brian submitted the paper for peer review, where it was praised overwhelmingly for its "power and honesty," but chose not to have a conference with the instructor. Here is his final paper, submitted for a grade. How would you evaluate this paper? What strengths and weaknesses would you target? What grade would you assign the paper above, given the conditions under which it was submitted?

Who's to Blame for Generation X?

The world around us is not of our creation. The environment into which we are born is not under our control. We can in no way affect the situation we are handed upon our arrival into society. Who can, better yet who did? Obviously, it is those who came before us. Each generation defines the parameters in which the next generation will operate. As the baby boom generation did for us, and as we will do for our own progeny. For twelve generations, our country has left a legacy of prosperity, education, and increased social harmony to it's children. This unique and wonderful tradition ended with the thirteenth generation of Americans, we are that generation. They have handed Generation X, our generation, a discarded, spent up shell of the american dream. They have left us with drastically reduced economic opportunity, a globally impotent educational system, and decrepit ideas of social interaction. Knowing this, they still have the gall to balk at the outcome. They would distance themselves from us and act as if they had nothing to do with our present state.

Let's now examine our present state from an economic standpoint. Since 1969 social security benefits have risen eighty percent, while AFDC benefits to poverty stricken children have dropped ten percent (Howe and Strauss 34).° The percent of elderly living in poverty has gone from twenty-five percent in 1980 to twelve percent in 1990, while the percent of under-eighteen persons living in poverty has gone from fifteen percent in 1970 to twenty-one percent in 1990 (Howe and Strauss 35). The term "age based entitlement" has come to be associated only with older Americans and never with children.

It is not the youngest Americans who have reaped the benefits of Social Security COLAs, runaway Medicare spending, S&L bailouts, senior saver discounts, unlimited mortgage deductions, CEO golden

---

Though the paper has internal documentation, Brian turned in no Works Cited page.

parachutes, and tax cuts for $100,000-plus households. It is not the oldest Americans who must pay the price for mounting budget deficits, unfunded benefit liabilities, dwindling savings rates, lackluster R&D, crumbling highways, and deepening foreign penetration. (Howe & Strauss 37)

Many of the aforementioned travesties were the policies of two presidents, Ronald Reagan and George Bush. Whose main support came from Americans thirty years old and up.

These are the people who have prospered at our expense. Our elders have overspent, overinvested, and overdrawn our economy. They have created a market of zero real wage growth and staggering unemployment figures. A market where young people can barely find full time work, and those that do still don't make enough to support themselves. Forget ever obtaining a pension and having a secure retirement. These are things only the privileged people over thirty will ever possess. We are the first generation that will not have a higher quality of life than our parents. I have personally seen interest rates on CDS, not savings accounts, CDS, go as low as one and three quarter percent. How is a young person to save for college, a house, a car, retirement, anything? We live in a nation committing fiscal child abuse.

Educationally our generation has not gotten the short end of the stick, they won't even tell us where they're keeping the stick hidden. We are the first generation to actually have funding cut from education. Our teachers are the lowest paid in real wages and weak on discipline, and we have been the guinea pigs for more experimental curricula then any other generation. Our college tuition costs are higher, in some cases ten and fifteen times higher, than ever before. Our elders have refused to modify education standards to keep up with the rest of the world, leaving us unable to compete for jobs in a global market. Almost twenty-five percent of our generation drops out of high school (Howe & Strauss 36). Why shouldn't they? A high school education gets them nowhere and they can't afford college. This is exceptionally frustrating to us when we see older Americans with the same or less education than we succeeding. Baby Boomers with a four-year degree are in the same position that we would have to have a master's or doctoral degree to obtain.

Not only are our educational opportunities seriously lacking, but we have been psychologically programmed not to succeed. Since the 1983 publishing of *A Nation At Risk* by the US Department of Education we have been told countless times that we are dumb. We are stupid, unskilled, unmotivated, lazy, and incapable of academic achievement. Any good parent knows you don't tell a child that he or she can't accomplish something, for it only gives them ample excuse not to accomplish it. This simple little thing that every good parent knows seems to have been forgotten by an entire nation. We are told of our ignorance and then cursed when we live up, or down, to their prophecies. We are told that we are ruining their country. It is high time they realized it is our country too, we want to ensure that it thrives as much as they do. We merely lack the opportunities that they did not bother to afford to us.

What positive social patterns from our formative years can we draw on as examples? Every day twenty-five hundred of us see our parents get divorced, thirteen of us commit suicide, six hundred and thirty of us are robbed, eighty of us are raped, and one hundred thousand of us feel as if we wouldn't be safe unless we carried a gun to school (Howe & Strauss 33). "From 1960 to 1986, the average parental time available to children dropped by ten to twelve hours per week, a decline of roughly forty percent" (Howe & Strauss 56). In

1988, only fifty point nine percent of children lived with their birth mother and father (Howe & Strauss 61). How is a generation supposed to function while bearing the burden of these kinds of statistics. The social aptitudes we lack stem directly from how we were raised. They tell us to be less violent, yet they won't create safe communities and schools. And then there's television. They tell us to learn to get along, and only one of two of their marriages succeed. They want us to learn to communicate, but leave us with the Muppets in the afternoon. It is a classic case of "Do as I say and not as I do." Children learn by example and we were given none to study.

As much as we would love to sit around having our little pity parties and grasping for sympathy, that is something we simply cannot afford to do. We must not become the self-absorbed, self-righteous, bloated, megalomaniacs that the Baby Boom, Silent, and G.I. Generations did. If that is what we become let us at least have the decency not to bother procreating. We must avoid this fate at all cost. We must turn things around in spite of what was handed us. We must insure that our children will never deal with the problems we faced. We have to reprogram our psyches. We have to clear out all the junk our elders have stuffed in there and replace it with a positive motivating force that will allow us to think beyond today. We do not have the luxury of carrying on a past dream for we have to create our own. This may be a blessing in disguise because in our dreams we are not confined to outdated concepts of morality, politics, economics, theology, and divisionism. We can move forward and create new institutions of learning, government, religion, and commerce. Our potential to make history is limitless if we can only come together. We have to stop killing each other, robbing and raping each other, educate ourselves (their not going to do it for us) and do away with the "Lookout for Number 1" attitude.

Beyond the Graded Paper

Beyond making comments on individual student papers, you have several other productive ways of keeping the student informed about her progress and helping her improve her writing throughout the semester. These are just a few of the techniques many composition instructors find helpful for their students.

Error Logs

Some instructors ask students to keep a log of all the errors on formally submitted papers, sorting them out into categories such as spelling, punctuation, syntax, format, and content problems. The student records each identified problem in the appropriate category, along with a correction. Then periodically (most easily in conferences) the instructor reviews the log with the student, handbook in hand, and helps him see the patterns his errors take. For instance, there may be confusion about the spelling of words containing the sound [dʒ]; are they spelled -*dge* or -*ge*? Is there a problem with doubling consonants when adding suffixes? As the student perceives the pattern of errors, the instructor can help her develop a private editing checklist that focuses her attention on the situations that lead to those errors. A frequent comma-splicer, for instance, might learn to examine commas before clauses beginning with "however" if this has been the occasion for error in the past. By keeping error logs, students learn to diagnose and remedy their most common writing problems, techniques that will be very useful when they leave the writing class and have no teacher to point out the weak spots. In special circumstances, you may wish to team up with the Writing Center or other campus support services (see Chapter 6) to help students improve.

Heuristics

Students can use systematic questioning strategies called *heuristics* to evaluate their own writing and alter their writing processes. These may be impressionistic lists of goals to achieve, such as the class standards for grading described in the previous chapter, or they may be more rigidly structured lists such as the late Robert Bain's "Framework for Judging" (1974). This list, which Bain later modified in courses at the University of North Carolina at Chapel Hill to incorporate nonsexist language and external concerns, begins with global writing concerns of purpose, structure, and audience and moves to smaller concerns such as support, language, choice, and mechanics, ending finally at concerns outside the actual writing process. It is framed in terms of a reader's response to a piece of writing, which forces writers to examine the impact each of their rhetorical choices has on a community as well. Moreover, because it addresses so many issues in a logical order from large to small, both thinkers and feelers, sensers and intuiters, can use it comfortably. Students can use the Framework to judge progress on a particular draft; moreover, if certain points (such as audience address or sentence structure) are habitual weak spots, the teacher and student working together can identify strategies to remedy individual weaknesses. Thus a student who often has problems with developing support may be encouraged to try several extra types of prewriting as he gathers material for a paper; a student who has trouble with paragraph development may ask all the paragraph questions for each chunk of her paper. Here is Bain's modified framework:

A Framework for Judging

1. A writer promises to do something. What does the writer of this paper promise to do? Can we state that promise in our own words? Does the writer keep that promise? If not, where and why does the writer fail to do so?

2. Is there a perceivable order to the presentation of the writer's feelings and ideas? Can we follow and describe that order? Does that order of presentation show how the writer has felt and thought about the subject? If we cannot follow the order of the presentation, where does the writer lose us and why? Can we suggest better strategies than those the writer has chosen? If so, how and why?

3. What seems to be the writer's attitude toward the audience—playful, sarcastic, condescending, serious? What does the writer's attitude toward the audience say about the relationship between that writer and the audience?

4. Has the writer omitted any important details or arguments that would contribute to our understanding of the writer's understanding and feelings? Has the writer included details or arguments not connected with the feelings and ideas under discussion? Where could the writer add to the paper and where subtract? How could the writer clarify these feelings and ideas?

5. Is the writer's attitude toward these feelings and ideas convincing? Is the

writer filling space or writing about feelings and ideas which matter? How can we tell?

6. Is the language of the paper appropriate to the author's voice and subject? If the writer uses big words, is it done to show off or to help the reader better understand? Is the language fairly free of clichés, jargon, and worn-out words and phrases? If the writer bends or breaks the conventions of language (making up new words or running them together), are there reasons for doing so?

7. Does each paragraph signal clearly to the reader the direction in which the writer's ideas and feelings are moving? Does each paragraph develop and complete the idea it introduces? If we lose our way in a paragraph, where and why do we get lost?

8. Are the rhythms and patterns of sentences appropriate to the writer's subject and voice? If the sentences seem to be "Dick and Jane" sentences, how could the writer combine sentences to break up this pattern? If the sentences are so long the reader gets lost in them, where could the writer break them into shorter units? Does the writer use the passive voice excessively? If so, is that usage justified?

9. Has the writer observed the conventions of grammar, punctuation, spelling, and capitalization? If not, is there a good reason why the writer has not done so?

10. Does the writer's paper demonstrate the skills asked for by the assignment? That is, if the assignment calls for an argument, is there an argument in the paper?

11. Have any external circumstances such as late submission, nonstandard form, plagiarism, or the like, influenced the reader's reaction to the paper? If so, can the writer overcome that influence?

Self-assessments

Students can evaluate their own progress through brief notes attached to the papers they submit. They need only answer two or three questions, perhaps writing on the back of the paper itself or on a separate sheet answers to these three queries: "What do you [the student] think has worked well in this paper? What in this paper gave you trouble? Are there goals or competencies you don't think you've achieved yet?" Students will usually answer those questions frankly, and you can use their responses to guide your evaluation of the text and to compose your endnote.

The Work of Grading Papers

In the end, of course, you have to grade some papers. For the beginning teacher this can be a time-consuming and excruciating process; novices frequently spend an hour or more on each paper. If you have a heavy course load or large enrollment, the task can seem impossible. In time, you'll learn to move more quickly, but still will need to spend at least 15-20 minutes on a 500-700 word paper. What follows are some practical tips to help you speed the grading process.

- Start with carefully designed assignments and give the students enough time to complete the assignment successfully. The clearer the assignment, the fewer variables left for you to cope with; the more adequate the time, the fewer hasty or careless errors you (should) have to contend with.
- Be realistic when telling students when they'll get papers back. Many authorities insist that teachers return papers at the first class meeting after the assignments are submitted. Sometimes, if the papers are short enough and the classes small enough, and the instructor's life uncomplicated enough, this is possible. Certainly it's ideal. Two class meetings—or a week—is more realistic. The students need at least one class meeting to review your comments and suggestions on one paper before submitting their next effort—and more time is helpful if they need a conference to discuss those comments with you. Schedule papers far enough apart to let you grade them carefully; and don't make promises you can't keep.
- Set a schedule for your grading and keep it. If you must grade 50 papers in 5 days, that's ten a day. At a half-hour per paper (a good beginner's rate), that's six hours of grading a day (you'll need a break or two to maintain your concentration). Resign yourself to setting the VCR, sending out for pizza, and becoming a hermit for that time. If the papers come in before a weekend, you'll have more time for your grading; it is possible to do 50 papers in two days, though your sanity at the end will be in serious jeopardy.
- Set reasonable time limits. Buy a timer and be ruthless about paying attention to it. Allow yourself a maximum time per paper—25 or 30 minutes for an average (500-700 word) paper for a beginner, 15-20 minutes as you get more experienced. Read the paper through once in its entirety before you mark anything,

even minor mechanical errors. This allows you to assess the biggest strengths and weaknesses, to target your attention. Reread the paper, making your minimal marks and marginal comments. Then skim it one more time and compose your end-note. (Sometimes the endnotes written by beginning teachers are a page or longer; you'll learn to control this with experience.) Again, the three-part formula—strengths, a few weaknesses, goals/strategies—can help you compose a response quickly.

- Often you'll find yourself calling on stock phrases to compose your endnotes; students rarely compare comments, so you needn't worry too much if every third endnote contains a sentence or two such as "Kelli, one of the strongest things about this paper are the quotes you use to support your opinions," or "The quotes you've chosen, Jim, really offer strong support for your assertions." As long as the comments are clear, precise, and appropriate for the student's paper, you needn't concern yourself unnecessarily with the originality of the sentiment. After all, students are shooting for similar goals; naturally, some will have similar successes and weaknesses.

- Write a good endnote. If you have clear grading standards, put a letter grade on the paper after you've written your endnote; if not, sort it into roughly-defined piles: the good ones, the okay ones, the problem ones, and go back to assign a grade later. If your time runs out, finish your note immediately and move on; you're probably asking the student to address too many issues. If the paper is a real disaster, set it aside; you'll want time to write a thoughtful note later. If you finish early, take a quick stretch and move on; you'll want that time later. Don't turn the endnote into a justification or apology for a low grade; use it as a chance to teach the student ways to improve. If you feel that assigning a very low grade would be detrimental to the student's progress, you can always mark it "No grade pending conference," discuss the paper with the student, and grade it after the student has revised it further. This solution works best when used sparingly and privately; otherwise you'll have B+ students clamoring for a chance to rewrite papers to get an A. (You can choose to allow such students to do so, of course, but be prepared to fight accusations of grade inflation.)

- Keep good records. Don't just put the grade on the paper; record it in your grade book or progress folder immediately. If you're keeping a progress chart for conferences, make a few sketchy notes now; you can go back and elaborate later if necessary. If you forget to record grades now you'll eventually find yourself in the position of returning a set of papers without recording the grades; then you have to go through all sorts of conniptions to get the papers back to record the grades. Such a time-consuming annoyance can be avoided by keeping records carefully from the beginning. If you're making up ongoing exercises taken from student papers (see Chapter 8), type those sample sentences onto your handout or disk now; it only takes a minute to give you a class activity for tomorrow (or down the road).

Evaluating Through Portfolios

In the last decade, some composition programs have imitated the example of our colleagues in the visual arts and elementary schools in finding a way to evaluate student work: the portfolio. A typical portfolio might allow students to select four or five pieces completed and revised in the semester to represent the student's work in the class. The materials may include preliminary drafts, peer reviews, journal entries, reflective assessments of the portfolio assembly process, and other creations as well as "finished papers"; last semester, I received my first videotape of a student performing some original songs he had written in my class as part of his portfolio. The chief advantage of a portfolio is that it lets a student demonstrate his or her growth as a writer over the course of time, rather than simply providing a collection of "snapshots" taken at various points throughout the semester. If portfolios are used program-wide, they are usually read by other faculty than the writer's own instructor, and judged either successful or unsuccessful (a pass/fail, pass/no credit, or satisfactory/unsatisfactory rating). If they are used in individual classrooms, the course instructor assigns some kind of ranking that converts into a grade (sometimes taking into account other work in the class, as in the sample syllabus in Chapter 5).

Portfolio grading, at its best, empowers students, and spurs revision; thus, it has drawn a great deal of attention in recent years as programs struggle with the whole question of evaluation. Moreover, it has become a way for teachers to document their own growth and reflective practice as well, and at some institutions has become an important part of hiring, tenure, and promotion decisions. By de-emphasizing grades throughout the semester, it's hoped, portfolios make students focus on continually reworking and refining their skills to become better writers, so that they have progress to show at the end of the course.

I've had mixed experiences with portfolios in the five years I've used them, and on reflection I put them down to three causes. First, the goals of my institution's writing program are hard to assess through a portfolio; second, the suspended judgement involved in portfolio assessment distinctly counters some students' learning styles; and finally, since I know how much (and you wouldn't *believe* how much) effort goes into compiling some of these portfolios, I find it hard to judge them just on the contents alone. I'm also a sucker for the artistic components students add—decorated covers, photographs, computer graphics, fancy binders—you name it, they'll use it. (Last fall I got one that included origami made out of the student's drafts; see what I mean?) Overall, I think portfolios benefit most students, in most situations. On the other hand, in a pilot study, I tried using them in a professional writing class where by School of Business policy the students' grades depend heavily on the format and appearance of the documents they produce. Since multiple revisions (and increased familiarity with desk-top publishing) tend to produce quite impressive-looking documents, I found that the portfolios severely inflated grades in the course. My course director and I have agreed to terminate this experiment.

Portfolios are not without their problems. If they are used program-wide, a clear description of the contents must be evolved, which may lead teachers to "teach to the portfolio" as high school teachers are accused of "teaching to the test." Developing an assessment rubric and assuring consistency of reading may also offer challenges. The sheer time involved—getting the portfolios from your class to the other teacher(s) who will read them and let you know whether your students have passed, and then returning the portfolios to the authors—can be a major management hurdle. And evaluating students only at the end of a course, when there's no time left to improve, can increase the stress level for some students and may do some of them an injustice.

If you're marking portfolios individually, the problems can swell alarmingly; rather than mark 25 papers nine times a semester, you'll have to mark 125 per class at one time. If you teach multiple sections, the problem will mushroom. You can lessen the burden by conducting a preliminary portfolio review at midsemester in preparation for the "real thing" at the end of term or by otherwise adjusting the due dates to meet your own—and the class's— needs. Moreover, since you've given a great deal of feedback all along, and the final papers are usually pretty good, the temptation to inflate grades on the portfolios may be dangerous. You'll still need to provide students with feedback on the individual papers so they know what points to work on and which papers to revise as their "best." Finally, portfolios most emphatically do *not* save time; because of all the responding, the many versions of texts you may see, and the record-keeping, portfolios increase your workload.

Don't be surprised, too, if some students are made very insecure and nervous by portfolios. They may need the security of an interim grade to build their confidence. On the other hand, some students at the extremes—both your most and least confident writers—may find the freedom from grades really exhilarating, and blossom as a result. I've seen reactions everywhere along this spectrum since I started using portfolios, and I find myself "winging it" every semester. Two articles in the anthology that concludes this volume, one by Chris Anson and one by Jeffrey Sommers, outline some of the possibilities portfolios offer a reflective teacher. If you have a supportive program, and lots of energy, I think portfolios are an idea well worth exploring.

Conferencing

You can also work individually with students on the development of papers. You could "evaluate" some papers in one-to-one conferences, assigning verbal grades of "excellent, very good, fair" and the like. Since these grades will likely be higher, reflecting your input into the project at many stages, you might then assign letter grades only to papers students produce independently, alternating conference and independent papers. This strategy reduces by half the number of written comments you must produce; its drawback is the amount of time such conference teaching requires.

Collaborating

A different kind of workload reduction can be achieved by letting your students do some of the work for you collaboratively. When students work effectively in small and large groups, they can identify writing problems at the draft stage and help their fellow students remedy weaknesses. Collaborative activities can fit at any developmental stage in a piece of writing, allowing you many opportunities to use this valuable technique. Group proofreading sessions likewise can find and solve many mechanical problems before they reach your desk. If you train the groups to look for the kinds of problems students are having, they can do a great deal of the diagnostic work for each other. You'll occasionally have to correct a faulty diagnosis, but will generally save time in this manner. If all students have access to computer facilities, you can encourage them to use spell checker programs and perhaps a few of the stylistic diagnostic programs as well. (Unfortunately, few of the latter are sophisticated enough to be of real practical use for collegiate discourse.) Students with cognitive problems can be referred to various kinds of campus assistance (about which see above, Chapter 6).

Student-set standards

You can also encourage students to set the standard for achievement in the class. You can use a model such as the Framework for Judging (discussed above) or your school's description of letter grades, if it provides one. Or, early in the semester, you can have students develop sets of criteria that characterize average, above average, below average, and excellent writing; then hold them to these in assigning grades. Duplicate the criteria and distribute them to the class members; use them to develop goals in assignments, to develop groupwork heuristics, and to support your comments.

Teaching in Practice

Below is the set of goals developed by one of my freshman writing classes two weeks into the course; they are challenging, even more so because the students developed them with only a few hints and leading questions from me. The wording is theirs; feel free to use it as an example.

We the members of English 101:L4 agree that these are our standards for writing in this class:

Average Writing (C to C+) has
- a sense of organization (transitions, thesis, etc.)
- adequate word choice and grammar
- average style—not great but not really rough
- some repetition
- some sketchy or missing development
- some boring sentence structure
- sometimes a weak intro or conclusion
- a "vanilla" writer writing for a "vanilla" audience

Above Average Writing (B to B+) has
- the strengths of average writing and more clarity
- a structure that really works but doesn't stick out
- good research, support, background, or details as needed
- a sense that the writer knows what he's doing and is addressing real people
- few mechanical problems
- sharp, almost professional appearance
- proofreading
- a good intro and conclusion

Excellent Writing (A) has
- the strengths of above-average writing and "flow"
- a real sense of the writer's competence
- a real sense of the writer's purpose
- something memorable
- really careful language use and style
- a positive impact on the audience
- a "professional" feel to it

Below Average Writing (D) has
- all of the weaknesses of average writing and roughness
- clichés or other thoughtless word use
- little sense of purpose or organization or support
- little sense of who's the writer or the readers
- problems with style, mechanics, and/or proofreading
- the characteristics of a rush job—sloppiness, skimpiness, and disorganization

Unsuccessful Writing (F) has
- many problems, such as the below-average problems, only worse

- failure to meet the assignment
- plagiarism
- excessive lateness
- a sense that the writer was unwilling or unable or unorganized or all of these things

When students are involved in setting these standards, you'll find that disputes over grades are less frequent, and that students will honestly assess for you what grades their efforts ought to receive. I ask each of my writing classes to develop a list like this (this is an exceptionally good one); then, with each paper, I ask them to include a note describing which of the standards they feel they've met and which they are having trouble meeting. Then I can address my comments to those points. Students frequently underestimate their performance at first, but as the semester progresses, many predict their grades quite accurately. I've found that letting students grade their own efforts, using a rubric they've developed, helps reduce some of the anxiety associated with portfolios graded at the end of the semester.

Evaluation Cans and Can'ts

Some teachers, particularly beginning ones, have an extremely idealistic view of evaluation. They see it as a cure-all, the rendering of advice which will, overnight, turn the student into the next Walker Percy or Toni Morrison. To gain these results, they write comments that may approach (or exceed) the original paper in length. The overwhelmed student may try to respond, but is usually daunted by all the advice and suggestions—and subsequent papers sometimes are disasters. Often, it seems the student ignores those responses altogether. The idealistic teacher, dreams shattered, wanders the hallways muttering about the intractability of students and the frustrations of the job. It's not a healthy situation for either party, because the perspectives on both sides get so far out of kilter.

Evaluating individual written products is a matter of seeing how well students have reached intermediate goals in the course. It's subjective and can't be done on the bell curve; writing progress is too individual a process for that. (While you'll want to apply the same standards to all students, you'll probably have to allow some leeway in measuring achievement. Students who master narrow competencies (such as mechanics or syntactic variety) quickly should receive credit for these successes, but should probably be judged more on how well they master more open matters—audience manipulation, voice, development, and so on. Students who have a great deal of difficulty mastering the narrow competencies—those who come from particularly weak backgrounds or who have dialect interference problems, for example—may have excellent ideas but difficulty in presenting them. They should be rewarded for the content of their papers but encouraged to master the conventions of academic discourse as well. Make it clear to students that you're not evaluating how well they compete against other students—or against your ideals—but how much progress they're making in achieving the goals set for all students.

You'll also have to guard against biased reactions to certain students. Too often we find ourselves saying "Oh, here's Lee's paper; it'll be another good one" or "Oh dear, let's see what kind of disaster Dana's committed this time" or "Chris has been such a know-it-all in class lately; I'll show him he still has things to learn." It's human to make these prejudgments, but to teach effectively you have to set them aside as you mark the actual paper and consider its strengths and weaknesses as objectively as you can. (Another reason why making evaluation criteria part of the assignment can help you: it assures each paper a fair reading.)

Likewise, you may be tempted to reward a student's effort on a paper rather than the product he actually produces ("This just doesn't hold together but Ming worked so hard; look at all these drafts!"); such sympathy may be human, but it's not going to help the student. Giving good grades for effort rather than for results provides students with a false assessment of their achievements. It's dishonest. Better to withhold a grade pending a conference and revision in such cases than to artificially inflate such student's expectations. Likewise, painful as it is, it's dishonest to give a student a passing grade, certifying the ability to read and write at the college level without reservation, when the student hasn't in fact demonstrated that ability. If the student hasn't responded to your help throughout the term, assign the failing grade and send the student to the writing center or other appropriate source for help before re-enrolling in the class.

Of course there are other kinds of evaluations that need to be made in writing courses. The next chapter will discuss those in more detail.

Scenario

Mai Lee has been unable to find a tenure track job after completing her dissertation, so she signs a contract for a three-year
appointment teaching composition at a community college. The
state is becoming more conservative and insisting on "standards"
and "quality" in state-supported schools like hers, and when she
arrives for the first day of orientation she learns what that will
mean for her as a teacher of composition. The Director of Writing
hands out a green form to each new teacher, saying "This is our
departmental grading checklist, which you are required to use in
grading papers. As you'll see, it sets standards for minimum content and correctness in our courses. The whole department has
voted to use this form, and the state Board of Regents may require
it statewide, so we're very proud to be leading this effort."

When Mai Lee looks at the sheet, she is shocked to see that
papers that do not meet the minimum requirements for content
or correctness on *one* or more items can receive grades of no
higher than 50 (F). The items identified for automatic failure are

For content:
  • Does not address the assignment appropriately
  • Does not meet the minimum length required
  • Lacks focus, coherence, or organization
  • Is superficial in thought
  • Lacks variety in word choice and sentence structure

For correctness:
  • Has repeated errors in grammar, punctuation, spelling, mechan-
    ics, or usage
  • Has two or more sentence fragments, run-on or fused sentences, or
    comma splices (or combination of these faults)

Below this list, Mai Lee sees with astonishment, are point deductions for other errors, including 10 points off for each misplaced
comma and 7 points off for each misspelled word. As a conces-
sion, the form allows students who receive less than a C on major
assignments to revise a maximum of two of them, but instructors can assign a grade no higher than C- for such revisions.

This policy violates everything Mai Lee believes about the
teaching of writing. But she has signed a contract. She needs the job.
What should she do?

Evaluating the Writing Course

A writing course is made up of three elements: the student writers, the instructor, and the course of instruction. The performance of each of these has to be assessed to determine the course's effectiveness. Traditionally such evaluations are carried out only at the end of the course; the drawback to such a tradition is that nothing can be done to remedy any weaknesses of the course for those students and that instructor in that particular situation. The failing or disappointing grades come as a *post mortem*, not a diagnostic. So the description of evaluation below will vary a bit from the traditional one to describe some kinds of evaluation that can take place while the class is in progress, the kinds of evaluation that may lead to remedying problems and encouraging student growth. Again, your selection of a system of evaluation will depend on whether you're evaluating papers individually or as an overall portfolio (both discussed in the previous chapter), as well as on what your institution demands.

Evaluating the Instructor's Performance

While we all like to think we're perfect—or nearly so—the sad truth is that many of us have areas of our teaching performance that could be shored up. It's hard to have the humility of Chaucer's Clerk—"Gladly wolde he lerne, and gladly teche"—yet that attitude is essential to teaching success. To do our best job in the classroom, we have to evaluate our strengths and weaknesses as honestly as we do those of our students. Thank heavens we don't have to do this alone; we have students and colleagues to help.

Student Evaluations

Student evaluations tell us one thing and one thing only: what the students perceive about our course. They're not experts in curriculum design or in the subject matter, but they are professional takers of courses. And their comments on evaluations tell us how we, and our courses, come across to them. If students think you tell too many bad jokes, or give out too many handouts, or really care about them, they'll say so when offered the chance. Ask for their honest responses, and listen and respond to what they tell you. Among my standard questions are "How can I make this course better? Which of your needs should I address more directly?" Sometimes I don't get a consensus in the answers, but I nearly always get thoughtful responses, to which I do pay attention. (The cookies I usually provide on evaluation days may have something to do with the quality of their responses; chocolate chips *can* stir thought.)

Colleagues' Evaluations

Evaluations conducted by colleagues are another feature of most writing programs. This is done on a more-or-less formal basis, depending on the school. Some ask the teacher being observed to submit a lesson plan to the observer in advance, have the observer record what goes on in the classroom, and arrange for observer and observed to meet and discuss the results. Other programs have a colleague drop in on a class and write an informal letter to the chair or director summarizing what went on. Such evaluations may or may not be used in hiring, reappointment, and promotion decisions.

You may also ask for informal peer observation if there are factors in your classroom performance that you'd like to improve or just would like to have assessed objectively. Here you can invite a friend or officemate to sit in on a class, record what goes on (what you say and do, what the students say and do, and when), and discuss it with you. These informal observations are often good practice if you're due for a formal observation shortly; there's nothing like a dry run to sharpen things up. If your school offers videotaping services, you might like to have your performance videotaped. Once you get over the embarrassment of watching yourself on tape, you can usually find some habits to correct or methods to work on. (I was horrified, when I was first taped, to see how much I fiddled with my rings. I've about conquered that problem, but from my last taping I've discovered that I now mutilate paper clips instead—and that my students watch me do it. Another habit to kick.)

Although opinion varies, I think it's best to inform students in advance when you'll be observed and why. This reassures them that they're not being judged and often wins you some extra cooperation. Most will come to class on observation day ready and willing to talk;

you may have trouble controlling discussion, instead of eliciting it! Even the quiet or distracting students usually contribute on observation days; somehow, students presume that how you perform depends on them. In these sessions, you may come as close to being a united writing community as you ever will be.

Self-Evaluations

Self-evaluation is the hardest part of evaluating your performance. It's hard to put all the comments, criticism, praise, and suggestions in perspective, especially when these remarks are in conflict. Half the class may love workshops; the other half may loathe them. Half may want to write more in class, while the other half wants to discuss essays. How do you strike a balance? A reasonable solution is to look at the trends the comments suggest, compare them to your colleagues' evaluations if available, and act on those suggestions that seem most reasonable to you. If you're perplexed, talk to an experienced teacher or your director and get some perspective. Evaluations, after all, don't really show what you do badly; they show you what you can do well and what you can do better.

Teaching Portfolios

Many programs now encourage or require instructors to compile teaching portfolios that document their work in a class, just as the instructors may require student portfolios. The value of such reflective tools for improving your teaching performance is immense, and more and more people are using them to improve their profile on the job market. The typical teaching portfolio includes both samples of your teaching—assignments, syllabi, handouts, videotapes of you in class, evaluations, etc.—and reflective commentary on the contents that help someone reviewing the portfolio assess their value within an appropriate context. Because effective teaching can be defined and demonstrated in many ways, a teaching portfolio lets you show yourself (first of all) and the world the kind of teacher you really are, rather than how well you match some abstract profile of "the good teacher." Your portfolio can document the evolution of your teaching over time, as well as permit you the luxury of reflecting on the past to assess the present and improve the future. Many people (myself among them) include student papers in their portfolios; most of the ones I have are good papers, but a few are perplexing ones that caused me to rethink some of my classroom practice. My commentary on these papers is part of the way I show my reviewers how I think about what I do and what my students do in the classroom.

Many portfolios also document the ways teachers stay current in their profession, including documentation of scholarship, professional activity (such as attending professional meetings) and service (such as mentoring other T.A.s). This can be formal evidence (certificates of attendance) or informal—thank you notes, follow-ups, and the like. It can also include testimony from students as to the quality of your influence on them. One of the pieces in my portfolio right now is an e-mail thank-you note from a student written the night of graduation last spring; I had seen him and had complimented him (deservedly so) to his family for his achievements. That night he e-mailed his thanks and those of his parents for taking the time to convey my pride to them. His note says, "After you left, my grandfather said, 'You must be pretty good to impress a professor, boy.' And you know, I felt that way too. I can only imagine what you feel when you see us go across the stage, but I hope you know that as we walk across and out into the world, we take a piece of you with us forever." That's the kind of comment I like having in my portfolio; it tells a reviewer something about the connections I established and the learning this young man accomplished.

Self-evaluations like teaching portfolios take a lot of time to put together, because they show so much about who we are. I have a new appreciation for what my students have gone through now that I have compiled my own. As an evolutionary process of helping you reflect on your own teaching and development, they are hard to beat. The scholarship on teaching portfolios continues to boom; we have included Chris Anson's article on them in the anthology at the end of this text. Some other recent excellent publications include P. Seldin, *The Teaching Portfolio: A Practical Guide to Improved Performance and Promotion/Tenure Decisions* (1991); R. Edgerton et al., *The Teaching Portfolio: Capturing Scholarship in Teaching* (1991); and David Way, "The Teaching Portfolio: A Tool for Seeking Employment and the Improvement of Practice," available at http://www.sas. cornell. edu/ois/portfolio/html.

Responding to Evaluations

Alas, not all evaluations are used only to improve teaching. Many institutions, as noted above, use them for hiring and promotion decisions; note the subtitles of Seldin's and Way's works in the paragraph above, for instance. That's why you should always look at your student and colleague evaluations. If your department keeps them on file, *always* add a short written response to them. You may wish to note special circumstances (the course was held from 8:00 to 9:30 p.m. in a small room that lacked air conditioning, and the students rightly rebelled; evaluations were distributed on a religious holiday when 25 percent of the students were absent) and, more concretely, your reaction to any criticisms or suggestions. These show that you take your teaching performance seriously and that you can deal constructively with criticism. You might want to indicate actions you're not going to take, as well ("Students claimed I graded too harshly; however, as 75 percent made a C+ or higher, I'm not worried that I am habitually underrating their performances."). It's not a bad idea, too, to draw attention to the strengths students note, in a low-key way, if your evaluations will be read. If students think workshops and conferences help them, point this out; only this may counterbalance a colleague's expressed surprise at your "failure" to lecture.

Assessing Overall Course Effectiveness

You can assess the strengths and weaknesses of the course you teach in many ways; if you're prudent, you'll do this while the course is in progress, so that you can adjust the syllabus or your teaching methods to meet student needs and help them reach their goals. You may, for example, wish to begin the course with some kind of attitude survey or poll that examines students' attitudes toward writing and language to measure how these attitudes change (I often cull platitudes from the "pop grammarians'" books, such as "A good sentence never ends in a preposition" or "Never use 'I' in serious writing" or "All successful paragraphs have a clear topic sentence" and see how strongly my students agree or disagree). These reactions provide fruit for class discussion and often suggest some provocative writing prompts.

A short, anonymous, in-class evaluation can be conducted quickly during the semester to keep tabs on the class' perception of its progress. (A model for such an evaluation is below.) In a quarter-length course, this might be used once; in a semester-length course, it might be used twice. Anonymity encourages students to answer honestly. You should discuss the results with the class to assure them that their suggestions are valuable and tell them what changes (if any) you'll make in response to their comments.

Midterm Evaluation

Answer each question by circling the letters that best describe your position on each question. Feel free to use the back of this sheet to make other comments. DON'T put your name on this survey. DY=definite yes; Y=yes; NC=not certain; N=no; DN=definite no

1. I'm doing at least 80 percent of the reading.
   DY   Y   NC   N   DN
2. I want to discuss the texts in more detail.
   DY   Y   NC   N   DN
3. I have a clearer notion of what good writing involves.
   DY   Y   NC   N   DN
4. Assignments and classwork have helped my writing to improve.
   DY   Y   NC   N   DN
5. I find conferences helpful.
   DY   Y   NC   N   DN
6. I find the writing groups helpful.
   DY   Y   NC   N   DN
7. The comments on my papers are clear and helpful.
   DY   Y   NC   N   DN
8. I feel free to ask questions, comment, and disagree.
   DY   Y   NC   N   DN
9. I know what's expected of me on assignments.
   DY   Y   NC   N   DN
10. I understand the goals I'm trying to reach.
    DY   Y   NC   N   DN
11. I can cope with the workload.
    DY   Y   NC   N   DN
12. I'm getting my money's worth from this course.
    DY   Y   NC   N   DN

What techniques, competencies, and class techniques would you like to spend more time on? What would you like to do less of? How can I make this course better for you?

As you can tell from these questions, such informal progress evaluations tell you how students are perceiving your course, and let you revise as necessary to make the course deliver what you have promised (and your institution demands) it will.

End-of-course evaluations have increased markedly in sophistication in recent years, though assessment has never been a wildly popular topic among composition and rhetoric scholars. (We tend to leave that for our colleagues in the school of education.) In the December 1982 issue of *College Composition and Communication,* Stephen Witte, John Daly, Lester Faigley, and William Koch presented some important research in evaluation, as well as some caveats for how that information should be used. They also describe an 80-item long evaluation and a 21-item short evaluation that have been tested and refined in writing courses nationwide. (A version of the short form is presented as the "Teaching in Practice" selection below.) Edward White, both an education and a writing specialist, has refined and expanded these ideas considerably in the second edition of his book *Teaching and Assessing Writing* (1994). These scholars remind us that as important as evaluations are, more important are the warnings that accompany them. The results can't just be calculated as raw scores; they must be calculated with standard deviations and assessed against a statistically valid sample in order to have meaning. They shouldn't be used in isolation to determine a teacher's hiring, promotion, or salary; rather, they should be viewed as reflecting student perception of the teaching performance and judged accordingly. And, of course, they should be conducted anonymously to ensure honest response without fear of repercussion. Like all other evaluations, you should prepare a written response to what your evaluations tell you and others about your teaching performance.

Teaching in Practice

This questionnaire has been adapted from the research of Witte et al. described above. This open-ended form elicits fairly reliable, fairly consistent data on student perceptions of a course. I always use those last five questions to ask about portfolios, our e-mail discussions, the information about learning styles, etc., so that I have quantifiable data to talk about when I write my summary evaluations for my annual report.

Writing Class Evaluation

Please follow your instructor's directions carefully as you fill out the identification section of the answer sheet. When your instructor tells you to begin, mark your responses to each item in the numbered spaces below. Use pencil and answer all of the questions, making sure that you record the answer to each question in the space that matches the number of the question. Items 22 to 26 are reserved for questions your instructor may wish to ask; these questions will be written on the board. Use the following code for recording your response:

1 Strongly agree
2 Agree
3 Undecided
4 Disagree
5 Strongly disagree

A member of the class will collect your responses and turn them in to the departmental office. Your responses will in no way affect your grade, and your instructor will not see them until final grades are turned in.

1. My instructor in this course is a very good one.
2. My instructor in this course is one of the most helpful instructors I have ever had.
3. My instructor is intellectually stimulating.
4. My work in this course is evaluated fairly.
5. The instructor does a good job of teaching students how to write different kinds of papers.
6. The instructor is good about teaching students how to argue a thesis or position.
7. The instructor puts too much emphasis on "correct" grammar in student writing.
8. The instructor clearly connects what he or she teaches in class with the writing assignments he or she makes.
9. The instructor is good about teaching me how to evaluate my own papers so that I can better revise them.
10. The instructor is good about teaching me to consider the needs of my audience when I am thinking about a writing topic.
11. The instructor is good about using class time to help me as I am writing my papers.
12. The instructor spends too much time on some things and not enough time on other things. (Which ones? Use the back!)
13. In evaluating my writing, the instructor uses standards that are too high.
14. The instructor's comments on my papers are easy to understand.
15. The instructor is good about teaching me how to support main ideas in my papers through examples and specific details.
16. The instructor is good about encouraging me to join in class discussions.
17. The instructor does a good job of using examples of writing in teaching students how to write.
18. The instructor is good about trying to increase my confidence about writing.

19. What this course teaches is very useful to me right now.
20. What I am learning in this course is valuable.
21. What this course teaches will be useful to me in the future.
22. (Items 22 through 26 are reserved for additional questions your
23.   instructor may have for your particular section.)
24.
25.
26.

One last point. Evaluations don't always tell us what we want to hear, but they usually tell us what we *need* to hear. There's a difference. If you're going to teach well, you have to be honest with yourself. All of us can always learn to do our jobs better. So listen to the messages your evaluations give you.

Scenario

This discussion about evaluation is excerpted from a conversation that took place between my electronic colleagues, Bobbie Silk and Jon Olson, on the WCENTER electronic discussion list on the last weekend of May, 1996, and is reprinted here with their kind permission. Bobbie is Co-Director of the Writing Lab at Clarke College; Jon is Writing Center Coordinator at Oregon State University, and the emoticons are Jon's own.

Jon: Don'tcha think writing instruction is sometimes just like when the car freezes in mid-air and *The Dukes of Hazzard* cuts to a commercial message?

Bobbie: All right, Jon. I think I see why writing instruction is sometimes just like that. (And how much of this show did you watch, anyway?) In fact, I like the analogy a lot. So, do some of our problems [in evaluation] arise from the fact that sometimes we—and certainly others—forget that the point of the instruction is the action, not the frozen image of action in the photo?

Jon: Yeah, Bobbie. Good question. And what I'm seeing in this picture you created is the teacher who gives the commercial message of writing essentials (of what's central to effective writing), a commercial which not only seems to freeze the action but also sometimes detours the writer off the road-which-connects-the-disciplines and sends the writer hurtling out over the void which the disciplines encircle. When the commercial message—what goes on in the classroom—is over, and the action resumes, if there is no center to connect to, the writer falls into the void.

Bobbie: Interesting. Hmmmmm. So some student writers have enough gas and momentum to finish the arc and come down on the other side. But they'll always be a little nervous, a little unsure about power and speed. So what is at the center of writing that they should have?

Jon: Bobbie, I don't know if student writers make the *Dukes of Hazzard* jump on their own or not. They might. But sometimes they get sent on the arc, *projected* by teachers (I intend the psychological resonance of that word) and frozen in mid-action. I'm thinking that teachers sometimes divert writing students from the track, and that teachers stop the students' writing action in mid-air over what the teacher perceives to be central. Teachers' writing instruction can often seem like a commercial for what they think is central or essential, but that commercial doesn't always have a lot to do with the force or purpose of the writer's action. (I think most writers have enough gas ;-)).

Bobbie and Jon use the freeze-frames of a familiar television show to try to develop a metaphor for the points where we stop and evaluate writing, either individual pieces or whole courses. Would you use this metaphor? Or what metaphor would you put in its place?

CHAPTER

11

Special Challenges in the Classroom

What has preceded this chapter has described teaching in mainstream college classrooms. Most of you will begin your teaching careers in such classes, with such students. But as the world of composition instruction evolves, inevitably you will find yourself dealing with some of the special challenges that writing teachers seem to end up facing more than other teachers. This chapter offers a brief overview of five of those challenges, with some suggestions as to how you might go about beginning to learn to meet them.

The Challenge of Basic Writers

Anywhere from 15 to 25 percent of all first-year writing students are classified as basic writers. The term is a catchall; "basic" writers may have weak academic backgrounds, or language interference problems, or learning disabilities; or may be poor standardized test-takers; or returning students too far removed from their high-school careers to take the regular first-year course; or be students the school expects to have trouble with academics for some reason. This problem isn't going away; some predictions claim that in another decade, more than half the students graduating from American high schools won't have English as a first language. When students with these problems are mainstreamed into the regular composition classroom, the resulting inhomogeneous mix can be hard to teach effectively. That's why basic writing teachers are some of the hardest-working, most devoted, and often most innovative teachers you'll encounter.

Some of these students may be beyond your help; if they have learning disabilities, for instance, you may need to refer them to special services on your campus where trained professionals can help them. (Some will have problems that fall under the Americans with Disabilities Act, in which case you are legally required to make accommodations for them; the counselor for students with disabilities on your campus will be able to tell you what is required.) If these students' problems stem from too little exposure to writing and formal language conventions, you may have to try to remedy the deficiencies of twelve years of formal education in a term. Students with dialect interference or ESL (English as a Second Language) problems may again need outside help, but primarily they'll need constant, close attention as they master the conventions of edited English. And students who lack familiarity with academic discourse may need similar attention; on the other hand, "rusty" students may just need frequent practice and light supervision to move to the next level of courses.

What do you do if you are asked to teach such students? Don't panic. First, try to assess the students' chief problems. You will probably find a wide variety, making you forego large-class teaching in favor of smaller group work. Placing students of like ability together may save you time, and them frustration. Use groupwork—peer discussions and editing, team research, reading groups, and the like—to help students help each other. Assign study buddies so that they can help each other. Hold frequent conferences, and give more frequent (if shorter) writing assignments so that the students get plenty of practice.

What should those assignments be? The romantic or expressivist school of writing theory suggests that these students write about their personal knowledge and experiences. Making them "experts" builds their confidence, helps them appreciate voice and audience, and builds trust between them and you, and them and their classmates. On the other hand, social-epistemic theorists believe that such students are not served well by focusing on themselves. Rather, they argue, such students should focus on the language of the academy, learn its conventions, appropriate its discourse for themselves, and thus enter a larger community of readers and writers. Bartholomae and Petrosky (1986) have put together an ambitious model program of college reading and writing, mostly drawn from other first-year courses, to challenge basic writers to "figure out" the rules of academic discourse—in Bartholomae's memorable phrase, to "invent the university" (see his essay in Part III). In actual practice, because students in any basic writing class tend to be so varied, you may need to mix the two kinds of assignments, and throw in some cognitive approaches as well. Basic writers benefit from a close examination of different writing practices, and from analyzing their own writing process; many need to learn the differences between revision and correction, and to learn the conventions for formal editing, as well.

The body of scholarship on basic writing is too extensive for me to do justice to here. Among the better journals focusing on basic writing are *The Journal of Basic Writing* and *The Journal of Developmental Education; Teaching English in the Two Year College* and *Focuses* also feature a number of articles on basic writing. The best books to start with are Mina Shaughnessy's *Errors and Expectations* (1977); Bartholomae and Petrosky's *Facts, Artifacts, Counterfacts* (1986); and *A Sourcebook for Basic Writing Teachers*, edited by Theresa Enos (1987). You'll find a number of other suggestions in the Bibliography.

The Challenge of Returning Students

As was noted in Chapter 5, the faces in your classrooms may look very different than did the faces in your own first-year writing class. In particular (and especially if you teach in a two-year college), you will probably see more older students—students anywhere from their mid-twenties to well into their nineties! It can be a strange experience teaching someone old enough to be your parent or grandparent; rest assured, the returning student feels equally strange. You may have to make a special effort to make returning students comfortable, but it's well worth it: they are highly-motivated, dedicated people, with a wealth of interesting experience (in life as well as learning) to contribute to your class. Traditional students can be motivated and challenged by returning students as well; I remember one time when a fiftyish woman received the highest grade on an assignment, and I praised her in class. Her classmates gave her a standing ovation when she yelled, "I'm taking this home and putting *it* on the refrigerator!" Not only was it a great moment, but it contributed greatly to the spirit of community in that class—a "refrigerator effort" became a buzzword that term.

But returning students may face challenges that traditional students can more easily handle. One of these is *confidence*: Returning students are out of practice with academic conventions and behaviors. Challenges to their confidence in such matters naturally carry over to their confidence in their academic abilities (this seems especially acute for women students). Financial, time, and family pressures may exacerbate this situation. These may show up in your classroom more sharply than others, because writing classes tend to be smaller and the relationship between student and instructor closer than in many other first-year courses. You may need to hold extra conferences, and you will certainly need to check that returning students can meet the schedules and goals you set for your class. A little flexibility with such students may go a long way in helping them succeed. An excellent source for teaching returning students is Robert F. Sommer's book *Teaching Writing to Adults* (1989); you will find other sources listed in the Bibliography.

Another challenge returning students face is *time management*. Many returning students are juggling full-time employment and/or families with their schooling; inevitably, there will be conflicts. Returning students especially need clear assignments and due dates, and appreciate assignments that are completed in smaller stages; they can juggle these deadlines more easily. Returning students' complex schedules, however, may make it hard for them to participate in activities outside of class or to arrange time for extra groupwork. You may have to make some concessions so these students get the same opportunities their traditional counterparts do. If the facilities exist, consider electronic collaboration; often students who can't get to campus can dial up their e-mail from home or work.

The Challenge of Language Differences

Students may be challenged by the many varieties of American English. Some students will know what "yabba" or "bumbershoot" or "woodpussy" will mean; the Southern student's "branch," however, is the Northeastern student's "creek." To get a hoagie in a Denver delicatessen, a Philadelphia student has to ask for a sub; in other parts of the country this sandwich is called a submarine, a grinder, a muffaletta, and a poorboy. A Rhode Island cabinet may look like a milkshake to people from Nebraska.

Sometimes students feel there's something "wrong" with them or their families because their language doesn't match that of some anchorperson or soap opera star or teacher. Of course, nothing could be further from the truth; all of our students need to know this, just as they need to know how to call on the particular varieties of language required in special discourse situations. The increasing population of non-native students has exacerbated the challenge of language differences; so has the call for "English as the Official Language" political policies.

This changing situation will require teachers to be more aware of language prejudices and interlanguage difficulties in the classroom, and to learn to do something about them. Most campuses offer some support for students and teachers who face second-language challenges; check the college bulletin or phone book, or ask your Director whether your campus has an English as a Second Language (ESL) program or office. Journals like *Teaching English as a Second Language* can offer assistance; you'll also want to consult George Gadda's article in Part III and his excellent bibliography for more sources. And, as he points out, different cultural backgrounds may well lead to different assumptions about writing; these are points you must appreciate, and can become productive sources of classroom discussion and writing in a multicultural environment.

Exercises to strengthen the students' fluency in several kinds of discourse can be helpful. For instance, students may collect dialect examples (some excellent suggestions are given in Roger Shuy's *Discovering American Dialects* [1967] if you want model surveys). Their results could be incorporated into family or community histories or analyses of how certain ethnic groups influenced the American language. Further research projects might send students to standard histories of the English language to learn how many words and phrases they take for granted are borrowed from other sources. (*Taco* they'll recognize as borrowed, but what about *cookie*?) Students can also experiment with inserting bits of nonacademic language in academic papers, or vice-versa, and discuss in their groups the effect of these on the audience. Students who have serious dialect interference problems, however, might need some private or outside help. Such situations are best handled in private conferences, where you and the student can work one-on-one. If you teach such students, check whether your school offers extra help for these students; they may need it. The Bibliography will point you to other excellent sources of information and ideas.

The Challenges of Gender and Gender Bias

It's true: teachers have different expectations for students of both genders. From the earliest grades, teachers expect girls to sit quietly and raise their hands; they expect boys to interrupt, jump up, and sometimes resist. Think of some of the other expectations you may have about gender and writing ability—boys will be messier, girls have better verbal abilities than boys do, boys are more logical, and so on. Such beliefs may hold some truth: for instance, research suggests women are more likely to construct deductive than inductive arguments, and that women use more tag questions to gain their readers' assent and approval. There's no doubt that English vocabulary preserves gendered linguistic stereotypes: consider, for instance, *governor/governess*, *doctor/nurse*, and similar pairs. And why is it more complimentary to call a girl a *tomboy* than it is for the Saturday night comedians to call a male a "girlie man"?

The students who come to your classrooms have been raised in these traditions, most without being aware of it. Not only should you be aware of these interactions of gender and language, but it's worth discussing them with your students as well. If there's an American Association of University Women (AAUW) chapter on your campus, see if you can borrow their videotape "Shortchanging Girls, Shortchanging America," which documents gender bias in schools. Have students collect campus slang, gendered pair words and pronoun references, and analyze the stereotypes those words promote and preserve. If your students have read controversial books like Deborah Tannen's *You Just Don't Understand*, ask them if she's right: can men and women really communicate? Or is gender an impassable barrier?

Some of these ideas are interwoven with the notion published by Mary Belenky and coworkers on "women's ways of knowing." In their complex book of that name (1986), they argue that women tend to be "separate knowers"—they subsume or remove any sense of their individuality from their writing so that it (and by extension they) cannot be attacked. But women are also inclined to work collaboratively, and so they can become "connected knowers"—letting their own voices come through, and encouraging and respecting others who do the same. By contrast, men are individualists, stressing their own achievements in contrast to other men, and see themselves as creators of authority, rather than subject to it.

Teachers need to help all students develop both their "male" and "female" sides. This means encouraging all students to see themselves as capable of creating meaning, and challenging received knowledge, and at the same time encouraging them to listen to others, to work collaboratively, and to construct consensuses. The works in the Bibliography will give you a number of excellent sources to help you tackle the question of gender.

Teaching in Progress

One of the assignments I ask my first-year students to participate in is compiling a current dictionary of campus slang. Students each compile a stack of 50 examples of slang words or phrases (using some simple guidelines and examples I provide), then we combine our examples into a dictionary. There'll be some repetition, but this usually gives us about 900 examples to work with. One of the markers they collect along with the words is the context in which it was used, including the speaker and the situation, so we have a lot of evidence to use.

Then we turn "language detectives," and break into teams. One group may take all the words that describe male-female relations, another group the words that describe campus subcultures (for instance Greek organizations, environmentalists), another the words that describe power relations (usually student-teacher or generational terms), and so on. Sometimes several teams take on the same group of words. Collaboratively, they first try to describe the attitudes they find in these words, and then to analyze why the words are present. For instance, why are there terms that praise men for having simultaneous romantic relations with women ("mattress cowboy," "top dog") but none that praise women for doing the same thing? Many of my students are vegans, and most are ardent recyclers; so why is "tree hugger" a negative term? The results they find tell them a great deal about the social and gender issues in language use, and make them question their own linguistic behaviors; individually, then, they write about these choices. One young woman last year wrote, "I always used the term 'ragging' before, but now that I understand the insulting background of this word, it's *out* of my dictionary!" Many of the students included their analyses of slang as part of their portfolio; they were proud both of the research they had done individually and collectively, and the writing it sparked.

The Challenge of Computers in the Classroom

Writing teachers tend to be enthusiasts; when a new technique comes along, we tend to embrace it wholeheartedly—and sometimes without good results. When computers entered writing classrooms, teachers

nts would revise more because no one could see
they made, and because making changes would
, punctuation, and other mechanical errors would
he past, because the computers could help students
e those problems. E-mail conversation would let us
give s... most simultaneous feedback, as well as providing
other forums for dialogue, collaboration, and conversation.

But like formal grammar instruction, computer use so far appears
neither to have a positive or a negative effect on writing improvement.
Computers are as effective as their users are. If student writers understand how to revise or create, they may well be able to do these
processes more efficiently using a computer. If students understand
the rules of editing and proofreading, the computer may make their
lives easier. The bottom line is that we still have to teach students how
to write well, as well as how to take advantage of computers. We can't
just plop students in front of machines and expect miracles.

I am an enthusiastic supporter of computers in writing classes,
and believe that, if used intelligently by both students *and* teachers,
they can be a great asset. Teachers and students in a computer classroom can become more equal partners, as the teacher releases some
of her or his authority to the learner and her or his computer. In
addition, computer "networks" allow more possibilities for collaboration and peer teaching, especially when students' schedules don't
allow for more traditional face-to-face collaboration. But to do so,
students need to use the computer as more than a glorified typewriter. This means learning to compare multiple documents, access
information sources, use support programs, collaborate via e-mail or
networks, submit papers electronically, become desktop publishers,
and the like. Too often teachers in a computer classroom end up
answering closed questions such as "Does this sound right?" or "Is
this comma in the right place?" or "How do I get this to print out?"
Those are services we provide our students, but they don't contribute
to much active learning.

At the same time, we must teach students the limitations of writing by computer. These shortcuts have their drawbacks as well as their
benefits. Spell checkers and grammar programs, for instance, are helpful—but they can't tell you if you've typed "fiend" when you meant
"friend," or correct similar errors. They're relatively deaf to the
nuances of style—try putting a paragraph or two of Martin Luther
King's "Letter from Birmingham Jail" through a commercial style pro-

gram. Such programs equate mechanical correctness and stylistic homogeneity with "good writing." That's simplistic, and mechanistic.

One promising field is "hypertext"—a way of operating that enables computers to connect distantly related subjects, import visual and aural detail, and move their users between subjects and ideas in a non-linear way. In other words, they contradict the notion of "fixed texts." This enables students to explore wider realms of connections. On the other hand, there's no evidence yet that it makes them better writers. This technology shows promise, but it hasn't yet delivered. It's an object lesson: nifty tools don't necessarily make better writers. Whether you use computers in your classroom or not, you still have to teach students the basics of writing. Using computers may make writing faster and more convenient for students, but only a thorough knowledge of writing will make them better writers. The Bibliography provides a number of articles that offer varying perspectives on the uses and values of computers in the writing classroom.

Teaching in Progress

"E-Mail Teaching," by Rob Brault, University of Minnesota

Since I got wired for e-mail at home, I've been giving students my e-mail address so that they could contact me about papers. The few who did usually asked fairly quick questions about readings, assignments, or deadlines. During my last course, however, a student began what turned out to be a fairly long and detailed conversation. Our exchange took some nasty turns, but in the end we ironed things out and I learned some valuable points about the use of e-mail as a teaching medium.

The exchange started with an assignment in which students describe the career field they want to enter to a person outside that field. After handing back rough drafts with my comments, I received my first e-mail message from Linda. She wanted me to clarify some of my comments; since I no longer had the drafts, I responded from memory. Linda seemed resistant to the idea that she would ever have to write to people outside her field; some of her responses to me closed off the conversation instead of opening up ideas for discussion. Some of her comments seemed a bit confrontational, but I decided this would not be uncommon in a face-to-face conversation. I responded with quick, short comments, treating it as an informal conversation, and didn't edit it for tone.

When I checked my e-mail the next morning, Linda's second message had appeared. She appeared angrier and more confrontational than ever. She took exception to several of my questions and comments, called the assignment description "woefully inadequate," and said that if I had particular requirements for the assignment, she "should have been made aware of that fact more than 14 hours before the assignment was due." Clearly something was going wrong; Linda was obviously unhappy and I felt she was faulting my teaching. This time, I consulted some colleagues before responding. They agreed that the student was being pretty harsh, even unfair in her complaints, and we discussed some of the anxieties she must have felt and how I could react to her. I answered via e-mail a little later, trying to point out diplomatically that the questions I had asked were also present in the assignment. I also described how her criticisms made me feel, and suggested that we meet in person, since a "real" conversation might be easier to handle than a virtual one.

The next day I found a third message and read it with trepidation. To my surprise, Linda's response bore a completely different tone. She was much more respectful and considerate, she qualified her previous harsh criticisms, and I learned more about her perspectives on the assignment. Again, I waited a little before replying and tried to be as diplomatic and as positive as possible.

The trouble in this situation began, I think, with my expectations about e-mail conversations. Typically, such correspondence is treated as informal electronic notes, so a relaxed, conversational tone is often acceptable. When I responded to Linda's first message as if it were an informal conversation, I forgot about the power differential in our positions and the inevitable importance of a discussion that has or can have an impact on a student's grade. When I read Linda's third message, I was pleased to see that we had reached an understanding of our respective positions and of our shared concerns. About e-mail exchanges, I had discovered that while sometimes we can use a relaxed, conversational style, a writing teacher must always consider the power situations and remember that any written comments dealing with writing assignments, even on e-mail, are emotionally loaded and should be made as diplomatically and as seriously as any written assessment.

Scenario

You teach at a state university in a state that has just eliminated all "remedial courses" from the curricula at state-supported institutions. Those courses are now supposed to be taught in local community colleges. But to protect enrollment, your institution has decided to continue admitting students who would previously have been placed in basic writing classes, "mainstreaming" them into regular sections of composition. Because of the balky computer registration system, you have no idea who these students are until you get a diagnostic writing sample from them on the first day of class. Then you discover that your class of 23 students has at least eight you would consider to be basic writers, not to mention a visually-challenged student and a man who looks old and stern enough to be your grandfather. How will you handle the dynamics of this classroom?

PART

3

RESOURCES FOR WRITING TEACHERS

Anthology

Bibliography

Anthology

As composition and rhetoric studies expand, so does the list of materials a reflective teacher can consult. Below you'll find a sampling of what's out there for you to learn about. First comes a group of articles that reflect some of the most up-to-date thinking on the topics this book discusses, so that you will have a sense of the many perspectives and approaches that distinguish our profession. I've selected articles by experienced, current classroom teachers who are also scholars, since these most often represent a useful balance between theory and practice and provide additional bibliographic support.

David Bartholmae and Kenneth Bruffee provide overviews of how the academic community constructs itself and determines what knowledge it values, and George Gadda complicates the picture by adding in the factor of multicultural discourse styles. Richard Straub provides perspectives on responding to student writing. Lisa Ede and Andrea Lunsford offer reflections on audience and the negotiation of meaning, while Jeffrey Sommers and Chris Anson discuss portfolios as valuable tools for both students and teachers. Bob Schwegler confronts the political issues involved in reading student writing, while Alison Warriner discusses the dynamics of classrooms where students read each other's writing.

Next comes a series of articles that tie to specific kinds of praxis: Chris Anson and Richard Beach demonstrate journaling, Richard Raymond discusses revising strategies, Glynda Hull offers ways of helping students overcome errors, and John Dawkins presents an audience-centered method of teaching punctuation. Finally, Mickey Harris reminds us why students can benefit from having outside readers and tutors for their writing.

It's always hard to decide which articles to retain from edition to edition of this book. Since some of our past favorites are now anthologized in a number of places, I have made a number of wholesale changes in this edition. The old favorites are still listed in the bibliography, and still provide advice and strategies that haven't been superseded.

Finally, the bibliography lists the works cited in this text with additional titles bearing on its discussion. It has been divided into sections roughly corresponding to chapters in the text, but some would easily fit in more than one section, so skim all the relevant sections to find the ones you need to consult.

Inventing the University

David Bartholomae

> Education may well be, as of right, the instrument whereby every indi-
> vidual in a society like our own can gain access to any kind of dis-
> course. But we well know that in its distribution, in what it permits
> and in what it prevents, it follows the well-trodden battle-lines of
> social conflict. Every educational system is a political means of main-
> taining or of modifying the appropriation of discourse with the
> knowledge and the powers it carries with it.
>
> —FOUCAULT, *The Discourse on Language*

> ... the text is the form of the social relationships made visible, palpable,
> material.
>
> —BERNSTEIN, *Codes, Modalities and the
> Process of Cultural Reproduction: A Model*

I.

Every time a student sits down to write for us, he has to invent the university for the occasion—invent the university, that is, or a branch of it,
like history or anthropology or economics or English. The student has
to learn to speak our language, to speak as we do, to try on the peculiar ways of knowing, selecting, evaluating, reporting, concluding, and
arguing that define the discourse of our community. Or perhaps I
should say the *various* discourses of our community, since it is in the
nature of a liberal arts education that a student, after the first year or
two, must learn to try on a variety of voices and interpretive

schemes—to write, for example, as a literary critic one day and as an experimental psychologist the next; to work within fields where the rules governing the presentation of examples or the development of an argument are both distinct and, even to a professional, mysterious.

The student has to appropriate (or be appropriated by) a specialized discourse, and he has to do this as though he were easily and comfortably one with his audience, as though he were a member of the academy or an historian or an anthropologist or an economist; he has to invent the university by assembling and mimicking its language while finding some compromise between idiosyncracy, a personal history, on the one hand, and the requirements of convention, the history of a discipline, on the other. He must learn to speak our language. Or he must dare to speak it or to carry off the bluff, since speaking and writing will most certainly be required long before the skill is "learned." And this, understandably, causes problems.

Let me look quickly at an example. Here is an essay written by a college freshman.

> In the past time I thought that an incident was creative was when I had to make a clay model of the earth, but not of the classical or your everyday model of the earth which consists of the two cores, the mantle and the crust. I thought of these things in a dimension of which it would be unique, but easy to comprehend. Of course, your materials to work with were basic and limited at the same time, but thought help to put this limit into a right attitude or frame of mind to work with the clay.
>
> In the beginning of the clay model, I had to research and learn the different dimensions of the earth (in magnitude, quantity, state of matter, etc.) After this, I learned how to put this into the clay and come up with something different than any other person in my class at the time. In my opinion, color coordination and shape was the key to my creativity of the clay model of the earth.
>
> Creativity is the venture of the mind at work with the mechanics relay to the limbs from the cranium, which stores and triggers this action. It can be a burst of energy released at a precise time a thought is being transmitted. This can cause a frenzy of the human body, but it depends on the characteristics of the individual and how they can relay the message clearly enough through mechanics of the body to us as an observer. Then we must determine if it is creative or a learned process varied by the individuals thought process. Creativity is indeed

> a tool which has to exist, or our world will not succeed into the future
> and progress like it should.

I am continually impressed by the patience and goodwill of our students. This student was writing a placement essay during freshman orientation. The problem set to him was: "Describe a time when you did something you felt to be creative. Then, on the basis of the incident you have described, go on to draw some general conclusions about 'creativity.'" He knew that university faculty would be reading and evaluating his essay, and so he wrote for them.

In some ways it is a remarkable performance. He is trying on the discourse even though he doesn't have the knowledge that would make the discourse more than a routine, a set of conventional rituals and gestures. And he is doing this, I think, even though he knows he doesn't have the knowledge that would make the discourse more than a routine. He defines himself as a researcher working systematically, and not as a kid in a high school class: "I thought of these things in a dimension of . . ."; "I had to search and learn the different dimensions of the earth (in magnitude quantity, state of matter, etc.)." He moves quickly into a specialized language that is an approximation of our jargon), and draws both a general, textbook-like inclusion— "Creativity is the venture of the mind at work . . ."—and a resounding peroration—"Creativity is indeed a tool which has to exist, or our world will not succeed into the future and progress like it should." The writer has even picked up the rhythm of our prose with that last "indeed" and the qualifications and the parenthetical expressions of the opening paragraphs. And through it all he speaks with an impressive air of authority.

There is an elaborate but, I will argue, a necessary and enabling fiction work here as the student dramatizes his experience in a "setting"—the sting required by the discourse—where he can speak to us as a companion, a fellow researcher. As I read the essay, there is only one moment when the fiction is broken, when we are addressed differently. The student says, "Of course, your materials to work with were basic and limited at the same time, but thought help to put this limit into a right attitude or frame of mind to work with the clay." At this point, I think, we become students and he the teacher giving us a lesson (as in, "You take your pencil in your right hand and put your paper in front of you"). This is, however, one of the most characteristic slips of basic writers. (I use the term "basic writers" to refer to university students traditionally placed in remedial composition courses.) It is very hard for them to take on the role—the voice, the persona—of an authority whose authority is rooted in scholarship, analysis, or research. They slip, then, into a more immediately available and realizable voice of authority, the voice of a teacher giving a lesson or the voice of a parent lecturing at the dinner table. They offer advice or homilies rather than "academic" conclusions. There is a similar break in the final paragraph, where the conclusion that pushes for a definition ("Creativity is the venture of the mind at work with the mechanics relay to the limbs from the cranium") is replaced by a conclusion that speaks in the voice of an elder ("Creativity is indeed a tool which has to exist, or our world will not succeed into the future and progress like it should").

It is not uncommon, then, to find such breaks in the concluding sections of essays written by basic writers. Here is the concluding section of an essay written by a student about his work as a mechanic. He had been asked to generalize about work after reviewing an on-the-job experience or incident that "stuck in his mind" as somehow significant.

> How could two repairmen miss a leak? Lack of pride? No incentive? Lazy? I don't know.

At this point the writer is in a perfect position *to* speculate, to move from the problem to an analysis of the problem. Here is how the paragraph continues, however (and notice the change in pronoun reference).

> From this point on, I take my time, do it right, and don't let customers get under your skin. If they have a complaint, tell them to call your boss and he'll be more than glad to handle it. Most important, worry about yourself, and keep a clear eye on everyone, for there's always someone trying to take advantage of you *anytime and anyplace.* (Emphasis added)

We get neither a technical discussion nor an "academic" discussion but a Lesson on Life.[1] This is the language he uses to address the general question "How could two repairmen miss a leak?" The other brand of conclusion, the more academic one, would have required him to speak of his experience in our terms; it would, that is, have required

a special vocabulary, a special system of presentation, and an interpretive scheme (or a set of commonplaces) he could have used to identify and talk about the mystery of human error. The writer certainly
had access to the range of acceptable commonplaces for such an
explanation: "lack of pride," "no incentive," "lazy." Each commonplace
would dictate its own set of phrases, examples, and conclusions; and
we, his teachers, would know how to write out each argument, just as
we know how to write out more specialized arguments of our own. A
"commonplace," then, is a culturally or institutionally authorized
concept or statement that carries with it its own necessary elaboration. We all use commonplaces to orient ourselves in the world; they
provide points of reference and a set of "prearticulated" explanations
that are readily available to organize and interpret experience. The
phrase "lack of pride" carries with it its own account of the repair-
man's error, just as at another point in time a reference to "original sin"
would have provided an explanation, or just as in certain university
classrooms a reference to "alienation" would enable writers to continue and complete the discussion. While there is a way in which these
terms are interchangeable, they are not all permissible: A student in a
composition class would most likely be turned away from a discussion of original sin. Commonplaces are the "controlling ideas" of our
composition textbooks, textbooks that not only insist on a set form for
expository writing but a set view of public life.[2]

When the writer says, "I don't know," then, he is not saying that he
has nothing to say. He is saying that he is not in a position to carry on
this discussion. And so we are addressed as apprentices rather than as
teachers or scholars. In order to speak as a person of status or privilege,
the writer can either speak to us in our terms—in the privileged language of university discourse—or, in default (or in defiance) of that, he
can speak to us as though we were children, offering us the wisdom of
experience.

I think it is possible to say that the language of the "Clay Model"
paper has come *through* the writer and not from the writer. The writer
has located himself (more precisely, he has located the self that is represented by the "I" in the page) in a context that is finally beyond him,
not his own and not available to his immediate procedures for inventing and arranging text. I would not, that is, call this essay an example
of "writer-based" prose. I would not say that it is egocentric or that it
represents the "interior monologue or a writer thinking and talking to
himself" (Flower, 1981, p. 63). It is, rather, the record of a writer who has

lost himself in the discourse of his readers. There is a context beyond the intended reader that is not the world but a way of talking about the world, a way of talking that determines the use of examples, the possible conclusions, acceptable commonplaces, and key words for an essay on the construction of a clay model of the earth. This writer has entered the discourse without successfully approximating it.

Linda Flower (1981) has argued that the difficulty inexperienced writers have with writing can be understood as a difficulty in negotiating the transition between "writer-based" and "reader-based" prose. Expert writers, in other words, can better imagine how a reader will respond to a text and can transform or restructure what they have to say around a goal shared with a reader. Teaching students to revise for readers, then, will better prepare them to write initially with a reader in mind. The success of this pedagogy depends on the degree to which a writer can imagine and conform to a reader's goals. The difficulty of this act of imagination and the burden of such conformity are so much at the heart of the problem that a teacher must pause and take stock before offering revision as a solution. A student like the one who wrote the "Clay Model" paper is not so much trapped in a private language as he is shut out from one of the privileged languages of public life, a language he is aware of but cannot control.

II.

Our students, I've said, have to appropriate (or be appropriated by) a specialized discourse, and they have to do this as though they were easily or comfortably one with their audience. If you look at the situation this way, suddenly the problem of audience awareness becomes enormously complicated. One of the common assumptions of both composition research and composition teaching is that at some "stage" in the process of composing an essay a writer's ideas or his motives must be tailored to the needs and expectations of his audience. Writers have to "build bridges" between their point of view and the reader's. They have to anticipate and acknowledge the reader's assumptions and biases. They must begin with "common points of departure" before introducing new or controversial arguments. Here is what one of the most popular college textbooks says to students.

> Once you have your purpose clearly in mind, your next task is to define and analyze your audience. A sure sense of your audience—knowing

> who it is and what assumptions you can reasonably make about it—is
> crucial to the success of your rhetoric. (Hairston, 1978, p. 107)

It is difficult to imagine, however, how writers can have a purpose
before they are located in a discourse, since it is the discourse with its
projects and agendas that determines what writers can and will do.
The writer who can successfully manipulate an audience (or, to use a
less pointed language, the writer who can accommodate her motives
to her reader's expectations) is a writer who can both imagine and
write from a position of privilege. She must, that is, see herself within
a privileged discourse, one that already includes and excludes groups
of readers. She must be either equal to or more powerful than those she
would address. The writing, then, must somehow transform the political and social relationships between students and teachers.

If my students are going to write for me by knowing who I am—
and if this means more than knowing my prejudices, psyching me
out—it means knowing what I know; it means having the knowledge
of a professor of English. They have, then, to know what I know and
how I know what I know (the interpretive schemes that define the
way I would work out the problems I set for them); they have to learn
to write what I would write or to offer up some approximation of that
discourse. The problem of audience awareness, then, is a problem of
power and finesse. It cannot be addressed, as it is in most classroom
exercises, by giving students privilege and denying the situation of
the classroom—usually, that is, by having students write to an outsider, someone excluded from their privileged circle: "Write about 'To
His Coy Mistress,' not for your teacher but for the students in your
class"; "Describe Pittsburgh to someone who has never been there";
"Explain to a high school senior how best to prepare for college";
"Describe baseball to an Eskimo." Exercises such as these allow students to imagine the needs and goals of a reader, and they bring those
needs and goals forward as a dominant constraint in the construction
of an essay. And they argue, implicitly, what is generally true about
writing—that it is an act of aggression disguised as an act of charity.
What these assignments fail to address is the central problem of academic writing, where a student must assume the right of speaking to
someone who knows more about baseball or "To His Coy Mistress"
than the student does, a reader for whom the general commonplaces
and the readily available utterances about a subject are inadequate.

Linda Flower and John Hayes, in an often quoted article (1981), reported on a study of a protocol of an expert writer (an English teacher) writing about his job for readers of *Seventeen* magazine. The key moment for this writer, who seems to have been having trouble getting started, came when he decided that teenage girls read *Seventeen*; that some teenage girls like English because it is tidy ("some of them will have wrong reasons in that English is good because it's tidy—I can be a neat tidy little girl"), that some don't like it because it is "prim" and that, "By God, I can change that notion for them." Flower and Hayes's conclusion is that this effort of "exploration and consolidation" gave the writer "a new, relatively complex, rhetorically sophisticated working goal, one which encompasses plans for a topic, a persona, and the audience" (p. 383).[3]

Flower and Hayes give us a picture of a writer solving a problem, and the problem as they present it is a cognitive one. It is rooted in the way the writer's knowledge is represented in the writer's mind. The problem resides there, not in the nature of knowledge or in the nature of discourse but in a mental state prior to writing. It is possible, however, to see the problem as (perhaps simultaneously) a problem in the way subjects are located in a field of discourse.

Flower and Hayes divide up the composing process into three distinct activities: "planning or goal-setting," "translating," and "reviewing." The last of these, reviewing (which is further divided into two subprocesses "evaluating" and "revising"), is particularly powerful, for as a writer continually reviews his goals, plans, and the text he is producing, and as he continually generates new goals, plans, and text, he is engaging in a process of learning and discovery. Let me quote Flower and Hayes's conclusion at length.

> If one studies the process by which a writer uses a goal to generate ideas, then consolidates those ideas and uses them to revise or regenerate new, more complex goals one can see this learning process in action. Furthermore, one sees why the process of revising and clarifying goals has such a broad effect since it is through setting these new goals that the fruits of discovery come back to inform the continuing process of writing. In this instance, some of our most complex and imaginative acts can depend on the elegant simplicity of a few powerful thinking processes. We feel that a cognitive process explanation of discovery, toward which this theory is only a start, will have another special strength. By placing emphasis on the inventive power of the writer, who is asked to explore ideas, to develop, act on, test, and regen-

> erate his or her own goals, we are putting an important part of creativity where it belongs—in the hands of the working, thinking writer. (1981, p. 386)

While this conclusion is inspiring, the references to invention and creativity seem to refer to something other than an act of writing—if writing is, finally, words on a page. Flower and Hayes locate the act of writing solely within the mind of the writer. The act of writing, here, has a personal, cognitive history but not a history as a text, as a text that is made possible by prior texts. When located in the perspective afforded by prior texts, writing is seen to exist separate from the writer and his intentions; it is seen in the context of other articles in *Seventeen*, of all articles written for or about women, of all articles written about English teaching, and so on. Reading research has made it possible to say that these prior texts, or a reader's experience with these prior texts, have bearing on how the text is read. Intentions, then, are part of the history of the language itself. I am arguing that these prior texts determine not only how a text like the *Seventeen* article will be read but also how it will be written. Flower and Hayes show us what happens in the writer's mind but not what happens to the writer as his motives are located within our language, a language with its own requirements and agendas, a language that limits what we might say and that makes us write and sound, finally, also like someone else. If you think of other accounts of the composing process—and I'm thinking of accounts as diverse as Richard Rodriguez's *Hunger of Memory* (1983) and Edward Said's *Beginnings* (1975)—you get a very different account of what happens when private motive enters into public discourse, when a personal history becomes a public account. These accounts place the writer in a history that is not of the writer's own invention; and they are chronicles of loss, violence, and compromise.

It is one thing to see the *Seventeen* writer making and revising his plans for a topic, a persona, and an audience; it is another thing to talk about discovery, invention, and creativity. Whatever plans the writer had must finally have been located in language and, it is possible to argue, in a language that is persistently conventional and formulaic. We do not, after all, get to see the *Seventeen* article. We see only the elaborate mental procedures that accompanied the writing of the essay. We see a writer's plans for a persona; we don't see that persona in action. If writing is a process, it is also a product; and it is the product, and not the plan for writing, that locates a writer on the page, that locates him in a text and a style and the codes or conventions that make both of them readable.

Contemporary rhetorical theory has been concerned with the "codes" that constitute discourse (or specialized forms of discourse). These codes determine not only what might be said but also who might be speaking or reading. Barthes (1974), for example, has argued that the moment of writing, where private goals and plans become subject to a public language, is the moment when the writer becomes subject to a language he can neither command nor control. A text, he says, in being written passes through the codes that govern writing and becomes "de-originated," becomes a fragment of something that has "always been *already* read, seen, done, experienced" (p. 21). Alongside a text we have always the presence of "off-stage voices," the oversound of all that has been said (e.g., about girls, about English). These voices, the presence of the "already written," stand in defiance of a writer's desire for originality and determine what might be said. A writer does not write (and this is Barthes's famous paradox) but is, himself, written by the languages available to him.

It is possible to see the writer of the *Seventeen* article solving his problem of where to begin by appropriating an available discourse. Perhaps what enabled that writer to write was the moment he located himself as a writer in a familiar field of stereotypes: Readers of *Seventeen* are teenage girls; teenage girls think of English (and English teachers) as "tidy" and "prim," and, "By God, I can change that notion for them." The moment of eureka was not simply a moment of breaking through a cognitive jumble in that individual writer's mind but a moment of breaking into a familiar and established territory— one with insiders and outsiders; one with set phrases, examples, and conclusions.

I'm not offering a criticism of the morals or manners of the teacher who wrote the *Seventeen* article. I think that all writers, in order to write, must imagine for themselves the privilege of being "insiders"— that is, the privilege both of being inside an established and powerful discourse and of being granted a special right to speak. But I think that right to speak is seldom conferred on us—on any of us, teachers or students—by virtue of that fact that we have invented or discovered an original idea. Leading students to believe that they are responsible for something new or original, unless they understand what those words mean with regard to writing, is a dangerous and counterproductive practice. We do have the right to expect students to be active and engaged, but that is a matter of continually and stylistically working against the inevitable presence of conventional language; it is not matter of inventing a language that is new.

When a student is writing for a teacher, writing becomes more problematic than it was for the *Seventeen* writer (who was writing a version of the "Describe baseball to an Eskimo" exercise). The student, in effect, has to assume privilege without having any. And since students assume privilege by locating themselves within the discourse of a particular community—within a set of specifically acceptable gestures and commonplaces—learning, at least as it is defined in the liberal arts curriculum, becomes more a matter of imitation or parody than a matter of invention and discovery.

To argue that writing problems are also social and political problems is not to break faith with the enterprise of cognitive science. In a recent paper reviewing the tremendous range of research directed at identifying general cognitive skills, David Perkins (in press) has argued that "the higher the level of competence concerned," as in the case of adult learning, "the fewer general cognitive control strategies there are." There comes a point, that is, where "field-specific" or "domain-specific" schemata (what I have called "interpretive strategies") become more important than general problem solving processes. Thinking, learning, writing—all these become bound to the context of a particular discourse. And Perkins concludes:

> Instruction in cognitive control strategies tends to be organized around problem-solving tasks. However, the isolated problem is a creature largely of the classroom. The nonstudent, whether operating in scholarly or more everyday contexts, is likely to find himself or herself involved in what might be called "projects"—which might be anything from writing a novel to designing a shoe to starting a business.

It is interesting to note that Perkins defines the classroom as the place of artificial tasks and, as a consequence, has to place scholarly projects outside the classroom, where they are carried out by the "nonstudent." It is true, I think, that education has failed to involve students in scholarly projects, projects that allow students to act as though they were colleagues in an academic enterprise. Much of the written work that students do is test taking, report or summary—work that places them outside the official discourse of the academic community, where they are expected to admire and report on what we do, rather than inside that discourse, where they can do its work and participate in a common enterprise.[4] This, however, is a failure of teachers and curriculum designers, who speak of writing as a mode of learning but all too often represent writing as a "tool" to be used by an (hopefully) educated mind.

It could be said, then, that there is a bastard discourse peculiar to the writing most often required of students. Carl Bereiter and Marlene Scardamalia (in press) have written about this discourse (they call it "knowledge-telling"; students who are good at it have learned to cope with academic tasks by developing a "knowledge-telling strategy," and they have argued that insistence on knowledge-telling discourse undermines educational efforts to extend the variety of discourse schemata available to students.) What they actually say is this:

> When we think of knowledge stored in memory we tend these days to think of it as situated in three-dimensional space, with vertical and horizontal connections between sites. Learning is thought to add not only new elements to memory but also new connections and it is the richness and structure of these connections that would seem ... to spell the difference between inert and usable knowledge. On this account, the knowledge-telling strategy is educationally faulty because it specifically avoids the forming of connections between previously separated knowledge sites.[5]

It should be clear by now that when I think of "knowledge" I think of it as situated in the discourse that constitutes "knowledge" in a particular discourse community, rather than as situated in mental "knowledge sites." One can remember a discourse, just as one can remember an essay or the movement of a professor's lecture; but this discourse, in effect, also has a memory of its own, its own rich network of structures and connections beyond the deliberate control of any individual imagination.

There is, to be sure, an important distinction to be made between learning history, say, and learning to write as an historian. A student can learn to command and reproduce a set of names, dates, places, and canonical interpretations (to "tell" somebody else's knowledge); but this is not the same thing as learning to "think" (by learning to write) as an historian. The former requires efforts of memory; the latter requires a student to compose a text out of the texts that represent the primary materials of history and in accordance with the texts that define history as an act of report and interpretation.

Let me draw on an example from my own teaching. I don't expect my students to be literary critics when they write about *Bleak House*. If a literary critic is a person who wins publication in a professional journal (or if he or she is one who could), the students aren't critics. I do, however, expect my students to be, themselves, invented as literary critics by approximating the language of a literary critic writing about *Bleak House*. My students, then, don't invent the language of literary criticism (they don't, that is, act on their own) but they are, themselves, invented by it. Their papers don't begin with a moment of insight, a "by God" moment that is outside of language. They begin with a moment of appropriation, a moment when they can offer up a sentence that is not theirs as though it were their own. (I can remember when, as a graduate student, I would begin papers by sitting down to write literally in the voice—with the syntax and the key words—of the strongest teacher I had met.)

What I am saying about my students' essays is that they are approximate, not that they are wrong or invalid. They are evidence of a discourse that lies between what I might call the students' primary discourse (what the students might write about *Bleak House* were they not in my class or in any class, and were they not imagining that they were in my class or in any class—if you can imagine any student doing any such thing) and standard, official literary criticism (which is imaginable but impossible to find). The students' essays are evidence of a discourse that lies between these two hypothetical poles. The writing is limited as much by a student's ability to imagine "what might be said" as it is by cognitive control strategies.[6] The act of writing takes the student away from where he is and what he knows and allows him to imagine something else. The approximate discourse, therefore, is evidence of a change, a change that, because we are teachers, we call "development." What our beginning students need to learn is to extend themselves, by successive approximations, into the commonplaces, set phrases, rituals and gestures, habits of mind, tricks of persuasion, obligatory conclusions and necessary connections that determine the "what might be said" and constitute knowledge within the various branches of our academic community.[7]

Pat Bizzell is, I think, one of the most important scholars writing now on "basic writers" (and this is the common name we use for students who are refused unrestrained access to the academic community) and on the special characteristics of academic discourse. In a recent essay, "Cognition, Convention, and Certainty: What We Need to Know about Writing" (1982a), she looks at two schools of composition research and the way they represent the problems that writing poses for writers.[8] For one group, the "inner-directed theorists," the problems are internal, cognitive, rooted in the way the mind represents knowledge to itself. These researchers are concerned with discovering the "universal, fundamental structures of thought and language" and with developing pedagogies to teach or facilitate both basic, general cognitive skills and specific cognitive strategies, or heuristics, directed to serve more specialized needs. Of the second group, the "outer-directed theorists," she says that they are "more interested in the social processes whereby language-learning and thinking capacities are shaped and used in particular communities."

> The staple activity of outer-directed writing instruction will be analysis of the conventions of particular discourse communities. For example, a main focus of writing-across-the curriculum programs is to demystify the conventions of the academic discourse community. (1982a, p. 218)

The essay offers a detailed analysis of the way the two theoretical camps can best serve the general enterprise of composition research and composition teaching. Its agenda, however, seems to be to counter the influence of the cognitivists and to provide bibliography and encouragement to those interested in the social dimension of language learning.

As far as basic writers are concerned, Bizzell argues that the cognitivists' failure to acknowledge the primary, shaping role of convention in the act of composing makes them "particularly insensitive to the problems of poor writers." She argues that some of those problems, like the problem of establishing and monitoring overall goals for a piece of writing, can be

> better understood in terms of their unfamiliarity with the academic discourse community, combined, perhaps, with such limited experience outside their native discourse communities that they are unaware that there is such a thing as a discourse community with conventions to be mastered. What is underdeveloped is their knowledge both of the ways experience is constituted and interpreted in the academic discourse community and of the fact that all discourse communities constitute and interpret experience. (1982a, p. 230)

One response to the problems of basic writers, then, would be to determine just what the community's conventions are, so that those conventions could be written out, "demystified," and taught in our classrooms. Teachers, as a result, could be more precise and helpful when they ask students to "think," "argue," "describe," or "define." Another response would be to examine the essays written by basic writers—their approximations of academic discourse—to determine more clearly where the problems lie. If we look at their writing, and if we look at it in the context of other student writing, we can better see the points of discord that arise when students try to write their way into the university.

The purpose of the remainder of this chapter will be to examine some of the most striking and characteristic of these problems as they are presented in the expository essays of first-year college students. I will be concerned, then, with university discourse in its most generalized form—as it is represented by introductory courses—and not with the special conventions required by advanced work in the various disciplines. And I will be concerned with the difficult, and often violent, accommodations that occur when students locate themselves in a discourse that is not "naturally" or immediately theirs.

III.

I have reviewed 500 essays written, as the "Clay Model" essay was, in response to a question used during one of our placement exams at the University of Pittsburgh: "Describe a time when you did something you felt to be creative. Then, on the basis of the incident you have described, go on to draw some general conclusions about 'creativity.'" Some of the essays were written by basic writers (or, more properly, those essays led readers to identify the writers as basic writers); some were written by students who "passed" (who were granted immediate access to the community of writers at the university). As I read these essays, I was looking to determine the stylistic resources that enabled writers to locate themselves within an "academic" discourse. My bias as a reader should be clear by now. I was not looking to see how a writer might represent the skills demanded by a neutral language (a language whose key features were paragraphs, topic sentences, transitions, and the like—features of a clear and orderly mind). I was looking to see what happened when a writer entered into a language to locate himself (a textual self) and his subject; and I was looking to see how, once entered, that language made or unmade the writer.

Here is one essay. Its writer was classified as a basic writer and, since the essay is relatively free of sentence level errors, that decision must have been rooted in some perceived failure of the discourse itself:

> I am very interested in music, and I try to be creative in my interpretation of music. While in highschool, I was a member of a jazz ensemble. The members of the ensemble were given chances to improvise and be creative in various songs. I feel that this was a great experience for me, as well as the other members. I was proud to know that I could use my imagination and feelings to create music other than what was written.
>
> Creativity, to me, means being free to express yourself in a way that is unique to you, not having to conform to certain rules and guidelines. Music is only one of the many areas in which people are given opportunities to show their creativity. Sculpting, carving, building, art, and acting are just a few more areas where people can show their creativity.
>
> Through my music I conveyed feelings and thoughts which were important to me. Music was my means of showing creativity. In whatever form creativity takes, whether it be music, art, or science, it is an important aspect of our lives because it enables us to be individuals.

Notice the key gesture in this essay, one that appears in all but a few of the essays I read. The student defines as his own that which is a commonplace. "Creativity, to me, means being free to express yourself in a way that is unique to you, not having to conform to certain rules and guidelines." This act of appropriation constitutes his authority; it constitutes his authority as a writer and not just as a musician (that is, as someone with a story to tell). There were many essays in the set that told only a story—where the writer established his presence as a musician or a skier or someone who painted designs on a van, but not as a person at a remove from that experience interpreting it, treating it as a metaphor for something else (creativity). Unless those stories were long, detailed, and very well told—unless the writer was doing more than saying "I am a skier" or a musician or a van-painter—those writers were all given low ratings.

Notice also that the writer of the "Jazz" paper locates himself and his experience in relation to the commonplace (creativity is unique expression; it is not having to conform to rules or guidelines) regardless of whether the commonplace is true or not. Anyone who improvises "knows" that improvisation follows rules and guidelines. It is the power of the commonplace—its truth as a recognizable and, the writer believes, as a final statement—that justifies the example and completes the essay. The example, in other words, has value because it stands within the field of the commonplace.[9] It is not the occasion for what one might call an "objective" analysis or a "close" reading. It could also be said that the essay stops with the articulation of the commonplace. The following sections speak only to the power of that statement. The reference to "sculpting, carving, building, art, and acting" attests to the universality of the commonplace (and it attests the writer's nervousness with the status he has appropriated for himself—he is saying, "Now, I'm not the only one here who has done something unique"). The commonplace stands by itself. For this writer, it does not need to be elaborated. By virtue of having written it, he has completed the essay and established the contract by which we may be spoken to as equals: "In whatever form creativity takes, whether it be music, art, or science, it is an important aspect of our lives because it enables us to be individuals." (For me to break that contract, to argue that my life is not represented in that essay, is one way for me to begin as a teacher with that student in that essay.)

All of the papers I read were built around one of three commonplaces: (1) creativity is self-expression, (2) creativity is doing something new or unique, and (3) creativity is using old things in new ways. These are clearly, then, key phrases from the storehouse of things to say about creativity. I've listed them in the order of the students' ratings: A student with the highest rating was more likely to use number three than number one, although each commonplace ran across the range of possible ratings. One could argue that some standard assertions are more powerful than others, but I think the ranking simply represents the power of assertions within our community of readers. Every student was able to offer up an experience that was meant as an example of "creativity"; the lowest range of writers, then, was not represented by students who could not imagine themselves as creative people.[10]

I said that the writer of the "Jazz" paper offered up a commonplace regardless of whether it was true or not; and this, I said, was an instance of the power of a commonplace to determine the meaning of an example. A commonplace determines a system of interpretation that can be used to "place" an example within a standard system of belief. You can see a similar process at work in this essay.

During the football season, the team was supposed to wear the same type of cleats and the same type socks. I figured that I would change this a little by wearing my white shoes instead of black and to cover up the team socks with a pair of my own white ones. I thought that this looked better than what we were wearing, and I told a few of the other people on the team to change too. They agreed that it did look better and they changed there combination to go along with mine. After the game people came up to us and said that it looked very good the way we wore our socks, and they wanted to know why we changed from the rest of the team.

I feel that creativity comes from when a person lets his imagination come up with ideas and he is not afraid to express them. Once you create something to do it will be original and unique because it came about from your own imagination and if any one else tries to copy it, it won't be the same because you thought of it first from your own ideas.

This is not an elegant paper, but it seems seamless, tidy. If the paper on the clay model of the earth showed an ill fit between the writer and his project here the discourse seems natural, smooth. You could reproduce this paper and hand it out to a class, and it would take a lot of prompting before the students sensed something fishy and one of the more aggressive ones said something like, "Sure he came up with the idea of wearing white shoes and white socks. Him and Billy 'White-Shoes' Johnson. Come on. He copied the very thing he said was his own idea, 'original and unique.'"

The "I" of this text—the "I" who "figured," "thought," and "felt"—is located in a conventional rhetoric of the self that turns imagination into origination (I made it), that argues an ethic of production (I made it and it is mine), and that argues a tight scheme of intention (I made it because I decided to make it). The rhetoric seems invisible because it is so common. This "I" (the maker) is also located in a version of history that dominates classrooms, the "great man" theory: History is rolling along (the English novel is dominated by a central, intrusive narrative presence; America is in the throes of a Great Depression; during football season the team was supposed to wear the same kind of cleats and socks) until a figure appears, one who can shape history (Henry James, FDR, the writer of the "White Shoes" paper), and everything is changed. In the argument of the "White Shoes" paper, the history goes "I figured … I thought … I told … They agreed …" and, as a consequence, "I feel that creativity comes from when a person lets his imagination come up with ideas and he is not afraid to express them." The act of appropriation becomes a narrative of courage and conquest. The writer was able to write that story when he was able to imagine himself in that discourse. Getting him out of it will be a difficult matter indeed.

There are ways, I think, that a writer can shape history in the very act of writing it. Some students are able to enter into a discourse but, by stylistic maneuvers, to take possession of it at the same time. They don't originate a discourse, but they locate themselves within it aggressively, self-consciously. Here is another essay on jazz, which for sake of convenience I've shortened. It received a higher rating than the first essay on jazz.

> Jazz has always been thought of as a very original creative field in music. Improvisation, the spontaneous creation of original melodies in a piece of music, makes up a large part of jazz as a musical style. I had the opportunity to be a member of my high school's jazz ensemble for three years, and became an improvisation soloist this year. Throughout the years, I have seen and heard many jazz players, both professional and amateur. The solos performed by these artists were each flavored with that particular individual's style and ideas, along with some of the conventional premises behind improvisation. This particular type of solo work is creative because it is done on the spur of the moment and blends the performer's ideas with basic guidelines.
>
> I realized my own creative potential when I began soloing....
>
> My solos, just as all the solos generated by others, were original because I combined and shaped others' ideas with mine to create something completely new. Creativity is combining the practical knowledge and guidelines of a discipline with one's original ideas to bring about a new, original end result, one that is different from everyone else's. Creativity is based on the individual. Two artists can interpret the same scene differently. Each person who creates something does so by bringing out something individual in himself.

The essay is different in some important ways from the first essay on jazz. The writer of the second is more easily able to place himself in the context of an "academic" discussion. The second essay contains an "I" who realized his "creative potential" by soloing; the first contained an "I" who had "a great experience." In the second essay, before the phrase, "I had the opportunity to be a member of my high school's jazz ensemble," there is an introduction that offers a general definition of improvisation and an acknowledgment that other people have thought about jazz and creativity. In fact, throughout the essay the writer offers definitions and counterdefinitions. He is placing himself in the context of what has been said and what might be said. In the first paper, before a similar statement about being a member of a jazz ensemble, there was an introduction that locates jazz solely in the context of this individual's experience: "I am very interested in music." The writer of this first paper was authorized by who he is, a musician, rather than by what he can say about music in the context of what is generally said. The writer of the second essay uses a more specialized vocabulary; he talks about "conventional premises," "creative potential," "musical style," and "practical knowledge." And this is not just a matter of using bigger words, since these terms locate the experience in the context of a recognizable interpretive scheme—on the one hand there is tradition and, on the other, individual talent.

It could be said, then, that this essay is also framed and completed by a commonplace: "Creativity is combining the practical knowledge and guidelines of a discipline with one's original ideas to bring about a new, original end result, one that is different from everyone else's." Here, however, the argument is a more powerful one; and I mean "powerful" in the political sense, since it is an argument that complicates a "naive" assumption (it makes scholarly work possible, in other words), and it does so in terms that come close to those used in current academic debates (over the relation between convention and idiosyncracy or between rules and creativity). The assertion is almost consumed by the pleas for originality at the end of the sentence; but the point remains that the terms "original" and "different," as they are used at the end of the essay, are problematic, since they must be thought of in the context of "practical knowledge and guidelines of a discipline."

The key distinguishing gesture of this essay, that which makes it "better" than the other, is the way the writer works against a conventional point of view, one that is represented within the essay by conventional phrases that the writer must then work against. In his practice he demonstrates that a writer, and not just a musician, works within "conventional premises." The "I" who comments in this paper (not the "I" of the narrative about a time when he soloed) places himself self-consciously within the context of a conventional discourse about the subject, even as he struggles against the language of that conventional discourse. The opening definition of improvisation, where improvisation is defined as spontaneous creation, is rejected when the writer begins talking about "the conventional premises behind improvisation." The earlier definition is part of the conventional language of those who "have always thought" of jazz as a "very original creative field in music." The paper begins with what "has been said" and then works itself out against the force and logic of what has been said, of what is not only an argument but also a collection of phrases, examples, and definitions.

I had a teacher who once told us that whenever we were stuck for something to say, we should use the following as a "machine" for producing a paper: "While most readers of ____ have said ____, a close and careful reading shows that ____." The writer of the second paper on jazz is using a standard opening gambit, even if it is not announced with a flourish. The essay becomes possible when he sets himself against what must become a "naive" assumption—what "most people think." He has defined a closed circle for himself. In fact, you could say that he has laid the ground work for a discipline with its own key terms ("practical knowledge," "disciplinary guidelines," and "original ideas"), with its own agenda and with its own investigative procedures (looking for common features in the work of individual soloists).

The history represented by this student's essay, then, is not the history of a musician and it is not the history of a thought being worked out within an individual mind; it is the history of work being done within and against conventional systems.

In general, as I reviewed the essays for this study, I found that the more successful writers set themselves in their essays against what they defined as some more naive way of talking about their subject—against "those who think that . . ."—or against earlier, more naive versions of themselves—"once I thought that. . . ." By trading in one set of commonplaces at the expense of another, they could win themselves status as members of what is taken to be some more privileged group. The ability to imagine privilege enabled writing. Here is one particularly successful essay. Notice the specialized vocabulary, but notice also the way in which the text continually refers to its own language and to the language of others.

> Throughout my life, I have been interested and intrigued by music. My mother has often told me of the times, before I went to school, when I would "conduct" the orchestra on her records. I continued to listen to music and eventually started to play the guitar and the

clarinet. Finally, at about the age of twelve, I started to sit down and to try to write songs. Even though my instrumental skills were far from my own high standards. I would spend much of my spare time during the day with a guitar around my neck, trying to produce a piece of music.

Each of these sessions, as I remember them, had a rather set format. I would sit in my bedroom strumming different combinations of the five or six chords I could play, until I heard a series which sounded particularly good to me. After this, I set the music to a suitable rhythm (usually dependent on my mood at the time), and ran through the tune until I could play it fairly easily. Only after this section was complete did I go on to writing lyrics, which generally followed along the lines of the current popular songs on the radio.

At the time of the writing, I felt that my songs were, in themselves, an original creation of my own: that is, I, alone, made them. However, I now see that, in this sense of the word, I was not creative. The songs themselves seem to be an oversimplified form of the music I listened to at the time.

In a more fitting sense, however, I was being creative. Since I did not purposely copy my favorite songs, I was, effectively, originating my songs from my own process of creativity. To achieve my goal, I needed what a composer would call "inspiration" for my piece. In this case the inspiration was the current hit on the radio. Perhaps, with my present point of view, I feel that I used too much "inspiration" in my songs, but, at that time, I did not.

Creativity, therefore, is a process which, in my case, involved a certain series of "small creations" if you like. As well, it is something, the appreciation of which varies with one's point of view, that point of view being set by the person's experience, tastes, and his own personal view of creativity. The less experienced tend to allow for less originality, while the more experienced demand real originality to classify something a creation. Either way a term as abstract as this is perfectly correct and open to interpretations.

This writer is consistently and dramatically conscious of herself forming something to say out of what has been said and out of what she has been saying in the act of writing this paper. "Creativity" begins in this paper as "original creation." What she thought was "creativity," however, she now says was imitation; and, as she says, "in this sense of the word" she was not "creative." In another sense, however, she says that she was creative, since she didn't purposefully copy the songs but used them as "inspiration."

While the elaborate stylistic display—the pauses, qualifications, and the use of quotation marks—is in part a performance for our benefit, at a more obvious level we as readers are directly addressed in the first sentence of the last paragraph: "Creativity, therefore, is a process which, in my case, involved a certain series of 'small creations' if you like." We are addressed here as adults who can share her perspective on what she has said and who can be expected to understand her terms. It she gets into trouble after this sentence, and I think she does, it is because she doesn't have the courage to generalize from her assertion. Since she has rhetorically separated herself from her younger "self," and since she argues that she has gotten smarter, she assumes that there is some developmental sequence at work here and that, in the world of adults (which must be more complete than the world of children) there must be something like "real creativity." If her world is imperfect (if she can only talk about creation by putting the word in quotation marks), it must be because she is young. When she looks beyond herself to us, she cannot see our work as an extension of her project. She cannot assume that we too will be concerned with the problem of creativity and originality. At least she is not willing to challenge us on those grounds, to generalize her argument, and to argue that even for adults creations are really only "small creations." The sense of privilege that has allowed her to expose her own language cannot be extended to expose ours.

The writing in this piece—that is, the work of the writer within the essay—goes on in spite of, or against, the language that keeps pressing to give another name to her experience as a songwriter and to bring the discussion to closure. (In comparison, think of the quick closure of the "White Shoes" paper.) Its style is difficult, highly qualified. It relies on quotation marks and parody to set off the language and attitudes that belong to the discourse (or the discourses) that it would reject, that it would not take as its own proper location.

David Olson (1981) has argued that the key difference between oral language and written language is that written language separates both the producer and the receiver from the text. For my student writers, this means that they had to learn that what they said (the code) was more important than what they meant (the intention). A writer, in other words, loses his primacy at the moment of writing and must begin to attend to his and his words' conventional, even physical presence on the page. And, Olson says, the writer must learn that his authority is not established through his presence but through his absence—through his ability, that is, to speak as a god-like source beyond the limitations of any particular social or historical moment; to speak by means of the wisdom of convention, through the over-sounds of official or authoritative utterance, as the voice of logic or the voice of the community. He concludes:

> The child's growing competence with this distinctive register of language in which both the meaning and the authority are displaced from the intentions of the speaker and lodged in the text may contribute to the similarly specialized and distinctive mode of thought we have come to associate with literacy and formal education. (1981, p. 110)

Olson is writing about children. His generalizations, I think I've shown, can be extended to students writing their way into the academic community. These are educated and literate individuals, to be sure, but they are individuals still outside the peculiar boundaries of the academic community. In the papers I've examined in this chapter, the writers have shown an increasing awareness of the codes (or the competing codes) that operate within a discourse. To speak with authority they have to speak not only in another's voice but through another's code; and they not only have to do this, they have to speak in the voice and through the codes of those of us with power and wisdom; and they not only have to do this, they have to do it before they know what they are doing, before they have a project to participate in, and before, at least in terms of our disciplines, they have anything to say. Our students may be able to enter into a conventional discourse and speak, not as themselves, but through the voice of the community; the university, however, is the place where "common" wisdom is only of negative values—it is something to work against. The movement toward a more specialized discourse begins (or, perhaps, best begins) both when a student can define a position of privilege, a position that sets him against a "common" discourse, and when he or she can work self-consciously, critically, against not only the "common" code but his or her own.

IV.

Pat Bizzell, you will recall, argues that the problems of poor writers can be attributed both to their unfamiliarity with the conventions of academic discourse and to their ignorance that there are such things as discourse communities with conventions to be mastered. If the latter is true, I think it is true only in rare cases. All the student writers I've discussed (and, in fact, most of the student writers whose work I've seen) have shown an awareness that something special or something different is required when one writes for an academic classroom. The essays that I have presented in this chapter all, I think, give evidence of writers trying to write their way into a new community. To some degree, however, all of them can be said to be unfamiliar with the conventions of academic discourse.

Problems of convention are both problems of finish and problems of substance. The most substantial academic tasks for students learning history or sociology or literary criticism are matters of many courses, much reading and writing, and several years of education. Our students, however, must have a place to begin. They cannot sit through lectures and read textbooks and, as a consequence, write as sociologists or write literary criticism. There must be steps along the way. Some of these steps will be marked by drafts and revisions. Some will be marked by courses, and in an ideal curriculum the preliminary courses would be writing courses, whether housed in an English department or not. For some students, students we call "basic writers," these courses will be in a sense the most basic introduction to the language and methods of academic writing.

Our students, as I've said, must have a place to begin. If the problem of a beginning is the problem of establishing authority, of defining rhetorically or stylistically a position from which one may speak, then the papers I have examined show characteristic student responses to that problem and show levels of approximation or stages in the development of writers who are writing their way into a position of privilege.

As I look over the papers I've discussed, I would arrange them in the following order: the "White Shoes" paper; the first "Jazz" essay; the "Clay Model" paper; the second "Jazz" essay; and, as the most successful paper, the essay on "Composing Songs." The more advanced essays for me, then are those that are set against the "naive" codes of "everyday" life. (I put the terms "naive" and "everyday" in quotation marks because they are, of course, arbitrary terms.) In the advanced essays one can see a writer claiming an "inside" position of privilege by rejecting the language and commonplaces of a "naive" discourse, the language of "outsiders." The "I" of those essays locates itself against one discourse (what it claims to be a naive discourse) and approximates the specialized language of what is presumed to be a more powerful and more privileged community. There are two gestures present, then—one imitative and one critical. The writer continually audits and pushes against a language that would render him "like everyone else" and mimics the language and interpretive systems of the privileged community.

At a first level, then, a student might establish his authority by simply stating his own presence within the field of a subject. A student, for example, writes about creativity by telling a story about a time he went skiing. Nothing more. The "I" on the page is a skier, and skiing stands as a representation of a creative act. Neither the skier nor skiing are available for interpretation; they cannot be located in an essay that is not a narrative essay (where skiing might serve metaphorically as an example of, say, a sport where set movements also allow for a personal style). Or a student, as did the one who wrote the "White Shoes" paper, locates a narrative in an unconnected rehearsal of commonplaces about creativity. In both cases, the writers have finessed the requirement to set themselves against the available utterances of the world outside the closed world of the academy. And, again, in the first "Jazz" paper, we have the example of a writer who locates himself within an available commonplace and carries out only rudimentary procedures for elaboration, procedures driven by the commonplace itself and not set against it. Elaboration, in this latter case, is not the opening up of a system but a justification of it.

At a next level I would place student writers who establish their authority by mimicking the rhythm and texture, the "sound," of academic prose, without there being any recognizable interpretive or academic project under way. I'm thinking, here, of the "Clay Model" essay. At an advanced stage. I would place students who establish their authority as writers; they claim their authority, not by simply claiming that they are skiers or that they have done something creative, but by placing themselves both within and against a discourse, or within and against competing discourses, and working self consciously to claim an interpretive project of their own, one that grants them their privilege to speak. This is true, I think, in the case of the second "Jazz" paper and, to a greater degree, in the case of the "Composing Songs" paper.

The levels of development that I've suggested are not marked by corresponding levels in the type or frequency of error, at least not by the type of frequency of sentence-level error. I am arguing, then, that a basic writer is not necessarily a writer who makes a lot of mistakes. In fact, one of the problems with curricula designed to aid basic writers is that they too often begin with the assumption that the key distinguishing feature of a basic writer is the presence of sentence-level error. Students are placed in courses because their placement essays show a high frequency of such errors, and those courses are designed with the goal of making those errors go away. This approach to the problems of the basic writer ignores the degree to which error is less often a constant feature than a marker in the development of a writer. A student who can write a reasonably correct narrative may fall to pieces when faced with a more unfamiliar assignment. More important, however, such courses fail to serve the rest of the curriculum. On every campus there is a significant number of college freshmen who require a course to introduce them to the kinds of writing that are required for a university education. Some of these students can write correct sentences and some cannot; but, as a group, they lack the facility other freshmen possess when they are faced with an academic writing task.

The "White Shoes" essay, for example, shows fewer sentence-level errors than the "Clay Model" paper. This may well be due to the fact that the writer of the "White Shoes" paper stayed well within safe, familiar territory. He kept himself out of trouble by doing what he could easily do. The tortuous syntax of the more advanced papers on my list is a syntax that represents a writer's struggle with a difficult and unfamiliar language, and it is a syntax that can quickly lead an inexperienced writer into trouble. The syntax and punctuation of the "Composing Songs" essay, for example, shows the effort that is required when a writer works against the pressure of conventional discourse. If the prose is inelegant (although I confess I admire those dense sentences) it is still correct. This writer has a command of the linguistic and stylistic resources—the highly embedded sentences, the use of parentheses and quotation marks—required to complete the act of writing. It is easy to imagine the possible pitfalls for a writer working without this facility.

There was no camera trained on the "Clay Model" writer while he was writing, and I have no protocol of what was going through his mind, but it is possible to speculate on the syntactic difficulties of sentences like these: "In the past time I thought that an incident was creative was when I had to make a clay model of the earth, but not of the classical or your everyday model of the earth which consists of the two cores, the mantle and the crust. I thought of these things in a dimension of which it would be unique, but easy to comprehend." The syntactic difficulties appear to be the result of the writer's attempt to use an unusual vocabulary and to extend his sentences beyond the boundaries of what would have been "normal" in his speech or writing. There is reason to believe, that is, that the problem was with *this* kind of sentence, in this context. If the problem of the last sentence is that of holding together the units "I thought," "dimension," "unique" and "easy to comprehend," then the linguistic problem was not a simple matter of sentence instruction. I am arguing, then, that such sentences fall apart not because the writer lacked the necessary syntax to glue the pieces together but because he lacked the full statement within which these key words were already operating. While writing, and in the thrust of his need to complete the sentence, he had the key words but not the utterance. (And to recover the utterance, I suspect, he would need to do more than revise the sentence.) The invisible conventions, the prepared phrases remained too distant for the statement to be completed. The writer would have needed to get inside of a discourse that he could in fact only partially imagine. The act of constructing a sentence, then, became something like an act of transcription in which the voice on the tape unexpectedly faded away and became inaudible.

Shaughnessy (1977) speaks of the advanced writer as one who often has more facile but still incomplete possession of this prior discourse. In the sense of the advanced writer, the evidence of a problem is the presence of assonant, redundant, or imprecise language, as in a sentence such as this: "so education can be *total*, it must be *continuous*." Such a student, Shaughnessy says, could be said to hear the "melody of formal English" while still unable to make precise or exact distinctions. And, she says,

> the pre-packaging feature of language, the possibility of taking over phrases and whole sentences without much thought about them, threatens the writer now as before. The writer, as we have said, inherits the language out of which he must fabricate his own messages. He is therefore in a constant tangle with the language, obliged to recognize its public communal nature and yet driven to invent out of this language his own statements. (1977, pp. 207-208)

For the unskilled writer, the problem is different in degree and not in kind. The inexperienced writer is left with a more fragmentary record of the comings and goings of academic discourse. Or, as I said above, he or she often uses the key words without the complete statements within which they are already operating.

Let me provide one final example of this kind of syntactic difficulty in another piece of student writing. The writer of this paper seems to be able to sustain a discussion only by continually repeating his first step, producing a litany of strong, general, authoritative assertions that trail quickly into confusion. Notice how the writer seems to stabilize his movement through the paper by returning again and again to recognizable and available commonplace utterances. When he has to move away from them, however, away from the familiar to statements that would extend those utterances, where he, too, must speak, the writing—that is, both the syntax and the structure of the discourse—falls to pieces.

> Many times the times drives a person's life depends on how he uses it. I would like to think about if time is twenty-five hours a day rather than twenty-four hours. Some people think it's the boaring or some people might say it's the pleasure to take one more hour for their life. But I think the time is passing and coming, still we are standing on same position. We should use time as best as we can use about the good way in our life. Everything we do, such as sleep, eat, study, play and doing something for ourselves. These take the time to do and we could find the individual ability and may process own. It is the important for us and our society. As time going on the world changes therefore we are changing, too. When these situation changes we should follow the suitable case of own. But many times we should decide what's the better way to do so by using time. Sometimes like this kind of situation can cause the success of our lives or ruin. I think every individual of his own thought drive how to use time. These affect are done from environmental causes. So we should work on the better way of our life recognizing the importance of time.

There is a general pattern of disintegration when the writer moves off from standard phrases. This sentence, for example, starts out coherently and then falls apart: "*We should use time as best as we can use about the good way in our life.*" The difficulty seems to be one of extending those standard phrases or of connecting them to the main subject reference, "time" (or "the time," a construction that causes many of the problems in the paper). Here is an example of a sentence that shows, in miniature, this problem of connection: "*I think every individual* of his own thought drive how to use *time.*"

One of the remarkable things about this paper is that, in spite of all the syntactic confusion, there is the hint of an academic project here. The writer sets out to discuss how to creatively use one's time. The text seems to allude to examples and to stages in an argument, even if in the end it is all pretty incoherent. The gestures of academic authority, however, are clearly present, and present in a form that echoes the procedures in other, more successful papers. The writer sets himself against what "some people think"; he speaks with the air of authority: "But I think.... Everything we do ... When these situation changes...." And he speaks as though there were a project underway, one where he proposes what he thinks, turns to evidence, and offers a conclusion: "These affect are done from environmental causes. So we should work...." This is the case of a student with the ability to imagine the general outline and rhythm of academic prose but without the ability to carry it out, to complete the sentences. And when he gets lost in the new, in the unknown, in the responsibility of his own commitment to speak, he returns again to the familiar ground of the commonplace.

The challenge to researchers, it seems to me, is to turn their attention again to products, to student writing, since the drama in a student's essay, as he or she struggles with and against the languages of our contemporary life, is as intense and telling as the drama of an essay's mental preparation or physical production. A written text, too, can be a compelling model of the "composing process" once we conceive of a writer as at work within a text and simultaneously, then, within a society, a history, and a culture.

It may very well be that some students will need to learn to crudely mimic the "distinctive register" of academic discourse before they are prepared to actually and legitimately do the work of the discourse, and before they are sophisticated enough with the refinements of tone and gesture to do it with grace or elegance. To say this, however, is to say that our students must be our students. Their initial progress will be marked by their abilities to take on the role of privilege, by their abilities to establish authority. From this point of view, the student who wrote about constructing the clay model of the earth is better prepared for his education than the student who wrote about playing football in white shoes, even though the "White Shoes" paper is relatively error-free and the "Clay Model" paper is not. It will be hard to pry loose the writer of the "White Shoes" paper from the tidy, pat discourse that allows him to dispose of the question of creativity in such a quick and efficient manner. He will have to be convinced that it is better to write sentences he might not so easily control, and he will have to be convinced that it is better to write muddier and more confusing prose (in order that it may sound like ours), and this will be harder than convincing the "Clay Model" writer to continue what he has already begun.

ACKNOWLEDGMENTS

Preparation of this chapter was supported by the Learning Research and Development Center of the University of Pittsburgh, which is supported in part by the National Institute of Education.

Notes

1. David Olson (1981) has made a similar observation about school-related problems of language learning in younger children. Here is his conclusion: "Hence, depending upon whether children assumed language was primarily suitable for making assertions and conjectures or primarily for making direct or indirect commands, they will either find school texts easy or difficult" (p. 107).

2. For Aristotle, there were both general and specific commonplaces. A speaker, says Aristotle, has a "stock of arguments to which he may turn for a particular need."

> If he knows the *topoi* (regions, places, lines or argument)—and a skilled speaker will know them—he will know where to find what he wants for a special case. The general topics, or commonplaces are regions containing arguments that are common to all branches of knowledge.... But there are also special topics (regions, places, *loci*) in which one looks for arguments appertaining to particular branches of knowledge, special sciences, such as ethics or politics. (1932, pp. 154-155)

And, he says, "the topics or places, then, may be indifferently thought of as in the science that is concerned, or in the mind of, the speaker." But the question of location is indifferent" only if the mind of the speaker is in line with set opinion, general assumption. For the speaker (or writer) who is not situated so comfortably in the privileged public realm, this is indeed not an indifferent matter at all. If he does not have the commonplace at hand, he will not, in Aristotle terms, know where to go at all.

3. Pat Bizzell has argued that the *Seventeen* writer's process of goal-setting

> can be better understood if we see it in terms of writing for a discourse community. The initial problem . . . is to find a way to include these readers in a discourse community for which he is comfortable writing. He places them in the academic discourse community by imagining the girls as students. . . . Once he has included them in a familiar discourse community, he can find a way to address them that is common in the community he will argue with them, putting a new interpretation on information they possess in order to correct misconceptions. (1982a, p. 228)

4. See Bartholomae (1979, 1983) and Rose (1983) for articles on curricula designed to move students into university discourse. The movement to extend writing "across the curriculum" is evidence of a general concern for locating students within the work of the university; see Bizzell (1982a) and Maimon *et al*. (1981) For longer works directed specifically at basic writing, see Ponsot and Deen (1982) and Shaughnessy (1977). For a book describing a course for more advanced students, see Coles (1978).

5. In spite of my misgivings about Bereiter and Scardamalia's interpretation of the cognitive nature of the problem of "inert knowledge," this is an essay I regularly recommend to teachers. It has much to say about the dangers of what seem to be "neutral" forms of classroom discourse and provides, in its final section, a set of recommendations on how a teacher might undo discourse conventions that have become part of the institution of teaching.

6. Stanley Fish (1980) argues that the basis for distinguishing novice from expert readings is the persuasiveness of the discourse used to present and defend a given reading. In particular, see the chapter. "Demonstration vs. Persuasion: Two Models of Critical Activity" (pp. 356-37).

7. Some students, when they come to the university, can do this better than others. When Jonathan Culler says, "the possibility of bringing someone to see that a particular interpretation is a good one assumes shared points of departure and common notions of how to read," he is acknowledging that teaching, at least in English classes, has had to assume that students

be students, ready to some degree participating in the structures of reading and writing that constitute English studies (quoted in Fish, 1980, p.
366).

Stanley Fish tells us "not to worry" that students will violate our enterprise by offering idiosyncratic readings of standard texts:

> The fear of solipsism, of the imposition by the unconstrained self of
> its own prejudices, is unfounded because the self does not exist apart
> from the communal or conventional categories of thought that
> enable its operations (of thinking, seeing, reading). Once we realize
> that the conceptions that fill consciousness, including any concep-
> tion of its own status, are culturally derived, the very notion of an
> unconstrained self, of a consciousness, wholly and dangerously free,
> becomes incomprehensible. (1980, p. 335)

He, too, is assuming that students, to be students (and not "dangerously
free"), must be members in good standing of the community whose
immediate head is the English teacher. It is interesting that his parenthetical catalogue of the "operations" of thought, "thinking, seeing, reading,"
excludes writing, since it is only through written records that we have
any real indication of how a student thinks, sees, and reads. (Perhaps
"real" is an inappropriate word to use here, since there is certainly a "real"
intellectual life that goes on, independent of writing. Let me say that
thinking, seeing, and reading are valued in the academic community *only*
as they are represented by extended, elaborated written records.) Writing,
I presume, is a given for Fish. It is the card of entry into this closed community that constrains and excludes dangerous characters. Students who
are excluded from this community are students who do poorly on written
placement exams or in freshman composition. They do not, that is, move
easily into the privileged discourse of the community, represented by the
English literature class.

8. My debt to Bizzell's work should be evident everywhere in this essay. See
   also Bizzell (1978, 1982b) and Bizzell and Herzberg (1980).
9. Fish says the following about the relationship between student and an
   object under study:

> We are not to imagine a moment when my students "simply see" a
> physical configuration of atoms and then assign that configuration
> a significance according to the situation they happen to be in. To be
> in the situation (this or any other) is to "see" with the eyes of its

interests, its goals. its understood practices, values, and norms, and so to be conferring significance by seeing, not after it. The categories of my students' vision are the categories by which they understand themselves to be functioning as students ... and objects will appear to them in forms related to that way of functioning rather than in some objective or preinterpretive form. (1980, p. 334)

10. I am aware that the papers given the highest rankings offer arguments about creativity and originality similar to my own. If there is a conspiracy here, that is one of the points of my chapter. I should add that my reading of the "content" of basic writers' essays is quite different from Lunsford's (1980).

References

Aristotle. (1932). *The Rhetoric of Aristotle* (L. Cooper, Trans.). Englewood Cliffs. NJ: Prentice-Hall.

Barthes, R. (1974). S/Z (R. Howard. Trans.). New York: Hill & Wang.

Bartholomae, D. (1979). Teaching basic writing: An alternative to basic skills. *Journal of Basic Writing, 2*, 85-109.

Bartholomae, D. (1983). Writing assignments: Where writing begins. In P. Stock (Ed.). *Fforum* (pp. 300-312). Montclair, NJ: Boynton/Cook.

Bereiter, C. & Scardamalia, M. (in press). Cognitive coping strategies and the problem of "inert knowledge." In S. S. Chipman. J. W. Segal. & R. Glaser (Eds.). *Thinking and learning skills: Research and open questions* (Vol. 2). Hillsdale, NJ: Erlbaum.

Bizzell, P. (1978). The ethos of academic discourse. *College Composition and Communication, 29*, 351-355.

Bizzell, P. (1982a). Cognition, convention, and certainty: What we need to know about writing. *Pre/text, 3*, 213–244.

Bizzell, P. (1982b). College composition: Initiation into the academic discourse community. *Curriculum Inquiry, 72*, 191-207.

Bizzell, P., & Herzberg, B. (1980). "Inherent" ideology, "universal" history, "empirical" evidence, and context-free writing: Some problems with E. D. Hirsch's *The Philosophy of Composition. Modern Language Notes, 95*, 1181-1202.

Coles, W. E., Jr. (1978). *The plural I.* New York: Holt, Rinehart & Winston.

Fish, S. (1980). *Is there a text in this class? The authority of interpretive communities.* Cambridge, MA: Harvard University Press.

Flower, L. S. (1981). Revising writer—based prose. *Journal of Basic Writing, 3*, 62-74.

Flower, L. & Hayes, I. (1981). A cognitive process theory of writing. *College Composition and Communication, 32*, 365-387.

Hairston, M. (1978). *A contemporary rhetoric.* Boston: Houghton Mifflin.

Lunsford, A. A. (1980). The content of basic writers' essays. *College Composition and Communication, 31*, 278-290.

Maimon, E. P., Belcher, G. L., Heam. G. W., Nodine, B. F., & O'Connor. F. X. (1981). *Writing in the arts and sciences.* Cambridge, MA: Winthrop.

Olson, D. R. (1981). Writing: The divorce of the author from the text. In B. M. Kroll & R. I. V., (Eds.), *Exploring speaking-writing relationships: Connections and contrasts.* Urbana, IL: National Council of Teachers of English.

Perkins, D. N. (in press). General cognitive skills: Why not? In S. S. Chipman, J. W. Segal, & R. Glas (Eds.), *Thinking and learning skills: Research and open questions* (Vol. 2). Hillsdale, NJ: Erlbaum.

Ponsot, M., & Deen. R. (1982). *Beat not the poor desk.* Montclair, NJ: Boynton/Cook.

Rodriguez, R. (1983). *Hunger of memory.* New York: Bantam.

Rose, M. (1983). Remedial writing courses: A critique and a proposal. *College English, 45*, 109-128

Said, E. W. (1975). *Beginnings: Intention and method.* Baltimore: The Johns Hopkins University Press.

Shaughnessy, M. (1977). *Errors and expectations.* New York: Oxford University Press.

Social Construction, Language, and the Authority of Knowledge: A Bibliographical Essay

Kenneth A. Bruffee

Until a very few years ago, I had never heard the term "social construction." Much less had I become acquainted with its implications for scholars and instructors of literature and composition, or its implications for those of us interested in broader educational issues such as the future of humanistic studies and liberal education in general.

During the past three or four years, pursuing some of these implications, I discovered that social constructionist thought can positively affect the way we address professional issues that increasingly interest many of us today. But I also discovered that attempts to address these issues in this way are limited because many of us—myself included—have not yet read deeply enough the relevant scholarly literature.

Kenneth A. Bruffee is professor of English and director of the honors program at Brooklyn College. He was for four years a member of the editorial board of *Liberal Education*. His publications include *Elegiac Romance* and several articles in *College English*. His *Short Course in Writing* was recently published in its 3rd edition.

In this respect we are not alone. Although social construction has a venerable history in twentieth-century thought and although writers in a number of fields are engaged in an effort to develop the disciplinary implications of a nonfoundational social constructionist understanding of knowledge, that history remains largely unacknowledged and the effort fragmented. Terminology proliferates. The result is that in some cases positions not only similar but mutually supportive seem alien to one another. Writers find it difficult to draw upon each other's work to pursue their own more effectively. Many of the most sophisticated and knowledgeable texts that I discuss in this essay—not only work in literary criticism and composition studies but in philosophy and the social sciences—evidence a lack of awareness of fertile, suggestive, parallel work in other fields.

One cause of this situation is that there seems to exist no bibliographical guide that brings social constructionist texts together in one place, presents them as a coherent school of thought, and offers guidance to readers wending their way through unfamiliar territory. This is the need I hope this essay will fill.

An Introduction to Social Construction

Most of us have encountered the assumptions of social construction at one time or another under other rubrics: "new pragmatism," for example, or "dialogism," or even simply "Kuhn." Recent social constructionist thought was sparked some twenty years ago, in fact, by Thomas Kuhn's *Structure of Scientific Revolutions,* Kuhn is widely known for his controversial understanding of change in scientific knowledge. Scientific change occurs, Kuhn argues, in a revolutionary rather than an evolutionary way. Scientists don't add to an evergrowing pile of received truth. They trade in old "paradigms" of thought and adopt new ones. This in any case is the reading of Kuhn that most of us are familiar with. It is a highly domesticated reading, however, emphasizing the least challenging aspect of Kuhn's book. Considerably more challenging is the understanding of the nature of scientific knowledge itself that Kuhn's conception of paradigmatic change is based on.

Kuhn's understanding of scientific knowledge assumes that knowledge is, as he puts it on the last page of his book, "intrinsically the common property of a group or else nothing at all" (201). For most of us, the most seriously challenging aspect of Kuhn's work is its social constructionist epistemological assumptions. A social constructionist position in any discipline assumes that entities we normally call reality, knowledge, thought, facts, texts, selves, and so on are constructs generated by communities of like-minded peers. Social construction understands reality, knowledge, thought, facts, texts, selves, and so on as community-generated and community-maintained linguistic entities—or, more broadly speaking, symbolic entities—that define or "constitute" the communities that generate them, much as the language of the *United States Constitution*, the *Declaration of Independence*, and the Gettysburg Address in part constitutes the political, the legal, and to some extent the cultural community of Americans.

The publication and widespread discussion of Kuhn's book was seminal in the recent development of this line of thought. Since then, Richard Rorty's *Philosophy and the Mirror of Nature*, synthesizing the ideas of Dewey, Heidegger, and Wittgenstein, has generalized Kuhn. Whereas Kuhn says that scientific knowledge is a social construct, Rorty says that all knowledge is a social construct.

Rorty's book demonstrates that although social constructionist thought has only recently been discussed beyond the rather arcane limits of academic philosophy and the history and philosophy of science, it has been responsible for placing the assumptions of the traditional cognitive theory of knowledge in serious question for almost a century. Thus, as a way of thinking that challenges traditional views, social construction claims a formidable modernist pedigree. This fact alone suggests the value of reading the central texts of social constructionist thought for literary critics and literary historians. An understanding of modernism and modernist literature that does not take social constructionist thought into account inevitably remains limited.

As any reader discovers right away, the contemporary scholarly literature of social constructionist thought is highly diverse. Some implications for academic disciplines of understanding knowledge as (in Rorty's phrase) "socially justified belief" are found in books and articles written in fields such as psychology, sociology, political science, and philosophy as well as literary criticism. But from whatever disciplinary quarter they may reach us, some of the implications of social construction have the potential to lead English teachers to seriously rethink many of our disciplinary and professional interests, values, goals, and practices.

An example of the disciplinary and professional implications of social construction is suggested by the anthropologist Clifford Geertz in his 1983 collection of essays, *Local Knowledge*. Geertz observes that "the hallmark of modern consciousness" is an "enormous multiplicity" of cultural mores and cultural values. Most college and university instructors need only to look at the backgrounds of the students who populate our classrooms to see the truth of this observation. Modern cultural diversity or multiplicity being the case, Geertz regards as "a chimera" the traditional goal of liberal studies that most of us have been brought up on, to provide "a general orientation . . . growing out of humanistic studies . . . and shaping the direction of culture." He points out convincingly that "not only is the class basis for such a unitary 'humanism' completely absent . . . the agreement on the foundations of scholarly authority . . . has disappeared" (161).

It is not hard to find illustrations of this profound and growing lack of agreement among humanists. One is the discussion by literary critics of the status of the received literary "canon." Those who challenge the traditional canon suggest that what we think of as "literature" these days already includes a diversity of texts that the likes of, say, Matthew Arnold would never have considered. Another illustration is the debate between textual critic Jerome McGann and those who hew to the position of Fredson Bowers. Those who challenge the strict empiricism of the Bowers approach to textual criticism argue that published works are more reasonably regarded as the product of a community made up of the author and the author's friends, editor, and publisher than they are of a single individual of genius.

From Geertz's social constructionist point of view, therefore, humanistic scholarship and liberal education must be modernized. To do this, he says, humanists will need to develop "a critical consciousness" that leaves behind what he calls "the epistemological complacency of traditional humanism" (23, 44). In its place, we must learn to conceive "of cognition, emotion, motivation, perception, imagination, memory . . . whatever"—entities we normally think of as strictly individual, internal, and mental affairs—"as themselves, and directly, social affairs" (153).

This statement, describing as social in origin what we normally regard as individual, internal, and mental, summarizes succinctly the social constructionist understanding of knowledge in general and, in particular, what we do as scholars, researchers, and college or university instructors whatever our field of expertise. Our scholarship and research and our role as classroom instructors are all themselves, and directly, social affairs. For many of us it is only when we see the implications of social constructionist assumptions spelled out in everyday professional life in this way that they may begin to seem, to say the least, exotic and perhaps downright nonsensical and dangerous. Asked to describe what we do by an on-the-street reporter, most of us would not be likely to characterize our scholarship, our research, and our performance as classroom instructors as "social affairs."

But despite this healthy skepticism, it seems to me of the greatest importance that scholars and teachers in English and in the humanities in general make an effort to suspend judgment and give some consideration to social constructionist thought as a potentially fertile conceptual resource. There are two reasons for making this effort, one disinterested, the other unabashed professional self-interest.

The first reason is the disinterested desire we all share to improve our understanding and expertise as scholars and teachers. Social constructionist thought offers a strikingly fruitful alternative to the way we normally think and talk about what we do. Normally, the language that most of us use to discuss and write about scholarship, research, and college or university instruction is cognitive in derivation. It is based on the foundational premises of traditional—mainly Cartesian—epistemology. This means that the way we normally think about our professional work as scholars and teachers derives from the epistemological tradition that every academic field of study has followed since at least the seventeenth century.

The depth to which we remain members of that tradition is evident in the degree to which the language we use to talk about knowledge, scholarship, research, and college or university instruction is saturated with visual metaphors. We find them all but impossible to escape. Even such a basic and almost indispensable term as "theory" implies a "viewing." "Theory" has the same etymological root as "theater." We "contemplate" (another "viewing"), we talk about "insights," we "imagine." We "admire" the "brilliance" of some people's work and deplore the "dullness" of others. And in this essay when I have "clearly" and "lucidly" explained my "point of view," I naturally hope that every reader will "get the picture" and exclaim, "I see!"

According to the social constructionist view, this visual metaphor, inherent and unavoidable in cognitive thought, accounts for the fact that so much of what we normally say about knowledge, scholarship, research, and college or university instruction is confined within a frustrating circularity oscillating between "outer" and "inner" poles of "objectivity" and "subjectivity." This polarity of cognitive language derives from the traditional epistemological notion that the human mind is equipped with two working elements, a mirror and an inner eye. The mirror reflects outer reality. The inner eye contemplates that reflection. Reflection and contemplation together are what, from this cognitive point of view, we typically call thought or knowledge.

The significance of this visual metaphor buried in our cognitive terminology may best be suggested by contrasting several aspects of our normal account of knowledge with the alternative offered by social construction. First, one of the important assumptions of cognitive thought is that there must be a universal foundation, a ground, a base, a framework, a structure of some sort behind knowledge or beneath it, upon which what we know is built, assuring its certainty or truth. We normally think of that ground or structure as residing either in the inner eye (a concept, an idea, a theory), or in nature as mirrored in the mind (the world, reality, facts). The social constructionist alternative to this foundational cognitive assumption is non-foundational. It assumes that there is no such thing as a universal foundation, ground, framework, or structure of knowledge. There is only an agreement, a consensus arrived at for the time being by communities of knowledgeable peers. Concepts, ideas, theories, the world, reality, and facts are all language constructs generated by knowledge communities and used by them to maintain community coherence.

Social construction does not of course deny the obvious, that, as Rorty puts it, "we are shoved around by physical reality." But it does stress that there is a difference between "contact with" something and "dealing with" something. The latter is what we call knowledge; the former is not. Furthermore, we do not generate knowledge, the social constructionist says, by "dealing with" the physical reality that shoves us around. We generate knowledge by "dealing with" our *beliefs* about the physical reality that shoves us around. Specifically, we generate knowledge by justifying those beliefs socially.

A second assumption we make when we talk in cognitive terms about knowledge involves reification of our unconfirmed and unconfirmable inferences about what happens in the "black box" of the mind. We assume that terms such as "cognitive processes," "conceptual frameworks," "intellectual development," "higher order reasoning," and so on, refer to universal, objectifiable, and perhaps even measurable entities. Social constructionist thought does not make this assumption. It assumes, on the contrary, that such terms do not refer to anything universal, objectifiable, or measurable. Rather, they are a way of talking about a way of talking. Social construction assumes, that is, that thinking is an internalized version of conversation. Anything we say about the way thinking works is conversation about another conversation: talk about talk. Social construction regards terms such as "cognitive processes," "conceptual frameworks," "intellectual development," "higher order reasoning," and even "idea" and "objectivity," as social constructs. They are representative terms of a particular vernacular language, a language that constitutes a certain community of knowledgeable peers of which, in fact, most college and university instructors, myself included, are confirmed members.

A third assumption we make when we talk in cognitive terms about what we do is that the individual self is the matrix of all thought: "I think, therefore I am." A great idea is the product exclusively of a single great mind. Each of us studies to make knowledge "our own." And so on. In contrast, social construction assumes that the matrix of thought is not the individual self but some community of knowledgeable peers and the vernacular language of that community. That is, social construction understands knowledge and the authority of knowledge as community-generated, community-maintaining symbolic artifacts. Indeed, some social constructionists go so far in their nonfoundationalism as to assume, along with the sociologist Erving Goffman for example, that even what we think of as the individual self is a construct largely community generated and community maintained.

A fourth assumption we make when we talk in cognitive terms about knowledge and what we do is that there is something inherently problematical about knowledge. The issue in this case is not that some things are complex or hard to learn, but that anything we might try to know is by its nature inaccessible. This situation is familiar to many of us from philosophy as being the key to "the problems of modern philosophy"—problems of the relation between mind and body, subjectivity vs. objectivity, and so on.

The inherently problematical nature of knowledge from the cognitive point of view is that the visual metaphor of cognitive theory provides no necessary connection between the mind's two pieces of equipment, the inner mirror and the inner eye. There is a gap between them that cognitive theory offers no help in bridging. Worse, the cognitive metaphor describes those two pieces of equipment as being so different in format and operation that they seem unconnectable—as if one were made by Apple and the other by IBM. This difference and lack of connection between the two pieces of mental equipment plays an important role in modern scholarly and intellectual life. Most modern "skepticism" as a philosophical position trades on emphasizing the gap between them. The presumed coherence of most cognitive and developmentalist thought and research, and the presumed coherence of most of our discussions about scholarship, research, and college and university instruction, depends on assiduously and self-defeatingly ignoring it.

The advantage of social constructionist thought is not that it provides some miraculous solution to the problems assumed by cognitive thought as inherent in the nature of knowledge. Social construction denies that the problems are inherent in the nature of knowledge, regarding them as inherent merely in the visual metaphor that informs cognitive thought. Begin thinking about knowledge as a social construct rather than a function of ocular equipment in a mental "black box," the social constructionist says, and the problems no longer exist. Naturally, new problems arise in their place. But it is possible to take the position that since knowledge is identical with language and other symbol systems, the problems presented by social constructionist thought are of a sort that humanists in general and English teachers in particular are especially well equipped to cope with, if not solve.

Obviously, then, the disinterested reason why English scholars and teachers and other humanists should examine the potential of social construction dovetails with our professional self-interest. For language, literature, and composition teachers especially, the cognitive understanding of knowledge has always been of limited value because it places language on the margin of knowledge as a mere medium or conduit—a set of "skills" by which "ideas" are "communicated" or "transmitted" from one individual mind to another. The social constructionist alternative identifies knowledge and language and regards them as inseparable. Placing language at the center of our understanding of knowledge and of the authority of knowledge, it thereby places reading and writing unequivocally where (in my professionally self-interested opinion) it belongs, at the center of the liberal arts curriculum and the whole educational process.

Furthermore, this relocation of reading and writing at the center of liberal education provides in turn a new way of thinking constructively about the purpose and practice of liberal education generally that makes its relevance to the life of future generations compelling.

During the past 75 years the benefits of the debate in cognitive terms about education—with its ethnocentric emphasis on universals and absolutes, its endless circularity oscillating between the "subjective" and the "objective," its alienating emphasis on individuality, and its need to continually ignore, suppress, or sidestep the unbridgeable abyss inherent in our cognitive vocabulary between learner and what is learned—has become increasingly dubious. It is arguable that pursuing this debate may in fact no longer be the best way to discover what, today, education must do—prepare us to live in the "enormous multiplicity" of our world that Geertz calls attention to. Social construction offers a language with which to cope with that diverse, rapidly changing world, a world in which relations between people and things have become subordinate in importance and long-range effect to relations among people and among communities of people. And on the latter, on relations among diverse—and frequently a good deal less than mutually sympathetic—communities of people, our very survival depends.

General Accounts

Readers just beginning to explore social construction will find a thorough introduction to the basic issues in Kenneth J. Gergen's "The Social Constructionist Movement in Modern Psychology." In this article, Gergen explains social constructionist principles and summarizes their history. Beyond this, as the title indicates, Gergen is interested in implications for his own field. He concludes, however, by speculating on the potential "variety of interesting changes [that] may be anticipated in the character of professional life" in general, with the further development of social constructionist thought (273). As a result, much that he says is readily applicable to English studies. Supplementing Gergen's outline, two articles of my own, "The Structure of Knowledge and the Future of Liberal Education" and "Liberal Education and the Social Justification of Belief," place social constructionist thought in the context of the ongoing debate on liberal education, offer a precis of Rorty's argument in *Philosophy and the Mirror of Nature,* and speculate on some possible curricular implications.

Readers who prefer to begin their study of social construction with primary sources may find the following sequence somewhat increases the accessibility of these texts: Kuhn's *The Structure of Scientific Revolutions,* Geertz's *Local Knowledge,* and Rorty's *Philosophy and the Mirror of Nature.*

Kuhn seems to be the father of current social constructionist thought insofar as direct influence is concerned. Behind Kuhn lies Wittgenstein, and behind Rorty (who generalizes Kuhn) lie Wittgenstein, Heidegger, and Dewey. George Herbert Mead anticipated much social constructionist thought but had little influence. Kuhn's thesis, roughly speaking, is that scientific knowledge is a social construct, not a discovery of "what is really there." Knowledge is identical with the symbol system (i.e., the language) in which it is formulated. The community of knowledgeable peers constituted by that symbol system constructs knowledge by justifying it socially, that is, by arriving at a sort of consensus. Knowledge ceases to be knowledge when the community disbands or its members die.

I also recommend reading the debate over Kuhn's terms that occurred after the first edition of his book was published. The relevant bibliographical citations appear in notes 3 and 4 on page 174 of the second edition.

Clifford Geertz's essays are a useful companion to Kuhn, because Geertz shows how readily Kuhn's view of scientific knowledge applies to other fields. Geertz's recent collection of essays, *Local Knowledge,* may be read in light of the discussion of knowledge understood as a social construct that he develops throughout several chapters of his earlier collection, *The Interpretation of Cultures.* Geertz argues in anthropological language what Rorty argues in philosophical language: "Human thought is consummately social: social in its origins, social in its functions, social in its forms, social in its applications" (360). Geertz develops this line of thinking most explicitly in "The Growth of Culture and the Evolution of Mind," "The Impact of the Concept of Culture on the Concept of Man," and parts IV and V of "Ideology as a Cultural System."

In *Local Knowledge,* published a decade after *The Interpretation of Cultures,* Geertz takes the issue of a social understanding of knowledge beyond anthropology to other fields, in particular the humanities and law. The book challenges undergraduate liberal education as currently practiced, but the challenge lies submerged beneath tactful treatment of, among others, Lionel Trilling. Dangerous edges of the iceberg are visible only rarely, for example with reference to traditional views of the nature and value of the humanities such as those expressed by, among others, Max Black (160-61).

The core of the book is a polite and tactful debate between Geertz and Lionel Trilling that occurred at the very end of Trilling's life. For the fullest understanding of the implications of Local *Knowledge* for liberal education and literary criticism, I suggest reading the chapters in the order they were originally published:

1. Chapter 3, supplemented and developed in chapters 4, 5, and 6.
2. Lionel Trilling's unfinished, posthumously published reply to chapter 3, "Why We Read Jane Austen," not included in the book.
3. Chapter 2, Geertz's response to Trilling's reply.
4. Chapters 1, 7, 8, and the Introduction, which develop the argument sketched in chapter 2.

Because Kuhn and Geertz raise the main issues of social construction in readable ways, they provide background for approaching Richard Rorty's *Philosophy and the Mirror of Nature*, the central text in the current discussion of the nature and authority of knowledge. Rorty's thesis is that "we understand knowledge when we understand the social justification of belief, and thus have no need to view it as accuracy of representation" (170). Portions of this book may be difficult for people lacking, as I do, fluency in the vernacular of twentieth-century Anglo-American analytical philosophy. But it is worth the effort. I recommend reading it backwards, Part III followed by Parts II and I, because Part III is especially accessible if you have read Kuhn.

For the purposes of non-philosophers, Rorty's book is perhaps most interesting as an essay on the history of ideas in the tradition of A. O. Lovejoy's *The Great Chain of Being*. I cribbed Rorty's argument earlier in this essay in saying that the controlling metaphor in "modern philosophy"—that is, Western philosophy since Descartes—views the human mind as a locale furnished with two pieces of equipment: a "Mirror of Nature" reflecting external reality and an "Inner Eye" comprehending that reflection. Rorty deconstructs this metaphor, in the sense that he takes it apart and leaves the bits and pieces around to be swept away or rust. He does so, he says, because the metaphor locks thought about knowledge (including theory of knowledge, cognitive psychology, and the philosophy and psychology of education) into a futile circularity. It leads to unresolvable problems about an irreducible inner something (variously called the self, subjectivity, feelings, reason, form, intellect, transcendent reality, and so on) and an irreducible outer something (variously called the world, things, reality, objectivity, nature, facts, and so on).

That the two pieces of metaphorical mental equipment are unrelated and unrelatable is the third element in the post-Cartesian mental equipment package (seldom directly named but sometimes referred to obliquely as an abyss, alienation, sin, anomie, the indeterminacy of knowledge, the inability "really" to know, and so on). Attempts to make the connection almost always turn out to be band-aid operations, although sometimes highly celebrated ones. Rorty suggests that we put behind us circular efforts to explain knowledge driven by this cognitive apparatus and talk instead about what is involved in knowledge understood as a social construct, about which we still have a great deal to learn.

His argument has three main tributaries, Wittgenstein, Heidegger, and Dewey. There is not yet to my knowledge a secondary source that explores social constructionist aspects of Dewey's thought in a way that gives nonphilosophers much help beyond Rorty's explanation. There is some help to be had with Wittgenstein and Heidegger. In *Wittgenstein: A Social Theory of Knowledge,* David Bloor explores one aspect of Wittgenstein that Rorty's argument draws on. Bloor also derives a useful set of categories for developing Wittgenstein's notion of language-game communities from the anthropologist Mary Douglas.

Charles B. Guignon takes on Heidegger in a similarly helpful way. For members of the huge, diffuse community loosely defined by adherence to the British tradition of empirical, analytical thought, as most of us are willy-nilly, Heidegger is at first a more difficult nut to crack than Wittgenstein. Guignon gives a ready explanation of the historical and conceptual relationships between Heidegger's masterwork, *Being and Time,* and the cognitive epistemological tradition.

Community Specific Accounts

It is tempting to regard the material in the sections that follow as offering practical applications of theory developed by Kuhn, Rorty, and Geertz. The tendency to classify our knowledge into "theory" and "practice" has its source in the cognitive understanding of knowledge. Cognitive thought assumes a vertical, hierarchical relation between theory and practice. It regards theory or concept making, products of the mind's "inner eye," as the more privileged, more powerful level of thought. And it regards practical application, a function of the "mirror of nature," as less privileged and less powerful. Theory is said to "ground" and sanction practice. Practice is said merely to be ways of behaving or methods of doing things that are grounded and sanctioned by—that is, are the "consequence" of—theory. The categories "theory" and "practice" implicitly express, therefore, what Stanley Fish calls "theory hope" (Mitchell 112). "Theory hope" is the belief that whatever a theory sanctions us to do is surely correct, whatever we learn under its aegis surely true, and whatever results we get using its methods are surely valid.

I would argue, however, that the categories used in this essay, "general" and "community specific" accounts, do not imply "theory hope." The distinction between the community specific texts that follow and the foregoing general accounts is not vertical or hierarchical, but horizontal. For the sake of convenience I use the term "general accounts" for texts that state and explain assumptions of nonfoundational social constructionist thought. I use the term "community specific accounts" for texts that make those assumptions tacitly and, as Fish puts it, "put [them] to work as an interpretive 'window'" for a particular knowledge community (Mitchell 130).

An example may clarify how social constructionist assumptions can be put to work as an "interpretive 'window.'" Michael Ignatieff's The *Needs* of *Strangers* does not, as it happens, fit neatly into any of the categories below because the knowledge community it addresses encompasses several disciplines. Drawing on sources in literature, religion, and philosophy, Ignatieff begins an important effort to account in terms of the history of social and political thought for what has brought us to think of ourselves and our knowledge in nonfoundational social constructionist rather than Cartesian foundational or cognitive terms.

Ignatieff's book quietly assumes that political, social, and emotional (or "spiritual") "needs are historical" (138). It also assumes that "human nature is historical" (14), and that, as a result, from time to time as languages and the communities they constitute change, some human emotional needs may "lack language adequate to their expression." When this happens, Ignatieff says, these human needs "do not simply pass out of speech: they may cease to be felt." This inability to express, and thus possibly the inability even to feel, certain basic human needs may be a serious, socially and personally disrupting affliction. As the title of the book suggests, words that particularly concern Ignatieff, "words like fraternity, belonging and community," have become for many of us today "so soaked with nostalgia and utopianism that they are nearly useless as guides to the real possibilities of civic solidarity" (138). To the degree that we are unable to use such words seriously, we have in effect dropped them from the vocabulary of the vernacular language that constitutes us as a community of civilized human beings. Lacking the language, we tend to lack the feelings as well.

What led to this situation, Ignatieff suggests, is that in the Enlightenment we lost irretrievably one of the two freedoms human beings had treasured. The one we kept and enhanced was the political and social freedom to choose. The one we lost, except in a restricted, local sense, was the freedom implicit in what Ignatieff calls the sense of having chosen correctly: the freedom we derived from certainties of religious belief that were obviated by the Enlightenment.

Ignatieff does not counsel trying to regain this pre-Enlightenment freedom; it is for most of us most of the time, as he says, quite irretrievable. Instead he explores the results of the loss. In chapters on *King Lear,* Augustine, Hume, Rousseau, and Adam Smith, Ignatieff defines what he sees as the immediate task. The challenge for him is social and political, growing, as it does for Geertz, out of the "enormous multiplicity"—the vast cultural diversity—of modern life. "Modern society," Ignatieff says, "is changing the locus of belonging.... We need justice, we need liberty, and we need as much solidarity as can be reconciled with justice and liberty. But we also need, as much as anything else, language adequate to the times we live in" (139, 141). The language Ignatieff seeks is a community vernacular that in some world-encompassing way will delineate a "home" for our "claims of difference," so that "our common identity" as human beings together can "begin to find its voice" (131). Robert N. Bellah's *Habits of the Heart* develops a related theme by documenting the difficulty Americans have translating individualistic "freedom from" into "commitment to" consensus and cooperative action.

Most of the texts listed below are clearly more discipline-specific than Ignatieff's book, and the communities they address are more clearly defined. The value to scholars and teachers interested in literary critical texts, composition studies, and undergraduate education generally will be apparent. The value to us of the texts addressed to academic psychologists, sociologists, political scientists, and philosophers may be less obvious. In my view, these are useful because they offer us language we can in many cases adapt to discussion in diverse fields, including English studies.

Literary Studies

There are currently two lines of social constructionist thought in literary criticism and literary history. One of these follows the work of

Mikhail Bakhin, a mid-twentieth century Soviet social construction-ist literary critic and contemporary of the Soviet social construction-ist child psychologist, Lev Vygotsky. Throughout Bakhtin's work, as in for example the essay, "Discourse in the Novel," Bakhtin stresses the "voices" in literary language, especially the language of fiction, that are traceable to a diversity of social groups and that result in what he calls the "dialogic" quality of literary language.

The other current line of social constructionist literary criticism follows Rorty's synthesis. Rorty himself, in "Criticism without Theory," especially in its "MLA Version," and in his contribution to Mitchell suggests that literary critics should assume no general or a priori truths about the nature of literature and language and no "grounds" underlying the critical discussion of literature. They should maintain that literature is a social artifact, but they should not assume that that understanding of literature is the "real truth" from which certain "consequences" inevitably follow. Literary criticism, Rorty sug-gests, should adopt the position that to regard literature in a social constructionist way opens some interesting, intellectually and aes-thetically rewarding lines of conversation that literary critics may not have taken before. That position, Rorty says, will lead us to "an Homeric, narrative style" of critical discourse (Rorty, "MLA" 1), a style that sketches a certain context, puts some texts in that context, and then describes the advantages that seem to accrue from having done so (Mitchell 134).

An approach related to Rorty's, calling itself, following the name Rorty uses for his philosophical critique, the "new pragmatism," is most clearly stated in the work of Stanley Fish. Fish argues in *Is There a Text in This Class? The Authority of Interpretive Communities* that "interpretive communities" construct authoritative interpretations of literary texts through a process similar to Rorty's social justification of belief. The relevant section of the book is Part Two, pages 303-71. The views of Rorty and Fish together have provoked a dispute over the nature and value of theoretical discussion in literary studies. These views challenge some of our most basic assumptions not only about the nature of interpretation, but about the profession of literary criti-cism and literary history, and, indeed, about the study of the humani-ties in general. The "new pragmatist" position on relevant professional issues has been most provocatively stated in an essay by Steven Knapp and Walter Benn Michaels. Both the Knapp-Michaels essay and responses to it are conveniently collected in Mitchell's *Against Theory*.

Jerome McGann's social constructionist view of textual criticism in *A Critique of Modern Textual Criticism* follows the lead of Rorty and Fish. In doing so, it pointedly documents Geertz's remark in *Local Knowledge* that "agreement on the foundations of scholarly authority" in the humanities "has disappeared." McGann's argument attacks established empirical doctrine and methods based on the work of Fredson Bowers, which is epistemologically cognitive in its assumptions. McGann takes Fish's position that the meaning of a text is a social construct a step further by arguing that the very text itself in its final hard copy version is a community generated artifact. The " 'mode of existence of a literary work of art,' " McGann says, "is fundamentally social rather than personal," since " 'final authority' for literary works rests neither with the author nor with his affiliated institution [in most cases, the publisher]; it resides in the actual structure of the agreements which these two cooperating authorities reach in specific cases" (8, 54).

Composition Studies

Most work done today on composition tends to be either empirical or rhetorical. Almost all of it is cognitive in its assumptions. The difference between saying that language *has* a social context and that language *is* a social construct defines a key difference between cognitive and social constructionist work in composition. Cognitive work is based on the assumption that writing is primarily an individual act. A writer's language originates within the inner reaches of the individual mind. We use language primarily to express ideas generated in the mind and to communicate them to other individual human minds in the "social context."

In contrast, social constructionist work in composition is based on the assumption that writing is primarily a social act. A writer's language originates with the community to which he or she belongs. We use language primarily to join communities we do not yet belong to and to cement our membership in communities we already belong to.

Rigorously nonfoundational social constructionist research and writing in composition studies is not easy to come by. The search is made easier by John Trimbur's annotated bibliography, "Collaborative Learning and Teaching Writing." Some of the most suggestive social constructionist work is by the mid-twentieth century Soviet social constructionist student of child development, Lev Vygotsky, whose *Thought and Language* and *Mind in Society* are books that many composition teachers are already familiar with. James Wertsch's *Vygotsky and the Social Formation of Mind* develops further implications of Vygotsky's thought. Vygotsky demonstrated experimentally the socio-linguistic process by which children learn to think analytically. His thesis is that we learn to use language instrumentally, "talking through" our tasks with another person and then internalizing that conversation as thought. In this way writing re-externalizes the language of internalized conversation. My "Writing and Reading as Collaborative or Social Acts" and *Short Course in Writing* make tentative gestures to explore the possibilities of this way of thinking about composition, some of the implications of which I have discussed in "Collaborative Learning and 'The Conversation of Mankind.'"

Perhaps the most scholarly social constructionist work in composition that I am aware of is Greg Myers's "The Social Construction of Two Biologists' Proposals." This essay explains in detail how changes occur (or fail to occur) in scientific knowledge through gradually negotiated changes in the language of what scientists write. A related essay by Myers traces the career of an article by each of two prominent biologists through comment by five journal editors and rejection by four of them (both essays were published on the fifth submission), together with the authors' revisions in response to comment. Myers demonstrates the extent to which what these scientists actually knew gradually changed as the community of knowledgeable peers they belonged to demanded change in the language of the articles they were writing. Myers's work complements a growing body of social constructionist work on scientific knowledge, much of it being done in Britain. An example that treats scientists' conversation as well as their writing—including scientific jokes, "proto-jokes," satire, and other forms of humor—is Gilbert and Mulkay's *Opening Pandora's Box*.

Myers and Gilbert and Mulkay document modern instances of the principles developed historically in Anderson's *Between the Library and the Laboratory*. Anderson accounts for changes in language used in talking about physical matter in eighteenth-century France during the period in which the vernacular of the phlogiston theory began giving way to the recognizably scientific vernacular of modern chemistry. Anderson shows how, during this transitional period, Lavoisier's arguments introduced a new category of inquiry using the same rhetorical manner and, with few exceptions, the same vocabulary the phlogistonists used. "The real field of inquiry" involved in the new category of study, Anderson argues, is "not primarily the laboratory; much of the difficult work is performed first through [the] process of refining the language in which the question is asked" (96). Thus chemistry became in the eighteenth-century what Myers shows that biology is today: a language exercise or, more broadly speaking, a symbol-system exercise. "The real difference between the work of [the phlogistonist] Macquer and Lavoisier," Anderson says, "grows out of [a] shift of emphasis away from seeing science as an individual operation performed on a language to one in which language sets the parameters for the writers"—that is, in which the language they write determines what they know (23).

Social Sciences

It is perhaps inevitable that social scientists should have been among the first to understand the importance and pursue the implications of social construction. Their work is of interest to English scholars and teachers because it offers terms and ideas adaptable to social constructionist approaches in literary criticism, literary history, and composition studies. John Shotter's *Social Accountability and Selfhood* is an example of this adaptability. What Shotter calls the "accounts" of human action that communities "give of themselves in their everyday social life" are roughly equivalent to Rorty's social justification of belief. Much that he says about these "accounts" might be applied directly to the study of, say, narrative fiction. The book's history of social constructionist thought from Vico to modern times in Chapter 8 is also of value.

Kenneth Gergen's *Toward Transformation in Social Knowledge* and Rom Harre's *Personal Being* both develop the case for a social-constructionist understanding of knowledge in the social sciences. Harre argues in particular that "the self" is a social construct. From the point of view of English teachers and other humanists interested in exploring implications of social construction, an especially useful feature of Harre's book is the "research menu" at the end of each chapter. Collectively, these demonstrate how very much we still have to learn when we adopt social constructionist assumptions. They also offer valuable suggestions for future study.

In *The Social Construction of Mind,* Jeff Coulter considers the implications of social constructionist thought for the social sciences in general, but especially for sociology. Much as Rorty argues that "we understand knowledge when we understand the social justification of belief," Coulter argues that we understand best other people's "subjective" states and processes (such as understanding, intending, remembering, being "high" on drugs, and being "mentally ill") not by postulating "mentalistic elements or psychological constructions of the individual" but by understanding the "socially available resources furnished by the culture," that is, by understanding ordinary linguistic and other symbolic usage (34).

Unlike sociologists, but like literary critics, political scientists seem only now to be taking up issues raised by social construction. What happens when authority regarded as a social construct is turned by political communities—that is, by governments—into power? What is the nature of that power, how is it wielded, how is it to be controlled, and how does it affect our everyday lives?

These issues are important because the assumptions and implications of nonfoundational social construction strike some people as politically dangerous. I suggest in response to comment on "Collaborative Learning and 'The Conversation of Mankind'" that it is on the contrary foundational notions that have proven to be politically dangerous, a danger to which social construction is potentially a democratic corrective. A book that takes up this issue indirectly through close reading of several political theorists is Don Herzog's *Without Foundations*. Herzog fills a gap that critics have complained about in the work of Richard Rorty. He concludes that "the quest for certainty" makes many historically important "foundational political theories" quite "eerily apolitical" (243).

Undergraduate Education

Social construction has not yet made much impact on our thinking about undergraduate education generally. I have contributed a sketch of possible curricular implications in "Liberal Education and the Social Justification of Belief" and, elsewhere, some discussions of the place of collaborative learning in an undergraduate education. Collaborative learning is related to social construction in that it assumes learning occurs among persons rather than between a person and things. Some teachers using collaborative learning who have adopted social constructionist assumptions have found that they understand better what they are trying to do and, understanding it better, have a better chance of doing it well. Harvey Wiener's "Collaborative Learning in the Classroom: A Guide to Evaluation" suggests ways to tell when teachers are using collaborative learning most effectively.

Although to date there is not much research on the effects of collaborative learning in college and university education, recent work on its effects in primary and secondary schools is relevant. Surveys of research by David Johnson and by Shlomo Sharan support the experience of college and university instructors who have used collaborative learning. Students learn better through noncompetitive collaborative group work than in highly individualized and competitive classrooms. Robert Slavin's *Cooperative Learning* reports similar results. Jeannie Oakes's *Keeping Track* adduces evidence that vertically or hierarchically structured educational institutions and classrooms deliver inferior education to all students and suggests that this situation be changed by making institutional and classroom structure horizontal and cooperative. Bibliography relevant to collaborative learning in college and university contexts may be found in my *Short Course in Writing* and in John Trimbur's "Collaborative Learning and Teaching Writing."

The most far-reaching statement about the implications of social construction for undergraduate education is Rorty's "Hermeneutics, General Studies, and Teaching." His position is that we are mistaken when we tie our study and teaching of the humanities to a notion of "truth as something which exists and endures apart from" human beings. Abstract thought, archetypal figures, mythology, notions of Reason with a capital "R" and Truth with a capital "T," notions of established order, universals of sound reasoning, and other such structuralisms and consecrated stereotypes, Rorty says, are all forms "of what Nietzsche called 'the longest lie'—the lie that there is something beyond mankind to which it is [our] duty to be faithful" (2).

In place of Platonic ineffables such as these, Rorty would have humanists provide students with "a sense of tradition, of community, of human solidarity" (3). Students should gain "a sense of [the human community] as standing on its own feet, choosing its own destiny" (6). One way to develop this sense of human community, he says, is to read the major humanistic texts not as accounts of people's "encounter with Reality or Truth," but as accounts of attempts people have made "to solve problems, to work out the potentialities of the languages and activities available to them . . . by transcending the vocabulary in which these problems were posed" (9).

From this perspective, the purpose of studying the humanities continues to be basically what most of us believe it is now, "to help us [rise above the language of the day] in order to become fully humane." In Rorty's view, however, we rise above the language of the day not by learning to think and write abstractly or by appealing to "something higher—Reason rather than Prejudice, Truth rather than Convention." Instead, we rise above the language of the day by using it "as one option among others." We should therefore not regard the "liberality of mind and critical thought" that we try to develop in our students as capacities to deal in abstractions but as the capacity to seek out and understand "alternative perspectives." "Critical thinking," Rorty argues, "is playing off alternatives against one another, rather than playing them off against criteria of rationality, much less against eternal verities" (11).

Rorty expresses in this article, in the least compromising, most concentrated way, what a social constructionist position might mean in the long run to scholars and teachers of English and other humanistic subjects. As Geertz points out, furthermore, the implications for change in our work that Rorty suggests are matched by similarly far-reaching implications for change in the nature of our professional lives. For example, from a social constructionist point of view, literary critical discourse does more than define the mores of a disciplinary community. As Geertz says in "The Way We Think Now: Toward an Ethnography of Modern Thought" (*Local Knowledge*), one's discipline also defines "a great part of one's life": who, what, and where we believe we are (155). It is in the end something on that order of magnitude that is at stake when we begin to explore the implications of social construction.

Works Cited

Abercrombie, M. L. J. *The Anatomy of Judgement.* New York: Basic, Hammondsworth. Eng.: Penguin, 1960.

Anderson, Wilda C. *Between the Library and the Laboratory.* Baltimore: Johns Hopkins UP, 1984.

Bakhtin, Mikhail M. "Discourse in the Novel." *The Dialogic Imagination.* Ed. Michael Holquist. Trans. Caryl Emerson and Michael Holquist. Austin: U of Texas P, 1981.

Bellah, Robert N., et al. *Habits of the Heart: Individualism and Commitment in American Life.* Berkeley: U of California P, 1985.

Bloor, David. *Wittgenstein: A Social Theory of Knowledge.* New York: Columbia UP, 1983.

Bruffee, Kenneth A. "Collaborative Learning and 'The Conversation of Mankind.'" *College English* 46 (1984): 635-52.

———. "Comment and Response." *College English* 48 (1986): 76-78.

———. "Liberal Education and the Social Justification of Belief." *Liberal Education* 68 (1982): 95-114.

———. "Liberal Education, Scholarly Community, and the Authority of Knowledge." *Interpreting the Humanities.* Princeton: Woodrow Wilson Foundation, 1985. Rpt. in *Liberal Education* 71 (1985): 231-39.

———. *Short Course in Writing.* 3rd ed. Boston: Little, 1985.

———. "The Structure of Knowledge and the Future of Liberal Education." *Liberal Education* 67 (1981): 177-86.

———. "Writing and Reading as Collaborative or Social Acts: The Argument from Kuhn and Vygotsky." *The Writer's Mind: Writing as a Mode of Thinking.* Ed. Janice N. Hays, et al. Urbana: NCTE, 1983.

Coulter, Jeff. *The Social Construction of Mind: Studies in Ethnomethodology and Linguistic Philosophy.* Totowa, NJ: Rowman, 1979.

Fish, Stanley. *Is There a Text in This Class? The Authority of Interpretive Communities.* Cambridge: Harvard UP, 1980.

Geertz, Clifford. *The Interpretation of Cultures.* New York: Basic, 1973.

———. *Local Knowledge.* New York: Basic, 1983.

Gergen, Kenneth J. "The Social Constructionist Movement in Modern Psychology." *American Psychologist* 40 (1985): 266-75.

———. *Toward Transformation in Social Knowledge.* New York: Springer-Verlag, 1982.

Gilbert, G. Nigel, and Michael Mulkay. *Opening Pandora's Box: A Sociological Analysis of Scientists' Discourse.* Cambridge: U of Cambridge P, 1984.

Guignon, Charles B. *Heidegger and the Problem of Knowledge.* Indianapolis: Hackett, 1983.

Harre, Rom. *Personal Being: A Theory for Individual Psychology.* Cambridge: Harvard UP, 1984.

Herzog, Don. *Without Foundations: Justification in Political Theory.* Ithaca: Cornell UP, 1985.

Ignatieff, Michael. *The Needs of Strangers.* New York: Viking, 1984.

Johnson, David W., et al. "Effects of Cooperative, Competitive, and Individualistic Goal Structures on Achievement: A Meta-analysis." *Psychological Bulletin* 89 (1981): 47-62.

Kuhn, Thomas S. *The Structure of Scientific Revolutions.* 2nd ed. Chicago: U of Chicago P, 1970.

Lewin, Kurt, and Paul Grabbe. "Conduct, Knowledge, and the Acceptance of New Values." *Journal of Social Issues* 1 (1945): 53-64.

McGann, Jerome J. *A Critique of Modern Textual Criticism.* Chicago: U of Chicago P, 1983.

Mitchell, W. J. T., ed. *Against Theory: Literary Studies and the New Pragmatism*. Chicago: U of Chicago P, 1985.

Myers, Greg. "The Social Construction of Two Biologists' Proposals." *Written Communication* 2 (1985): 219-45. Compare Myers, "The Social Construction of Two Biology Articles." Unpublished paper delivered at the Conference on College Composition and Communication. New York, March 31, 1984.

Oakes, Jeannie. *Keeping Track: How Schools Structure Inequality*. New Haven: Yale UP, 1985.

Rorty, Richard. "Criticism Without Theory (MLA Version)." Unpublished essay, MS, 1983.

———. "Hermeneutics, General Studies, and Teaching." *Synergos: Selected Papers from the Synagos Seminars*. Vol. Z. Fairfax, Va.: George Mason UP, 1982.

———. *Philosophy and the Mirror of Nature*. Princeton: Princeton UP, 1979.

Sharan, Shlomo. "Cooperative Learning in Small Groups: Recent Methods and Effects on Achievement, Attitudes, and Ethnic Relations." *Review of Educational Research* 50 (1980): 241-71.

Shotter, John. *Social Accountability and Selfhood*. Oxford: Blackwell, 1984.

Slavin, Robert E. *Cooperative Learning*. New York: Longman, 1983.

Trilling Lionel. "Why We Read Jane Austen." *Times Literary Supplement* 5 March 1976: 50-52.

Trimbur, John. "Collaborative Learning and Teaching Writing." *Perspectives on Recent Research and Scholarship in Composition*. Ed. Ben W. McClelland and Timothy R. Donovan. New York: MLA, 1985.

Vygotsky, L. S. *Mind in Society*. Ed. Michael Cole. Cambridge: Harvard UP, 1978.

———. *Thought and Action*. Ed. and trans. Eugenia Hofmann and Gertrude Vakar. Cambridge: Harvard UP, 1962.

Wertsch, James V. *Vygotsky and the Social Formation of Mind*. Cambridge: Harvard UP, 1986.

Wiener, Harvey S. "Collaborative Learning in the Classroom: A Guide to Evaluation." *College English* 48 (1986): 52-61.

Writing and Language Socialization Across Cultures: Some Implications for the Classroom

George Gadda

All of us recognize differences between languages—we know that the sounds of Spanish differ from those of Chinese. If we've studied a language other than English, we're probably also aware that languages differ from each other in the way they form words and combine words to create sentences. We know that students' first languages can influence their English, and that the pronunciations or constructions likely to prove difficult for speakers of one language will differ from those difficult for speakers of other languages. Language teachers know how to predict these differences, and all of us are aware of them to some extent.

What may be much less clear to us is that languages also differ in their rhetorics—that is, in the way they use language to accomplish various purposes, particularly in writing. Along with the structural elements of language—sounds, words, syntax—we all learn rules about what can and should be said, and how, and when. Some of this rhetoric is formally taught in school; some of it we internalize in less direct ways, simply by observing what is typical and esteemed in our culture. Since few native speakers of English have the advanced literacy required to be native-like writers in a second language, very few of us have had the experience of conceptualizing the way things are most usually and effectively said or written in a language not our own. Differences in rhetoric may be opaque for us, and as unexpected as my own surprised realization in first year French that place names change from language to language.

This chapter has three parts. First it considers some of the differences among written texts identified by the study of contrastive rhetoric. Then, drawing on the work of Shirley Brice Heath, it addresses the related question of how children are socialized to use language and how that socialization may or may not aid them in the kind of analytical thinking and writing typical of higher education in the West. Finally the chapter suggests some uses that we as teachers can make of the insights derived from the work of contrastive rhetoricians and ethnographers of language, including a rationale for the approaches to teaching offered in Chapters 2, 4 and 5 *[of the book where this essay appeared]*.

Contrastive Rhetoric

Since 1966 scholars in a discipline called contrastive rhetoric have examined the writing produced in English by writers schooled in other countries to determine the ways in which their texts differ from those produced by native speakers of English. Although all of their work is exploratory rather than definitive, it does give us as teachers insight into some ways in which non-native speakers' writing in English may not meet the English-speaking reader's expectations.

The still-significant first study, Robert Kaplan's "Cultural Thought Patterns in Inter-cultural Education," was in fact motivated by the desire to explain why papers by foreign students often generated from instructors comments like, "The material is all here, but it seems somehow out of focus" (Kaplan, 1966, p. 3). Kaplan analyzed hundreds of expository compositions written in English by students whose first languages included Arabic, Chinese, Korean, and Spanish to determine how their paragraphs were organized.[1] He concluded that there were predictable differences between paragraphs written in English by students with the various first languages; to describe these differences Kaplan wrote that "superficially, the movement of the various paragraphs ... may be graphically represented in the following manner:

English   Semitic   Oriental   Romance   Russian

Kaplan cautions, however, that "Much more detailed and more accurate descriptions are required before any meaningful contrastive system can be elaborated" (p.15).

Based on the available evidence, however, Kaplan observes that in Arabic "paragraph development is based on a complex series of parallel constructions, both positive and negative. This kind of parallelism may most clearly be demonstrated in English by reference to the King James version of the Old Testament." Of Chinese and Korean compositions, he observes that

> Some Oriental writing, on the other hand, is marked by what may be called an approach by indirection... [It shows the subject] from a variety of tangential views, but the subject is never looked at directly. Things are developed in terms of what they are not, rather than in terms of what they are. Again, such a development in a modern English paragraph would strike the English reader as awkward and unnecessarily indirect. (p. 10)

Kaplan contrasts both of these models of development with the "linear" coherence of the textbook English expository paragraph, whether it is structured inductively (specifics leading to a generalization) or deductively (generalization followed by supporting details).[2]

Subsequently there have been a number of studies of the texts produced in English by writers schooled in other languages and rhetorical traditions. Among the topics such studies have examined are paragraph structures, means of highlighting topics, and ways of establishing coherence between sentences and paragraphs. Some studies have also considered the differences between whole texts produced by native English speakers and non-natives in response to the same stimulus. Two interesting studies have compared stories written by native speakers with stories written to the same topic by non-natives.

One of these studies compared the narratives written by 223 students in a group of eight Australian schools in 1984. The students were 6th and 11th grade native speakers of Arabic, Vietnamese, and English; the writing they produced for the study was "a bedtime story to a child younger than the writer" written in a 40 minute class period (Soter, 1988, p. 181). The researcher, Anna O. Soter, found that all three language groups produced stories with setting, character, and action, though the elements were used in different proportions. The native speakers of English approximated the conventions of conventional bedtime stories most closely, with their focus on the plot of the story conveying "a strong sense of forward movement" (p. 195). In contrast, the Vietnamese students placed less emphasis on plot, more on the relationship between characters and their inner states. Their concern with character manifested itself in a much greater proportion of dialogue in their stories than in those of the other two groups; Soter reports that Vietnamese informants identify these traits as typical of Vietnamese narratives in general. The Arabic speakers were also influenced by the style of narratives in their first language, Soter suggests; in comparison with the other two groups, the Arabic writers devoted considerably more attention to setting than did the native English speakers or the Vietnamese. She also notes that some of the narratives by Arabic speakers in 11th grade would not be culturally appropriate as bedtime stories in the West.

A similar study by Chantanee Indrasuta (1988) compares stories or narrative compositions written in English by 30 American high school seniors with those written by 30 Thai high school seniors in both Thai and English. Indrasuta found that the American and Thai compositions written to the topics "I Made a Hard Decision" and "I Succeeded, At Last" were similar in the kinds of cohesive ties they used, in their reliance on chronological organization, and in the proportions of description, dialogue, and generalization they included.

But there were also significant differences, differences often explained by interviews with the writers and their teachers. Though both American and Thai teachers and students agreed that the purpose of narrative is "to inform and to entertain," the Thai writers, perhaps influenced by the Buddhist tradition, conceived of narrative as intended to instruct, to point to a stated moral. Thai writers also thought their stories had to be true; if they had no real experience that fit the specifications of the title, they didn't create one. Finally, Thai students used considerably more figurative language than Americans, perhaps "because analogy appears to be the preferred way of describing things in Thai" (p.219). In contrast, American students understood the primary purpose of narrative to be capturing their audience's interest. Because they believed their primary task was to entertain the reader, they felt able to create a story or to reconceive a true one "to create surprise and suspense" (p. 221). The language of the American compositions was considerably less formal than that of the Thai compositions—much less likely to use figurative language, and much more likely to approximate colloquial speech. In all, Indrasuta suggests that the Thai and American students were reproducing two different cultural models of narrative, even when they were responding to the same writing assignment.

How Children are Socialized to Use Language: *Ways with Words*

Such differences in ideas about language use can exist between subcultures as well as between cultures. The most comprehensive study of such differences is Shirley Brice Heath's *Ways with Words*, the result of ten years of ethnographic work the author did in the Piedmont Carolinas in the 1960's.[3] This was a period of transition in Carolina schools similar to the flux currently being experienced in California schools; in the Carolinas, however, the students newly entering the schools were not immigrants from many nations, as in California today, but the black children who had been excluded from the white school system before the Supreme Court struck down "separate but equal" schooling in 1954's Brown v. Board of Education. A linguist and anthropologist, Heath was at the time working in teacher-training and in-service programs.

When elementary and high schools were desegregated in the Piedmont area of the Carolinas in the late 1960's, middle-class teachers were suddenly faced with classes that included black children whose ways of using language—not just or even primarily the forms of that language—made it difficult for them to meet their teachers' expectations for performance in class, or even to understand what they were. The teachers' classes had always included the children of white mill workers, whose performance did not match that of children from mainstream "townspeople" families. However, the addition of a group of children whose socialization was apparently so different from that of the other two groups made the need for background information crucial to the teachers.

As a result, for the next several years Heath frequently visited a community of working class white mill workers she calls "Roadville" and a working class black community she calls "Trackton." Out of her long-term observation of both communities, Heath draws portraits of the radically different ways in which children learned to use language in them. When compared with a similar portrait of the way children were socialized to use language in "townspeople" families, both black and white, this information allowed teachers to reconsider their own ways of using language in the classroom and to clarify and define their own expectations about how students will perform there.

From the beginning children in Roadville were engaged in dialogues by their parents and other adults, who used those dialogues to teach children how to do things "right." When naming things and displaying other knowledge, including knowledge about behavioral rules and moral judgments, Roadville children were always expected to produce a particular expected answer, even if other answers were accurate given the stimulus. Just as the fundamentalist Protestantism in which they were raised relied on the exact recall and literal interpretation of the Bible, so did everything else in the Roadville children's linguistic environment encourage the assumption that there was a single right answer to every question.

The experience of black children in Trackton was very different. Adults in Trackton did not modify their speech to children, and seldom did they engage them in dialogues. When they did, the purpose of those dialogues was never to have children display knowledge that adults already possessed. Especially if they were male, children were expected to find ways to assert themselves and to perform on the stage formed metaphorically by the open area at the center of the community and the porches that bordered it. In its oral communication, the community valued word play, imaginative and often fictionalized retellings of actual incidents, and, in general, the adroit use of language to mediate shifting moods and power relationships in Trackton itself. Children in Trackton were not always held to literal accuracy and were not usually asked to hypothesize. They were not encouraged to think of themselves as addressing audiences outside Trackton itself.

From the time their children were very small, Townspeople of both races modified their speech to make it comprehensible to children and engaged them in dialogues whose purpose was usually to teach the children or to assess what they knew. From an early age, parents read books with children; these encounters were filled with questions in which children were asked to provide information about the text or the pictures ("What's in front of the house?") or to form hypotheses about it ("What will happen next?"). In all, children were encouraged to use language in ways that fostered a view of themselves as able to report information, to manipulate it to form hypotheses and interpretations, and to assume a role in public discourse in which these activities would be pursued among people who were not members of the child's immediate community.

These differing backgrounds had given the three groups of children understandings of what counts as a "story" as different as those of the Arabic, Vietnamese, Thai, and native English speakers described above. For children in Trackton, a story was a narrative calculated to show off their creativity as story-tellers. While often based in fact, the story didn't need to be; it would be esteemed by the Trackton audience to the extent that it was clever (for example, by paraphrasing a familiar story or by commenting obliquely on a relationship in the community) and verbally inventive (for example, by playing with proverbs or with quotations from songs, television shows, or other parts of popular culture). Everything in their pre-school environment led Trackton children to think that to "tell a story" was to make one up and to embellish and perform it engagingly. These expectations contrasted sharply with those of Roadville. Among Roadville families, a "story" was a strictly true report of an actual incident told to illustrate a moral based on the model of often re-told stories from the Bible. Such stories were told only by members of the community who were agreed to be skilled story-tellers, and they had as their purpose reconfirming the moral and underlining human frailty. In ways predictable from Roadville's fundamentalist Protestantism, fictionalizing actual experience in any particular was considered to be a "lie." Among the Townspeople, in contrast, a "story" could be a factual account, but was more usually a fictional story introduced by a formula like "Once upon a time"—a story whose purpose was neither to instruct in Roadville's terms or to entertain in the particular ways valued in Trackton. Clearly, the request to "tell a story" will produce in children from these three communities quite different sets of expectations; equally clear is the fact that the understanding most in line with the school's expectations is the one controlled by the children of the Townspeople. As a result, they were most likely to respond to assignments in ways that their teachers would value.

The differences between the ways in which these three groups of children had been socialized to use language had important influences on their chances for success in school in other ways as well. The kinds of questioning to which they'd been exposed was particularly important. Children from Trackton were completely unaccustomed to—even bewildered by—the kinds of questions they were asked from the beginning of their formal schooling: questions that asked them to name objects, describe their properties—in many ways to display knowledge they knew the teacher already had. Children from Roadville did well with these questions in grades 1 through 3 but began to fall behind as the curricular emphasis in grades 4 and 5 shifted from display of memorized knowledge to its application in new situations (Heath, 1982, p. 64). The children who did best in meeting the demands of the school's curriculum as it became steadily more demanding conceptually were those of the mainstream families. It might be said that all of their socialization in language had given them a view of themselves as purposeful communicators—people who could observe, discuss what they observed, evaluate, and solve problems with language the view that the high school curriculum also presupposed.

Heath undertook her ethnographic research as a way of helping teachers change their teaching in ways that would offer a greater chance of success to children whose previous experiences with language in their homes and communities were different from those the school assumed and would draw upon. Once they had this information, teachers could begin to make the expectations of their classrooms clearer to children whose previous experience had not already accustomed them to its patterns. Based on her own observations and on other research, Heath identifies several uses of language as both central to success in school and practiced in the mainstream home:

- labeling parts of the environment;
- discussing their features;
- considering their uses and origins;
- hypothesizing alternatives about them.

The challenge for teachers is to help students add these uses of language to the repertoire they bring with them to school.

Approaching the question of educational success from a different perspective—the perspective of what college and university writing assignments require—in 1988 William Walsh and I identified a parallel list of abilities. To perform well on writing assignments designed to elicit analysis—writing intended to define and explain the significance of subject matter—we concluded that students needed these abilities:

- reading closely for important details and for organizing patterns, including those hitherto unrecognized or thought insignificant;
- selecting and organizing those details and patterns;
- drawing defensible inferences and generalizations from what is read or observed;

- evaluating and reevaluating the usefulness of those inferences and generalizations, testing them against competing ideas and the data. (Gadda and Walsh, 1988, p. 20)

In describing the purposes of college and university writing assignments, we quote ESL researcher Daniel Horowitz's conclusion that "most professors who have been trained in English-language universities place a high value on reintegration of data and that many writing tasks are, in fact, expressly designed to provide opportunities of demonstrating this ability" (1986, p. 458).

Thus, we support Horowitz' view that, to help language minority students succeed in higher education, we must do more than teach them the forms and structures of English. We must also help them understand how English is used for academic purposes in our schools and what kinds of discourse we value. As much as possible, we must help our students become comfortable with those ways of using language and claim them as their own.

Language Socialization and Language Minority Students

How do these insights gained from native speakers affect our work with language minority students? What has been observed about the ways in which language minority students are socialized to use language and the ways in which that socialization matches the expectations of our schools?

There has been no language socialization study of any group of language minority students as encompassing as *Ways With Words*. In the volume *Beyond Language,* however, Shirley Brice Heath reports on work undertaken in the last ten years by graduate student ethographers at UC Berkeley and at Stanford. We will focus here on what they have observed about language socialization among Chinese families and among working class families that have recently emigrated from rural Mexico. These groups are of particular interest given the number of students from these backgrounds that California's schools will serve through the foreseeable future.

Working Class Mexican Families Recently Arrived from Mexico

The researchers whose work Heath reports describe the language socialization of children in working class families recently emigrated from rural Mexico. The thrust of this socialization focused on training children to fulfill their expected roles in the family. Parents and elders are figures of authority; children are expected to be polite and respectful to their elders, and it is this aspect of language use on which parents focus their attention and their teaching. Adults and children form separate conversational groups on social occasions; children listen to elders, obey them, and answer questions they are asked, but they do not ask adults questions or begin conversations with them themselves. Often adults tease children, commenting playfully on the child's distinctive characteristics, relationship to the teaser, or suggesting a cruel but obviously fictional action. As the child responds, the exchange underlines and reinforces the familial or social relationship between the two. Much parental teaching proceeds by modeling rather than by verbal instruction: parents show children what to do and correct them as they imitate rather than explaining a whole process or asking questions designed to lead the child to the next step. (Middle class Mexican mothers use the latter strategies, however; in a 1974 study of Mexican mothers of various socioeconomic backgrounds teaching their children new tasks, Laosa [1977] found that Mexican mothers with high school educations more frequently used the questioning method typical of similarly educated Anglos.)

We have already seen the significance of the kinds of questions parents typically ask their children for the children's easy acculturation to the school. The kinds of questioning ethnographers have observed as typical of the working class Mexican home differ from those of Roadville, Trackton, and the Townspeople. Heath reports that recently emigrated working class Mexican parents "seldom ask questions that require children to repeat facts, rehearse the sequence of events, or foretell what they will do" (1986, p.161). When children are asked to name things, Heath notes, it is usually in the context of large social gatherings, not day-to-day family interactions, and the items labeled are likely to be people's names, parts of the body, or ongoing activities. In other words, the questioning activity once again serves a primary purpose of reinforcing relationships within the family and its immediate social situation. Questions seldom focus on information derived from outside the family circle, for example from media or public life, and parents do not usually ask questions about information they already possess. They may ask questions aimed at learning about behavior in contexts they don't know: "Were you good in school today?" Again the emphasis of the language exchange on appropriate behavior seems clear.

Working class families recently arrived from rural Mexico may not have children's books at home; Heath notes that story books are available in Mexican schools, but that publishers in Mexico do not promote books for children in the way that publishers in the United States and Europe do. (Heath emphasizes that lack of children's books in the home is thus not a sign that families are not concerned about supporting children's readiness for school.) Whether or not they have books, children from these families do have experience with story-telling, Heath notes that "stories fill many hours in Mexican-American homes; young and old tell scary *bruja* (witch) tales, as well as stories about real events embellished with new details and about historical figures and events" (p. 174). But these stories may not match the American school's definition of story, and the American school's emphasis on individual work conflicts with a much stronger group orientation in Mexican education.

Chinese Families

Like working class Mexican families, Chinese families socialize children to use language in ways that reinforce a social system. In this case, the social system is one that Heath characterizes as valuing "age, authority, perfection, restraint, and practical achievements" and as focusing on the importance of social roles determined by sex and age rather than individual characteristics or preferences (p. 158). Describing the general plan for raising children, Heath says:

> Parents see themselves as primary agents in directing children to assume in appropriate fashion the roles that the community expects of boys and girls, and later young men and women. Children must defer to adults, who determine what their children can do and tell them when they should do it. Children are encouraged to model themselves after authorities, to listen to authorities and watch what they do, and finally to practice again and again to achieve perfection. Learning is centered on the situation rather than the individual.... (p.158)

While socialization in the working class Mexican family focuses on producing a dutiful and respectful child with close affectional ties to others in the immediate environment, the Chinese process places primary emphasis on excellence in fulfilling a role prescribed by a larger social system.

Specifically in terms of language socialization, this respect for the authority of role means that parents control verbal interactions with their children. They choose topics for discussion and direct the flow of conversation; they pay attention to what their children say and correct them when necessary, treating language like any other kind of behavior. Unlike working class Mexican parents, Chinese parents ask children factual questions and talk about the steps they are following as they perform a task. Mothers in particular may read to young children and lead them in art projects or other educational activities. It could be said, then, that Chinese parents see themselves as active teachers of language.

We have seen the importance of questioning in relation to other groups and the expectations of schooling. Chinese parents have been observed to ask questions about fact, requesting names of things in the environment or the appropriateness of various behaviors for people of a certain age or sex. Chinese parents also ask children to describe processes, activities, and books. Heath notes, however, that these questions are likely to mirror the general preference for reinforcing the behavior appropriate to social roles rather than individual emotion:

> [Questions] from parents to children do not usually include expressions of emotional evaluations . . . Adults' comments about books or acquaintances do not model . . . interpretations based on emotions; for example, parents are not likely to say of a storybook character who has lost his way in the forest, "He's probably very sad and wishing he were home with his mother right now." They are much more likely to say, "He's lost in the forest. How could that happen to a little boy?" (1986, p. 172).

The questions Chinese parents ask thus prepare their children for many of the school's demands, but not necessarily for the Western school's openness to individual interpretation.

What is the result of this language socialization? In a 1989 article Fan Shen, who grew up in China and is now a graduate student in English at Marquette University, discusses her need to value individual perception much more highly in the U.S. educational system. Responding to Chinese culture's respect for authority, she recalls once in China "willfully attributing some of my own thoughts to 'experts' when I needed some arguments but could not find a suitable quotation from a literary or political 'giant'" (Shen, 1989, p. 460). In the U.S., on the other hand, her task in writing has been to construct a *persona* that is sufficiently confident and assertive, though "immodest" in Chinese terms. Confirming Kaplan's observations, she also comments on her need to learn a new way of thinking about the sequence of ideas in writing.

In her autobiography *Fifth Chinese Daughter,* Jade Snow Wong suggests some similar discontinuities between her home culture and that of U.S. academics. Wong, who grew up in a Chinese family in San Francisco during the 1930's and 40's, recalls her bewilderment in her first college class using the Socratic method:

> What was disturbing in the first weeks at Mills [College] was that her lifelong perfected system of learning failed her. At the end of several weeks, she had only a handful of lecture notes. The instructor of the labor course, a brilliant and direct man as interested in the practical workings of theory as in the theory itself, taught by encouraging questions. But at the end of every never-dull class period, Jade Snow did not have one lecture note.
>
> How was she going to study without notes? Accustomed to specific assignments in orderly fashion, and habitually thorough, she became concerned by the vagueness of these subjects which defeated her ability to memorize—an ability carefully perfected by her Chinese studies and which had heretofore always worked.
>
> Impressed by the informality and approachability of her professors, she gathered her courage to speak to her labor instructor. "I have a problem in not being able to take any lecture notes from you. At junior college, we were given definite outlines to follow and study for examinations."
>
> Her instructor seemed amused. "Why do you think that you learn only from lecture notes?"
>
> Jade Snow had no answer to this unexpected question.
>
> He continued, "Here we want to know each one individually. Instead of reading a set of prepared notes, I study my students' minds and ideas. By the conversational method, I try to develop your minds, not give you sets of facts. Don't you know that you can always go to the library to look up facts?"
>
> Jade Snow could not immediately grasp this new concept of individual training. She had never thought of the purpose of academic training as being anything else than that of disseminating superior information. (Won, 1945, pp. 161-62)

Wong's language experience at home, and even in American schools, had not given her the concept of analysis as we've defined it here.

What Can We as Teachers Do?

Everything in this chapter so far must be understood as reporting some cultural differences in discourse and language socialization as they are currently understood. One thing we must *never* do is assume that these descriptions define the experience or characteristics of any particular student. Researchers typically report as large a range of difference between members of a group as between groups; the fact that Jade Snow Wong and Fan Shen report having internalized authoritarian ideas about schooling does not suggest that any individual Chinese student will share their experience. In other words, we must avoid stereotyping.

Another thing we can't do is to restructure our classrooms or our curricular expectations to match what we suspect our students' backgrounds may be. Such changes would not be possible even if all our students came from one ethnic or national group, one socio-economic class, and one educational background—as of course they don't. The individual differences already referred to would also render such a plan useless, not to mention the needs and expectations of the society for which we prepare students.

What we can do is find teaching strategies that help students of all language socializations and discourse experiences participate in the school's culture of literacy. It's worth reflecting that the culture of the school is not the home culture of *any* student. Though the alignment between the cultures of the school and that of homes like those of Heath's Townspeople may be relatively close, any experienced teacher of writing to college-age native speakers from Townspeople homes knows that they don't achieve proficiency in what this chapter calls analytical writing without explanation, instruction, and conscious practice. The suggestions for teaching that follow are not for non-native speakers of English only; they are useful and effective with all groups of students. But these strategies are particularly useful for students whose home cultures are at some distance from our schools' expectations about language use for academic purposes.

As Heath notes, "The school can promote academic and vocational success for all children, regardless of their first-language background, by providing the *greatest possible range of oral and written language use*" (1986, p. 144). Encouraging students to write and talk about mathematics or history in a broad range of ways will support both their mastery of language itself and their comprehension and retention of subject matter. Where possible, Heath suggests adapting forms of speech already used in the community to academic purposes (rap songs to teach biology, for example), as well as providing instruction and guided practice in forms of speaking and writing with which students may not already be familiar. Collaborative learning techniques can allow students who are relatively skilled in these language uses to help those who aren't. A wide range of language uses for sheltered classrooms can be found in Chapter 2 and many suggestions for writing-tolerance in Chapter 5 [of Gadda's book].

Discussing with students *models of the kinds of writing they must produce* is a useful instructional practice with all populations. If students have never studied effective persuasive essays or lab reports, the likelihood that they'll write them successfully is small. Useful for all students, modeling is particularly important for students whose internalized sense of the way written texts work may differ from those of the English-speaking reader. In demonstrating analytical writing, it may be particularly useful to focus attention on these features:

- how the writer introduces the subject or issue;
- how the writer states his or her own position or thesis;
- how the writer incorporates or acknowledges the writing of others;
- how the text achieves coherence, both through linked ideas and through text features like transitions.

One caution: it's usually best to provide at least two good models of any one kind of writing. Contrasting the two pieces can help students see the range of possibilities within the form as well as what's essential to it.

Fostering a critical attitude toward written texts may be particularly useful for students whose home cultures regard texts as uniquely authoritative *because* they are written. Many cultures do not share the Western habit of regarding texts as invitations to interpretation and response. Carolyn Matalene notes that in China her students would tell her, "'We have *learned* the story,'" and they would in fact have memorized it. The usual Chinese response to a literary text is to repeat it, not to paraphrase, analyze, or interpret it (1985, p. 791). Students who deal with texts in this way will benefit from activities that cause them to manipulate texts, to articulate their own ideas about the issues the texts raise, and to see themselves as interpreters. Besides supporting their acquisition of written language, the activities presented in Chapter 4 to exemplify the "into, through, and beyond" model will help students become comfortable with the attitudes toward texts that Western academic analysis requires. Teachers can also model the process of reading a text actively, questioning its premises and the reasons for its stylistic choices. A similar questioning attitude toward their own texts and those of their peers lies behind the commenting models provided in Chapter 5.

Explaining Western ideas about using others' texts in one's own writing can be particularly important for students whose cultures employ allusion to well-known texts as an esteemed feature of style. Matalene (1985) notes that:

> It is, any literate Chinese will insist, "an absolute fact" that to be a good writer requires wide reading in the Chinese classics. Only through such readings in classical Chinese can a writer become equipped with the phrases, sayings, and literary allusions necessary to "ornament and enliven" discourse.... (p. 793)

Such quotations are not identified as such; neither are quotations from the Koran which Arabic-speaking students may incorporate in their writing. While it's true Western writers can incorporate or allude to extremely well-known quotations from the Bible or from Shakespeare without quotation marks or documentation, in writing for school and most other public purposes we assume that words, syntax, and ideas are those of the writer unless we're explicitly told otherwise. This expectation of Western readers may need to be made equally explicit to writers from other cultures. Of course, helping students acquire academic conventions of using and citing texts is a major concern of those who teach writing to native speakers as well.

Finally, *using students as informants about their own language use* can help teachers understand how to help their students meet the English-speaking reader's expectations more effectively. We have seen how different cultural and subcultural groups have different ideas of what a story is; clearly it's impossible for us as teachers to know all the ideas about various forms of discourse our individual students bring with them to the classroom. But we can ask them. If the texts our students produce seem to violate our expectations in systematic ways, we can ask them why—individually, or, if the puzzling traits are common, as a class. Here are some questions we might pose:

- Why did you begin and end the piece this way?
- How do you think this kind of writing should sound?
- What do you think your readers already know about what you say?
- What do you think you have to tell them?
- How do you expect your readers to follow you from point 1 to point 2?
- What do you expect your readers to understand by this?
- How do you expect this piece of writing to affect your readers?

By asking students to tell us how they arrived at texts that we find puzzling, we may be able to learn what conceptions they have that conflict with ours. And doing that may help us to see ourselves with different eyes as well.

Notes

1. This article named contrastive rhetoric and initiated its study. Kaplan's method in it has been questioned; in particular, it has been asked whether the "cultural thought patterns" referred to in the title can be reliably gauged from writing produced in English, and whether these are as deterministic as Kaplan's references to the Sapir/Whorf hypothesis might seem to claim. Whatever these reservations, later studies confirm the basic accuracy of Kaplan's observations; see, for example, Fan Shen's comments on the structure of Chinese discourse (Shen, 1989, pp. 462-465) and Shirley Ostler's on discourse in english by Arabic speakers (Ostler, 1987).

2. Kaplan provides a useful overview of work in contrastive rhetoric in "Contrastive Rhetoric and Second Language Learning: Notes Toward a Theory of Contrastive Rhetoric" (Kaplan, 1988). Among the recently published collections of work in contrastive rhetoric are those edited by Ulla Connor and Robert B. Kaplan (*Writing Across Languages: Analysis of L2 Text*, 1987) and by Alan C. Purves (*Writing across Languages and Cultures*, 1988).

3. Heath cautions that portraits like the ones synthesized here should not be considered definitive studies. They are derived from extended observations in particular families, and have been verified by members of the groups involved to be consistent with their own experience and their knowledge of the culture. Nonetheless, Heath notes that "Within the next few years, the publications of research currently underway by these and other scholars will, no doubt, both alter and greatly augment these beginning efforts to describe the sociocultural foundations of language development among the language minorities of California" (1986, p. 160).

References

Frodesen, J. (1991). Grammar in writing. In M. Celce-Murcia (Ed.). *Teaching*

English as a second or foreign language. Second edition. New York: Newbury House.

Gadda, G., Peitzman, F., and Walsh, W., eds. (1988). *Teaching analytical writing.* Los Angeles, CA: California Academic Partnership Program.

Heath, S. B. (1982). What no bedtime story means: Narrative skills at home and school. *Language In Society,* **II (2)**, 49-76.

Heath, S. B. (1983). *Ways with words: Language, life, and work in communities and classrooms.* Cambridge, England: Cambridge University Press.

Heath, S. B. (1986). Sociocultural contexts of language development. In *Beyond language: Social and cultural factors in schooling language minority students.* Los Angeles, CA: Evaluation, Dissemination and Assessment Center, California State University, Los Angeles.

Horowitz, D. (1986). What professors actually require: Academic tasks for the ESL classroom. *TESOL Quarterly,* **20**, 445-462.

Indrasuta, C. (1988). Narrative styles in the writing of Thai and American students. In A. C. Purves (Ed.), *Writing across languages and cultures: Issues in contrastive rhetoric.* Beverly Hills, CA: Sage Publications.

Kaplan, R.B. (1988). Cultural thought patterns in intercultural education. *Language Learning,* **16**, 1-20.

Kaplan, R.B. (1988). Contrastive rhetoric and second language learning: Notes toward a theory of contrastive rhetoric. In A C. Purves (Ed.), *Writing across languages and cultures: Issues in contrastive rhetoric.* Beverly Hills, CA: Sage Publications.

Laosa, L.M. (1977). Socialization, education and continuity: The importance of the sociocultural context. *Young Children.* 21-27.

Matalene, C. (1985). Contrastive rhetoric: An American writing teacher in China. *College English,* **47**, 789-808.

Reid, J.M. (1987). The learning style preferences of ESL students. *TESOL Quarterly,* **21 (1)**, 87-101.

Shen, F. (1989). The classroom and the wider culture: Identity as a key to learning English composition. *College Composition and Communication,* **40**, 459-466.

Soter, A.O. (1988). The second language learner and cultural transfer in narration. In A. C. Purves (Ed.), *Writing across languages and cultures: Issues in contrastive rhetoric.* Beverly Hills, CA: Sage Publications.

Trueba, H.T. (1987). *Success or failure? Learning and the language minority student.* New York: Newbury House.

Trueba, H.T. (1989). *Raising silent voices: Educating the linguistic minorities for the 21st century.* New York: Newbury House.

Wong, J.S. (1945). *Fifth Chinese daughter.* New York: Harper and Brothers.

Teacher Response as Conversation: More than Casual Talk, an Exploration

Richard Straub

It has become a commonplace in scholarship on teacher response: viewing comments as a dialogue between teacher and student, an ongoing discussion between the teacher reader and the student writer, a conversation. Erika Lindemann advises teachers to make comments that "create a kind of dialogue" between teacher and student and "keep the lines of communication open" (216). Chris Anson encourages teachers to write comments that are "more casual than formal, as if rhetorically sitting next to the writer, collaborating, suggesting, guiding, modeling" (352-53). Nina Ziv asserts that comments "can only be helpful if teachers respond to student writing as part of an ongoing dialogue between themselves and their students" (376). Comments that create real dialogue on the page, these authors suggest, allow students to see value in what they have to say and assume greater control over their own writing choices. Peter Elbow, explaining his reasons for framing his comments as a letter to the student, says: "When I write in the form of a letter I feel I am engaged in a writerly *conversation*—I am *talking* to the student—rather than trying to 'mark' or 'edit' or 'correct' the paper" (10). In an essay devoted to the subject, "The Voice in the Margins: Paper-Marking as Conversation," M. Francine Danis describes the benefits of looking at teacher commentary as similar to a "good talk with a friend." Viewing comments as a conversation, she says, "encourages me to regard myself in a positive light and to work toward an image of myself that I would want to write for. I would rather think of myself as a collaborator—a midwife, a coach—than a ruthless judge. So I'm faced with the challenge of responding in such a way that students will hear in my comments the kind of voice that I'm trying to project" (19).[1]

This metaphor of response as conversation has come about as a corrective to the traditional use of comments simply to label errors and mark problems. C. H. Knoblauch and Lil Brannon, reacting to the absence of anything approaching communication in most teacher commentary, argue that all too typically teachers are so concerned with their own agendas when they read student texts that they fail miserably at adapting their own writing, their written comments, to the rhetorical situation in front of them:

> There's a curious disjunction between what . . . teachers tell students about projecting outward as the starting point of communication and what they do themselves as aspiring communicators. For in their ways of talking to students, and especially in their habits of responding to student writing, they tend . . . to ride their own hobby-horses—sometimes to the extent that their students fail utterly to conceive what they might be talking about. . . . (*Rhetorical Traditions*, 119)

Such responders establish a one-way line of communication, dictating changes to be made and robbing students of the opportunity to make decisions about their own meanings and purposes. Instead, Knoblauch and Brannon advise teachers to adopt the role of helpful readers and to see in their responses "the possibility of real communication, the chance to make intellectual progress through purposeful dialogue" (*Rhetorical Traditions*, 119).

But what does it mean to treat teacher commentary as a dialogue? What makes teacher comments "conversational"? And how do such comments initiate revision and help students develop as writers? In this essay I define the basic features of conversational response and, then, working within and against this popular notion, develop a more rigorous definition of response as conversation. I suggest how the metaphor may be used more productively to help teachers make responses that turn students back into the chaos of revision, foster independent, substantive thought in their writing, and engage students in learning how writers and readers work intersubjectively through texts to achieve understanding.

In a way, we can tell pretty easily when a set of comments is conversational. Take a look, for instance, at the following sample comments, made in response to a rough draft by a first-year college writer. The essay, titled "Attention: Bass Fishermen," was handed in for an assignment that asked students to explain an idea or activity they are knowledgeable about to readers who are not as knowledgeable about the subject.[2] The draft frequently shifts from an expository account to a narrative of personal experience, as in the following passage:

> Lake Ivenho is unique because the only thing between you and the fish are the occasional patches of lillypads. The best solution to this problem is to work a top-water buzz bait in the early morning or late afternoon. I have hooked some big bass using this technique, but if the bass is big enough to give a good long fight it can be very difficult to get it through the lillypads. After fishing the lillypads that morning my next move was to work a plastic worm under the giant oak trees that hang out over much of Lake Ivenho. Bass like to hang out in these shady areas during the heat of the day so they can better spot unsuspecting prey swimming by. This didn't produce the monster bass I was looking for so my next move was to work a spinner-bait along the southeast bank of the lake.

All six of the teachers' responses appear as end notes, either after the essay or on a separate page:[3]

Sample Responses to "Attention: Bass Fishermen"

1. The fine details convey a real sense of what fishing is like. But the paper keeps shifting in mode: sometimes it is simply descriptive, sometimes a personal narrative of the day. The best tone for this assignment is the one you set in your opening prgh, in which the details show what is special for you about fishing. Hold onto this perspective all the way through in your revision. (EW)

2. Your choice of subject is a good one. You do, apparently, have considerable knowledge of it, and that was a requirement for the topic. Now, what must you do to make succeeding drafts of this paper better? First, you're going to have to focus on the assignment. This is not a personal experience essay. Too much of your paper is given over to your love of fishing for bass in

Orlando and an account of one day's fishing on Lake Ivenhoe. After you've announced the prey, large mouth bass, you should immediately begin with your discussion of habitat. After that, talk about equipment. You also move, without transitions, from a semi-abstract discussion of bass fishing to references to a particular day's fishing. A reader can get confused by that kind of maneuver. Remember your *first* obligation is to tell the reader where the fish are, what to use, and how to catch them. Having established that structure for the paper, you can put in the necessary details and then end with your zinger the story of the big bass you caught. (DS)

3. Well, let's take a look at your second draft of the newspaper piece here. . . . Ok, let's see. Let me give you some impressions I had of the draft first and try to raise some questions for you to think about, ok? Um, first of all, one thing . . . is this question of how much "you" you want here and how much you want to, uh, well essentially how much of yourself and your impressions and experiences you want to be in this piece. . . . And I think that's a judgment call. . . . . . . Um, what you could do is go through your paper and strip out everything about yourself and there wouldn't be much left but it would be purely informational—for example, "all these were formed by sink-holes thousands of years ago." That's purely informational and not really . . . you're doing a kind of encyclopedic writing there. And then at the other extreme, when you say, "During my early childhood the first fun thing that I was taught to do by my grandfather was fish for bluegill," which is a purely personal, narrative style of writing And the two of them are really mixed together, which happens a lot in this kind of writing. So I would encourage you to think about how much you want of yourself and your experiences, and . . . how much straight information you want to provide. (CA)

4. Your choice of topic is excellent because you clearly know a great deal about bass fishing. Your description of Orlando's lakes and of Lake Ivenho in particular gives me a real feeling for the place and for fishing there— because you include so many concrete examples and details, but these accounts also raise some problems. When you begin to recount specific experiences they tend to take over. Instead of explaining fishing you move into a narrative of one event. This is particularly true beginning in the middle of page 2 with the section that begins "After fishing the lillypads that morning. . . ." This account leads into the narrative that closes the paper. By concentrating on this event you abandon your role as expert explaining bass fishing. As you revise this essay try to concentrate on

explaining bass fishing rather than telling the story of one fishing trip. You can certainly draw on your own experiences to illustrate points you make, but try to prevent the narrative from taking over. (AG)

5. I like the feel of this draft. You've captured something of the pleasure and skill involved in bass fishing Details like using top-water buzz bait in patches of lillypads will make your readers want to buy some waders and head on out to Ivenho. In your next draft, keep those wonderful details, but pay attention as well to how you can make this more an expository essay than a personal experience piece. If I had to pick a title for this draft, it would be something like: "The Day I Caught My Monster Bass." What would you need to do to your paper to make the following title fit it: "Fishing in the Lakes of Central Orlando." (GH)

6. I felt something interesting going on here. Seemed as though you had the assignment in mind (don't just tell a story of your experiences but explain a subject)—for awhile—but then gradually forgot about it as you got sucked into telling about your particular day of fishing (You'll see my wiggly lines of slight bafflement as this story begins to creep in.) The trouble is I like your stories/moments. My preference would be not to drop them ("Shame on you—telling stories for an expository essay") but to search around for some way to save it/them as part of a piece that does what the assignment calls for. Not sure how to do it. Break it up into bits to be scattered here and there? Or leave it a longer story but have material before and after to make it a means of *explaining* your *subject?* Not sure: tricky problem. But worth trying to pull off. Good writers often get lots of narrative and descriptive bits into expository writing. (PE)

All six sets of comments are thoughtful and well-crafted. They offer the student useful ideas about how the essay might be improved, in ways he would be able to understand. All of them, in fact, were made by teachers who are well informed about recent composition studies and have contributed to the scholarship on evaluating and responding to student writing: Edward White (set 1), Donald Stewart (set 2), Chris Anson (set 3), Anne Gere (set 4), Glynda Hull (set 5), and Peter Elbow (set 6).[4] But not all of these responses are "conversational."

Intuitively, it seems to me, the last four sets of comments have the feel of conversations: They simply have the sound of someone talking with someone else. It is this quality that would lead us to see the third set of comments as the most conversational in the list. With good reason. The response is an excerpt of Anson's tape-recorded message to the student. The first two sets of comments, by contrast, are more autonomous and discursive, more authoritative. What is it, though, that makes some responses, and not others, take on this sense of talk, the feel of an implicit dialogue with the student? On closer inspection, the last four responses display certain fundamental characteristics of conversational response, features that make them, in the popular sense of the term, "conversational."

The Basic Features of Conversational Response

First of all, the last four end notes have an informal, spoken voice. They talk *with* the student rather than talk to him or speak down at him. At its most elemental level, of course, achieving a conversational style of response means just this: getting the gestures, tone of voice, and sense of speech in one's written comments. As Danis notes, picturing response as conversation "does for us as teachers what our advice about picturing an audience is meant to do for our students: it concretizes the awareness that we're communicating *with someone*" (19). The following comments in particular have this spoken quality:

- Well, let's take a look at your second draft of the newspaper piece here. (Response 3)
- Your description of Orlando's lakes and of Lake Ivenho in particular gives me a real feeling for the place and for fishing there.... (Response 4)
- I like the feel of this draft. (Response 5)
- Not sure how to do it. Break it up into bits to be scattered here and there? (Response 6)

Much of this informality is achieved through the teacher's simple word choice. The last four sets of commentary are marked by a minimal use of technical language and teacher talk. They rely instead on a common, everyday language:

- One thing... is this question of how much "you" you want here and how much you want to, uh, well essentially how much of yourself and your impressions and experiences you want to be in this piece. (Response 3)
- You can certainly draw on your own experiences to illustrate points you make, but try to prevent the narrative from taking over. (Response 4)
- If I had to pick a title for this draft, it would be something like "The Day I Caught My Monster Bass." (Response 5)

- Seemed as though you had the assignment in mind (don't just tell a story of your experiences but explain a subject)—for awhile—but then gradually forgot about it as you got sucked into telling about your particular day of fishing. (Response 6)

The first two sets of comments, by White and Stewart, do not have a lot of teacher talk. But they have more of it than the others: "the fine details"; "the best tone"; "the paper keeps shifting in tone"; "This is not a personal experience essay"; "You also move, without transitions, from a semi-abstract discussion of bass fishing to references to a particular day's fishing."[5]

Less obviously, the last four sets of comments make frequent use of text specific language—language that, in Nancy Sommers' phrase, is "anchored in the particulars of the students' texts" (152) and that is specific and precise, as in the following comments:

- What you could do is go through your paper and strip out everything about yourself and there wouldn't be much left but it would be purely informational—for example, "all these were formed by sink-holes thousands of years ago."
- Instead of explaining fishing you move into a narrative of one event. This is particularly true beginning in the middle of page 2 with the section that begins "After fishing the lillypads that morning. . . ." (Response 4)
- Details like using top-water buzz bait in patches of lillypads will make your readers want to buy some waders and head on out to Ivenho. (Response 5)

By dealing in the actual words of the student's text, these responders establish a common ground with the writer, showing that they have come to terms with what he has to say and giving their comments a local habitation and a familiar name. White and Stewart are clear and precise about what they expect the student to do by way of revision. Stewart also goes into specific detail about what he'd like to see revised. But their comments are cast in the teacher's language, not the language of the student's text. White does not ground his statement about how the essay shifts from a "simply descriptive" account to "a personal narrative" in the student's text. Stewart casts almost all of his comments in his own terms: "announced the prey," "habitat," "semi-abstract discussion of bass fishing," "that kind of maneuver," "the necessary details." He does little to link his guidelines for revision to the student's own language and meanings.[6]

The last four sets of comments also display one other feature that is central to an effective conversational style, in the conventional sense of the term: They all focus on what the writer has to say and engage him in a discussion of his ideas and purposes.[7] As Knoblauch and Brannon point out, "if teachers seriously aim to communicate with students about their writing and thereby affect students' performance, they must begin with what matters most to those writers, namely, the making of meaningful statements consistent with the writers' own purposes and their own estimations of how best to achieve them" (*Rhetorical Traditions,* 122). All four of these teachers go out of their way to understand and appreciate the writer's intentions and to play back their way of interpreting the text. Anson plays back his sense of where the writing gets "informational" and where it gets "personal." Gere gives her reading of how the writer's experiences begin to take over the paper and points out specific passages where she sees the shift occur. Hull praises the writer's success at capturing "the pleasure and skill involved in bass fishing" and makes special note of one particularly effective detail. Elbow presents less specific playback than the others, but he makes a point of providing his gloss on the writing before getting into his ideas about revision.

The first two readers focus on the overall purpose of the writing, but they do less by way of playing back their reading of the text. White praises the paper for conveying "a sense of what fishing is like," but his reading stops here, at this general level. Stewart indicates that he has closely read the writing, but he frames his reading as criticism: "Too much of your paper is given over to your love of fishing for bass in Orlando and an account of one day's fishing on Lake Ivanhoe." Such comments create White and Stewart as critics or editors, while the last four sets of comments create the teachers as readers first and critics, teachers, advisers, facilitators, and mentors only second, after they have completed this central task of showing that they have tried to understand what the writer is saying. To be a conversational responder is to be, first of all, a reader—one who listens to what the writer says and lets him know what she has heard.

Teachers who make comments that are conversational in this popular sense of the term, then, employ three basic strategies:

1. They create an informal, spoken voice, using everyday language.
2. They tie their commentary back to the student's own language on the page, in text-specific comments.

3. They focus on the writer's evolving meanings and play back their way of understanding the text.

Together, these qualities enable responders to meet what Danis calls one of the greatest challenges facing most student writers, the effort "to imagine the receiver, to compensate for that person's physical absence" (19), and what Sommers calls the key purpose of commenting on student writing, "to dramatize the presence of a reader" (148).

But it seems to me that these last four teachers are doing more than just creating a conversation in this basic sense of the term. Moreover, the three features identified above seem to capture only part of what the term may more productively come to mean. Because our talk about conversational response has emerged from a rejection of prescriptive commentary, we have come too quickly to associate this concrete, talkative style of response with casual, facilitative commentary. The idea of response as a *conversation* has become a catch-all for any teacher response that is informal, positive, and nurturing, or even for any response that is nonprescriptive.[8] The term has come to refer to any response that puts the teacher in the role of reader or coach rather than the role of critic or judge. It has consequently come to have the sound of other concepts in composition that have become hard to speak against and even more difficult to pin down, like "writing as process" and, more recently, "writing in community" and "writing as collaboration." When we think of response that is "conversational," we think of comments that are easy, gentle, and friendly, comments that, from another perspective, may be too readily dismissed as "soft."[9]

We would do well, of course, to be more casual and friendly in our comments, especially given teachers' historically bad reputation as harsh critics. Comments that have a spoken, casual quality help open lines of communication between teacher and student, and they are more likely to get read. But comments may be friendly and "conversational" without being facile and nonchalant, and they have to be more than informal, specific, and friendly if they are to accomplish the large goals we have come to expect of them. An easy, informal voice and an emphasis on playing back the text as a reader are important to any concept of response as conversation, but they alone will not make comments into productive conversations.

The Features of Conversational Response as an Exploration

If we look more closely at the last four sets of comments, it is clear that they do more than carry on an informal chat with the student. More than sounding casual or friendly, more than taking on the role of a reader, facilitator, or coach, these responders make comments that are tough, incisive, and critical. They are not only friendly and helpful; they are also expectant and probing. They engage in conversations with the student, but they are conversations that are at once relaxed *and* serious. They turn their comments into an inquiry into the writing, an exploration of the text and the student behind the text. The meaning I have in mind is suggested in Boswell's *Life*, where Johnson, after a time spent involved in what Boswell too casually calls "a *conversation*," proclaims: "No, sir ... we had talk enough, but no conversation; there was nothing *discussed*."[10] Here conversation is defined not so much by its casualness as by its engagement with a subject and a real exchange between two parties. In this sense response becomes a conversation when the teacher makes her comments into a give-and-take discussion with the student—an exchange that defines both parties as investigators and that may lead to a richer understanding of the subject and to more productive writing, reading, revision, and learning.

What do the last four sets of teacher comments do that makes them conversational in this richer sense of the term? How do they create such inquiries on the page? In addition to simply making use of concrete language and a talkative style, these responders practice three strategies that help turn their comments into examinations of the subject, real conversations:

4. They make critical comments but cast them in the larger context of help or guidance.
5. They provide direction for the student's revision, but they do not take control over the writing or establish a strict agenda for that revision..
6. They elaborate on the key statements of their responses.

Beyond assuming the role of reader or coach, the last four responders take on the roles of teacher, demanding reader, and co-investigator. This interplay of roles is created through, and reflected in, the modes of response these teachers employ—that is, the ways they frame their comments and in doing so establish various relationships with the student. White's and Stewart's endnotes are dominated by directive commentary, in which the teacher, adopting the stance of a critic or judge, takes control over the writing and lays out what is not working and what should be changed:

- The paper keeps shifting in mode: sometimes it is simply descriptive, sometimes a personal narrative of the day. The best tone for this assignment is the one you set in your opening prgh, in which the details show what is special for you about fishing. Hold onto this perspective all the way through in your revision. (Response 1)

- First, you're going to have to focus on the assignment. This is not a personal experience essay. Too much of your paper is given over to your love of fishing for bass in Orlando and an account of one day's fishing on Lake Ivenhoe. After you've announced the prey, large mouth bass, you should immediately begin with your discussion of habitat. After that, talk about equipment.... (Response 2)

Anson, Gere, Hull, and Elbow, on the other hand, make *some* use of these directive modes, but it is limited and moderate. They all present evaluations of the writing and indicate how the student might take up changes in his revision. But the control they exert over the student is tempered by the content, voice, and form of these directive comments. Instead of presenting outright criticisms, they present *qualified evaluations:*

- When you begin to recount specific experiences, they tend to take over. (Response 4)
- Seemed as though you had the assignment in mind (don't just tell a story of your experiences but explain a subject)—for awhile—but then gradually forgot about it as you got sucked into telling about your particular day of fishing. (Response 6)

Instead of requesting changes, they offer *advice:*

- So I would encourage you to think about how much you want of yourself and your experiences, and ... how much straight information you want to provide. (Response 3)
- You can certainly draw on your own experiences to illustrate points you make, but try to prevent the narrative from taking over. (Response 4)
- In your next draft, keep those wonderful details, but pay attention as well to how you can make this more an expository essay than a personal experience piece. (Response 5)
- My preference would be not to drop them ... but to search around for some way to save it/them as part of a piece that does what the assignment calls for. (Response 6)

These moderate modes give these evaluations and directives the feel of helpful, constructive criticism.[11]

The last four responders further temper their control and make their commentary interactive by surrounding the critical, directive comments they do make with a variety of nonjudgmental comments. They play back their reading of the text in interpretive comments, offer additional advice and questions for the student to consider, and provide examples and explanations of their responses. In doing so, they create a sense of mutual exchange between reader and writer, teacher and student, and turn their commentary into conversations in this richer sense of the term. It is not the case, then, that conversational comments cannot employ criticism or calls for revision. They can. In fact, they must, if they are to probe into the writing and push the writer to engage in richer pursuits of meaning. They just cannot have so much directive commentary—or so much directive commentary left unmodified by nondirective comments—that they define the teacher predominantly as a critic or a judge over the role of reader, adviser, facilitator, or mentor.

What most makes the last three sets of comments conversational in the more encompassing sense of the term is the depth of the responses: the extent to which these teachers give substance to and elaborate on their primary comments. It is obvious that Gere, Hull, and Elbow simply have *more* to say in their comments. But it is what they do in these additional comments that makes these responses distinctive. They don't just provide more comments or cover more ground; they deal more fully with the issues they take up. White's and Stewart's comments are one-dimensional. They make a statement and directly move on to another statement at the same level of generality.[12] The comments are listed, not developed. By contrast, the last three sets of comments are layered; they have a rich texture. One statement leads into, and is enriched by, another.

Early in her response, for instance, Gere elaborates on her main criticism of the essay, about how the writer's experiences dominate the writing:

1 When you begin to recount specific experiences they tend to take over.

    2 Instead of explaining fishing you move into a narrative of one event.

The second statement goes back over the ground of her initial state-

ment, adding to it, explaining it. She then follows up on this statement.
She grounds it in the student's text and clarifies it—and then, further,
explains the consequences of this decision. As she clarifies the problem for herself, she also draws the student into her way of seeing the
paper and clarifies the problem for him:

1 When you begin to recount specific experiences they tend to take
over.

   2 Instead of explaining fishing you move into a narrative of
   one event.

      3 This is particularly true beginning in the middle of page
      2 with the section that begins "After fishing the lillypads
      that morning...."

   4 This account leads into the narrative that closes the paper.

      5 By concentrating on this event you abandon your role as
      expert explaining bass fishing.

The response moves from a qualified evaluation expressing her concern about the mixed genres to four follow-up comments—all of them
nondirective—that serve to explain and work out the primary comment. By leading the student deliberately across the path of her thinking, she leads him to take up a like-minded investigation of these
issues. In the process her comments model a writer using writing as a
way of thinking.

To get a better appreciation of Gere's use of elaboration in her
response, all we have to do is consider the comments as they would
appear if she simply presented her general criticisms of the writing
and her calls for revision by themselves, without any elaboration:

> Your choice of topic is excellent because you clearly know a great deal
> about bass fishing. You include so many concrete examples and details,
> but these accounts also raise some problems. When you begin to
> recount specific experiences they tend to take over. As you revise this
> essay try to concentrate on explaining bass fishing rather than telling
> the story of one fishing trip.

By going back over the ground of these general comments, elaborating
on them at a more specific level, working directly with the words of
the student's text, and framing her comments in interactive modes,

Gere is able to pursue her thoughts about the paper and turn them simultaneously into a conversation and an inquiry. She gets engaged in the subject, explores the issues that are raised for her, and initiates a real, open exchange with the subject and the writer. The student is called to consider how to integrate his personal experiences with his advice about bass fishing, but he is also left to decide what specifically to do with them on his own.

The same kind of strategies for developing comments may be found in Hull's response. Generally, Hull says nothing more than she likes the draft but wants the writer to make it more fully into an expository essay. But instead of saying this and this alone, she defines what she likes about the writing and considers how it may be revised. Here is the response, again set off in levels to highlight the relationships among the individual comments:

1 I like the feel of this draft.

    2 You've captured something of the pleasure and skill involved in bass fishing.

        3 Details like using top-water buzz bait in patches of lilly-pads will make your readers want to buy some waders and head on out to Ivenho.

4 In your next draft, keep those wonderful details, but pay attention as well to how you can make this more an expository essay than a personal experience piece.

        5 If I had to pick a title for this draft, it would be something like: "The Day I Caught My Monster Bass."

        6 What would you need to do to your paper to make the following title fit it: "Fishing in the Lakes of Central Orlando."

Hull revisits each of her two general comments and, reaching to see better what she means, specifies what she has in mind. Notably, the comments she adds by way of elaboration are cast in interactive modes. She uses an explanatory comment and an example to give substance to her opening statement about what is captivating about the piece, and she adds an interpretive comment and an open question to talk more explicitly about how the writer might attend to making the piece into more of an expository essay. Even as she adds to her comments, she does not add to her control as a responder. She shares responsibility with the student, allowing him to decide what to do by way of revision. Now that the teacher has said what she has to say, the student is invited to have his turn at speaking.[13]

Similarly, Elbow follows up briefly on each of his main comments. Instead of telling the student what to do or laying out specific changes, he thinks out loud about how the student might find a way to keep the personal anecdotes in the revised essay:

1 Not sure how to do it.

> 2 Break it up into bits to be scattered here and there?

> 3 Or leave it a longer story but have material before and after to make it a means of *explaining* your *subject?*

4 Not sure; tricky problem. But worth trying to pull off.

> 5 Good writers often get lots of narrative and descriptive bits into expository writing.

His comments present one side of what is clearly intended as a two-sided investigation into the subject of how this writing may be improved. Like Gere and Hull, even as he elaborates his primary comments, Elbow allows the student to retain a good measure of control over the writing. Will the student decide to scatter these moments from his experience across the essay? Will he try to find a way to use this long account of his own day at the lake? Given these constraints—and this direction—he is left to take up the investigation for himself.

It is this kind of elaborating, more than anything else, that makes Gere's, Hull's, and Elbow's commentary more than simply talkative. They seem to imagine their comments as a kind of essay in its own right, an attempt to get at in their own minds, in their own words, a teacher's reading of the writing. What is the essay saying? Where does it work well and where can it be made to work better? How can it be turned into an occasion for learning? We can see just how important elaboration—and, in particular, elaboration cast in interactive modes— is to this richer sense of conversational response by comparing Anson's and Stewart's responses to "Attention: Bass Fishermen"—this time, using the fuller versions of what they said to this writer.[14]

In his original response, Anson follows his opening comments with a number of more specific, exploratory comments (in boldface), all of them designed to follow up on his advice that the student "think

about how much you want of yourself and your experiences, and...
how much straight information you want to provide":

> Now, my impression right now, and we'll see how the others react, is
> that you're probably a little bit over toward the extreme of personal
> memory as opposed to the informational. So that there are some places
> where you might try out the "so what" test: "I grew up on them and I
> know most of the hidden underwater structures, like fallen trees." Ok,
> if somebody's interested in perhaps going to Orlando to fish, ... know-
> ing that you know where all the hidden structures are isn't going to be
> useful information, if you see what I mean. Useful in a narrative about
> your childhood, maybe, but not, um, you know, for an article on these
> great fishing spots. Something that would be useful to know is that
> this lake, Ivanho (is that spelled like the novel, maybe?)—that this lake
> is a great fishing lake. And the information that you then go into here
> on, uh, that the lake is fishable from the shoreline and so on, would be
> appropriate.

> Um, so. So one big issue to think about for revision, then, is how much
> information you want to take out which might not be of great interest
> to the reader and then what other sorts of information they might
> want to know.[15]

Anson uses five comments to develop his basic comments. He points
to a specific example from the text and illustrates, through two
explanatory comments, how one might go about deciding what to
keep and what to omit by considering the needs of a prospective
reader. He then goes on to suggest, in two additional comments, the
kind of information that might be helpful. The added commentary is
probing and reflective, creating the sense of someone working alongside the writer, looking to see what might be done to pursue these
ideas and form them into a more thoughtful, focused piece of writing.
In the process Anson offers more lines of thought to consider, more
direction for the student, yet also manages to exert only a moderate
control over the text. Notably, these additions are nondirective: They
do not lay out a plan for revision so much as they consider an issue the
student would do well to think about. The comments do not emphasize informal talk at the expense of exploring ideas for revision, and
they do not emphasize exploration at the expense of communicating
easily with the student. They demonstrate how the best conversational responses integrate informal dialogue *and* serious inquiry.

While elaboration usually helps make a set of responses less directive, not all elaboration necessarily leads to conversation. Stewart's fuller original response is a case in point. Following his opening comments, where he presents in no uncertain terms his concern about the writer's failure to fulfill the expository aims of the assignment, Stewart adds nine comments by way of elaboration (in bold):

> Too much of your paper is given over to your love of fishing for bass in Orlando and an account of one day's fishing on Lake Ivenhoe. ... While your personal experience can certainly be incorporated into this kind of paper, it's not what the editor of *Field and Stream* wants. After you've announced the prey, large mouth bass, you should immediately begin with your discussion of habitat. **This is the place to bring in the information you have provided in your narrative about the habits of the bass, under differing conditions.** After that, talk about equipment. **You mention two types of lures, but you never tell us what kind of rod you use, how to cast for bass, and what motions to impart to the lure to attract bass.** You also move, without transitions, from a semi-abstract discussion of bass fishing to references to a particular day's fishing. A reader can get confused by that kind of maneuver. **Remember: your first obligation is to tell the reader where the fish are, what to use, and how to catch them. When those are your emphases, you can work in the other material. For example, you could say that bass prefer certain kinds of lakes at certain temperatures with certain kinds of hiding places and certain kinds of food.**
>
> **After that you can tell us that the particular lake you like meets these qualifications superbly. Having established that structure for the paper, you can put in the necessary details and then end with your zinger: the story of the big bass you caught. In this paper, you give us only two sentences after hooking it. That's not enough. The reader wants a longer report of the battle you had landing this big fish. Otherwise, the paper ends on a terribly abrupt and anticlimactic note.**[16]

All nine of these comments, however are framed in authoritative modes: four as unqualified criticisms, five as requests for specific changes In contrast to Anson's commentary, none of these follow-up comments is presented as an explanation, an option, or a question. None of them explores the subject or examines possible alternatives the student may consider. Instead, they are presented as a kind of blueprint for revision. Adopting the role of editor, Stewart sets out his own rather rigid agenda for revision. He does not open up an inquiry or engage in a give-and-take exchange with the student, and as a result his comments fall well short of creating a conversation.[17] While Stewart's commentary, then, is detailed and specific, it is not exploratory. Only by elaborating one's comments in a way that opens up the matters under discussion for a mutual investigation by writer and reader can a teacher make his comments conversational in the sense I am pursuing here.[18]

In summary, then. Anson, Gere, Hull, and Elbow put into practice a number of responding strategies that turn their conversations into explorations:

1. They create an informal, spoken voice, using everyday language.
2. They tie their commentary back to the student's own language on the page, in text-specific comments.
3. They focus on the writer's evolving meanings and play back their way of understanding the text.
4. They make critical comments but cast them in the larger context of help or guidance.
5. They provide direction for the student's revision, but they do not take control over the writing or establish a strict agenda for that revision.
6. They elaborate on the key statements of their responses.

All six of these strategies are important to conversational response in this richer, exploratory sense of the term. The first three strategies help create the sense of someone talking with someone else on the page and develop a sense of exchange between teacher and student. The last three strategies are the keys to creating responses that are discussions and explorations.[19]

Anson, Gere, Hull, and Elbow are not intent simply on exchanging informal talk with the student or communicating their views about the writing to the writer. Their attention is not fixed above all other concerns on turning their comments into a kind of informal reader-based prose. These responders seem to concentrate on the subject at hand, not on the student reading the comments, and engage the writing in a way that they hope will engage the writer. By constructing themselves as investigators, the teachers implicitly construct the student writer as an investigator. By treating the issues raised in the writing as real issues, real matters to be discussed and considered, they accept the student as someone who has something to say, something well worth exploring. By talking about the text as an act of writing and reading, they create the student as someone who is both capable of, and interested in, working through these issues of writing and improving himself as a writer. The more they delve into their responses, the more they establish their roles as writers and readers in an intersubjective dialogue, as partners in an ongoing conversation, and the more likely they may bring the student both to participate further in the conversation and learn something more about the ways writers and readers share understanding through texts.

What makes response to student writing "conversational" in this rich, Johnsonian sense of the term is the teacher's double focus: On the one hand, she is trying to talk with the writer about what he has to say; on the other, she is trying to explore and exploit the possibilities in the writing, to suggest what else might be done with it *and* what else might be learned about how writers and readers use texts to come together and make meaning.[20] Because the comments are written in a casual manner and are more detailed, they are engaging and understandable. Because they are searching and provisional, they challenge and encourage the student to explore his options as a writer. Because they are interactive and open-ended, they allow the teacher to negotiate two contrary but equally necessary strategies of teacher response: They give the student more help and direction, yet they keep a good deal of control and responsibility in his hands. The comments do not lay out an agenda for revision so much as they dramatize the act of reading the text and push the student back into the writing, calling on him to consider the sufficiency of his choices and possibilities for further development in this text and in his overall work as a developing writer and reader.

Viewing response as both a conversation and an exploration encourages teachers to avoid making comments that are cryptic, anonymous, and overly directive. It encourages them to write comments that dramatize the presence of a reader, keep a good deal of control over the writing in the hands of the writer, and lead students back into the chaos of revision—three goals that have come to dominate our talk about responding to student writing.[21] But the metaphor of response as conversation goes beyond these goals. It emphasizes, in addition, the importance of making judgments about the content of student writing, offering students direction and pushing them to reach for more to say in their writing. The conversational responders whose work is reviewed here do not eschew all forms of directive and evaluative response; in fact, their commentary in many ways is shaped around such commentary. But their evaluative and directive comments are used selectively, and the ones that are presented are augmented by an array of interactive responses. Since their comments are designed to promote richer inquiry, they provide more direction and exert greater control over student writing than recent models of teacher response seem to recommend.

Viewing response as a conversation also encourages teachers to adopt a reader's perspective and play back for students how well they are communicating their intentions to an audience. As Knoblauch and Brannon remind us, "We comment on student essays to dramatize the presence of a reader who depends on the writer's choices in order to perceive the intent of a discourse. Thoughtful commentary describes when communication has occurred and when it has not, raising questions that the writer may never have considered from a reader's point of view" ("Teacher Commentary," 1). But the metaphor of response as conversation asks teachers to do more than assume the role of a target audience; it urges them, in addition, to create themselves as demanding, expectant readers and lead students to look for more from their writing than clear communication alone. Writing itself, the metaphor reminds us, is a searching, a shaping, an interchange of ideas. It suggests that teachers would do well to strive toward a Burkean identification with students in their comments and construct themselves and their students as fellow inquirers. If teachers respond as interested *and* expectant readers, looking to promote richer inquiry and not just writing that is better formed, students will exert more effort at constructing something worthwhile to say and finding ways to share this understanding more fully with others.[22]

The metaphor of response as conversation also dramatizes the processes by which writers and readers come together intersubjectively through a text to construct meaning. The rich interaction that conversational response creates between writer and reader promotes what Deborah Brandt sees as the key knowledge of literate development: "knowing how people read and write, how they do the work of it" (6):

> Writers and readers in action are deeply embedded in an immediate working context of aims, plans, trials, and constructions. . . . The language that they write and read finds meaning only in relationship to this ongoing context—a context more of work than of words. Further,

> reference in literate language is also contextbound and essentially deictic, pointing not in at internal relations of a text but out to the developing here-and-now relationship of writer and reader at work. Texts talk incessantly about the acts of writing and reading in progress. No matter what their ostensible topic, written texts are primarily about the writing and reading of them. What they refer to is not an explicit message but the implicit process by which intersubjective understanding is getting accomplished. That is what you have to know in order to read and write. (4)

When teachers treat their response as a conversation—not just feedback—they model for students how readers and writers muster and manage language, metacommunicative cues, and context in order to create meaning. They provide the kind of knowledge about texts and text-making that Brandt finds crucial to literacy learning, by giving students "not merely experience with texts but ample access to other people who read and write and who will show you why and how they do it" (6). Teachers who make their comments part of a larger conversation with the student do not view the text as an autonomous artifact: they view the text as a meeting place for writers and readers, a "public social reality," a means for intersubjective dialogue. Their comments say, here's how I understand what you are saying, here's what I'm thinking about it, and here's what you might consider if you want me to meet you somewhere further along in this discussion. Conversational comments bring the meaning a reader creates from the text back out, through the reader's comments into the arena of social exchange, where meaning may be refined, redirected, and developed. Writing is reciprocated with writing, exchange with both an exchange and an invitation to further writing and inquiry. Because writers and readers do not merely have to keep a message going but also have to keep a whole process going, any response that promotes a detailed, honest interaction about a piece of writing will contribute to the student's work in revision and her ongoing development as a writer.

Conversational Response: Theory into Practice

Looking at the length and involvement of these sample comments, many teachers will think that, sure, conversational response may be a viable option for that small cluster of teacher-theorists who teach just one or two writing classes a year and who have the luxury of giving such attention to their comments on student writing, but they are not for me. Faced with the baffling prospect of teaching three or four sections of writing with 20-30 students per section, these teachers may wonder about the feasibility of a method of response that asks even more of them as teachers than they are already getting worn out trying to do. They may wonder how they could give more time and attend more fully to the content and thought of student writing in the ways we see here. And with good reason. The fact is, they will not be able to write these kind of involved comments in the time they could spend dealing with the traditional, formalistic concerns of student writing, in a traditional, editorial way.

Nevertheless, teachers can somehow adopt the principles of conversational response without spending any more time than they now spend in responding to student writing. They can focus more of their comments on the ideas of the student's writing and find ways to condense the commentary they make on matters of style and correctness. They can limit their comments to one or two issues per paper—and concentrate on only two or three places where these issues arise. They can deal extensively with the content and thought of their students' writing in the first half of the course and hold off on doing more with sentence structure and correctness until the second half. They can concentrate on writing fewer but fuller marginal comments and write only brief overview comments at the end of a paper. Several well-developed marginal comments will take less time than a full endnote, yet they can go far toward leading the student back into the writing.[23] Teachers can also respond more fully at the start of the course and, as the course progresses, place more and more responsibility on students to respond to one another's writing. They can even give more or less involved comments alternately to various groups of students, rotating the groups across the term.

With only a little more time to respond to each set of papers, teachers can make a practice of clarifying and extending some of the key comments they do make. In fact, by making their comments exploratory and conversational, they will more than likely make much better use of the time they do spend on responding to student writing and reap better dividends for their efforts. Much of the time teachers devote now to their comments, the research suggests, is wasted. I suspect this is true—not because teacher comments are not useful but because the ways we have come to make comments on student writing are unconsidered. Our comments fall on deaf ears or simply do not get read, I suspect, largely because they do not deal with what the student has to say or might say in a piece of writing and because they are written in a language and style that, far from inviting interest, thwart the student from reading what we have to say. By engaging ourselves in what our students have to say and inviting them to read what we have to say in response—and by making response a significant matter for the larger classroom conversation—we may make whatever time we do spend on responding to student writing truly worthwhile. Comments that are shaped into a real conversation blur the lines between writing and reading, and allow teachers to actively model and encourage acts of making meaning. They create a shared responsibility for writing and revision and enable a real *discussion,* a two-way conversation, to take place between reader and writer, teacher and student. Such conversational responses will engage students in looking again into their writing and challenge them to take up their part of the dialogue, continue the discussion, and continue their work as writers.

Notes

1. I would like to thank Peter Elbow and David Foster (*RR* peer reviewers), whose responses on the drafts of this essay took on all the marks of both a conversation with me and an exploration into the ideas presented here. I am grateful for their helpful, challenging commentary.

2. The essay and the assignment are presented in a book-length study of teacher response coauthored by Ronald F. Lunsford and me, *Twelve Readers Reading: Responding to College Student Writing* (Cresskill, NJ: Hampton, 1995).

3. These six sets of teachers' comments are taken from *Twelve Readers Reading,* which examines the responding styles of 12 well-recognized composition teachers. Several sets of these comments—namely, sets 1, 2, 4, and 6—include several additional comments in the margins of the student text, not represented here.

4. Stewart's (set 2), Anson's (set 3), and Elbow's (set 6) endnotes are not presented in their entirety—in part, due to space considerations, since each of their comments runs to at least twice the length of the excerpt.

5. The following sample endnotes, taken from a study of another group of teachers, present more obvious examples of language that is technical and teacherly and responses that are not conversational:

1. You need to work on your tenses, your clarity of sentence structure and paragraph structure. You jump around with your thoughts. They are not in order. You also need to explain some terms.

2. You need work on paragraphing. All of the ideas are put into just two paragraphs. There needs to be better organization. A paragraph needs to have a topic sentence, and all of the information in it needs to be on that particular topic. Think about organization. Plus the paper needs a better focus. Concentrate on topics.

3. After you discuss the advantages of Lake Ivenho, your paper digresses from its controlling idea about the lakes of central Orlando being the greatest natural fishing holes. The paper, at this point, becomes a narration/process paper about fishing this particular lake. You seem to lose sight of your purpose. You need to reevaluate your purpose and revise to create a *unified* paper. Do you want to write about the good bass fishing in the Orlando lakes, or do you want to write about a fishing experience on Lake Ivenho?

6. The other responders might also do well to write more of their comments in the language of the student's text—especially in those comments where they are giving their reading of the writing. Elbow's commentary, in particular, could use more text-specific commentary. He *indicates* ideas and passages he is referring to, but he does not *use* any of the actual words from the student's text.

7. The more a teacher tries to cover a full range of concerns, including sentence structure, paragraphing, arrangement, and correctness, and makes no distinctions about which is more important than others, the more difficult it is to make those comments conversational. Of course, teachers *may* take up a number of concerns and turn them into a conversation. as long as they are willing to make longer responses and deal principally with what the writer has to say. See, for example, Chris Anson's responses in *Twelve Readers Reading*.

8. One doesn't have to look long or hard to find the association of conversational comments with friendly or nurturing commentary. In pointing to the benefits of response as conversation, Danis, for example, writes: "First, and perhaps most importantly, thinking of paper-marking as conversation helps me enjoy myself as I respond to papers. A good talk with a friend or two is a pleasure: I like hearing other people's views and ways of putting things, and of course I enjoy sharing my own thoughts and feel-

ings, especially when I know that someone is really interested" (19).

9. That we've come to associate conversational response with easygoing facilitative response is easily illustrated by the fact that we would very likely hesitate to call the following response conversational: "Listen, Steve, you may have a few pretty good lines here about bass fishing and this day spent fishing the Orlando lakes, but it's just not anywhere near where it needs to be yet. It's too scattered and unfocused. I mean, page two is full of quick stops and turns. There's no way a reader'll be able to keep up with the way you constantly shift from one thing to another." Although the response has a conversational tone, it is simply too critical to be considered "conversational" in the way we have come to use the term.

10. The nature of "conversation" is a subject that frequently arises in Boswell's biography—and not always only with this meaning.

11. Notably, all six responders make a point of praising something in the student's work. The last three responders, though, devote more of their response to acknowledging what this student did well in the draft. Gere praises the writer's choice of topic and his description of the Orlando lakes; she goes on to explain what accounts for these positive reactions: his use of concrete examples and detail. Hull gives half of her comments to expressing how the detail engages her in the writing. In the excerpt here and in the rest of his response, Elbow makes no fewer than four comments that praise the writing: "I enjoyed reading your piece"; "I even enjoyed the metaphor of seeing a fish on the hook—and then realized it's merely the conventional term"; "What I like is your voice and presence and the sense of immediacy through lots of detail. I marked places that I especially liked"; and "The trouble is I like your stories/moments." It is not the case that these responders balance positive and negative comments; the point is that they make sure to acknowledge what is working well and give substance to their praise. It seems that once they have played back their reading of the text and pointed to what works in the piece, they feel as though they are in a better position to call on the student to look back on the writing and make revisions. This observation would confirm the many studies calling for greater use of praise in teacher commentary. It would also urge teachers to employ, in particular, genuine praise.

12. I am relying here on Francis Christensen's concept of "levels of generality" and his "generative rhetoric" of the paragraph, where sentences in a sequence of sentences are seen in relation to other surrounding sentences. See his *Notes Toward a New Rhetoric*. I should note here also that I have modified Stewart's and Anson's responses to this essay in order to dramatize certain characteristics of their responding styles.

13. I am reminded of a talk I heard by Nancy McCracken at a 1993 NCTE pre-
    convention workshop in Pittsburgh, in which she examined teacher
    response in relation to Mary Louise Pratt's speech-act theory.
14. By adding these comments to the pared-down versions I presented earli-
    er, I hope to dramatize more fully the effect of these follow-up comments.
15. Here is the original, full version of the first half of Anson's commentary,
    which makes up half of his overall response. Anson assumes that the
    writer has already received peer responses in small groups and has sub-
    mitted his own tape-recorded concerns about the writing to Anson with
    his draft. His basic comments are in regular type; the rest (in bold face)
    elaborate on these comments:

> Hi Steve. Well, let's take a look at your second draft of the newspaper piece
> here. . . . Ok, let's see. Let me give you some impressions I had of the draft first
> and try to raise some questions for you to think about, ok? Um, first of all, one
> thing . . . is this question of how much "you" you want here and how much you
> want to, uh, well essentially how much of yourself and your impressions and
> experiences you want to be in this piece. . . . And I think that's a judgment call,
> **because the *Trib* article you attached to your tape is obviously, um, a good**
> **example of how somebody can provide information . . . to readers who might**
> **be interested in getting that information and yet do so from a, uh, a kind of**
> **narrative perspective, uh, where in addition to saying, "Here are some places**
> **to go and here's, you know, this is a good restaurant and don't try skiing too**
> **late in the spring, and try the fondue here or here's a great little place to get**
> **wine and cheese"—in addition to giving that sort of information, he's also**
> **sharing, speaking from experience and sharing some of those experiences:**
> **"We liked the food at 'Le Petit Cafe' at the foot of Zermat," or "we were simply**
> **appalled at the cost for a lift up to the top of the Matterhorn," or whatever.**
> **And I think the two of them can go together just fine; otherwise it comes off**
> **like, um, you know, so purely informational that the reader might not trust**
> **the writer for making certain judgments.**
>
> But I think it's really a question of balance. Um, what you could do is go
> through your paper and strip out everything about yourself and there
> wouldn't be much left but it would be purely informational—**for example, all**
> **these were formed by sink-holes thousands of years ago." That's purely infor-**
> **mational and not really . . . you're doing a kind of encyclopedic writing there.**
> And then at the other extreme **when you say, "During my early childhood the**
> **first fun thing that I was taught to do by my grandfather was fish for bluegill,"**
> which is a purely personal, narrative style of writing. **And the two of them are**

really mixed together, which happens a lot in this kind of writing. So I would encourage you to think about how much you want of yourself and your experiences, and ... how much straight information you want to provide. Now, my impression right now, and we'll see how the others react, is that you're probably a little bit over toward the extreme of personal memory as opposed to the informational. So that there are some places where you might try out the "so what" test: **"I grew up on them and I know most of the hidden underwater structures, like fallen trees."** Ok, if somebody's interested in perhaps going to Orlando to fish, this might be useful information. But knowing that you know where all the hidden structures are isn't going to be useful information, if you see what I mean. Useful in a narrative about your childhood, maybe, but not, um, you know, for an article on these great fishing spots. Something that would be useful to know is that this lake, Ivanho (is that spelled like the novel, maybe?) —that this lake is a great fishing lake. And the information that you then go into here on, um, that the lake is fishable from the shoreline and so on, would be appropriate. Um, so. So one big issue to think about for revision, then, is how much information you want to take out which might not be of great interest to the reader and then what other sorts of information they might want to know.

16. Stewart's excerpt here makes up about two-thirds of his overall response. The rest of the end note deals with a few editorial problems.

17. Some teachers, like White and Stewart, might take exception to such a view of conversational response because they feel it is too open-ended and does not provide enough direction to students. These teachers probably emphasize the written product and expect their comments to lead students to produce formally complete writing. Other teachers, like Brannon and Knoblauch, might say that this view of conversational response may take too much control out of the hands of the writer. They are probably committed to either a process or a collaborative view of writing instruction, and believe that the more students are left to experience and assess their own writing and reading processes, with less teacher intervention, the more proficient they will become. The view of conversational response developed here works in between these two views of writing instruction. It looks to exploit the possibilities in the developing draft and lead the writer to produce fuller and more thoughtful texts, yet it also strives to keep the student in control of his own ideas and tries to attend to the student's gradual development as a writer. Teachers and students alike have come to prefer the outward forms of writing, the obvious features of the formal text, to the less tangible domain of thought. But, as

James Moffett reminds us, "Teachers have no business preferring either and have no choice but to work *in the gap* between thought and speech," between, that is, the student's ways of thinking and the manifestation of that thought in a text.

18. Notice how the tone of the following end note changes—and becomes more conversational in the sense I am pursuing here—when such open-ended elaboration (in boldface) is added to the basic comments of the response:

> It is difficult, to determine exactly what you are writing about—is it the lakes of Orlando or a particular fishing trip or how to catch fish? At times I get the feeling that it's one, but then I think it's another. While your paper has possibility, you need to reorganize and decide exactly what you are trying to relate. I wonder what you could do to help me out. **Maybe you could cut your personal anecdotes and focus on presenting your advice on bass fishing. (How important is it that we know that you know where all these "underground structures" are? Would it be important to know this story about your day fishing?) Or maybe you could work your personal experiences into an essay that is mostly about how to fish for bass—for instance, by just making brief mention of them to illustrate your advice.**

19. The concept of response as conversation that I develop here goes beyond the one Ronald F. Lunsford and I present in *Twelve Readers Reading* (Chapter 5). Our use of the term in the book is consistent with the generally accepted understanding, which emphasizes the teacher-student relationship and interpersonal communication. In this essay I am pursuing a more specific and potentially more useful definition of the term. which emphasizes the teacher-text relationship and exploration.

20. Those who have championed the idea of response as an informal dialogue, like Danis and Knoblauch and Brannon, might say that pushing students to explore their ideas further might work against the basic goal of conversational response—to establish an informal, cooperative relationship between teacher and student, one that minimizes the teacher's authority as a responder and emphasizes the teacher's role as a supportive reader. Of course, teachers would do well to look to their comments, first of all, to open up an informal, cooperative dialogue with their students. But, having achieved such a give-and-take relationship, they might take a greater initiative in leading students to develop the thought of their writing and push themselves as developing writers.

21. See, for example, the pioneering articles by Nancy Sommers and Lil

Brannon and C. H. Knoblauch, "Responding to Student Writing" and "On Students' Rights to Their Own Texts: A Model of Teacher Response."

22. It is important to note that looking at response as both a conversation and an exploration does not assume any one particular theory of teaching writing. It may be used by teachers who base their classes on a social constructionist approach, a process approach, a rhetorical approach, a cognitive approach, or an expressivist approach. Looking at commentary as a conversation allows teachers to emphasize the particular concerns of these various approaches even as it allows them to attend more fully to the content and thought of student writing.

23. Although a conversational style is most readily achieved in endnotes or in letters, it can also be achieved in marginal comments. The key to making such comments in the margins lies in making use of text-specific combination comments, where the teacher presents two or more comments on a given area of the writing. Beyond simply making evaluations or presenting advice or commands, the responder plays back the text, raises questions for the student to consider, and offers explanations, all the while trying to maintain an open-ended discussion with the writer, as in the following comments:

> I see you moving here from talk about bass fishing to a specific account of one day's fishing at Lake Ivanhoe. I think it might help to stick with explaining the delights of bass fishing in Orlando rather than telling about a specific day of fishing—or perhaps to find a better way to use this one experience to illustrate how to fish for bass in these Orlando lakes.

> This is useful information about fishing around lily pads. Do you fish during the early morning and late afternoon because those are the times when bass would be feeding here? I wonder if all good fishermen have a knack for where to fish at what times and when to move on to new locations.

> Okay, so you're real familiar with these lakes. What can you tell us about how you determine the best places to fish there? Do you go to different areas depending on the time of day, the type of weather, or the time of the year?

> Finding out about how bass hang out around shady areas during the day and how they react to changes in barometric pressure teaches

me a lot about bass fishing. I'd like to hear even more of this detailed insider knowledge.

Ultimately, it is of little consequence whether the comments appear in the margins of the text or in an end note. What is important is that the teacher speak in specific terms about the content of the writing and use those comments to create a give-and-take discussion with the student—a conversation that is informal and expectant, one that is geared toward turning students back into their texts and their thinking.

Works Cited

Anson, Chris. "Response Styles and Ways of Knowing." *Writing and Response: Theory, Practice, Research.* Urbana IL: NCTE, 1989. 332-66.

Boswell, James. *Life of Johnson.* Ed. R. W. Chapman. Oxford: Oxford UP, 1904.

Brandt, Deborah. *Literacy as Involvement: The Acts of Writers, Readers, and Text.* Carbondale: Southern Illinois UP, 1990.

Brannon, Lil, and C. H. Knoblauch. "On Students' Rights to Their Own Texts: A Model of Teacher Response." *College Composition and Communication* 32 (1982): 157-66.

Christensen, Francis. *Notes Toward a New Rhetoric.* New York: Harper, 1967.

Danis, M. Francine. "The Voice In the Margins: Paper-Marking as Conversation." *Freshman English News* 15 (1987): 18-20.

Elbow, Peter. "Principles That Underlie My Teaching." Unpublished material submitted to Richard Straub and Ronald F. Lunsford's *Twelve Readers Reading: Responding to College Student Writing.* Cresskill, NJ: Hampton, 1995.

Knoblauch, C. H., and Lil Brannon. *Rhetorical Traditions and the Teaching of Writing.* Upper Montclair, NJ: Boynton/Cook, 1984.

———. "Teacher Commentary on Student Writing: The State of the Art." *Freshman English News* 10 (1981): 1-4.

Lindemann, Erika. *A Rhetoric for Writing Teachers.* 2nd ed. New York: Oxford UP, 1987.

Moffett. James. "Integrity in the Teaching of Writing." *Coming on Center.* Montclair, NJ: Boynton/Cook, 1981.

Sommers, Nancy. "Responding to Student Writing." *College Composition and Communication* 32 (1982): 148-56.

Straub, Richard, and Ronald F. Lunsford. *Twelve Readers Reading: Responding to College Student Writing.* Cresskill NJ: Hampton, 1995.

Ziv, Nina. "The Effect of Teacher Comments on the Writing of Four College Freshmen." Richard Beach and Lillian Bridwell. *New Directions in Composition Research.* New York: Guilford, 1984. 362-80.

Representing Audience: "Successful" Discourse and Disciplinary Critique

Andrea A. Lunsford and Lisa Ede

> We are wedded in language, have our being in words. Language is also a place of struggle.
>
> —BELL HOOKS (*Yearning* 146)

In his February, 1994 *CCC* editor's column, Joseph Harris provides a brief overview of the kinds of work he hopes to publish in the journal, noting, among other things, that he is "especially interested in pieces that take a critical or revisionary look at work in composition studies" (7). Given the contemporary turn to self-conscious disciplinary critique, Harris' call is hardly surprising. In its relatively brief disciplinary history, in fact, composition studies has engaged in a great deal

---

Andrea Lunsford and Lisa Ede, who have been writing together for some fifteen years now, here follow their practice of alternating the order of their names as one small way of resisting the academy's privileging of first authorship and as a way of acknowledging their deeply interconnected ways or thinking and writing. Lisa Ede is the Director of the Center for Writing and Learning and Professor of English at Oregon State University. She is the author of *Work in Progress* and is currently at work on a study tentatively titled *Situating Composition: Composition Studies and the Politics of Location*. Andrea Lunsford is Distinguished Professor and Vice Chair of English at Ohio State University and editor, most recently, of *Reclaiming Rhetorica: Women in the History of Rhetoric*.

of revisionary looking back, as can be seen in the several paradigm shifts or theoretical revolutions the field has experienced during the span of the last three decades. This disciplinary critique has for the most part, however, been carried out in the agonistic manner characteristic of traditional academic discussion, with each wave of criticism, each revisionary look establishing its own efficacy by demonstrating the flaws of prior conceptions.[1]

The notion of disciplinary progress—or success—enacted by these discourses has in many ways served our field well. For though composition studies could hardly be described as an established or mainstream academic discipline, it has succeeded to a considerable extent in legitimizing and professionalizing its position in the academy. And the critical discourse of such theorists as Janet Emig, James Berlin, and Susan Miller have, we believe, contributed substantially to our understanding of how very much is at stake when scholars in composition studies profess the teaching of writing.

We are grateful for this tradition of critical discourse. Indeed we wish to respond to Harris' call to participate in a "critical or revisionary" look at work in composition studies by building on this tradition—albeit with one significant exception. We attempt here to resist traditional oppositional critique, with its tendency to focus (usually in a negative way) on the work of others. Instead, we propose here to attempt a self-critique by revising an essay of our own, "Audience Addressed/Audience Invoked: The Role of Audience in Composition Theory and Pedagogy" (AA/AI, hereafter), the essay that (if citations, analyses, and reprintings are any indication) of all our coauthored work might be said to have been judged most "successful" by others in our field.

We've put "successful" in quotation marks for a reason. The conventional western understanding of success emphasizes the role that individual agency plays in achievement. In this view, particularly as played out most often in American mythologies, success comes to those individuals who work hard for it, and who thus deserve it. Business persons who work hard, who fight the good fight, are successful. Writers who write well, who use the resources of language to persuade others, similarly merit whatever recognition and achievement come their way. As conventionally understood, success in the academy is measured by "objective" and largely individualist criteria, such as publications and reprintings, citations, and the degree of response the writing engenders.

That such a view of success—and of language—has been challenged on a number of fronts goes without saying. We may write language, but language also writes us. We may desire to express our ideas, but the ideas we express may reveal more than we have intended. Rather than emphasizing individual agency, this post-structuralist view of discourse calls attention to the role that shared assumptions and ideologies play in enabling or hindering communication. It reminds us as well of the locatedness and situatedness of all texts—and of the need to inquire into what Gesa E. Kirsch and Joy S. Ritchie in a recent *CCC* essay refer to as a "politics of location" (7). Such an effort challenges researchers, Kirsch and Ritchie argue, to "theorize their locations by examining their experiences as reflections of ideology and culture, by reinterpreting their own experiences through the eyes of others, and by recognizing their own split selves, their multiple and often unknowable identifiers" (8). It is in the spirit of Kirsch and Ritchie's call that we turn to our earlier essay.

In attempting such a self-critique we wish to be as clear about our goals as possible. In this essay, we intend to subject our earlier work to critical inquiry in an effort to foreground the rhetoricity of this work and to explore and learn from the cultural, disciplinary, and institutional forces at play in it. In so doing, we attempt to illuminate both the absences and presences in AA/AI, but to do so in a way that resists the lure of totalizing, oppositionalizing readings. We do not, in other words, wish to construct a bad-old-Ede-and-Lunsford which we—in traditional agonistic fashion—will strike down in the service of representing an all-new-and-improved-Lunsford-and-Ede on audience. In revisiting our essay, then, we wish neither to reject nor defend AA/AI but rather to embrace multiple understandings of it, and to acknowledge the extent to which any discursive moment contains diverse, heterodox, and even contradictory realities—confirming (once again) the acuity of Kenneth Burke's observation that "if any given terminology is a *reflection* of reality, by its very nature as a terminology it must also be a *selection* of reality; and to this extent it must function also as a *deflection* of reality" (45). As a result of such multiple understandings, we hope to raise heuristic questions not only about our own work but also about conventional narratives (and genres) of disciplinary progress and about the relationship between "success" and traditional academic critique.

Audience and the Subject(s) of Discourse

At the time that it was written, AA/AI entered an ongoing debate on the nature and role of audience in discourse. Responding to a number of essays on the concept of audience that appeared in the late 1970s and early 1980s, AA/AI attempted to redirect current discussions of audience by arguing that previous commentators had generally taken a partial view of an unusually rich and complex concept. Some theorists, such as Ruth Mitchell and Mary Taylor, privileged what we called the *audience addressed,* "the concrete reality of the writer's audience . . . [and assumed] that knowledge of this audience's attitudes, beliefs, and expectations is not only possible (via observation and analysis) but essential" (AA/AI 156). Others, such as Walter Ong and Russell Long, emphasized the extent to which writers create or *invoke* audiences by using "the semantic and syntactic resources of language to create cues for the reader—cues which help to define the role or roles the writer wishes the reader to adopt" (160). Our own approach was to challenge the helpfulness of such dichotomous and polarizing views of audience as either wholly addressed or wholly invoked and to argue for a syntheses of these perspectives, one that acknowledges the creativity and interdependence of writers and readers, writing and reading, and that recognizes the "fluid, dynamic character of rhetorical situations" (165). Audience can perhaps best be conceptualized, we argued, as a complex series of obligations, needs, resources, and constraints that both enable and constrain writers and readers (165).

Ten years later, we still resist efforts to characterize audience as solely textual (invoked) or material (addressed), and we continue to affirm the importance of considering audience in the context of the rhetorical situation. Rereading our essay, we note its refusal to generate pedagogical formulas or rules for teachers and students and its attempt to argue that the most complex understanding of audience is—theoretically and pedagogically—the most useful. We also recognize, however, a number of absences in AA/AI—absences that reflect our personal and professional desire to turn away from the potential difficulties and costs entailed in successful communication.

By insisting that the concept of audience involves textual and material constraints as well as opportunities, and that it must always be considered in the context of the larger rhetorical situation, AA/AI sets the scene—but then fails to explore—the ways in which audiences can not only enable but also silence writers and readers. In addition, although AA/AI recognizes the possibility of readers rejecting "the role or roles the writer wishes them to adopt in responding to a text" (166), our essay consistently down-plays the possibility of tension and contradiction, presenting the interplay of audience addressed and audience invoked as potential opportunities for the writer "catalyzed and guided by a strung sense of purpose to reanalyze and reinvent solutions" (164). With good will and rhetorical sensitivity, AA/AI implicitly suggests, writers will be able to negotiate their ways into positions of discursive power, will achieve and maintain communicative success.

Such an understanding of writing assumes a negotiation of meaning among if not literal equals then among those with equal access to the resources of language. Such an understanding also necessitates, of course, a parallel series of assumptions about writers and readers, as well as about the genres they attempt to inhabit. We have already indicated that the subject of discourse invoked in AA/AI is a subject who feels both agency and authority—that subject is also implicitly stable, unified, and autonomous. Although we recognize in AA/AI that students have less power than teachers and thus less freedom in some rhetorical situations in there, we do not pursue the multiple ways in which the student writer's agency and identity may be shaped and constrained not only by immediate audiences but also, and even more forcefully, by the ways in which both she and those audiences are positioned within larger institutional and discursive frameworks. Nor do we consider the powerful effects of ideology working through genres, such as those inscribed in academic essayist literacy, to call forth and thus to control and constrain writers and audiences.[2] That a student might find herself full of contradiction and conflict, might find the choices available to her as a writer confusing and even crippling— might in fact find it difficult, even undesirable, to claim the identity of "writer"—did not occur to us.[3]

That such ideas did not occur to us is a mark of the extent to which the students invoked in AA/AI were in important ways the students we had been—eager, compliant, willing to shape ourselves to rhetorical situations. Our desire to invoke such students and to (re)write experience in such a way as to highlight success not failure, consensus not conflict, progress not struggle, is, we have realized, deeply imbedded in our relationship to schooling as well as to discourse. In working on this essay, for instance, we have each recalled memories of struggle and failure, of negative educational experiences that reminded us of the degree to which, as students, we molded ourselves as willing sub-jects of education. Andrea found herself reflecting most often on her early grade school years, recalling, for instance, a moment when she perceived that a teacher simply did not like her—and noting the ways in which that perception led her not to challenge the teacher's views of goals but to attempt to remake herself in the image of a dutifully schooled subject less likely to invoke a hostile teacher audience. Lisa found herself drawn to memories of graduate school experiences and to the ways in which she repressed her confusion and anger as differ-ent courses required her to become not only a different audience for each professor but a different subject as well.

In reflecting on these memories, we have begun to explore the extent to which, very early in our educations, we identified with the goals and institutions of schooling. Our home communities were ones in which school was generally defined as a place for positive change and advancement. But our identification with schooling involved more than mere acceptance of these attitudes. Academic good girls, we studied, even excelled, and in so doing we came to associate both schooling and the writing we did in school with a positive sense of self, a means of validation and "success," and of hailing appreciative audiences. So powerful was this identification, in fact, that we recast those painful memories of struggle that we could not repress, reinter-preting experiences that might have led to resistance and critique as evidence of individual problems that we could remedy if only we would work harder, do (and be) better. Such an approach is congruent, of course, with the individualism inherent throughout our culture, educational institutions, and scholarly disciplines, an individualism that traditionally writes the kind of struggles we experienced as stu-dents as inevitable, even necessary and salutary aspects of the western narrative of individual success that AA/AI implicitly endorses.[4]

Does this critique suggest that we have now rejected our identifi-cation with schooling and its traditional individualist assumptions? It does not or not monolithically at least, for it would be disingenuous indeed for us to ignore or devalue what we have gained both intellec-tually and materially as a result of our schooling. So while we recog-nize that schooling subjects and disciplines students and that writing is not necessarily and certainly not always a venue for power, we also recognize—and honor—the potential of both writing and schooling to enable students to enact subjectivities that they experience as positive and authorizing. Thus like the audiences that it hails, schooling is both deeply situated and inherently paradoxical—full of contradictions and complexities—and opportunities. In this analysis of our earlier work our goal is neither to embrace schooling unthinkingly (as we once did) nor to condemn schooling out of hand. Rather, we seek to recognize its multiple complexities and to understand as fully as possible our positioning among them as we strive not only to acknowledge but also to take responsibility for our own politics of location.

Part of this positioning of course involves our experiences and identities not only with schooling in general but with the field of composition in particular. When we reflect upon the disciplinary moment in which we wrote AA/AI, we find ourselves with multiple understandings and responses. From our current perspective, one informed by recent research in feminism, poststructuralism rhetorical theory and critical pedagogy, it is easy to look back at research in composition in the mid-1980s—with its emphasis on the writing process and cognitive models of that process—and note the field's generally uncritical identification with and appropriation of the goals of schooling. Paradoxes of institutional placement that now seem obvious—such as the tension inherent in our field's asserted desire to empower students and its curricular positioning as gatekeeper and certifier—were repressed in much of the work of the time, including our own. We want now to acknowledge and understand the implication of such repression as well as to relinquish at least some of the dreams of disciplinary progress, of moving inexorably toward a time when we can "know" audiences much less teach students to use such knowledge in straightforward ways to achieve "success" in writing. Yet we would not want to give up our field's commitment to teaching. Thus when we return to such efforts as Mina Shaughnessy's *Errors and Expectations,* or to early writing process studies we find much to celebrate in their commitment to teaching, to opening up spaces in the academy for traditionally excluded students and to the importance of striving for social and political change. We want now, at *this* disciplinary moment, to reaffirm these commitments, while acknowledging the importance of inquiring into the nature of both teacher and student subjectivities and of recognizing the implications of our cultural, political economic and institutional embeddedness. Teachers and students are—we understand better now than in the past—not free individual agents writing their own destinies but rather constructed subjects embedded in multiple discourses, and the classroom is not a magic circle free of ideological and institutional influence. Such understandings have been and continue to be chastening to us; they encourage humility and modesty in teaching and research and an increased attentiveness to the motivated and situated—that is to say deeply rhetorical—nature of our assumptions and practices.

Audience, Ideology, and the Rhetorical Tradition

As we have tried to suggest, the writers and teachers speaking through AA/AI are, in many important ways, the writers and teachers we wanted and still want to be: negotiators of rhetorical situations who can gain a place for ourselves, our students, and our field at the academic and social conversational table. But we can also now see repressed in our essay—metaphorically smoothed or trolled out—traces of difficulties, of pain, failure, misunderstanding, and conflict. Such repressions were both encouraged and made possible not only by our personal identification with schooling and with the emergent field of composition studies, but also by our deep—and ongoing—commitment to the discipline of rhetoric.

In AA/AI, this commitment to traditional views of rhetoric, and particularly to the heuristic potential of the concept of the rhetorical situation, offered us a powerful framework for analyzing and enriching understandings of audience, a framework we still find useful. But this commitment also almost certainly insured that we would not notice the tradition's insistent impulse toward successful communication on the one hand and exclusion on the other. Indeed, the rhetorical tradition's focus on success in communicating with and persuading others is longstanding and enduring, discernible in the western emphasis on efficiency, "getting the job done," and clarity, as well as in traditional theories and definitions of rhetoric. Think, for instance, of Aristotle's definition of rhetoric as "the faculty of discovering in the particular case what are the available means of persuasion" (7) or of Richards' view of it as "the study of misunderstanding and its remedies" (3).

This focus on successful communicative negotiation inevitably, albeit silently, casts misunderstanding, miscommunication, disagreement, resistance, and dissent as failure and, as such, as that which is to be avoided or "cured." Today it seems to us that this emphasis on "success" has exacted a high hidden price. For how better to avoid misunderstanding and failure (and to make "successful" communication more likely) than to exclude, to disenfranchise those who by their very presence in the arena of discourse raise increased possibilities for communicative failures. The student writers invoked in AA/AI, for instance, are always already within and compliant to academic discourse, and thus willing and able to "adapt their discourse to meet the needs and expectations of an addressed audience" (166). While we still hope to help students meet such needs and expectations, we would also hope to bring into relief the exclusions that will almost certainly be necessary to do so, as well as the choices students must consider in deciding to inhabit academic discourse in this way.

That the rhetorical tradition is one of persistent exclusion goes without saying. But seeing the desire for successful communication as deeply implicated in the tendency to exclude those (like women and slaves in the ancient world) who might tend to disrupt or stand in the way of that success seems to us particularly noteworthy. For the dual moves toward exclusion and successful persuasion tend to hide from view any value that misunderstanding, resistance, or similar "failures" might have in complementing and enriching our notion of "success" by opening up spaces for additional voices, ways of understanding, conversations, and avenues of communication. It's interesting to consider, in this regard, the ways in which exclusionary tendencies of the rhetorical tradition are tied to a view of the human subject as coherent autonomous, and unified. Such a view assumes that writers and readers have no options but to be either in—or out of—a particular rhetorical situation.

Suppressed by the double impulse toward exclusion and success are the ways in which lived experiences can cause people to create internalized audiences that can lead not only to successful communication but also to disabling silences or to attempts at manipulative control, or the ways in which the materiality of people's lives can have the same effects, can result in communicative failure, in audiences ignored, rejected, excluded, or denied. Most deeply suppressed in the persistent gesture toward success, with its accompanying silent embrace of sameness, is a concomitant inattention to issues of difference. Thus while traditional Western conceptions of rhetoric as a system do, we still wish to argue, leave a space for difference in the concepts of rhetorical situation and of audience, that space has been, in practice, more often apparent than real. But not always. For as bell hooks and many others traditionally excluded from the dominant discourse continue to demonstrate, the "place of struggle" that rhetoric encompasses *can* be broadened (albeit with difficulty) to enact differences. In terms of verbal communication this rhetorical space is what we have to work with and in. And in order to do so in a way that makes that space as open and inclusive as possible, we must work hard to understand the complex choices, multiple responsibilities, and competing representations that communication always entails. Only thus can we open up more spaces for dialogue with others; only thus can we understand, with hooks, that:

> Spaces can be real and imagined. Spaces can tell stories and unfold histories. Spaces can be interrupted, appropriated, and transformed through artistic and literary practice. (*Yearning*, 152)

Re-Presenting Audience

As we hope this discussion has suggested, situating AA/AI in a web of personal, professional, and disciplinary contexts draws attention to those multiple and sometimes conflicting desires that speak through our effort to communicate with others, to both address and invoke audiences. As we noted early on in this essay, however, this attempt at a rereading of our work has aimed not to dismiss or discredit the work we have discussed, and in this sense not to engage in the agonistic activities so characteristic of the academy and the rhetorical tradition. Rather, we have attempted to demonstrate here the value of reading one's own research with the same kind of rhetorical care often reserved for the work of others and to suggest that this kind of reading—which calls attention to absences as well as presences, to multiplicity, tension, and competing motives in discourse—can enrich our understanding in ways that oppositional or totalizing readings do not.

Reading AA/AI against the backdrop of our own commitment to and identification with schooling, for instance, helped us to understand that although we intended AA/AI both to invoke and address a broad range of audiences, it speaks most strongly to those whose identifications and experiences mirror our own, while turning away from the potential difficulties and costs often inherent in the effort to achieve the kind of academic "success" that our essay takes for granted as well as from those who would wish to subvert such "success." Similarly, reading AA/AI in the context of research in the field emphasizes the degree to which our text fails to examine common-sense understandings of the nature, purposes, and impacts of education. In addition, a single-minded focus on students' success, without an interrogation of the definitions and foundations of such success, effectively prevents us from fully recognizing the contradictions and conflicts inherent in our own (and students') positionings. Finally, seeing these desires for success and suppression of conflict as implicated in the larger project of the western rhetorical tradition helps us to understand not only how implicated we are in that tradition but also the exclusions at that tradition necessarily entails.

Put another way, reading AA/AI in terms of its place in the field of composition studies as well as in the rhetorical tradition as we have just done requires us to acknowledge the extent to which our essay both inhabits and expresses what Lynn Worsham terms our field's modernist commitment "to the Enlightenment dreams of communications and consensus, emancipation and empowerment" (100). That we now question some aspects of these dreams is evident in our desire to interrogate AA/AI in order to reveal at least some of its exclusions and repressions. These exclusions and repressions need to be acknowledged, we believe, if (as both writers and teachers) we are to work effectively to further those goals that we remain unwilling to relinquish. For with Stanley Aronowitz and Henry Giroux, we believe that "those ideals of the project of modernity that link memory, agency, and reason to the construction of a democratic public sphere need to be defended" (59).

Our understanding of what it means to work to further the goals of democratic education has changed, however, since we wrote AA/AI. We have learned to be suspicious, for instance, of claims to empower or do something "for" others, especially when that claim entails representations that may essentialize those on whose behalf these claims are made. (Current arguments about basic writing programs turn at least in part on this issue.) We have also learned to reassess what it means to be "successful" as both writers and teachers, and we have become aware of the ways in which "success" disciplines and shapes what we are allowed—generically, theoretically, pedagogically—to do. Perhaps most importantly, we now know in our bones that there is no pure or separate space from which we nay write or teach. Representation, of ourselves as well as of those audiences that we both invoke and address, can never be innocent—whether that representation involves writing an essay (such as the one you are now reading) or teaching a class. Nevertheless, without representation we cannot engage in discourse, nor can we create spaces that, potentially at least, enable others—as well as ourselves—to speak. And without representation, we cannot teach writing or reading, for those acts depend absolutely on a willingness to represent and be represented.

Coda

In this rereading of AA/AI, we have attempted to engage in a series of reflections about what it means to represent audience, and, in doing so, to raise some questions about "successful" discourse, disciplinary critique and progress. We have looked at AA/AI as an example of "successful" discourse and attempted to examine the nature of that success. In so doing, we have tried to indicate that "success" is—in every case—more charged with tensions, competing motives, and trade offs than we had imagined, tensions that we have been at pains to suggest, can and should inform our teacherly and writerly practices.

In writing this essay we have also attempted to resist the impulse to engage in traditional academic critique by overturning our previous work. We have done so primarily because we have come to feel that such critical maneuvers, while necessary and helpful in many ways, make it particularly easy for us to forget how multiple, heterodox, and situated both teaching and writing are. They also contribute to a rhetoric of disciplinary progress that tends to exempt those effecting critique from inquiry into their own ethical responsibilities and choices. No critical reading can insure or guarantee that our field will effect positive pedagogical change, and we have no doubt that our analysis has failed to illuminate some of the ethical responsibilities and choices implicit in our earlier work. Nor do we doubt that the essay presented here could be effectively subjected to the same kind of positioning and exploration and critique. (Indeed, some of our reviewers have provided us with the beginnings of such a critique.)

What seems finally most important to us, however, is not the particular product of a particular critique of the intensely self-reflective kind attempted here, but the process, the intellectual habit of mind, necessary to doing so. In the long run, we have written (not to mention re-written and re-written) this essay over a period of some two years now because we are trying to enact a practice that can inform our teaching as well as our scholarship. What, after all, do we have to offer our students if we cannot pass out universal laws of correctness, absolute textual meanings, and guarantees of communicative success along with our syllabi? What we have to offer, we believe, is a way of being in language and a way of both inhabiting and shaping knowledge structures, ways that strive to be critically self-reflective, multi-perspectival, and complex.

In short, what we have been trying to do here is consonant with what Don Bialostosky argues we must teach our students to do: to interrogate not only the discourses of schooling but personal, communal, and professional discourses as well. For students, the cultivation of such habits of mind can lead, Bialostosky believes, to the development of "doublevoiced" texts that are self-reflexive, aware of the situated nature of the words they write and speak (18). Such a pedagogy should, Bialostosky implies, not stop with students' awareness of their own situatedness but instead move toward a commitment to representing themselves as fully and ethically as possible—and toward an increased responsibility for their written and spoken words.

We should not, however, expect our students, as Bialostosky says, "to examine the words they arrive with" unless we ourselves are also engaged in just such an ongoing project (17). It is, we know from experience, much easier to call for scholarly and pedagogical changes than to enact such changes In a footnote to "Beyond the Personal: Theorizing a Politics of Location in Composition Research," for instance, Kirsch and Ritchie acknowledge "the irony of the text . . . [they] have produced: a relatively univocal, coherent text that argues for experimental, multivocal writing" (27). And we can certainly find similar examples of such unintended discursive irony in texts we have authored or coauthored and in much other "successful" work in our field. Part of the burden of this essay has been to question the ground of such discursive "success," but to do so in ways that suggest the possibility of non-agonistic disciplinary critique, a critique that we believe necessarily entails self-critique and self-reflection. We are not, however, arguing for the imposition of some new, singular norm of scholarly practice. Rather, we hope that others will join us in articulating the multiple ways in which scholars may productively "examine the words they arrive with" whenever they engage in the representation of self and audience.

Acknowledgments
We are grateful to friends and colleagues who responded to sometimes wildly varying drafts of this essay: Sharon Crowley, Russell Durst, Tom Fox, Suzanne Clark, Vicki Collins, Cheryl Glenn, Anita Helle, and Gesa Kirsch.

Notes

1. In "Wearing a Pith Helmet at a Sly Angle: or, Can Writing Researchers Do Ethnography in a Postmodern Era?", Ralph Cintron comments, for instance, on the extent to which "academic debates are to a significant degree performances. Differences—and they do exist—push themselves forward by creating caricatures of each other. Although it may seem paradoxical, differences are deeply relational: To denounce the other's position is to announce one's own" (376).

2. Many feminist scholars are working to challenge the generic constraints associated with the traditional academic essay and are aiming the essay in fact as a site of intense struggle and exploration. The student writer we invoke in AA/AI is involved in no such struggle, seeking instead to inhabit tradition successfully.

3. We have been particularly aided in recognizing the potential conflicts and contradictions inherent in inhabiting various writerly identities by reading the many works of bell hooks—whose reflections on audience in particular (see, in this regard *Talking Back: Thinking Feminist, Thinking Black*) and literacy in general reflect her powerful understanding of how much is at stake in acts of reading and writing. We are aware of other projects that will help illuminate our understanding of these issues, such as Juanita Comfort's dissertation, "Negotiating Identity in Academic Writing: Experiences of African American Women Doctoral Students."

4. In "On Race and Voice: Challenges for Liberal Education in the 1990s," Chandra Talpade Mohanty makes a similar point when she observes that "if complex structural experiences of domination and resistance can be ideologically reformulated as individual behaviors and attitudes, they can be managed while carrying on business as usual" (157).

Works Cited

Aristotle. *The Rhetoric of Aristotle.* Trans. and ed. Lane Cooper. Englewood Cliffs: Prentice, 1932.

Aronowitz, Stanley, and Henry A. Giroux. *Postmodern Education: Politics, Culture, and Social Criticism.* Minneapolis: U of Minnesota P, 1991.

Bialostosky, Don H. "Liberal Education, Writing, and the Dialogic Self." *Contending with Words: Composition and Rhetoric in a Postmodern Age.* Ed. Patricia Harkin and John Schilb. New York: MLA, 1991. 11-22.

Burke, Kenneth. *Language as Symbolic Action: Essays on Life, Literature, and Method.* Berkeley: U of California P, 1966.

Cintron, Ralph. "Wearing a Pith Helmet at a Sly Angle: or, Can Writing Researchers Do Ethnography in a Postmodern Era?" *Written*

Communication 10 (1993): 371-412.

Comfort, Juanita. "Negotiating Identity in Academic Writing: Experiences of African American Women Doctoral Students." Diss. Ohio State U, 1995.

Ede, Lisa and Andrea Lunsford. "Audience Addressed/Audience Invoked: The Role of Audience in Composition Theory and Pedagogy." *CCC* 35 (1984): 155-71.

Harris, Joseph. "CCC in the 90s." *CCC* 45 (1994): 7-9.

hooks, bell. *Talking Back: Thinking Feminist, Thinking Black*. Boston: South End, 1989.

———. *Yearning: Race, Gender, and Cultural Politics*. Boston: South End, 1990.

Kirsch, Gesa E., and Joy S. Ritchie. "Beyond the Personal: Theorizing a Politics of Location in Composition Research." *CCC* 46 (1995): 7-29.

Long, Russell C. "Writer-Audience Relationships: Analysis or Invention?" *CCC* 31 (1980): 221-26.

Mitchell, Ruth and Mary Taylor. "The Integrating Perspective: An Audience-Response Model for Writing." *College English* 41 (1979): 247-71.

Mohanty, Chandra Talpade. "On Race and Voice: Challenges for Liberal Education in the 1990s." *Between Borders*. Ed. Henry A. Giroux and Peter McLaren. New York: Routledge, 1994. 145-66.

Ong, Walter J. "The Writer's Audience Is Always a Fiction." *PMLA* 90 (1975): 9-21.

Richards, I. A. *The Philosophy of Rhetoric*. London: Oxford UP, 1936.

Shaughnessy, Mina P. *Errors and Expectations*. New York: Oxford UP, 1977.

Worsham, Lynn. "Writing against Writing: The Predicament of *Ecriture Feminine* in Composition Studies." *Contending with Words: Composition and Rhetoric in a Postmodern Age*. Ed. Patrica Harkin and John Schilb. New York: MLA, 1991. 82-104.

Portfolios for Teachers: Writing Our Way to Reflective Practice

Chris M. Anson

In 1986 George Hillocks published his now well-known work, *Research on Written Composition*. This was the first "metaanalysis" in a maturing field, a sign that the study of writing had reached a critical mass sufficient to let us stand back and assess how far we had come and to find out what works in the teaching of writing. The result was a useful set of delivery modes that described the dominant ways in which composition classrooms are organized and taught followed by an empirical assessment of these modes' effictiveness.

If Hillock's painstaking synthesis clearly reflected our preoccupations, then formal inquiry into composition had been driven by a hunger for abstractions, not by a desire to understand what happens in the minds of individual teachers who are influenced by personal experiences and act on self-constructed theory. As Susan Miller characterizes this focus on the abstract, it has left little room for "interpretive theory in composition, an approach that privileges the subject in, and the subjectivity of, composition as an intellectual pursuit" (120). Such an approach relies on accounts of teaching that weave through the thoughts, ambitions, and struggles of individual teachers as they breathe life into their own personal curriculum.

Unfortunately, the scholarly research community often devalues story-telling as a type of inquiry. In *The Making of Knowledge in Composition*, North defends the practice even as he acknowledges that "its credibility, its power vis-a-vis other kinds of knowledge, has gradually, steadily diminished" (21). In an effort to raise the intellectual stature of narratives about classroom experience, Brannon argues that it is primarily through storytelling that we come to know about teaching. Proposing a dialectic between the "softness" of classroom narratives and the "hardness" of scientific truth that has dominated our scholarly journals, she argues that it is time for each to inform the other, time to rediscover "reliability" of our own reflected practice. Brannon is not alone in this belief. Recent work such as Witherell and Noddings' collection, *Stories Lives Tell: Narrative and Dialogue in Education,* as well as extensive research by Lee Shulman, suggest a growing awareness of teachers' reflected practice as an arena of authentic study. These voices challenge us to redefine what should count as knowledge of the writing classroom and ask why it is that teachers' stories are not widely written and heard.

Recently, through such organizations as the American Association of Higher Education, teachers and administrators have taken a keen interest in an innovation that places personal accounts of teaching at the center of instructional development: the *teaching portfolio* (see Edgerton, Hutchings and Quinlan). Teaching portfolios invite teachers to tell the story of their work and in doing so to become more reflective of their own practice. As such, teaching portfolios respond directly to calls, like Brannon's, to legitimize classroom experience as real teaching and instructional inquiry.

To composition scholars, teachers, and administrators who have campaigned vigorously for student portfolios, the teaching portfolio makes good sense. Yet we still have much to learn about the method, both as a tool for appraising teachers' performance and as a way to encourage faculty development collaboration, and professionalism. This chapter describes the teaching portfolio and its goals, offers a rationale for its centrality to our profession, suggests some ways in which it can be adapted to specific kinds of writing programs, and raises questions for further exploration and study.

The Nature and Structure of Teaching Portfolios

Most approaches to teaching portfolios define them as a collection of materials, assembled by a faculty member, that document or reflect teaching performance. Some approaches emphasize the "communicative" goals of portfolios as a way to share one's teaching, others stress its role in assessment, still others its potential to encourage development. Wolf's description in "The School Teacher's Portfolio" perhaps best sums up these various functions:

> A [teaching] portfolio can be defined as a container for storing and displaying evidence of a teacher's knowledge and skills. However, this definition is incomplete. A portfolio is more than a container—a portfolio also represents an attitude that assessment is dynamic, and that the richest portrayals of teaching (and student) performance are based upon multiple sources of evidence collected over time in authentic settings.

While the portfolio may seem at first glance like a typical faculty "file," it differs from standard dossiers in important ways. First, although it can contain personal material, it benefits from agreements among a community of teachers about what it should contain and what purposes it should serve. Individual faculty dossiers, by contrast, represent mostly private efforts (often symbolically "off-limits" in a locked department file). Second, the teaching portfolio is not simply a repository of the outcomes of teaching; it contains documents that show teachers in action, both creating their teaching and reflecting on it during moments of introspection. Finally, the teaching portfolio may contain much more material than might be forwarded to a hiring committee or faculty evaluation team. The portfolio may become several portfolios, each displaying different materials depending on its purpose and audience.

Ideally, a teaching portfolio should contain both primary and secondary documents. Primary documents are actual materials from classroom instruction including, but by no means limited to, the following:

- Syllabi
- Course overviews or descriptions
- Assignments of all kinds
- Exams
- Study Guides
- Student papers, perhaps with teacher comments
- Classroom materials such as overheads or handouts
- Innovative instructional materials (computer programs, etc.)
- Logs from class visits
- Student evaluations

Secondary documents are materials that demonstrate active, critical thinking about instructional issues and materials. They might include the following:

- Reflections on peer-observations or videotapes
- Reflections on course evaluations
- Self-evaluations of all kinds
- Narrative accounts of problem-solving
- Responses to case studies and scenarios about teaching
- Journals documenting thoughtfulness about instructional issues
- Goal statements and philosophies
- Letters of assessment from others

From a developmental perspective, these secondary documents are essential if portfolios are to be used for something more than what Wolf, in "Teaching Portfolios," calls "amassing papers." Instead, they must be "*structured* around key dimensions of teaching, such as planning, teaching, evaluating students, and professional activities. . . . [T]he portfolio should be more than a few snapshots, but should reflect a person's accomplishments over time and in a variety of contexts" (2).

Most published descriptions of teaching portfolios also stress their collaborative potential. Portfolios should not only bring teachers together to talk about and share in the activity of teaching, but should also represent the influences of colleagues, students, and theorists. They should, then, be understood first as something programmatic or anchored in a community, not as a "file" stored away in a department cabinet.

Teaching Portfolios at the Center of Writing Programs

Teaching portfolios seem especially well-suited to the field of composition, whose scholars and teachers are experts in writing assessment just as they understand and strongly promote the use of writing as a mode of learning. Three important subject positions of teachers among our community nicely match the less discipline-specific goals of the teaching portfolio.

Teacher as Writer

More than in any other teaching-oriented field, composition celebrates the value of writing for improved instruction and deeper reflection. In most nationally prominent workshops on the teaching of writing, participants' experiences drafting, sharing, and revising their own texts become the seeds of personal and professional growth Such experiences "enact the belief that the best writing teachers are teachers who write" (Faery); participants learn how to teach writing "from the inside out" (Healy).

As Durst points out, however, many teachers write less than their own students:

> For most elementary, secondary, and community college teachers . . . writing is not a necessary part of the job. On the contrary, the responsibilities of their jobs generally work *against* finding time and energy for writing. And, of course, there are few job-related rewards for being a teacher who writes. (262).

Institutions that expect publication do, of course, encourage their faculty to write. Yet to survive in these settings, the faculty may end up working exclusively on articles and books unrelated to teaching.

Teaching portfolios must be *written*. While most primary documents placed in a portfolio have an independent life as part of classroom instruction, the portfolio casts a new light on such documents and gives their creators a different sense of audience. Through the imagined eyes of a colleague or administrator, the college teacher now rethinks the overly dictatorial tone in her course syllabus. Anticipating the scrutiny of a hiring committee looking at his portfolio, the recent Ph.D. wonders whether his sample assignment seems clear enough to demonstrate his best work. Knowing she will soon be sharing her comments on student papers with her peer teaching team, the instructor at a community college begins reflecting on her style of response. The various audiences invited into these teachers' portfolios inspire them to think in more principled ways about how their teaching materials are written, and this process leads to revision, new thought and new action where perhaps otherwise there would be little change.

But it is the secondary documents that really encourage teachers to write. Teaching philosophies, observation reports, discussions of course designs, explanations of assignments, analyses of comments of student papers, reflections on sets of student evaluations—these become the threads of a narrative, a kind of professional autobiography of a teacher's classroom life. It is difficult to imagine anyone invested in their daily work as a teacher giving short shrift to a statement of their beliefs about how best students learn and how best we might teach them. Ideally, teachers can meet in small focus groups to circulate and discuss drafts of their reflections and philosophies. Revisions of primary or secondary documents can then lead to changed attitudes and improved teaching strategies.

Teacher as Scholar

The dominant rhetoric in higher education unnecessarily splits teaching and scholarship, often through systems that reward one more richly than the other. "Research universities" stand in stark contrast to "teaching colleges." In spelling out the criteria for success, promotion and tenure codes usually separate the activities of "research and scholarship" or "publishing" from the activities of "teaching and advising students," as if the two were unrelated. In its report on the rising costs of higher education, the U.S. House Select Committee on Children, Youth, and Families argues that "the focus on higher education today is on research, not teaching" (3). Offering statistics that show the decline of attention to teaching and advising relative to the rise in emphasis on research, the report suggests that

> conducting research has become such an overwhelming focus on today's campuses that those professors who still manage to teach more than a few hours a day are actually looked down upon by their peers, to say nothing of the negative effect teaching has on their chances for tenure, pay, and promotion. (3-4)

Such dichotomizing characterizes teaching as a deliberately unscholarly kind of work requiring the endurance of tedium in contrast to the more demanding and intellectually rewarding work of research. In a valiant effort to tear down this barrier between the personal life of the laboratory or office and the public life of the classroom, Ernest Boyer offers four specific ways in which teachers can be scholars: through the scholarship of discovery (such as research), the scholarship of integration (such as writing a textbook), the scholarship of application (such as consulting), and the scholarship of teaching. Uniting all the professional activities of college faculty under the banner of scholarship restores teaching to its rightful intellectual place. "At bottom," Edgerton, Hutchings, and Quinlan claim, " the concept entails a view that teaching, like other scholarly activities ... relies on a base of expertise, a 'scholarly knowing' that needs to and *can* be identified, made public, and evaluated; a scholarship that faculty themselves must be responsible for monitoring" (1).

By creating and developing teachers' base of expertise through inquiry into the real problems and experiences of the classroom, teaching portfolios encourage this scholarly view of teaching. In the field of composition, "teacher research" has already gained prestige as a kind of inquiry rooted in classroom experience but branching into the world of theory and investigation. As William Schubert argues, even the teacher lore so often denigrated as unprincipled chit-chat is actually highly relevant to "the theory and practice of curriculum, teaching, supervision, and school improvement . . . To assume that scholarship can focus productively on what teachers learn recognizes teachers as important partners in the creation of knowledge about education" (207).

Teacher as Professional

Faculty members in higher education, particularly at research-oriented universities, often define their professional lives in terms of scholarship. In spite of the increased demand for a stronger commitment to teaching in American universities, the public itself perpetuates the image of experts in disciplines whose intellectual missions exist at some remove from teaching. The popular press stereotypes "absent-minded professors" as intellectuals immersed in the stuff of their disciplines. TV shows and movies depict faculty as distant, hard-to-reach scholars who hurry from their lectures for fear of being harassed by students. Much rarer are images of compassionate teachers willing to sit down with students and help them to learn, and who think conscientiously about their own instruction.

This tendency to privilege field-specific knowledge as the grist of one's professional life systematically devalues teachers (especially in public schools) whose professions are necessarily rooted in classrooms. Howard Gardner has described this situation as a paradox: "Few societies have paid as much lip service to the importance of education . . . yet it seems necessary to say as well that education—and particularly the schools—have often held a dubious position in the value scheme of the larger society" (98). Perhaps no sign more strongly defines the belief in professionalism-as-scholarship than the organization of the faculty vita. Publications, research grants, conference papers, and other artifacts of scholarship almost always appear before (and more prominently than) lists of courses, names of advisees, instructional innovations, and other outcomes of teaching.

Teaching portfolios not only display a teacher's best work but invite readers into the teacher's studio, where strategies for principled instruction are conceived and created. Portfolios provide glimpses— and sometimes longer, studied gazes—of teachers at work as professionals. In this sense, the portfolio encourages teachers to think of themselves as experts whose decisions are reflected in the professional artifacts of their instruction Their expertise as *conveyors and ochestrators* of specialized knowledge stands side-by-side with that specialized knowledge itself.

Adapting Teaching Portfolios to Specific Contexts

Most of the literature on teaching portfolios agrees that portfolios give teachers a way to work on and document not just the outcome of their efforts but also their reflection, improvement, and growing expertise. Individuals or committees charged with evaluating teachers (for performance appraisals, merit pay, or hiring) come away from a portfolio with a much clearer and more comprehensive picture of a teacher's work than brief testimonials and statistics from student evaluations. And, in composition, portfolios define a space for teachers to work on their own writing or, with other teachers, collectively focus on a large area of their professional lives.

Yet in spite of this conceptual agreement about teaching portfolios, important practical questions remain. Without decisions about the contents and uses of portfolios, they can become merely random repositories—haphazardly organized collections of student evaluations, old syllabi, and hastily photocopied handouts. And if they are used solely for assessment, teachers may soon look on them with feelings of fear and doubt rather than a sense of personal ownership in their work.

To be effective, portfolios must be adapted to teachers' and administrators' specific needs. If a program of faculty development wants to emphasize teaching style, the documents might go so far as to include a videotape of all or part of a class session along with a self-analysis. If participants in a writing-across-the-curriculum program want to improve the way they read students' work, then the portfolio might contain some examples of students' final and/or draft papers representing a range of quality, along with the teacher's commentary on those and an accompanying reflection on the nature of the teacher's responses. Specific questions can be designed as prompts ("Characterize your response style by examining a classful of your papers, and include a sample; what are your goals in responding to student writing? How do your comments achieve those goals?") If a department wants to work in a given year on the principles of effective writing assignments, the portfolio might include three sample assignments with accompanying descriptions of their place in the scheme of a course and a rationale for their design. The following year, the focus might shift to advising students—and the portfolio contents for that year should reflect the shift. Central to the adoption of portfolio contents is the constant need to guide reflection and encourage change in keeping with the missions of particular departments and institutions.

To illustrate this adaptive potential further, let's consider three fictitious writing programs where teaching portfolios play a role in faculty development and the evaluation of teaching. Each site uses portfolios for different purposes among quite different teachers.

Site 1 is Jonesville College, a small liberal arts school with a strong writing-across-the-curriculum program. The program is supported by teaching portfolios among all faculty assigned to "writing-intensive" (WI) courses. WI courses have a smaller class size than most other courses and also carry a special incentive bonus paid by the central administration. New teachers of WI courses meet monthly throughout their first year to participate in workshops, discuss the integration of writing into their coursework, and share ideas and samples of student writing. Coordinators of the WI program use portfolios initially to support faculty development. However, because competition to teach WI courses is keen, faculty are reappointed to these courses yearly. An evaluation committee coordinated by the director of writing across the curriculum examines the portfolios of present WI teachers who wish to continue teaching the following year. Criteria for reappointment include evidence of principled assignment design, integration of writing fully into the coursework, reflections on the nature of students' writing, and year-end self-assessments with commentary for further improvement. At Jonesville, therefore, the portfolios begin cumulatively and developmentally for teachers-in-training, and turn recursive and evaluative in future years. Model portfolios from experienced WI teachers provide ideas and techniques for teachers new to the program and demonstrate the principles of reflective practice.

Site 2 is the English department at Smithtown Community College, a midsize campus near a major metropolitan area. The department coordinates a single first-year composition course staffed largely by annually renewed instructors, some of whom teach at other local colleges and spend little extra time on campus. Five years ago, the instructors lobbied the department to examine its rather haphazard process of faculty evaluation after several younger instructors were eliminated following a budget cut. The chair decided to begin a teaching portfolio program as a way to assess the instructors' performance and create a better community of more committed teachers.

The model he chose is recursive: each portfolio must include, at a minimum, a full syllabus for each course taught, along with a two-or three-page rationale for its design; three samples of student writing from each course in the categories "strong," "typical," and "weak," along with the original responses and a one-page analysis explaining the papers' relative strengths and weaknesses and how the responses encouraged revision or further learning; two-page post-course self-assessments for all classes taught, with accompanying student evaluations from one of those classes; and a cover essay articulating a philosophy of teaching. Optional but strongly encouraged are informal write-ups of conference sessions, workshops, or readings relating to teaching.

The portfolios represent Smithtown's mission by focusing on student performance relative to strong, student-centered teaching. In successive years, teachers must revise or replace these documents but must refer to the changes they have made in their methods or beliefs. The chair discusses the portfolio with each instructor at the time of reappointment. It is generally understood that seniority will not count as much as a continued commitment, demonstrated in the portfolio, to change, renewal, and improvement in teaching. While the instructors continue to lobby against the inequities of annual renewals, they feel that the portfolios more fairly reflect their abilities at the time of reappointment.

Site 3 is a large composition program at Johnson State University, staffed almost entirely by teaching assistants pursuing Ph.D.s in the Department of English. As part of its TA development program, the program begins teaching portfolios in the first year of the TAs' five-year appointments. The model shown in Figure 14-1 is cumulative: the directors feel that as TAs move through their teaching appointments, they naturally attend to different concerns at different

Year	Focus	Entries
1	Experiential	Reflections on visits Teaching reflections Responses to student writing
2	Logistical	Syllabus with rationale Extended descriptions of assignments with rationales Narrative philosophy of teaching
3	Theoretical	Revised philosophy of teaching New rationales based on theory Student surveys of techniques, with analysis and reflection
4	Experimental	Post-course self-assessments Analyses of experimental techniques Revised philosophy of teaching
5	Professional	Best samples of all work (new portfolio for job search)

Figure 14-1 A Cumulative Model for Teaching Portfolios

levels of instructional sophistication. Since most of their new TAs have never taught before, Year I focuses on strategies for leading discussion, running small groups, working individually with students, and managing time. All TAs are given a common course design that they may slightly modify after consultation. During the year, each TA must visit another instructor's class at least twice and be visited at least twice. Small teams discuss, revise, and enter into the portfolio their write-ups of these visits, as well as reflections on samples of student writing. At several points during the year, the instructors write "teaching reflections" in which they analyze specific successes and failures in their classroom instruction. The writing program administrators and their assistants respond to the portfolio entries as they are cycled into the portfolio.

In Year 2, the TAs begin designing their own versions of the composition courses offered at JSU. Now the focus is logistical. Documents placed in the portfolio include a full syllabus, an accompanying rationale, and extended descriptions of each assignment along with explanations of its goals, contents, and sequence in the course. Instructors also write narrative-like philosophies of teaching. By the time they move to Year 3, the TAs must begin reading more extensively in the area of composition theory and research. A graduate course optionally supports this new theoretical focus. Now the TAs must reinterpret their classroom activities, course design, and philosophy through the new perspectives offered in their readings. Documents include revised statements of philosophy, deeper rationales for pedagogical choices, and at least one carefully administered student survey focusing on a specific technique used in the classroom, along with an analysis of the results.

In Year 4, TAs move into a more experimental stage during which they try out new and often innovative ideas in the classroom. In addition to post-course self-assessments, each TA must place into her portfolio at least two analyses of experimental or innovative instructional strategies. The best of these are photocopied and circulated among all the instructors. Finally, between Years 4 and 5, TAs prepare a professional teaching dossier from the materials they have accumulated in their teaching portfolios. These include the very best examples of syllabi, assignments, descriptions of innovations, reflections, post-course self-assessments of students' evaluations, and teaching philosophies. In this way, JSU's program uses teaching portfolios initially as a development tool and gradually "professionalizes" them to support teachers' job searches when they complete their graduate programs.

Clearly, each of these sketches raises concerns just as it suggests innovations. Most such concerns, however, will not arise from the "developmental" potential of teaching portfolios but from their use in the evaluation of teaching. No one will argue against creating a space for deeper reflection, greater collaboration, and more effective instruction. But many will question the method as a way to make judgments about teaching ability. To this issue we now briefly turn.

The Problem of Assessment

At the heart of the teaching portfolio lies the belief that excellent teachers possess a special expertise, what Shulman calls the "pedagogy of substance," that allows them to transform discipline-specific material into learnable concepts and methods. Shulman's research suggests that it is possible to gauge or measure this expertise and the attempt to achieve it. Because it provides rich descriptions and actual materials from teachers' instruction, the teaching portfolio opens up that possibility for measurement in a way that has excited many educators concerned about the public cry for accountability in higher education.

As experts in the assessment of student writing and thinking, compositionists interested in teaching portfolios as an evaluation tool face the mixed blessing of working out criteria for successful performance. Primary documents appeal to be the easiest to codify in this way: most teachers can distinguish between an especially strong course syllabus and an undeveloped or quickly drafted one. The unimaginative or thoughtlessly written assignment stands in stark contrast to the assignment that reflects clear goals and will interest and motivate students. Secondary documents, on the other hand, present more interesting puzzles. How might we measure "the ability to reflect"? What really counts for good response to students' in-process drafts? How might we sort strong from weak rationales for specific writing assignments?

Consider, for example, excerpts from the observation logs of two teaching assistants in the early years of their teaching careers. The teachers, both women, have observed the class of a colleague, kept a descriptive log of what happened during the class, and met briefly with the teacher to discuss the log.

Excerpt 1

[The teacher has visited a colleague's class on a day when the students worked on rough drafts of papers in small groups.]

Four of the five students apparently had little difficulty with the assignment, although not having read the papers I could only judge by watching their interaction. The fifth was out of her element, a high-school student who did not understand the assignment or seemed unable to carry it through. The teacher was extremely empathetic to her and gave her many openings to verbalize her understanding of the assignment and the essay she was analyzing; however, she was unable to do so. He finally excused her by saying she was apparently just "letting it sit for a while."

The quality of the students' comments varied, but they stayed quite general. The high-school student offered no contribution, except to say that she could not read one copy of the rough draft that she had been given. The teacher, unquestioningly the main critic here, offered comments and questions to each of the writers. All of the information flowed through him, rather than from student to student.

Paper 1. The paper was more analytical than evaluative. Student comments were made on clarifying audience, using more detail, and asking for elaboration and expansion at specific points. The best student response came for this paper, which was apparently quite funny. The teacher pointed out that the rhetorical strategies needed clarification. . . . Paper III. This "undeveloped" paper has already been mentioned. The instructor's tact was impeccable, and he gave her a chance to start over if she needed it. In the postobservation conference, the instructor related that this student did not ever take his offers of extra help. Her attendance is good, although she is in over her head. *I would infer that because this student is in high school she probably thinks that if she continues to come to class she will pass, regardless of her written performance. . . .*

Excerpt 2

[The teacher has visited a colleague's class on a day when the students have brought in short responses to a chapter about journal writing.]

. . . At this juncture, X solicited responses from the class. "Ok, what did it you think about the reading ? How did you react to it?" There is general silence; students flipping through the pages. X tries again. "Was this useful, do you think, as a way to start writing?" Students seem to nod in assent, but still no response. X starts talking about the concepts in the chapter. Two ways to use the techniques, as learning tool to explore material, and as writing tool to gather thoughts and draft. 7 minutes; X still talking. Then he asks if there are any questions. A student says she keeps a journal anyway, and can she turn in pages from it in this journal or somehow do both at the same time. X cracks a joke that loosens up the class a little. Then he sobers, advises her to do more academic kind of work in the course journal. Leave other stuff out. One student doesn't see the difference. He explains; locus is always on course or paper. Then quickly moves to transition into his explanation of the next assignment.

Two issues emerged for me from this part of the observation. The first is the questioning style and the silence. I find this so typical in my own teaching. You throw out a question and . . . nothing. I think X lost a chance to capitalize on the s's freewrites. Maybe by prefacing: "Take a look for a minute at your freewrites about the chapter, and star or circle any responses that stand out for you." Give them 30 seconds or so, then follow up. If the response seems limited, maybe just call on them, or do a safe-circle round-robin kind of thing, so everyone has a voice. X filled in the silence, but in our pre-ob he said he was trying to make his course as active as possible. So this wasn't a case of mini-lecture, of presenting vital information, but it came off like a lecture.

The other issue (a little thornier?) is the journal. The most exciting part of the first part of the class came when the student asked about her own journal writing. The st. thought there wasn't any difference between the two types (actually he asked, but it was almost an implication). I might have let this run a bit. The journal is slippery; maybe X could have asked #6 to describe what sort of stuff she writes in her personal journal, to gauge if it could fit into the course journal. Also, if the initial class discussion had been richer, the question might have come up in that context, instead of a "Is it ok to do such-and-such" question. I know how X felt. There hadn't been any discussion, he was put off, had other stuff to cover, and maybe just shut down a potential theoretical problem with the journal. He did loosen them up, which seemed a wise move if you're uncertain yourself. I'm not sure. But the openness he wanted didn't seem to be there. In my own use of journals in the classroom, I try to... [paragraph].

After describing the next assignment, X asked students . . .

As shown in the italicized material, the first teacher provides almost no reflection on her observation. She is witness to, but not interpreter of, the classroom she observed. In contrast, the second teacher stops in the middle of her account to discuss her own use of journals and how she might have handled a moment of silence. If we assume that the presence of such meta-commentary reflects positively on a teacher's ability to monitor her own teaching and continually improve her instruction, the second teacher would seem far ahead of the first.

Anyone who uses such material for assessment, however, will soon have the gnawing suspicion that the presence or absence of reflection may not predict teaching ability—just as talking a lot in class may not predict a student's intellectual acumen, ability to write, or accumulated knowledge. Critics in the creative arts have long claimed that artistic ability may be largely unconscious. Writers, painters, and composers are often unable to say exactly what made them describe a scene in such lugubrious words, choose burnt umber for the edge of the moon, or suddenly shift to the minor key in the middle of a movement; yet they may still create brilliant works.

Comparisons of what defines "quality" in teaching—between individual teachers, between departments, or between discipline—can also illustrate quite clearly the present dubiousness of specifying universal criteria or standards for such quality. Edgerton, Hutchings, and Quinlan, for example, include in their monograph *The Teaching*

Portfolio a sample entry from Harvard University history teacher James Wilkinson. Wilkinson's entry includes a student's typed book review, on which Wilkinson has made marginal annotations and an end comment. In his reflective statement accompanying the student paper, Wilkinson describes his reasons for writing what he did, and what the sample tells him about his own practice. This and other examples of portfolio entries are reproduced in order to "look at the particulars that might comprise a teaching portfolio" (13).

From the perspective of a history department, Wilkinson's entry no doubt shows a concerned faculty member who takes the time to design good assignments, read his students' work carefully, and write useful comments. While not intended to be a model of excellence, Wilkinson's entry clearly reveals a dedicated teacher at work, someone able to stand back from his teaching enough to know that he is offering "encouragement, even where there is need for improvement," and not "writ[ing] out what [students] should have said, but instead giving them general guidelines" (39). Most advocates of writing across the curriculum would react enthusiastically to such an entry, inspired that writing can be used effectively in all disciplines.

But if we switch the setting for purposes of illustration, the history department's criteria seem more localized. From the perspective of a faculty member teaching advanced composition, Wilkinson's commentary may seem inadequate, or "differently adequate," lacking developmental insight or advice about the writing process in order to draw the student's attention to the material of history. From the perspective of a psychology department with large classes void of writing assignments, Wilkinson's response may seem absurdly diligent. Once we acknowledge such multiple perspectives coming from widely different disciplinary, departmental, or institutional settings, the problem of establishing universal criteria for "good teaching" takes on considerable complexity. Perhaps evaluating teaching using documents in a portfolio (especially secondary ones) may have to remain the responsibility of individual departments within specific universities.

To release themselves of such dilemmas, most administrators argue that specifying exactly what should be in the portfolio and then describing strong and weak examples of those contents *encourages certain kinds of thinking* conducive to good teaching. This privileges neither the "science" of teaching, which assumes an objectivist and sometimes clinical view, nor the "art" of teaching, which often resigns ability to intuition, magic, and God-given dispositions. Reflection blends the two approaches by assuming that teaching can be discussed and improved consciously even if it can never be understood entirely clinically. If the ability to reflect on and problematize teaching activities really is associated with expertise, then evaluation programs can play a powerful role in improving instruction across entire campuses by raising to consciousness at least some of those decisions, actions, and experiences that lead to success in the classroom.

Without explicit, theoretically informed criteria for such portfolio contents as observation logs, reflections on student evaluations, or rationales for assignments, teaching portfolios can still encourage accountability, which in turn can be linked to assessment. A program of faculty or TA development, for example, can list documents that must be placed into a teaching portfolio over a certain time period. More ambitious programs can provide models of well-written, reflective documents, and can encourage faculty collaboration, perhaps by setting up small teams or pairing novice teachers with mentors. In such a context, both teacher A and teacher B above could carry on a useful discussion of their observations. Teacher A might express some interest in teacher B's feelings about journal writing, or strategies for engaging the class when a question to students meets with deafening silence. Both teachers could profit from such interaction. In responding to Teacher B's questions about her observation, Teacher A might begin expressing her own values and ideas more fully. Did she think that the teacher was treating the high school student differently? What might this suggest about the "levels" of students in mixed classrooms and how to deal with such differences in small groups? What might one do in a small group when the discussion is staying too "general"? What happens when students find a peer's paper "funny" or enjoyable but the teacher thinks it needs more work on "rhetorical strategies"? Simply establishing Teacher A's interpretation and evaluation of the classroom scene might then lead into substantive issues of classroom organization, interaction, and teaching style. Good *reflection* may naturally follow from good *discussion* and vice versa.

An agenda of research and development for the teaching portfolio within the field of composition might begin by acknowledging that no monolithic concept of "good teaching" exists; indeed, the entire field devotes most of its energy to this very question, without ever reaching closure. Having put aside the trepidation of such a totalized view, discussions within departments might turn to principled ways of achieving established goals. Such a situation already exists, though not always explicitly, across different writing programs around the country. One school's philosophy and goals may justify a heavy emphasis on the relationship between reading and writing especially in traditional library research, while another's emphasizes the development of critical awareness of cultural difference, using a major "ethnographic" paper as its pivotal writing assignment. Within each context, however, there are certainly better and worse ways to teach the research paper or the ethnographic exploration. Open discussion of such methods can, in turn, raise questions about the program's larger goals, creating curricular change just as it changes and improves the teaching of individual faculty.

Whether or not the field can ever reach consensus about "good teaching," the evaluative criteria for performance should be shaped in the context of each teacher's work. A good teacher may not be someone who consistently uses small-group conferencing just because a national board of consultants or a group of composition scholars have deemed them crucial to the development of students' writing abilities. Rather, a good teacher may be someone who tried small-group conferences early on, abandoned them because they didn't seem to be working, and now, urged on by the portfolio, is revisiting this method, experimenting with it, and asking sensible questions about its role in the classroom. Administrators, merit-pay committees, and others charged with evaluating teaching may have to intuit improvement and hard work from the available document—a prospect that itself might encourage teachers to be more explicit about their goals, methods, and reflections as teachers.

Clearly, much work remains to be done—most of it fortuitous for the field. In the need to establish standards for such seemingly routine tasks as responding to and evaluating student writing, designing a theoretically informed composition course, or integrating reading and writing in a principled way, we may as a field push our own investigations of writing curriculums and teaching methods a bit further. And that, in turn, will create better abstract models upon which living, breathing teachers can, in all their complexity, act.

References

Boyer, Ernest. *Scholarship Reconsidered: Priorities of the Professoriate.* Princeton, NJ: Princeton UP, 1990.

Durst, Russel K. "A Writer's Community: How Teachers can Form Writing

Groups." *Teacher as Writer: Entering the Professional Conversation.* Ed. Karin L. Dahl. Urbana, IL: National Council of Teachers of English, 1992, 261-271.

Edgerton, Russell, Patricia Hutchings, and Kathleen Quinlan. *The Teaching Portfolio: Capturing the Scholarship in Teaching.* Washington, D.C.: American Association of Higher Education, 1991.

Faery, Rebecca B. "Teachers and Writers: The Faculty Writing Workshop and Writing Across the Curriculum." Midwest Modern Language Association. November 1992. St. Louis, MO.

Gardner, Howard. *Multiple Intelligences: The Theory in Practice.* New York: Basic Books, 1993.

———. "The Difficulties of School." *Literacy: An Overview by 14 Experts.* Ed. Stephen R. Graubard. New York: Noonday Press, 1991. 85-114.

Healy, Mary K. "Writing Communities: One Historical Perspective" *Teacher as Writer: Entering the Professional Conversation.* Ed. Karin L. Dahl. Urbana, IL: National Council of Teachers of English, 1992. 253-260.

Hillocks, George Jr. *Research on Written Composition: New Directions for Teaching.* Urbana, IL: National Council of Teachers of English, 1986.

Miller, Susan. *Textual Carnivals: The Politics of Composition.* Carbondale, IL: Southern Illinois UP, 1992.

North, Stephen. *The Making of Knowledge in Composition: Portrait of an Emerging Field.* Portsmouth, NH: Boynton/Cook, 1987.

Schubert, William H. "Teacher Lore: A Basis for Understanding Praxis." *Stories Lives Tell: Narrative and Dialogue in Education.* Eds. Carol Witherell and Ned Noddings. New York: Teachers College Press, 1991. 207-233.

Shulman, Lee. "Paradigms and Research Programs in the Study of Teaching: A Contemporary Perspective." *Handbook of Research on Teaching.* Ed. Merlin C. Whitrock. New York: Macmillan, 1986. 3-36.

United States Cong. House Select Committee on Children, Youth, and Families. *College Education: Paying More and Getting Less.* 102nd Cong. Washington: GPO, 1992.

Witherell, Carol, and Ned Noddings. Eds. *Stories Lives Tell: Narrative and Dialogue in Education.* New York: Teachers College Press, 1991.

Wolf, Kenneth P. "The Schoolteacher's Portfolio: Practical Issues in Design, Implementation, and Evaluation." *Phi Delta Kappan,* October, 1991. 129-136.

———. *Teaching Portfolios: Synthesis of Research and Annotated Bibliography.* San Francisco: Far West Laboratory for Educational Research and Development, 1991.

Bringing Practice in Line With Theory: Using Portfolio Grading in the Composition Classroom

Jeffrey Sommers
Miami University—Middletown

Portfolio assessment in the composition classroom offers not a methodology but a framework for response. Rather than provide definitive answers to questions about grading criteria and standards, the relationship between teacher and student, and increased paper loads, the portfolio approach presents an opportunity for instructors to bring their practice in responding to student writing in line with their theories of composing and pedagogy. My essay proposes to take an exploratory look at how portfolio evaluation compels instructors to address a number of important, and long-lived, issues underlying response to student writing. When an instructor chooses to use a portfolio system, certain other decisions must inevitably follow, and it is the implications of these decisions that I propose to examine most closely.

As the writing process has become the focus of composition classes over the past three decades, it seems an almost natural evolution for portfolio evaluation to have entered the classroom. Emphasizing the importance of revision to the composing process—regardless of which theoretical view of composing one takes—ought to lead to a classroom practice that permits, even encourages, students to revise. While such revision can, of course, occur in a classroom in which the writing portfolio is not in use, the portfolio itself tends to encourage students to revise because it suggests that writing occurs over time, not in a single sitting, just as the portfolio itself grows over time and cannot be created in a single sitting. Elbow and Belanoff argue that a portfolio system evaluates student writing "in ways that better reflect the complexities of the writing process: with time for freewriting, planning, discussion with instructors and peers, revising, and copyediting. It lets students put these activities together in a way most productive for them" (this volume 14).

Additionally, the portfolio approach can help students discover that writing is indeed a form of learning. Janet Emig has argued that writing "provides [a] record of evolution of thought since writing is epigenetic as process-and-product" (128). Portfolios provide a record of that record. Emig also describes writing as "active, engaged, personal—notably, self-rhythmed" (128). The notion that writing occurs over time in response to the rhythms created by the individual writer—a notion that makes eminent sense when one considers that no two writers seem to work at precisely the same pace and that no two pieces of writing seem to take form at the same pace even for the same writer—is another excellent argument for using portfolios. The portfolio approach allows writers to assemble an *oeuvre* at their own pace, within the structure of the writing course and its assignments, of course. Nevertheless, the portfolio by its very nature suggests self-rhythm because some pieces will require more drafts than others, even if explicit deadlines are prompting their composition.

For good cause, then, have portfolio systems of evaluation become commonplace in composition classrooms. But with these portfolios also come serious issues about grading standards and criteria, about how teachers and students relate to one another, about how teachers handle increased paper loads. Before examining how these issues might be resolved, perhaps it is time to acknowledge that this essay has yet to define *portfolio*. I have deliberately avoided doing so for two reasons: first, *portfolio* is a familiar-enough term and not really all that mysterious, and thus what I have written so far should be comprehensible to my readers; second, no consensus exists about just what a portfolio is or should be, however familiar the concept may seem. In fact, two distinctly different models of portfolios exist, each compelling its adherents to address the central issues of response in very different theoretical ways.

The first model is described well by James E. Ford and Gregory

Larkin, who use as an analogy an artist's portfolio. Each student's work is "collected, like the best representative work of an artist, into a 'portfolio'" (951). We are to see students in the role of free-lance commercial artists approaching an art director at an advertising agency with a large portfolio case containing their "best representative work." Such a model is easily transferred into the writing classroom. Students in the writing course produce a certain number of written documents during the term, agreeing in advance that only a specified number of those documents will be graded by the instructor. Commercial artists would never compile a portfolio that consisted of every piece of work they had done and neither do the students; the idea is to select a representative sampling that shows the creators at their best.

This portfolio model most likely grows out of instructors' concern with grading criteria and standards. Ford and Larkin, as the title of their article suggests, came to the portfolio as a means of guaranteeing grading standards. Instructors are justified in upholding rigorous standards of excellence because their students have been able to revise their work and select their best writing for evaluation. As Ford and Larkin comment, "A student can 'blow' an occasional assignment without disastrous effect" (952), suggesting that the instructor is being eminently fair. Elbow and Belanoff, in the context of a programmatic portfolio-assessment project, make a similar argument, one equally applicable to the individual composition classroom. "By giving students a chance to be examined on their best writing—by giving them an opportunity for more help—we are also able to demand their best writing" (this volume 13). This portfolio system "encourages high standards from the start, thereby encouraging maximum development" (Burnham 137).

To Ford and Larkin, Burnham, and Elbow and Belanoff, a portfolio is a sampling of finished products selected by the student for evaluation. Although the instructor using this model may very well be concerned with the students' development as writers, as Burnham's remark indicates, essentially this portfolio model is grade driven and could be accurately labeled a *portfolio grading system*. It is grade driven because the rationale for using the portfolio framework grows out of an understanding that the student's written work will ultimately be evaluated.[1]

However, portfolio grading, paradoxically, not only grows out of a concern for eroding standards, but also out of a concern for the overemphasis upon grades in writing courses. Christopher Burnham calls the students' "obsession" with grades a "major stumbling block" (125) to effective learning in the composition classroom and turns to portfolio grading as a means of mitigating the students' obsession with grades. Burnham concludes that the portfolio system "establishes a writing environment rather than a grading environment in the classroom" (137).

Thus, by addressing the issue of responding to the student's writing, Burnham wants to change the relationship between the student and the instructor. He wants to create a more facilitative role for the instructor, in accordance with suggestions about response from Donald Murray, Nancy Sommers, and Lil Brannon and C. H. Knoblauch. He not only wants to allow students to retain the rights to their own writing, he wants them to assume responsibility for their writing, asserting that portfolio grading "creates independent writers and learners" (136).

The question then of when and what to grade becomes quite significant. Although grading criteria must be established by instructors who employ portfolio grading, new criteria for grading the final drafts do not generally need to be developed. Presumably, instructors will bring to bear an already developed set of criteria for grading, applying these criteria rigorously to designated papers, thus protecting the integrity of their standards. Nonetheless, a crucial question arises: when will student work receive a grade: at midterm, only at the end of the term, with each submission? Some instructors grade every draft and revision as students submit them, some grade only the revisions, some grade only papers designated as final drafts. In some portfolio-grading systems, the students select a specified number of final drafts at midterm and a second set at end of the term, while in other systems, all grading occurs at the end of the term.

Instructors using portfolio grading must decide when to offer grades. Grading every draft keeps the students informed, but, because even a temporary grade has an air of finality to many students simply because it is a grade, this policy may undercut the idea that each draft may potentially develop into a finished product. Grading revisions only may encourage the grade-obsessed student to revise if only to obtain a grade, thus introducing revision to some students who may otherwise lack the motivation to revise, but also reinforcing the primacy of grades.

By deferring grades until the end of the term, instructors can extend the duration of the "writing environment" that Burnham hopes to substitute for the "grading environment" in the course. However, if students are indeed obsessed with grades, as he argues, then it seems likely that for a substantial number of students, or perhaps for all of the students to varying extents, there will always be a grading environment lurking beneath the writing environment of the course. If instructors respond effectively and frequently and confer with students individually, they can keep students informed of their approximate standing in the course, possibly deflecting their grade anxiety, but it is disingenuous to claim that portfolio grading removes grade obsession. If the portfolio ultimately produces an accumulation of individual grades, grade obsession cannot really be eliminated although it certainly can be reduced.

Yet a larger issue arises, an issue related to one's pedagogical assumptions about the significance of grades. Burnham discusses the portfolio system as a means of leading to student development, a development inevitably measured by the final grades earned by the student's portfolio. Inherent in this model is the idea that students can improve the writing, and thus the grade, by revising and selecting their best work. Inevitably, then, instructors using portfolio grading must address the issue of grade inflation. Although one of the motivating forces behind portfolio grading, as we have seen, is protecting grading standards, the system itself is designed to promote better writing by the students, and it stands to reason that many students are going to be submitting portfolios that consist of writing better than they might be able to produce in a classroom employing a traditional grading system. Will instructors raise the standards so high that even the improved writing in the portfolios falls into the usual grading curve? Or, and this seems much more likely, will the grades themselves on the whole be somewhat higher because of the portfolio approach despite higher standards? Should higher grades be of significant concern to instructors? Do higher grades mean "grade inflation"? What is the role of grades in writing courses? Portfolio grading compels instructors to consider these important questions.

Finally, portfolio grading presents problems to instructors in handling the paper load. Since most programs suggest or stipulate a certain number of assignments per term, instructors using the portfolio system must determine how they will count assignments. Will newly revised papers count as new assignments? By doing so, the instructor can keep the paper load from mushrooming. Let's focus on a course that requires seven papers in a semester (the situation at my institution), with the understanding that the portfolio will consist of four final drafts selected by the student. If instructors count revisions of papers 1 and 2 as papers 3 and 4, their paper load will be less because students will still only produce seven drafts for them to read. On the other hand, the students' options at the end of the term will be reduced by this method of counting; they will have to select four final drafts from only five different pieces in progress. To ensure students the full choice of seven, however, instructors commit themselves to more responding. In our hypothetical case, they will read at least nine drafts, seven first drafts, and revisions of the first two papers. Thus a routine decision actually has important pedagogical implications.

Several methods of controlling the paper load do exist. One is to divide the term in half, asking students to produce two miniportfolios. At midterm, for instance, in the situation already described, students are required to submit two final drafts for grading out of the first four assigned papers. At the end of the term, students must select two of the final three assigned papers for grading. Thus the paper load is under greater control because the students cannot continue work on the first four papers after midterm. On the other hand, Burnham's desire to create a writing environment rather than a grading environment will be affected because grades will become of primary concern not once but twice during the term.

Another method for controlling the paper load is to limit the number of drafts students may write of individual papers. Without such a limit, some students will rewrite and resubmit papers almost weekly, adding greatly to the paper load; of course, one can argue that such students are developing as writers in an important way. Deadlines for revisions of papers can also be used to control the paper load since "real" writers always work under deadlines. They may revise and revise and revise, but ultimately they must conclude. Instructors may allow students to revise a given assignment as often as they wish but within a designated period of time. Another method of controlling the paper load is to limit the number of revisions students may submit at one time or to designate specific times when revisions may be submitted. Late in the term, industrious students may have revisions of three or four different assignments ready to be submitted; some limit on the number they may hand in at one time can help instructors manage the course more effectively. Stipulating that revisions can be handed in only on certain days can allow instructors to plan their time for responding more efficiently.

Eventually, the end of the term arrives, and for many instructors using portfolio grading, the paper load explodes. Portfolios of four papers or more per student come in at the end of the term and must be graded quickly in order to submit final grades on time. Holistic grading can make the paper load manageable as instructors offer no comments but just a letter grade on each final draft. Grading portfolios at the end of the term undeniably requires more time than grading a single final exam or final paper would. However mundane these questions of handling the paper load may seem, the answers one supplies affect the entire portfolio grading system because many of these decisions may influence the relationship between students and their instructors, and some may influence, or be influenced by, instructors' grading criteria and standards.

To sum up then, a portfolio grading system defines a portfolio as a sampling of students' finished writing selected by the students for evaluation. Portfolio grading offers instructors a means of keeping their grading standards high while employing their usual grading criteria, it presents one potential method for reducing students' obsession with grades and transforming the classroom environment into one more engaged with writing than grading, and it increases instructors' paper loads. Instructors' decisions about when to grade and how to manage the paper load raise complications because they affect the relationship between instructors and their students. Thus, teachers planning on implementing portfolio grading need to consider carefully how they will do so in a way that will keep their practice in line with their own theoretical assumptions about writing and about composition pedagogy.

The second, newer, portfolio system model I will call the "holistic portfolio." The holistic portfolio is a response to continued theorizing about the nature of the composing process. Louise Wetherbee Phelps argues that theories underlying teaching practices evolve toward greater depth, and she sketches a hierarchy of response models to student writing beginning with one she labels "evaluative attitude, closed text" (49). In this model, the instructor treats the student text as "self-contained, complete in itself... a discrete discourse episode to be experienced more or less decontextually" (50). This concept of response to a text views reading as evaluation; instructors responding in this model may speak of "grading a stack of papers." The next response model described by Phelps is one she calls "formative attitude, evolving text" (51). Instructors read students' drafts as part of a process of evolution, thus entering into and influencing the students' composing process. In this model of response, instructors locate "learning largely in the actual composing process" (53).

Phelps describes a third model of response as "developmental attitude, portfolio of work": "Whereas the first group of teachers reads a 'stack' of papers and the second reads collected bits, scraps, and drafts of the composing process, the third reads a 'portfolio' of work by one student" (53). Phelps elaborates on two ways to work with portfolios, describing first the portfolio grading model we have already examined, which she dubs "the weak form." In this approach, she writes, "teachers continue to read and grade individual papers, attempting to help students perfect each one" (53). As Phelps has described the models of response, we can see that she has first described portfolio assessment used in a programmatic approach to large-scale decision making about student proficiency and placement. Her second model fairly accurately describes the portfolio-grading approach of Ford and Larkin and Burnham, elaborated upon somewhat in her depiction of "the weak form" of her third response model.

In the second method of using portfolios, Phelps also describes a different portfolio system. Some instructors employ portfolios because they wish to respond from a *"developmental* perspective." From this perspective, the student writing "blurs as an individual entity" and is treated as a sample "excerpted from a stream of writing stimulated by the writing class, part of the 'life text' each literate person continually produces" (53). Phelps concludes:

> The reader's function is [to read] through the text to the writer's developing cognitive, linguistic. and social capacities as they bear on writing activities. The set of a single writer's texts to which the reader has access, either literally or through memory, is the corpus from which the reader tries to construct a speculative profile of the writer's developmental history and current maturity. (53)

This definition of portfolio no longer serves as an analogy to the commercial artist's carefully assembled portfolio of a representative sampling of her best work. Instead it more closely resembles an archivist's collection of a writer's entire *oeuvre*. Instructors do not deal with selected writings but evaluate the entire output of the student writer. The implications of such a definition are quite different from those of the portfolio grading model defined by Ford and Larkin, Burnham, and Elbow and Belanoff.

While portfolio grading systems are driven by pedagogical concerns with fair grading as well as with composing process theory, the holistic portfolio system is primarily driven by a pedagogical concern with composing process theory. Although Knoblauch and Brannon's polemic *Rhetorical Traditions and the Teaching of Writing* does not discuss portfolio evaluation, its view of the composing process might very readily lead to it. Knoblauch and Brannon describe the "myth of improvement" that has stifled writing instruction by focusing on the kind of evaluation Phelps details in her first model of response (evaluative attitude, closed text). Knoblauch and Brannon suggest that "the most debilitating illusion associated with writing instruction is the belief that teachers can, or at least ought to be able to, control writers' maturation, causing it to occur as the explicit consequence of something they do or ought to do" (165). This illusion is reductionist, leading to a view of the writing course "in minimal functionalist terms" (165). This "myth of improvement" has produced a definition of teaching and curricular success that stresses "trivial but readily demonstrable short-term 'skill' acquisitions" and has led some teachers "to imagine it is fair to 'grade on improvement,' mistaking a willingness to follow orders for real development" (165).

While Knoblauch and Brannon's book remains controversial, their critique of "the myth of improvement" cogently articulates many instructors' reservations about grading practices based on the artificial academic calendar, a system that demands students learn at a given pace, defined by a ten-week quarter, a fourteen-week trimester, or a sixteen-week semester. Knoblauch and Brannon conclude by arguing that "symptoms of growth—the willingness to take risks, to profit from advice, to revise, to make recommendations to others—may appear quickly, even if improved *performance* takes longer" (169).

For instructors whose conception of the composing process is compatible with the developmental schemes underlying Knoblauch and Brannon's book and Phelps's third model of response, the holistic portfolio should have great appeal. It presents these instructors with difficult decisions, however, in the same areas that the portfolio grading system presented its practitioners: grading criteria and standards, the teacher-student relationship, and handling the paper load.

While upholding grading standards was the catalyst for portfolio grading, holistic portfolio systems appear to be less concerned with the notion of grading standards, at least in traditional terms. Because the holistic portfolio system does not focus instructors' attention on specific final drafts, it does present instructors with some major decisions about criteria for the final evaluation.

Several possibilities exist. Instructors may create a grading system that weights final drafts but also grades draft materials, notes, peer commentary, and so on. Counting the number of drafts or the variety of included materials is a way to "grade" preliminary materials. However, any counting method might distort the course's emphasis on development by encouraging students to create "phony" drafts, drafts written after the fact simply to pad the portfolio (just as many of us used to compose outlines *after* completing high school term papers as a way of meeting a course requirement).

Another way to grade the final portfolio is more holistic, and thus probably "purer" in the sense that it avoids treating individual drafts as "collected bits, scraps, and drafts" and treats portfolios as part of "the life text" (Phelps 53). The instructor looks for "symptoms of growth," to borrow Knoblauch and Brannon's phrase—"the willingness to take risks, to profit from advice, to revise, to make recommendations to others." Those students who demonstrate the greatest growth receive the highest grades, assuming that the instructor has developed a scale that measures growth—no small assumption.

While the holistic portfolio can fit very nicely into a developmental view of the composing process, it presents great difficulties in fitting at all into a traditional academic grading system and poses serious questions for instructors about how they see their writing courses fitting into the academy. This method of evaluation works most readily in a passing no-pass grading situation, and indeed is an argument for such a grading system. But pass/no pass writing courses are the exception rather than the rule. Unfortunately, neither Knoblauch and Brannon nor Phelps really addresses the issue of how to grade in a writing course that emphasizes a developmental perspective on writing. It is conceivable that an instructor holistically evaluating a set of portfolios could assign an entire class of industrious students grades of A, having developed grading criteria that emphasize "symptoms of growth"; such an instructor can have rigorous standards in that only those students who have made the effort and demonstrated the growth receive the As. However, one suspects this instructor would face a one-to-one meeting with a concerned writing program administrator or department chair sometime after submitting the final grades.

Some compromise or accommodation must undoubtedly be made by instructors, perhaps along the lines discussed earlier of weighting final drafts. The important point to make here is that instructors should be aware of how the grading criteria they develop correlate with the theory underlying their use of portfolio evaluation.

Given the problematic nature of grading holistic portfolios, why would instructors adopt this model of the portfolio system? The holistic portfolio system offers distinct advantages in defining a healthy teacher-student relationship. Burnham's hopes of creating a writing environment rather than a grading environment are more readily realized in the holistic portfolio system. Because the final portfolio will not be graded in any traditional sense, because individual grades on drafts do not occur, in theory the classroom using the holistic portfolio can indeed become a writing environment, since there is no reason for it to become a grading environment, and the instructor can truly doff the evaluator's role and don instead the facilitator's role.

Burnham praises portfolio grading for encouraging students to assume responsibility for their learning; portfolio grading "creates independent writers and learners," he concludes (137). His point is that when students know that they can control their grades through extra effort in revising and through the selection process available to them prior to final evaluation, they become more responsible and more independent; in today's terminology, they become "empowered." However, the motivation comes from a concern with grades.

In the holistic portfolio system, the students are also afforded the opportunity to become more responsible, not for their grades so much as for their development. They can indeed become independent learners, independent of traditional grading obsessions as well. The teacher and student can become "co-writers," in Phelps's phrase. The emphasis in the course falls not on improving texts as a means of improving a grade but instead falls on developing as a writer, understanding that this development is more important than grades on individual texts.

Both models of portfolios, then, hope to free students of the tyranny of the grade. The portfolio grading system does so temporarily, but also readily accommodates the traditional institutional need for grades. The holistic portfolio system can indeed free students to become learners and writers for the duration of a writing course but only if instructors have resolved the essential conflict between their course and the institution's demand for traditionally meaningful grades.

In the final area of paper load, it seems most likely that the holistic portfolio system will produce a heavier paper load than the portfolio grading system will. Any schemes to limit students' output would likely conflict with the theoretical assumptions that lead to using the holistic portfolio system. Thus students' portfolios are likely to grow in length as well as in the hoped-for depth of development. At the end of the term, instructors must read not merely a specific number of selected final drafts, but entire portfolios, certainly a slower process. Periodic reading of the growing portfolios—which instructors taking such a developmental perspective will probably wish to do—may reduce the paper load at the end of the course since instructors can scan the familiar materials in the portfolio, but it will not significantly reduce the paper load so much as spread it out over the course of the term.

Instructors contemplating a portfolio system of either sort, or a hybrid version of the two models described, are faced with the need to answer some important questions for themselves before incorporating the system into their writing classes. Louise Wetherbee Phelps concludes her discussion by commenting that her depiction of response models represents an increasing growth on the part of instructors. She argues that "experience itself presses teachers toward increasingly generous and flexible conceptions of the text and the reading task" (59). If she is correct, as I think she is, then the movement in composition classrooms toward portfolio systems of one sort or another will accelerate as the emphasis on the composing process as central to writing courses continues.

As the profession continues to refine its thinking about composition pedagogy, portfolio systems seem destined to proliferate in use and to grow in significance. The portfolio system of evaluation has tremendous advantages, which are described throughout the rest of this book, but it also requires great thought on the part of instructors because a portfolio system implemented in a scattershot manner may well undercut the goals of a writing course. The portfolio offers instructors wonderful opportunities to bring their teaching practice in line with their theoretical assumptions about writing and about teaching, but that convergence can only occur if instructors ask themselves the right—and the tough—questions and work out the answers that best provide what both instructors and students need in the writing course.

Note

1. I am assuming that instructors themselves will grade the papers. Ford and Larkin describe a programmatic use of portfolio grading wherein the portfolios are graded by a team of graders not including the students' instructor. My interest in this essay, however, is in the issues faced by individual instructors who do not have the power to implement such grading practice but must conduct their own evaluations.

Works Cited

Burnham, Christopher. "Portfolio Evaluation: Room to Breathe and Grow." *Training the New Teacher of College Composition.* Ed. Charles Bridges. Urbana. IL NCTE, 1986.

Elbow, Peter, and Pat Belanoff. "Portfolios as a Substitute for Proficiency Examinations." *College Composition and Communication* 37 (1986): 336-39.

Elbow, Peter, and Pat Belanoff. "State University of New York at Stony Brook Portfolio-Based Evaluation System." *Portfolios: Process and Product.* Ed. Pat Belanoff and Marcia Dickson. Portsmouth: Boynton-Cook/Heinemann, 1991.

Emig, Janet. "Writing as a Mode of Learning." *College Composition and Communication* 28 (1977): 122-28.

Ford, James E. and Gregory Larkin. "The Portfolio System: An End to Backsliding Writing Standards." *College English* 39 (1978): 950-55.

Knoblauch, C. H., and Lil Brannon. *Rhetorical Traditions and the Teaching of Writing.* Portsmouth, N.H.: Boynton/Cook, 1984.

———. "Teacher Commentary on Student Writing: The State of the Art." *Freshman English News* 10 (Fall 1981) 1-4.

Phelps, Louise Wetherbee. "Images of Student Writing: The Deep Structure of Teacher Response." *Writing and Response: Theory, Practice, and Research.* Ed. Chris M. Anson. Urbana, IL NCTE, 1989.

The Politics of Reading
Student Papers

Robert A. Schwegler
University of Rhode Island

In the year following my father's death, my mother sorted through the cartons in the basement of their home and began sending me envelopes filled with sepia-toned photographs of great aunts and great uncles. Among these was a carefully posed picture of a group of men standing by a horse-drawn merchant's wagon, some in suits, others with the open collars and rolled-up sleeves of workingmen from the early 1900s. The stiff poses of the men convey a sense of awkward pride and dignity. The wagon, looking newly painted and hitched to a well-groomed horse, announces in shiny letters the wares of "Schwegler & Levea—Greengrocers."

My father's drive to succeed, his willingness to work at two jobs—teacher and pharmacist—stemmed in part from the threat of poverty that came at age twelve when my grandfather died. But the feelings of fear and loss that drove my father had other roots as well, beginning with the threat to social status posed by the bankruptcy of the greengrocer business, my grandfather's subsequent injury while working as a laborer at the Pierce Arrow plant, and his physical decline and death.

At least this is how I received the story as a child and a teenager, sensing with it my father's pain and accepting the framework of values: a desire for material achievement and security as well as a sense that social (class) identity is both essential and fragile.

As I read student papers, I am especially moved by stories of loss or threats to the writer's social identity or economic security. I value as well the efforts of a student who struggles for grades and praise not as steps toward a career or even as validations of the writer's efforts but for their message of belonging and security: "Yes, this is how an educated person writes. You are one of us, a college student, a member of this social class." I enjoy, of course, an accomplished student essay that goes beyond formulas to blend personal voice with skillful use of rhetorical strategies. But I am also drawn to the paper whose struggles with academic diction and awkward but ambitious phrasing seem to whisper frantically, " I can do it. Let me stay!"

Other teacher/readers, I suspect, respond likewise to the values embodied in student papers and composing behaviors. Some may be drawn to particular images and values they encounter in narratives of growing up. Or they may perceive special force and pertinence in arguments about pornography or gun control congruent with their own outlooks while exhibiting a sharp critical awareness of the reasoning in papers supporting positions they oppose.

At the same time, it is difficult for most instructors to conceive of a positive role for responses conveying their moral, social, or political attitudes. In his anatomy of the possible roles for readers of student texts, Alan Purves leaves little room among categories such as "common reader," "editor," and "critic" for the instructor who interacts with values in a paper or who acknowledges to students that her perception of a text's meaning is conditioned by her social, cultural, or political concerns. While some of the most influential discussions of response and evaluation have encouraged teachers to provide "genuine personal reactions" (Knoblauch and Brannon 132) to student texts, they have at the same time viewed the teacher/reader as a "sounding board" whose job is to identify authorial meaning and intent and report on the "communicative effectiveness" of a text (Brannon and Knoblauch 166; also Sommers).

Despite acknowledgments that reading is an active, or transactive, process (Probst; Griffin), discussions of response and evaluation have continued to focus primarily on textual meaning. The content of readers' responses—specifically the values that permeate teacher/readers' reactions and help constitute the mental texts they create as part of the transaction of reading—has been largely ignored. Lacking any clear role for value-laden responses, most instructors have tried to suppress or displace them, lumping them with other inappropriate kinds of comments: those that "perpetuate archaic modes of expression, propagandize for a particular style, or coerce agreement with a sociopolitical attitude" (Sloan 35).

Like many other composition instructors, I, too, have feared that value-laden responses will lead me to be partial or to impose some ideological "ideal text" on student essays. Thus, in reading and evaluating student papers, I have often relied on formal criteria: coherence, evidence, thesis statements, stylistic clarity, and correctness. I have tried to guide my personal responses to reflect "community" standards, sometimes unconsciously echoing the language of textbooks. Detailed assignments, grading sheets, and peer evaluation guided by comment sheets have also put distance between my social and political values and the comments I make on student writing. When possible, I have tried take my commentary direct and personal, but also to remain in the role of an "assistant in the student's effort to make meaning" (Probst 74), focusing on authorial intention and negotiating with the student over the effectiveness of particular choices in form or content.

These techniques are familiar and useful elements of contemporary pedagogy. Yet they also can be, and often are, part of an elaborate set of strategies instructors employ to suppress or displace value-laden and political readings of student papers by putting the locus of evaluation outside the individual reader, situating it instead either in the text itself or in a supposedly community-wide set of standards expressed either in formal terms (thesis statement, clarity, logic) or in the responses of a putative "average reader." What we must remember, however, is that none of us can escape our personal histories as readers of texts. To the extent that our histories and ourselves are socially constructed, all readings of student papers must be in some measure political and value-laden. So, too, are the relationships we establish with students. In leaving the political dimensions of reading and teaching unacknowledged, we do not banish them; instead, we conceal them, often moving them beyond both recognition and control so that they can undermine teaching and learning.

Three sets of professional practices and assumptions have encouraged composition instructors to suppress value-laden responses to student writing and ignore the political dimensions of their reading and teaching practices:

1. The belief that reading and evaluation of student papers ought to be objective.
2. Simplistic models of the cognitive process of evaluation, and

3. Some often unexamined but widely held paradigms governing the relationship of teacher/readers and student/writers.

I would like to examine the implications of these assumptions and offer in their place perspectives incorporating the inevitable social and ideological grounding of response and evaluation into the act of composition teaching.

Objective/Subjective

During this century, composition teachers have generally viewed the reading and evaluating of student papers as, ideally, an objective rather than subjective process. Of course, few have argued that it can ever be objective in a technical sense, since different readers cannot be counted on to give identical scores to a text. Nonetheless, objectivity has been a goal in two informal senses, that is, in tying evaluation to the features of the text (the object) and not the reader's responses to it, and in trying to create uniformity among readers' perceptions and judgments.

The act of reading student papers has thus been often conceptualized as the identification of textual or content features assumed to be marks of writing quality to the exclusion of readers' responses to ideas, values, and stylistic force. Moreover, the role of the reader has been conceptualized as that of a representative of the standards of a larger audience, perhaps as embodying the tastes of the general educated readership for expository essays or the discourse preferences of a specific interpretive community. Hence the reader of student writing has been defined as an authoritative reader (a generalized or decontextualized subject) and not as an individual respondent.

In the first half of the century, research and pedagogy emphasized the use of grading scales and commentary cards that focused primarily on the formal features of texts and attempted to make the teacher's job of grading papers easier while at the same time eliminating inequality (or unreliability) in grading (Gere, "Empirical Research" 115-118). In the second half of the century, driven in part by the need for interrater reliability in research and in large-scale assessments and in part by a recognition that both untrained and trained readers relying on grading scales varied widely in judgments of papers (Gere, "Empirical Research" 115-116; Diederich), attention shifted to readers, specifically to methods such as holistic scoring, as ways of eliminating reader bias and achieving regularity (reliability) in response (Hillocks, 100-102; Gere, "Empirical Research" 117-118).

Neither grading scales nor holistic scoring attempts to make the individual reader disappear. After all, it is the reader who applies the scale or generates a holistic score. Nonetheless, the reader—the responding subject—is in both cases assumed to be of less importance than the text and to be in need of control. As Anne Gere puts it, "The interaction between reader and writer, the context in which the writing is produced, and the textual representation created by the reader are subsumed by pervasive attention which focuses on the written text and emphasizes reader consensus in response to this text" ("Written Composition," 47).

These developments have run parallel to the rise and dominance of formalist literary criticism, characterized by an emphasis on form, on determinate meaning, and on the decontextualization of interpretive reading, as well as by a hostility to reader-response approaches and a flight from the social and political implications of texts. It would be foolish, therefore, to ascribe the struggle for objectivity in reading and evaluation simply to forces in composition research and pedagogy. And there are certainly laudable motives in the struggle to achieve some sort of "objectivity"—a desire for fairness, a fear of undue partiality, and the search for a reliable method of scoring to counter arguments for indirect, multiple-choice assessments of writing ability (White; Odell). Nonetheless, these motives are often mingled with an excessive suspicion of subjectivity in interpretation and assessment along with a belief in the determinate meaning of texts and its centrality in reading. One may speculate as well on the extent to which the tendency of instructors to impose ideal texts of their own on student work (Brannon and Knoblauch) derives from the assumption that there are universal, objective standards that can be used to judge the quality of writing.

The following summary comment on a student paper illustrates how response strategies centered on formal elements and employing a distanced, authoritarian "teacher role" (Fuller) can displace personal reactions and values. Anson offers these comments as an example of a "dualistic" response style, fitting them into a classification derived from William Perry's developmental and epistemological scheme. I have borrowed the example as a way of suggesting that phenomena we have grown used to discussing in psychological terms may also be analyzed within social or political frames.

> Overall, the paper shows sensitivity and understanding. What the paper does not have is a coherent paragraph organization and composition. This is unfortunate because it mars the effectiveness of what has been for you clearly a painful but educative experience. Try to organize your thoughts in terms of paragraphs that explore and describe *one* thought at a time. It would also have helped if you had established a "theme" (simply an overall controlling idea) for the paper in the opening paragraph. The paper also has an awkward, contradictory and repetitive sentence structure. You make a free use of contractions that are much too casual and not used in formal writing, you have clauses in the same sentences that contradict each other, and you make the same statement several times without adding anything substantial to what you have already said ("I knew I had made the right decision" is an example). So, overall I would say, in the future exercise more caution in planning your paper and more control in writing clearer, more precise and effective sentences. (Anson, "Response" 347)

The only time "I" appears in this passage to denote the respondent is in the final sentence, directed to future writing activities. In the opening sentence, however, the instructor's personal responses to the paper's ideas, values, and rhetorical force appear to be displaced onto the paper itself by being treated as attributes of the text ("the paper shows sensitivity and understanding") rather than as evaluations offered by the reader (e.g., "I found your treatment of the subject sensitive and filled with understanding"). A student might assume, therefore, that if "sensitivity and understanding" are qualities of the text, they should be apparent to any competent reader, though the forms of expression might need to be corrected and polished. Pedagogically, however, it is far more important for a student to recognize that "sensitivity and understanding" are qualities a reader has perceived—that they are responses to the text. Such recognitions may well foster a rhetorical and flexible awareness of audience, a perspective that characterizes the thinking of successful student writers (Roth).

Formalist strategies of reading and response have been effectively criticized for their failure to attend to student texts as meaningful communicative events (Gere, "Written Composition"). In analyzing the instructor's comment cited above, for example, Chris M. Anson observes,

> What stands out here is [the instructor's] cursory *response* to [the stu-

dent's] writing as a reflection of a human being coming to terms with her commitments. The *meaning* of [her] text . . . suddenly fades from view, and the assignment becomes a kind of rhetorical trick simply to get [her] to reveal her practices in paragraph structuring and adherence to the conventions of "formal" discourse. Whatever beliefs [the student] has developed about the world, she may begin to think that the written language, in the rigidity implied by [the instructor's] constraints on organization and development, is not the medium through which to explore them. ("Response," 347)

Such approaches have also been criticized for their negative effects on student writing and their composition of a teacher's authority over texts that rightfully belong to the student/writer (Sommers; Brannon and Knoblauch).

Still, even those who call for readings that pay attention to the meaning of student texts or for "ordinary" rather that "teacherly" readings (Fuller) seem unwilling to endorse responses that are individual, subjective, and value-laden, preferring instead of some form of displacement like, "I believe most readers would find your arguments here unsettling or unconvincing because of the lack of evidence." Or a primarily positive focus: "I can really share the anguish and frustration of the victim's parents here." They draw back from a reaction like

> I think you ought to know that I get really distressed when people try to convince me that capital punishment is good because it will save money (just as you argue here). I feel that this argument ignores the fact that living, breathing people are going to die. I suppose I might find this argument easier to accept if you explained that the money saved would enable the government to do some really good things, such as helping homeless families, but even then I'm not sure how convinced I would be. I don't want to put too much pressure on you here or to seem too closed-minded, but I also want to let you know that I'm a bit of a tough audience in this matter.

In encouraging teachers to leave control in the hands of student/writers and to refrain from imposing their Ideal Texts on student' efforts, Brannon and Knoblauch envision for teacher/readers only a limited, reactive involvement in questions of meaning. The instructor's role is to recognize the intended meanings in a student's text and to report on how satisfactorily they are conveyed, thereby initiating negotiation over "ways to bring actual effect as closely in line with a desired intention as possible" (162). In this arrangement, ideas and values are created by and belong to the writer, not the reader; "negotiation" is limited primarily to matters of form and expression. Even Thomas Newkirk's call for "a dialectical encounter between teacher and student" (328) stops well short of envisioning the teacher/reader's response as offering an antithesis to the student's thesis, though Newkirik does attempt to delineate and active role for readers in the "constant interplay between audience and intention" (329).

What are the causes of this hesitation between acknowledging the primacy of meaning and accepting a teacher/reader's subjective constructions of meaning or of responses making plain an instructor's social or personal biases; moral or political positions; or even reactions like boredom, sympathy, or irritation? We ought not underestimate the continuing force of formalist approaches to reading and literary criticism, especially what Stanley Fish identifies as the "formalist assumption...that subjectivity is an ever present danger and that any critical procedure must include a mechanism for holding it in check" (9). Even more likely explanations, I think, are that we hesitate to remove the tacit restraints that now limit response because of our experiences with authoritarian approaches to reading and evaluation and because we are aware that the imbalance of power in instruction can give a teacher's comments coercive force.

Nonetheless, once we recognize the extent to which we are constituted as reading subjects by the social and interpretive communities we inhabit, we ought to be able to deal directly with the lingering fear that subjectivity leads to chaos; to unstructured, incoherent responses; or to the expression of idiosyncratic biases. We might see, for example, that subjective response need not be authoritarian. I sometimes use a paper entitled "A Two-Foot Hole or a Two-Inch Hole?" in evaluation workshops. The paper argues in graphic terms for allowing police to use heavier-caliber weapons that are more likely to cause disabling injuries that halt the flight of criminals and are also less likely to cause ricochets that harm bystanders. Those instructors who wish to express disapproval of the author's arguments or the values implied by them generally take one of two paths. Some reveal their distaste briefly but then focus on formal aspects of the paper. This approach tells a student little about how to respond to the concerns of her audience other than by working on the formal elements of the text and encourages her to view the teacher as a somewhat mysterious, disapproving, and authoritative other. On the other hand, a few instructors respond with comments like, "I find this statement and the examples that follow upsetting because. . . ." This approach gives the student information she can use to restructure, recontextualize, or simply enhance her arguments, and it encourages her to view the teacher as a reasoning and reasonable respondent.

The authoritarian or coercive force of a teacher's comments depends, as I will argue later, on the relationships of power and responsibility established between teacher/readers and student/writers. When conflicts (or agreements) between a student's values and those of an instructor are acknowledged or explained, they can be valuable for learning. Unacknowledged or unexplained reactions still shape reading and evaluation, but they have the power to distort learning.

Cognition and Evaluation

I am not suggesting that every comment on a student paper or every remark in a conference be grounded in questions of value. Rhetorical strategies and stylistic matters are certainly important subjects for discussion. Sometimes students are best served by a reader who acts as a sounding board, other times by one who functions as a helpful editor. We can choose, however, to make value-laden responses—to foreground them—because they are always available. Our readings are never neutral: they are always, inevitably, ideological and political—at least to some extent—and we can choose to foreground or suppress this aspect.

Despite widespread recognition that reading is an active, constructive process, the cognitive process of evaluation has been assumed to be simple and straightforward, concerned primarily with form and authorial intent. Even sophisticated discussions of assessment rest on an assumed model of judgment similar to that outlined in a popular textbook:

> Evaluation of a literary piece, as for any other creative endeavor, is meaningful only when based somehow on the answers to three question: (1) What was the author's purpose? (2) How successfully was it fulfilled? (3) How worthwhile was it? . . . Many things are written and published that succeed very well in carrying out the author's intent—but are simply not worthwhile. (Decker and Schwegler 44)

Though in answering question 2 ("How successfully was it fulfilled?") the teacher/reader might be assumed to be participating in an act of evaluation, she does so only in a limited sense, estimating a correlation between intention and accomplishment, and excluding questions of value and ideology. Such an exclusion is apparent in the formulation offered by Brannon and Knoblauch:

> And when evaluation is undertaken, as a last step in the process we propose, the standards invoked do not have to do with fixed preconceptions about form or content as stipulated by some Ideal Text. Instead, they relate to communicative effectiveness as an experienced reader assesses it in a particular writing situation. The standards of communicative effectiveness are how well the writer's choices achieve stated or implied purposes given the needs and expectations of an intended audience. If the evaluator finds the writer's choices to be *plausible* (as opposed to "correct") all of the time, the grade for that writing is higher than if the choices occasionally or frequently create uncertainties that cause failures in communication. (166)

Implicit in both these typical discussions is a view of reading, especially of the student papers, as a two-part operation consisting of interpretation (including an estimate of communicative effectiveness) followed at times by judgments of value. Though estimates of communicative effectiveness are certainly evaluations, this rough model absorbs them into the process of understanding, which is assumed to be nonpolitical in the sense that it does not rely on social or moral criteria or draw to any great extent on the reader's personal experience and attitudes. Judgments of value are presumed to be more or less separate from the act of interpretation. The role of an individual reader's values in such judgments is downplayed because she is encouraged to adopt the role of a reader whose social situation and outlook are most favorable to the intended purposes of the text.

This model reenacts a fact/value split that guided literary criticism and scholarship for much of this century, though it has recently been subjected to trenchant criticism (Smith 5-15). One particularly clear statement of the fact/value distinction is E. D. Hirsch's sharp differentiation between, on one hand, acts of understanding and interpretation directed to textual meaning (including attention to the relationship of intention and accomplishment) and, on the other hand, judgments of a text's significance as it relates to readers' values as well as events, personalities, and other texts. Moreover, the assumption that a reader can arrive at estimates of communicative effectiveness more or less independently of her values, preconceptions, and social situatedness in turn implies a view of reading as a linear process of meaning transferal.

At first glance, contemporary discussions of writing and response may seem to have abandoned these models of reading and evaluation in favor of social, interactive perspectives paralleling developments in reception theory, poststructuralist thought, and reading theory (Harker). Deborah Brandt, for example, argues that both comprehension and composition take place in actual or projected social contexts. A similar concern for context and interaction is apparent in an increasing focus on the process of teacher-student negotiation during revision (Onore) and in calls for greater attention to "dialectic encounter" in the relationship of teacher/readers and student/writers (Newkirk 328).

Nonetheless, Louise Phelps's observation that "theories of teacher response lag behind" the recent shift in rhetorical theory to an emphasis on "activity in context" (61-62) is accurate. For example, Martin Nystrand's discussions of the social nature of writing and reading skirt questions about the roles of values and ideology and concentrate instead on identifying the conditions for clear, meaningful communication (Nystrand, "Social-Interactive"; *Structure*; "Sharing"). Chris M. Anson's discussion of the role of ideology in response to student writing is more promising, though his view of the values involved in response is restricted to "instructional ideologies": "the teacher[s'] values, beliefs, and models of learning . . . their awareness of student development and intellectual style, their knowledge of educational theory and research or their exposure to a variety of instructional modes and techniques" ("Response" 354). What we need, then, is a model of the cognitive process of reading and evaluating—with special emphasis on response to student texts—that makes plain the extent to which the process is grounded in personal, social, and cultural ideology and experience. Such a model can also serve to remind us that as instructors we do not have the choice of making our readings of student texts ideological or non-ideological. The choice rather concerns which elements of the experience to foreground in our responses and to acknowledge as we arrive at an evaluation.

Elsewhere (Schwegler) I have described in detail some of the components of a model of the cognitive process of reading and evaluating student papers that is built on contemporary reading and rhetorical theory (van Dijk and Kintsch). The discussion that follows highlights the socially and culturally grounded elements of the process. Central to this alternate perspective are two assumptions designed to replace these that lie behind traditional views of reading and evaluation. In place of the assumption that reading to understand and estimate communicative effectiveness and reading to respond to values and evaluate are different and separable tasks, the new perspective assumes that all acts of reading are simultaneously acts of understanding, interpretation, evaluation, and response to values. In place of the assumption that it is primarily the features and information in the text and not the reader's knowledge, values, or interpretive strategies that shape reader response and judgment, the new approach assumes that response and judgment are shaped by the reader's knowledge; ideology (personal, social, cultural); social situation; and interpretive strategies (often shaped themselves by social and cultural ideology and class [Bourdieu] as well as by textual features and content). From this perspective, then, the reading of student papers and acts of response and evaluation are problematic, socially situated processes taking place at all times within the value frameworks (ideologies) of the teacher/reader.

When an instructor begins reading a student paper, she draws cues from it or the context and blends these with background knowledge (stored in schema) to arrive at an initial estimate of the text's purposes and design. Most instructors are aware, of course, of the role of expectations in evaluation of the formal or generic qualities of texts, especially insofar as a writer's understanding of generic constraints and skill in employing them can contribute to the communicative effectiveness of a text: "Because you are trying to get readers to agree with your point of view you ought to state your thesis early in the paper." Because genres are cultural conventions, they also entail social and ideological expectations based on readers' associations of a genre with a particular discourse setting (Couture 70-85). When a text confirms expectations for organization and broad logical relationships, as in the case of a report in a technical writing class that embodies the teacher's (or textbook's) conception of the finished product, then the values entailed in matters of genre often are not apparent to the person reading and evaluating. But when a text departs from generic expectations, as in the case of feminist literary criticism that employs personal narrative rather than expository patterning, it may pose a direct challenge to the reader's ideological expectations. And when a text clearly mishandles generic conventions, readers may question not only the writer's skill, but also maturity (in the case of student writers), understanding of the social setting, or failure to appreciate the cultural and social background of the intended audience.

More important than matters of genre, however, are those features of discourse addressed by the term *register*. *Register* refers to the "meaning potential" of reader-writer-text interactions: "the range of meanings and register of a discourse type or setting include its characteristic vocabulary, sentence structures, organizational patterns, modes of interpersonal expression, or logical patterns of reasoning and evidence" (Bernhardt 191). As M. A. K. Halliday points out (111), registers are manifested in language, but are themselves social and ideological structures, not linguistic forms. Thus, a student paper on a controversial issue will likely elicit in an instructor's mind knowledge of generally accepted ways of formulating the issue and similar issues; an understanding of the appropriate discourse styles and strategies; and an awareness of how other texts have addressed the issue, especially those with cultural and social importance.

The following opening paragraph from a student essay is probably conventional enough to prompt little personal moral response from an experienced composition instructor:

> There are many solutions to the drug problems of junior high and high schools, one of which is not mandatory drug testing. Because of the numerous opposers and conflicting viewpoints it is difficult to find a universal solution. I believe that a more probable solution rests in the education of students, rather than in disciplinary action.

The context of production, the manner of topicalization, and the style identify this paragraph as part of a student essay. Inscribed in the register for such texts is a set of hierarchical social relationships identifying the relative power and status of reader and writer. Thus, simply by deciding to read a text as a student paper, an instructor becomes socially (and ideologically) situated with regard to it, though her own values may of course determine the way she evaluates departures from or adherence to the constraints of the register. And by the same token, the student writer of the paragraph above acknowledges his inferior status in the phrase "the numerous opposers and conflicting viewpoints," an attempt to incorporate the language of the teacher and the textbook: "opposition," "opposing points of view." While some students respond with defiance to the constraints of the student register (Freedman, "Register" 342), the majority take on willingly the tasks of the novice, one of which is to employ the technical language of the field—of chemistry, or of literary criticism, or in this case, of composition, but this writer's failure to employ the language in the correct form or in a manner we might recognize as characteristic of the "best students" or "most accomplished writers" marks him as a novice or perhaps (I would argue) as an outsider who does not quite understand the stylistic mores and the special language of the discourse setting.

To draw on Pierre Bourdieu, we might say that the student acknowledges the value of "educational capital" but reveals through the false note of a word like "opposers" that he is still not fully competent at the game of discourse that certifies its attainment (see Bourdieu 65-70). Indeed, I would argue that the factors of class; of monetary, cultural, and educational capital; of power and hierarchy that Bourdieu sees as determining judgments about and the distribution of cultural good (including written discourse) are manifested in the expectations that constitute registers. At the same time, how a particular instructor response to conflicts between her expectations and the register of a student text—with helpful advice or with brusque, negative comments—is likely to depend on a number of things, including the instructor's view of the social role of education.

Even a common and seemingly neutral assignment such as "Prepare an essay analyzing the point of view in 'A Rose for Emily'" entails expectations whose ideological grounding becomes evident when a paper fails to fulfill them. Consider, for example, a student paper that opens with these statements:

> In William Faulkner's short story "A Rose for Emily," he uses a narrator in the first person to help convey the main idea behind the story, which is one of loneliness, something almost everyone can relate to. When I first read the story, I couldn't understand why the author would spend so much time describing a strange old lady. Then I looked at our textbook and I started thinking that maybe he was illustrating the theme of "Complexities of Love" which I think is very important.

Responses such as "high schoolish," "unsophisticated," "uncritical," or even "ignorant" and "childish" are likely to occur to an instructor, to be suppressed, perhaps, in favor of pedagogically oriented responses designed to help the student think and write critically about the story. But both sets of responses—the directly evaluative and the corrective—may be viewed as reactions to the way the act of analysis has been defined, as ethical rather than aesthetic or formalist, and to the manner of expression, which does not display the language or the stance expected in academic literary study, even at a novice level. As Bourdieu has demonstrated (11-96), there is generally a strong correlation between superior social status and formalist, decontextualized approaches to art, on one hand, and between ethical approaches and lower social status on the other. I would contend that these relationships, reproduced in the forms of expectations for novice critical discourse, can lead to responses like "uncritical" and "unsophisticated." The hostility with which some instructors greet departures from the norms for student literary analysis ("This student barely knows how to read, much less write a good critical paper") suggests that in violating expectations, a student may also be perceived as calling into question the value of the cultural and educational capital that constitutes the teacher's authority.

A clash of registers in the reading and evaluation of student texts is therefore likely to be more than a case of differing expectations for style of expression. Conflicts between registers involve differing conceptions of the task, the context, and reader-text-writer relationships, conceptions that are part of the frameworks of social and cultural values—ideological networks—that underlie all acts of reading and writing (Belsey; Macdonell).

Ideology, broadly defined as "the conscious or unconscious beliefs, habits, and social practices of a particular society" (McCormick, Waller, and Flower 285) and including personal beliefs and attitudes, also plays an important role in the next stage of reading, the attempt to build a coherent mental representation of a text's meaning. Working within a scaffold of expectations for a particular text, a reader tries to build a coherent mental image of its meanings and purposes using cues and information from the text as well as inferences from prior knowledge. Inference serves to fill in those many elements of the representation not explicitly detailed in the text. Perceptions of coherence and incoherence in student papers as well as judgments of the adequacy of detail and support can vary according to the assumptions and knowledge of the teacher/reader. So too can estimates of a paper's focus, development, and organization.

Register and the social relationships it manifests also play an important role in the mental images instructors create of student authors. Barritt, Stock, and Clark have noted the tendency of readers of placement exams to create mental images of the authors as prospective students and to frame their responses to the text in terms of these images. In examining think-aloud protocols of composition instructors reading student papers, I have noted that readers often draw information from the text and from prior experience with student writers to create images of what might be called "inferred authors." These images take several forms:

Author as student
This is the type of student that you hope you have one of in every class, I have one this semester who I had before and she wrote a paper interestingly very similar to this.

Author as strategist
Again the um details that the student has chosen tell me that they do understand the material, they researched it well.

I don't know if this student really, really remembers Mammy, too young for Jolson. I suspect not but if this person could have used uh Bartlett's Familiar Quotations, I suspect.

Author as individual (personal characteristics and attitudes)
I am saying *she* all the way through, that may be sexism, this may be a man. But it's written like what I would think a woman, a woman's writing would be.

Instructors sometimes use an inferred author—or the inferred traits and attitudes of a known author—as part of value judgments, comparing, for example, the supposed maturity or critical ability of the student to those of other students. Most often, however, inferring an author is a strategy that enables teacher/readers to view a text as a communicative, social act, something produced by a writer to share thoughts with a reader. This not only places a discourse in a social context but also encourages readers to respond to and evaluate it as a moral and social act.

Paradigms

As I have argued, differing views of the role of the teacher in evaluation and response can lead to either foregrounding or repressing questions of value. Views of the teacher's role as authoritative, authoritarian, and prescriptive have dominated traditional approaches to composition instruction and have led to an emphasis on form (Purves; Knoblauch and Brannon; Fuller). Contemporary approaches that view the teacher as a general reader or a writing coach have placed more emphasis on a paper's content and message. Cognitive models may either disguise or highlight the inevitable contributions of ideology. Moreover, the paradigms we employ to conceptualize the relations between teacher/readers and student/writers in a composition class are political. First, they guide the distribution and exercise of power in the classroom society. Second, they reproduce in various ways the relationships that characterize the larger societies to which we and our students belong. Complex and shifting though these paradigm are, they do at the same time form some relatively clear pattern. To identify these, it may be helpful to view the classroom writing situation as consisting of three primary components—writer, reader, and text—each varying in authority. In addition, it is helpful to regard the relationship of writer, text, and reader in the classroom as one form of the broader relationship among producers, cultural goods, and consumers, similar to that linking, for example, authors, novels, and reader, though it may feel uncomfortable to apply economic and political language to what most of us experience as a personal and "humanistic" relationships.

In taking this approach, I am drawing on the concept of "overdetermination," which suggests that the relationships within any segment of a society are shaped by the multiple effects (interaction) of the relationships in the rest of the society so that no social entity can be considered independent of other (Resnick and Wolff 1-25). And I am also making use of Louis Althusser's observation that one of the main functions of education (and of other institutions such as the legal system, the family, and the communications industry) is "reproduction of the relations of production" (146) as they exist in the practices and dominant ideology of a society. This is not to say that teaching practices simply replicate or blindly inculcate the characteristic relationships and attitudes of management and workers, for example, or of professionals and administrators in a particular social and economic system, though they may do this. As Althusser and others have pointed out, education is a relatively autonomous site at which the dominant ideology in a society or culture comes into contact and struggle with competing ideologies (Althusser; Macdonell 33-36). And it is a site where the participants may accept, refuse, or struggle to change the roles offered to them by a society and culture (Macdonell 39-40).

To put these concepts in more familiar terms, a composition class offers a number of roles, some reflecting widely accepted attitudes (teacher as authority, student as learner), others reflecting different degrees of disagreement with or rebellion against typical teacher-student relationships (teacher as writing coach, teacher as fellow writer). To take on a role is to be constituted as a subject by it and to step into relationships of authority and power that may reflect a dominant ideology or resistance to it. Most composition instructors are likely to recognize the various roles they and their students can perform (Purves; Horvath). Most are also likely to admit that struggle is a regular part of writing classes, whether it be over the need to revise, the proper response to an essay, the appropriate grade for a paper, etc. What many fail to recognize, however, are the political dimensions of these roles and struggles, and the extent to which they enact power relationships and can become avenues for repression or for growth and change.

In a traditional composition classroom, the instructor specifies the nature of the text to be produced by creating a detailed assignment, choosing specific models, focusing class discussion, responding to student writing, etc. A student's role is to understand the task and to reproduce its specifications in a paper while adding "value" to the product in the form of style, content, and insight. Though such an arrangement leaves open some power for students as creators of a text, most authority accrues to the instructor, who functions both as a reader of the text and as its writer.

It is arrangements of this sort that Brannon and Knoblauch have in mind when they criticize writing instruction that imposes on a student writer an instructor's vision of an "Ideal Text" and in so doing usurps the writer's text and intentions. Such relationships are not limited to composition courses in which the instructor imposes a particular rhetorical pattern on student writing. It can apply as well to a literature course in which students must enact a strict thesis and support structure, or to a writing-across-the-curriculum course with a different formal requirement.

Teaching that centers power in the expectations and responses of a teacher/reader can be considered authoritarian even when it attempts to encourage and reward critical thinking and even when it aims to empower students by helping them master the discourses of various academic disciplines. This pattern centralizes power in ways similar to the worker-management relationships that characterize much industrial production in our society and the hierarchical patters found in many companies and government agencies.

Students in authoritarian classes frequently complain that they are required to write the paper the instructor wants and that, despite talk about "learning to think critically" and "expressing your ideas clearly and fully," their real task is to "psych out the instructor." At the same time their instructors may complain about the lack of real critical thinking in student essays or wonder why these essays are simply "manicured corpses" devoid of imagination and insight. While instructors may sometimes be correct in pointing to lack of critical thinking ability, psychological immaturity, or appropriate background knowledge as the cause of problems in writing, I suspect that these explanations often have a repressive function. They encourage us to view a conflict or struggle as a problem. They make students rather than the power structure the locus of the problem. And they provide grounds for ignoring signs of defiance: boredom, cynical adherence to trite formats, cheating, and other reactions characteristic of settings in which one's efforts are undervalued or not valued at all.

In contrast, the paradigm of "ownership" or "rights" that dominates contemporary discussions of evaluation and response (Brannon and Knoblauch; Onore; Phelps) transfers considerable authority to student writers. Proponents of this approach argue that a shift of authority from teacher/reader to student/writer is necessary because

> As long as judgments of what may be "better" or "worse"—that is, of what constitutes improvement in writing—remain the province of teachers alone, then the writer cannot fully and authentically engage in choice making and problem solving. And without the authority to make choices, the writer can never understand how central are the consequences of any meaning-making activity in writing. (Onore, 231-232)

Within this paradigm, the authority of the instructor as reader is greatly reduced, especially when peer groups and collaborative learning are employed in ways that make students not only the writers but also the primary readers of the texts produced in a course. Though this arrangement may seem radical, it nonetheless reflects and reproduces some of the dominant relationships of power and production in contemporary American society.

Under the "student ownership" or "rights" paradigm, an instructor retains ultimate responsibility for initiating student writing, but the emphasis on revision and on formative responses to successive drafts serves to shift authority to the writer. The importance of the initial assignment lessens as a student discovers, with the aid of her instructor, her "real" intentions for the text. The language commonly used to describe this process emphasizes the importance of student control over the evolving text and stigmatizes forms of response and evaluation that appropriate students' texts (Sommers). In one form, this approach casts teachers first in the role of listeners—to the students' texts and to the students as readers and evaluators of their own texts—and then as questioners whose responses help students pay attention to the effectiveness with which a text conveys meaning (Murray). In another form, the instructor responds as a "real" reader, concerned primarily with what the author has to say, not with identifying errors (Fuller).

The relationship of writer and reader(s) is viewed as one of "negotiation," not, as the term might suggest, between parties with differing interstices and values, but between parties who agree on the primacy of the writer's meanings and have also agreed to cooperate on refining the meanings and their expression: "a process of negotiation, where writer and peers or writer and teacher (or tutor) work together to consider, and if possible to enhance, the relationship between intention and effect" (Brannon and Knoblauch, 163). Recent expressions of the paradigm have tried to allow readers a more active role and to move toward a dialectical view of negotiation without abandoning the primacy of the writer's rights in a text:

> In arguing for a process pedagogy, we are arguing at the very least for a writer's right to his own texts and not so subsidiarily for the right of the classroom community to interpret and feed meanings back to the writer. Paradoxically, while a focus on meaning-making requires individual ownership of a text, it simultaneously requires that a writer negotiate with that community his or her intended meanings so that neither pure idiosyncracy nor tyranny results. (Onore 232).

Paradox is probably an appropriate word for this position since it tries to maintain "ownership" or "right" as a governing concept without modifying it in response to the competing concept also acknowledged as central, the "right" of readers to assert their perceptions of a text's meaning.

Use of "ownership" and "right" as metaphors for a particular approach to response and evaluation rests on the assumption that private property—including the rights to intellectual and cultural property—is a dominant value in our society. Thomas Newkirk is correct in pointing out that metaphors used to discuss the relationship of reader and writer within this paradigm "echo private property and contractual law" (328). At the same time, however, the projected relationships of production in the classroom under this paradigm do not seem to be reflections of the dominant conditions of production in the society in quite the straightforward manner of those predicated by the authoritarian paradigm, though they may well be reflections of the complicated processes of cultural production in our society.

What I am suggesting is that the "ownership" paradigm reflects a certain confusion over the most effective conditions for production—industrial as well as cultural—and over the proper roles for labor and management, producer and consumer, teacher and student. In both practice and theory, this approach to writing instruction is less satisfactory than it might seem at first. For example, one of the clearest impressions left by Sarah Freedman's detailed study of response to student writing in two classrooms is the extent to which all writing activities are shaped by the teachers' values despite the teachers' obvious respect for students' ownership of texts: "As with Peterson's [class], every activity in Glass's classroom is informed by her philosophy of teaching writing. Thus, assignments, whole-class discussion, and peer-group work address collectively her hopes for her students' cognitive and academic growth" (*Response* 133). It seems likely, then, that though pedagogies based on this paradigm may lead to an improvement in student writing, they do so only through a superficial transfer of authority.

It makes little sense to criticize this approach as superficial and ameliorative rather than radical, however, for the benefits of even a limited transfer of authority over writing are plain in the reports from practitioners (see Anson, *Writing*). A more serious criticism is that in both theory and practice, this approach involves unresolvable contradictions and repressions that undermine it.

To limit the role and authority of the teacher/reader to that of a "soundingboard" (Brannon and Knoblauch) is to risk suppressing the value-laden, ideological, socially situated responses that constitute constructive reading, thereby making the reader a mere adjunct to the act of writing. On the other hand, to recognize reading as a meaning-making act and acknowledge the authority of the teacher/reader, while maintaining the primacy of student rights over a text, is to create a paradox, consisting of two separate rather than contingent authorities:

> To a degree, the student owns his or her paper, but the paper is *intended* for others in the way property isn't; and so, to a degree, the writing is also owned by its readers. No one (I hope) condones the practice condemned by Knoblauch and Brannon in which students must guess at some Platonic text that exists in the teacher's imagination. But by the same token, the expectations of the teacher, the course, and the academy must interact with the intentions of the student. Intention, in other words, cannot be an absolute, a "God-term." (Newkirk 329)

This contradiction can be overcome if both instructors and students are willing to play "paradoxical roles," at once asserting their own authority and recognizing the authority of the other, a process that takes place through negotiation (Newkirk; Onore). Negotiation, however, deals with differing perceptions of meaning and judgments of the effectiveness of expression, differences that can be resolved by focusing on a common goal: the articulation and development of the writer's intention. Negotiation, that is, involves a willingness on the part of teachers and student to alter their perspectives and, I would add, a willingness on the part of both to ignore contrasting values whose examination might heighten their differences.

Much of what this paradigm has to offer to composition instruction is laudable. What I find most remarkable about the various discussions of it, however, is the lack of recognition that reader-writer contacts can (and often should) lead to a sharpening of difference (or conflict) between values and ideologies, or perhaps to the strengthening and extension of mutual beliefs. By restricting the process of negotiation to creating agreement, the current practice of negotiation excludes possibilities for articulating questions of value, for identifying agreements, and disagreements, and for productive conflict that encourages change.

These exclusions point to the outlines for a third paradigm of teacher/reader-student/writer relationships, one that encourages the foregrounding of values and ideology in response and evaluation while focusing on reader-writer differences as occasions for growth and change. According to this perspective, the classroom is a site of struggle between the legitimate authority of both readers and writers, their contrasting positions in the educational hierarchy, and their respective values. Seen in this way, the act of reading and responding to student papers reproduces the struggles that characterize our evolving society: conflicts over modes of industrial production and exchange; changes in ethnic and cultural patterns; questions of educational and social structure; issues of race, gender, and class.

By assuming that the interactions of values and ideologies, not simply the communication of meaning and information, is an important purpose for writing and reading, teachers and students in composition classes can view each other as contingent rather than hierarchical authorities. To do so is to acknowledge the ways in which production and consumption can be said to "produce" each other (Holub 126). That is, this paradigm offers a way to regard writers and readers as standing in a dialectical relationship, with neither having priority. This paradigm differs from the other two not so much in the recognition of a dialectical relationship but in its refusal to grant priority to either and in its belief that this dialectic ought to be characterized by struggle and conflict as well as by cooperation.

When the authorities of readers and writers are treated as contingent, writing becomes the inevitable product of their interaction—and the quality of this product becomes the focus of attention. This is especially true when both the writing and response deal with questions of value or involve interchanges of reader and writer. They are made accessible to critical examination and become sites for struggle and change.

Admittedly, the power of teachers is greater than that of students, so to speak of contingent authorities is not to envision equal power. The relationships of power within American education and society sharply limit the extent to which authority can be effectively redistributed in any classroom. In addition, a teacher's knowledge, skill, and experience relative to that of students often creates an imbalance in authority. Nonetheless, teachers can use their authority to create significant roles for both writers and readers. They can choose to foreground rather than suppress questions of value and ideology. Susan Wells, for example, argues that even a course as instrumental in aim and as closely tied to the dominant power relationships as a technical writing course can be conducted in a manner that directs critical attention to the social relations inscribed in discourse, thereby opening possibilities for empowerment and change.

Instructors can also structure the occasions for writing in ways that give authority to students. Open topics allow for some transfer of control, though they are often variations on a theme established by an instructor. Encouraging students to redefine a writing task in consultation with the teacher is a further step, especially if the instructor is willing to voice disagreements or misgivings while being open to reasoned persuasion. Open or writer-generated assignments can be effective as well when they call for consultation between student(s) and instructor and when the instructor's opinions are not given undue weight. Collections of reading in cultural or media studies and the methods of analysis used in these fields offer other ways to foreground ideology. Moreover, depending on how they are employed, traditional collections such as argument readers and thematic literature anthologies provide similar opportunities. So, too, do case-study projects and simulation exercises. In all cases, however, the choice of materials and activities should be open to challenge from students.

The potential for difference, struggle, and student criticism in all these approaches is essential, both because it can lead to growth and change and because it can set limits on the authority of the teacher/reader. Moreover, though they represent a new paradigm, none of these strategies is difficult to implement in a contemporary composition class. In contrast, it is much harder to envision a language and procedures for evaluations grounded in value. One problem is that we have been trained to regard these judgments as inherently suspect and unfair. Another problem is that there is no easily available body of lore to provide practical strategies.

The language of marginal and summative commentary we have learned from handboooks, our teachers, and teacher training is predominantly formalist and often implicitly authoritarian. To escape the constraints of this language, those who argue for readings that focus on a writer's intentions have begun demonstrating what form appropriate responses might take: "Are you saying that it doesn't really matter? Do you believe that?" " I can't tell whether your purpose here is just to make someone feel better or really to argue that all colleges are alike and that going or not going is an unimportant decision: in either case, do you really believe your statement?" (Knoblauch and Brannon 127-128). A similar effort is necessary for responses to the quality of ideas, the depth and persistence of reasoning, the patterns of belief, and the underlying ideologies in student writing:

> This section of the paper displays what I consider an excellent understanding of the tensions between siblings and the mingling of love and anger that I recognize from my own experience as a brother and as a parent.

> I know you offer a good deal of evidence, but the arguments for gun-control here still appear rather superficial when I contrast them with those offered in class discussion last week.

> Unconvincing. The scene just doesn't come alive for me, and I feel no sympathy for your uncle despite your extended description of the events.

> The behaviors you describe as a way of poking fun at the overdressed couple in the elegant restaurant have a different effect on me. I see them as signs that the social background of these people has not given them the upper-class manners to enable them to "fit in." And I feel sorry for them. I'm not sure there is any way to reconcile our outlooks, though. If you wish to take my reaction into account, you might drop the exaggerated details in the last two sentences of the third paragraph. I say this tentatively, realizing that it is these sentences that most pleased the other students in your group.

Judgments like these should not be the sole ground for response and evaluation, but they can be an important element.

If we make plain in class discussion and in response to drafts what we consider a forceful argument, a moving example, and an intriguing insight as well as unpersuasive lines of reasoning and objectionable perspective on these expectations through revision, then we should feel free to employ them in evaluating a finished paper without fear that we are unduly constraining student expression.

Though the outline of this third paradigm has been sketchy, I believe it offers worthwhile alternatives for reading and evaluating student writing and for composition instruction. It is by no means an ideal solution and may in turn prove to contain its own repressions, though in ways different from its predecessors. As is so often the case, however, repression may become the impetus for further development.

Works Cited

Althusser, Louis. *Lenin and Philosophy and Other Essays*. Trans. Ben Brewster. London: NLB, 1971.

Anson, Chris M. "Response Styles and Ways of Knowing." In *Writing and Response: Theory, Practice, and Research*. Ed. Chris M. Anson. Urbana, IL: NCTE. 1989, 332-366.

———, ed. *Writing and Response: Theory, Practice, and Research*. Urbana, IL: NCTE, 1989.

Barritt, Loren, Patricia L. Stock, and Francelia Clark. "Researching Practice: Evaluating Assessment Essays." *CCC* (1986): 315-327.

Belsey, Catherine. *Critical Practice*. London: Routledge, 1980.

Bernhardt, Stephen A. "Applying a Functional Model of Language in the Writing Classroom." In *Functional Approaches to Writing: Research Perspectives*. Ed. Barbara Couture. Norwood, NJ: Ablex, 1986, 186-198.

Bourdieu, Pierre. *Distinction: A Social Critique of the Judgment of Taste*. Tr. Richard Nice. Cambridge: Harvard University Press, 1984.

Brannon, Lil, and C. H. Knoblauch. "On Students' Rights to their Own Texts: A Model of Teacher Response." *CCC* 33 (1982): 157-166.

Courture, Barbara. "Effective Ideation in Written Text: A Functional Approach to Clarity and Exigence." In *Functional Approaches to Writing: Research Perspectives*. Ed. Barbara Couture. Norwood, NJ: Ablex, 1986, 69-92.

Decker, Randall E., and Robert A. Schwegler. *Patterns of Exposition* 12. Glenview, IL: Scott, Foresman/Little, Brown, 1990.

Diederich, Paul B. *Measuring Growth in English*. Urbana, IL: NCTE, 1974.

Dijk, Teun A. Van, and Walter Kintsch. *Strategies of Discourse Comprehension*. Orlando: Academic, 1983.

Fish, Stanley. *Is There a Text in This Class?* Cambridge: Harvard University Press, 1980.

Freedman, Sarah Warshauer. *Response to Student Writing*. Urbana, IL: NCTE, 1987.

———. "The Registers of Student and Professional Expository Writing: Influences on Teacher's Response." In *New Directions in Composition Research*. Eds. Richard Beach and Lillian S. Bridwell. New York: Guilford, 1984, 334-347.

Fuller, David. "A Curious Case of Our Responding Habits: What Do We Respond to and Why?" *Journal of Advanced Composition* 8 (1988): 88-96.

Gere, Anne Ruggles, "Empirical Research in Composition." In *Perspectives on Research and Scholarship in Composition*. Eds. Ben W. McClelland and Timothy R. Donovan. New York: MLA, 1985, 110-124.

———. "Written Composition: Toward a Theory of Evaluation." *College English* 42 (1980): 44-58.

Griffin, C. W. "Theory of Responding to Student Writing: The State of the Art." *CCC* 33 (1982): 296-301.

Halliday, M. A. K. *Language as Social Semiotic*. Baltimore: University Park Press, 1978.

Harker, W. John. "Literary Theory and the Reading Process: A Meeting of Perspectives." *Written Communication* 4 (1987): 235-252.

Hilgers, Thomas L. "Toward a Taxonomy of Beginning Writers: Evaluative Statements on Written Compositions." *Written Communication* 1 (1984): 365-384.

Hillocks, George, Jr. *Research on Written Composition*. Urbana, IL: National Conference on Research in English, 1986.

Hirsch, E. D., Jr. *Validity in Interpretation*. New Haven: Yale University Press, 1967.

Holub, Robert C. *Reception Theory: A Critical Introduction*. London: Methuen, 1984.

Horvath, Brooke K. "The Components of Written Response: A Practical Synthesis of Current Views." *Rhetoric Review* 2 (1984): 136-156.

Knoblauch, C. H., and Lil Brannon. *Rhetorical Traditions and the Teaching of Writing*. Portsmouth, NH: Boynton/Cook, 1984.

Kucer, Stephen L. "The Making of Meaning: Reading and Writing as Parallel Processes." *Written Communication* 2 (1985): 317-336.

McCormick, Kathleen, Gary Waller, and Linda Flower. *Reading Texts: Reading, Responding, Writing*. Lexington, MA: Heath, 1987.

Macdonnell, Diane. *Theories of Discourse: An Introduction*. Oxford: Blackwell, 1986.

Murray, Donald M. "Teaching the Other Self: The Writer's First Reader." *CCC* 33 (1982): 140-147.

Newkirk, Thomas. "The First Five Minutes: Setting the Agenda in a Writing Conference." In *Writing and Response: Theory, Practice, and Research*. Ed. Chris M. Anson, Urbana, IL: NCTE, 1989, 317-331.

Nystrand, Martin. "A Social-Interactive Model of Writing." *Written Communication* 6 (1989): 66-85.

———. " Sharing Words: The Effects of Readers on Developing Writers." *Written Communication* 7 (1990): 3-24.

———. *The Structure of Written Communication: Studies in Reciprocity between Writers and Readers*. Orlando: Academic Press, 1986.

Odell, Lee. "Defining and Assessing Competence in Writing." In *The Nature and Measurement of Competency in English*. Ed. Charles R. Cooper.

Urbana, IL: NCTE, 1981, 95-138.

Onore, Cynthia. "The Student, the Teacher, and the Text: Negotiating Meanings through Response and Revision." In *Writing and Response: Theory, Practice and Research.* Ed. Chris M. Anson. Urbana, IL: NCTE, 1989, 231-260.

Phelps, Louise Wetherbee. "Images of Student Writing: The Deep Structure of Teacher Response." In *Writing and Response: Theory, Practice, and Research.* Ed. Chris M. Anson. Urbana, IL: NCTE, 1989, 37-67.

Probst, Robert E. "Transactional Theory and Response to Student Writing." In *Writing and Response: Theory, Practice, and Research.* Ed. Chris M. Anson. Urbana, IL: NCTE, 1989.

Purves, Alan C. "The Teacher as Reader: An Anatomy." *College English* 46 (1984): 259-265.

Resnick, Stephen A., and Richard D. Wolff. *Knowledge and Class: A Marxian Critique of Political Economy.* Chicago: University of Chicago Press, 1987.

Roth, Robert G. "The Evolving Audience: Alternatives to Audience Accommodation." *CCC* 38 (1987): 47-55.

Schwegler, Robert A. "Discourse Theory and the Reading of Student Texts." Paper delivered at New Directions in Communication Research, University of New Hampshire, 1986.

Sloan, Gary. "The Perils of Paper Grading." *English Journal* 66 (1977): 33-36.

Smith, Barbara Herrnstein. "Contingencies of Value." In *Canons.* Ed. Robert von Hallberg. Chicago: University of Chicago Press, 5-39.

Sommers, Nancy. "Responding to Student Writing." *CCC* 33 (1982): 148-156.

Wells, Susan, "Jurgen Habermas, Communicative Competence, and the Teaching of Technical Discourse." In *Theory in the Classroom.* Ed. Cary Nelson. Urbana, IL: University of Illinois Press, 1986. 245-269.

White, Edward M. "Holisticism." *CCC* 35 (1984): 400-409.

"I Didn't Think They Had it in Them": Students Learning from Students

Alison Warriner

The quotation in the title above is from Tom, a student commenting on the performance of his fellow classmates in a final course evaluation. His opinion reflects surprise that his classmates helped him learn so much, and results from an unconventional pedagogy tried in three courses at a small comprehensive university on the East Coast. These three courses all satisfied the Advanced Composition requirement, but they focused on different topics: Women Essayists (WE), Language Awareness (LA), and Advanced Argumentation (AA). Both Women Essayists and Language Awareness were filled with students who needed Advanced Composition because it was required for their major. Although Advanced Argumentation did fulfill the Advanced Composition requirement, only two (as far as I knew) of the students were taking it because they "had" to. Although Women Essayists *became* a course that felt like an elective, Language Awareness always felt like a required course to some students, especially for those in Media Studies and Education who initially resented having to take it. Even those students, though, felt that they benefited from the unconventional pedagogy, and almost every student in all three classes wrote in their final evaluations not only that they preferred learning from their peers, but that they felt they had learned *more*. During the three years in which these courses were offered, the students responded to questionnaires and evaluations to help me determine the strengths and weaknesses of the way I designed and conducted the courses.

Some years ago I had been wanting to change the way I teach when I read Jane Tompkins' "Pedagogy of the Distressed." I subsequently forgot the details, but I must have unconsciously retained the spirit, since several of her thoughts reappear in these classrooms, especially "I trust the students" and "less is more" (659). I also remember that the motive for her innovations had been fatigue (660). While I was not at the same stage of weariness the first time I tried this, I was discouraged by the passivity of my students and wanted to change the dynamics of the classroom.

I did not think, however, that my classroom at that point was very traditional. I was familiar with Freire's theory of the banking model of education and had already abandoned lectures. I had followed Erika Lindemann's advice that "teachers may give students responsibility for devising their own assignments, assigning one another research and writing tasks, setting appropriate deadlines, and revising drafts together. *Collaboration, community,* and *responsibility* are the watchwords" (255). I had agreed with Wendy Bishop, Patricia Bizzell, Jim Corder and Kathleen Boardman that teachers who wrote with their students found themselves more actively involved. I had shared my writing with students. I understood with Carol Gilligan and the *Women's Ways of Knowing* collective (Belenky *et al*) that non-hierarchical structure could be empowering to non-traditional students. I encouraged collaborative small groups and oral reports. I believed in and practiced a student-centered pedagogy, I thought—and yet, there were still too many days when the students seemed to feel it was my responsibility either to entertain them or to think for them.

Three years ago, I became ready to change my teaching practice when I was listening to my first-year students present oral reports on their research papers at the end of the semester. I was relaxed—most of my work was finished, and now the students would speak. The presenters had prepared for days, maybe weeks; they were nervous, intense, and deeply committed to their projects. The class was engaged, listening carefully to the report and discussing the topic afterwards. I hardly spoke, but they did not need me to speak. We were pressed for time for the students' presentations, and the class wanted the discussions to go on (they had ten minutes for each).

I wondered if I could create a course that motivated this level of engagement.

About a month later I considered this question at a summer workshop at the Institute for Writing and Thinking at Bard College. We were writing about an early learning experience, and since I couldn't think of one beyond tying my shoelaces, I tried to recall my most intense learning experiences in college, none of which seemed to involve a professor directly. They seemed, rather, to involve working on my own. I think I was remembering these experiences *because* I was writing; I had not thought of them in years and doubt whether I could have remembered them had I not been physically writing. I was connecting this workshop experience with my own teaching situations. Although I had often promised myself to allow more time for the kind of in-class writing that was inspiring me at Bard, it was the first to go when time got short. And, while I encouraged independent work, I had been reluctant to give over class time to students beyond brief oral reports and collaborative group work.

In that Bard workshop, those of us who related our early learning experiences had written about our own enterprise. As the workshop progressed, we read what Bruner, Piaget, and Vygotsky had to say about how people use what they know to learn more, especially by "doing" rather than just listening. I was particularly struck that summer by how much knowledge we workshop participants already had but did not know we had until we discovered it ourselves. We used three heuristics that could be transferred to the classroom: the act of writing, independent research, and teaching others.

My first try to change classroom social relations involved turning students into teachers; I followed Lucy McCormick Calkins' advice. As she says of herself, "When I know I will be teaching a class on a topic, I become a powerful learner. Everywhere, I see related anecdotes, ideas, and quotations. Because I teach, I learn" (qtd in Nelson, 72). I discovered that student teachers were just as good as, and perhaps better than, I was myself at enabling the class as a whole to learn. Students learn from each other, and the experience is better than learning from the teacher. Of the forty-three students in these three experimental courses, only two wished they had had more "instruction" from me.

In certain basic ways I turned the course over to the students. At first they did not believe it. My experiment was similar to Tompkins'; I also see that others have tried what she calls the "dialogic" classroom with less success, especially when it comes to students' designing the course and determining the reading. For example, Frederic Gale, in "Something Old, Something New, Something Borrowed" talks about how difficult it is to maintain a true dialogic classroom; he points out that the ideal is that "students would participate actively in the classroom conversation, if not lead it, and be active in the development of a reading list, but that is something to be hoped for and not often achieved" (31). He adds that "the students ought to select the reading materials, and one of them should lead the group discussion the week that his or her choice of readings is discussed. I have found it ... difficult to achieve this ideal" (33). I was also skeptical after my first try in my course, Women Essayists, because that course seemed special in so many ways that I was almost ready to dismiss it as one of those lucky "good" classes. My second and third attempts, respectively in the courses "Language Awareness" and "Advanced Argumentation" worked just as well. These three good experiences persuaded me that this is pedagogy worth sharing. As I trace the experiences in these classes that led to my belief that students learn best from each other, I will also point out the drawbacks. Some cannot be avoided, but most can be ameliorated with preparation.

Because my premise is students learn best from teaching, the only "requirement" in each course was long presentations by students. In the syllabi I included lists of several topic areas from which students could choose, although they were not limited to these. I did not want the lists to be prescriptive or proscriptive. Many students used an item on the list as a prompt for their "class." I also gave students a packet of writing-to-learn exercises that included instructions on free writing, looping, clustering, mapping, outlining, collages, found poems (very popular), dialectical notebooks, SLU (seen, lurking, unseen), and other heuristics culled from Aristotle to Zinsser.

Because they initially did not trust their peers to be sources of knowledge ("I didn't think they had it in them"), students in all three classes expressed serious doubts about this approach: "I resented Dr. Warriner's almost blatant refusal to lead the class or at least to set up the requirements. I did not want to trust my peers to make such choices about a class I was in" (Julie, WE). "Allowing us to take charge of this class ... is a bad idea. Bad meaning that it will allow us to concentrate on the course and get more involved [!] but I don't think to give us that much power is good" (Anthony, LA). "I think the idea of the students running the class is crazy. . . . I'm sort of lazy and would rather have someone tell me what I will be doing then I will just do it" (Heather, LA). Other students didn't believe that I would follow through—"you say we would be *completely* in charge—I doubt that"

(Anthony) and still others were excited at the prospect: "This class is *just* what I need!" (Jim, LA).

I explained that the course must meet college standards and expectations, so they should try to make it rigorous enough to satisfy an accreditation committee. Even though they may not have known exactly what that meant, they responded to the implication. Usually there were some who considered slacking off ("you mean we can write NO papers?") but most students restrained those who tried to make it too easy. Still, they were not comfortable with the degree of responsibility. My class notes from Women Essayists indicate their stress: they didn't know the writers or the material, I was supposed to be the teacher, it was my responsibility to make the assignments, I was the one with the knowledge, they would trust me. Each semester I had to be firm in my insistence that they were capable of designing the course themselves, and eventually they would work together, negotiating, arguing, compromising, not compromising, until they hammered out their course agreements (see Appendix).

Each time when the agreements were completed, a surprising change occurred. The students suddenly felt responsible for the class. Most of them began research on their presentations immediately, and all consistently completed the assignments given by fellow students. They felt less compelled to finish *my* assignments, on the few occasions when a class fell to me. In all the courses, and more so in the ones with fewer students, I was responsible for some of the classes. Kelly (WE) reflected that "each piece of writing was an extension of myself ... nothing was written up just so I could make my one entry per week quota." Daniela (WE) speculated that a student might think that "you may subconsciously go easy on yourself if you are giving yourself the work, and that maybe you aren't getting your money's worth. But the thing is that once you are forced to make your own decisions, you also set your standards higher because you feel an obligation to yourself to really try and see just how creative, ambitious, and hard working you can be." Ernesto (LA) responded to the students' assignments this way: "I really live with them, inside, and I feel that my cells eat the knowledge ... with voracity: this is so nutritious!"

One demonstration of the students' achievements was that seven of them felt confident enough about their writing to submit to outside sources. While a few were in the school newspaper, most were in the *Hartford Courant* or *The Connecticut Post*. Daniela, above, sent me her published article (*The Hartford Courant*, 6 March, 1994) with this note

written in the margin: "Look! RIGHT ABOVE Ellen Goodman!"
Kathleen (AA) submitted her essay on organic gardening to local
newspapers after the students in the class urged her to try.

The students' investment manifested itself in forms other than
writing. One snow day, when only seven out of twenty students could
get to campus, the students (in Language Awareness) decided to stay
in spite of the ice building up outside, and concentrate on style. We
spent the session working with each other's writing style. The atmosphere was adventurous, as is often the case in "survival" situations,
and the students felt that it was their class, and they didn't want to
waste it. When a student missed a presentation because of illness or
other emergency, the class did not look to me to fill in for the absent
one, partly because I refused to do it anyway. On one occasion when I
was late for my "turn" teaching, Melissa (AA), a young woman trained
in formal logic, took over and was explaining Toulmin's informal logic
on the board. She had found an excerpt from *The Uses of Argument* in
our *Course Reader* and was helping others with the idea of "warrants."
That class served as an example to me of when I should restrain my
contributions. I was tempted several times to interrupt and make this
difficult exercise easier, but they eventually figured out a number of
warrants without help. Had I taken over, it would have slowed their
growing senses of achievement, autonomy, and conviction that they
could learn what they needed from each other.

The students' investment also showed in their attitudes towards
other class members. They were enthusiastic, prepared and respectful.
Sometimes, classes were chaotic or divisive. The students cared about
the material, and were less reluctant to argue with a student presenter
than with an instructor. A few of the students in their final evaluations (especially in Women Essayists) wished I had stepped in more
often to calm down some of the more hostile encounters, and sometimes I wished I had too, but I also wonder if my intrusion would have
defeated the sense of responsibility students felt for the class. One student (WT) wrote anonymously, "while it was good to vent anger and
feelings (which may have sparked reactions that led to writing), I wish
there had been fewer episodes because they did not conclude anything." Others mentioned how much they had learned about how to
argue and to respect others' viewpoints *because* I refrained from stepping in: "Sometimes the class got into heated discussions, which I felt
was a great way to learn" (Also anonymous, WE).

A conflict that exemplifies the nature of the friction in the Women

Essayists class occurred with Julie's assignment, which asked the students to compare the *styles* of Susan Sontag in "Women's Beauty: Put Down or Power Source" and Alice Walker in "Beauty: When the Other Dancer is the Self." "My topic," Julie explained, "was supposed to be a comparison of the style of the two essays, to analyze both of their approaches. But, for some reason (?), the topic of the conversation became 'Beauty,' which was fine with me." Although Julie said it was fine, she regretted the loss of a discussion on style, and what happened in class that day set a tone of antagonism that lasted several class sessions. One of the students had been "demoted [at work] unfairly due to discrimination (I wasn't pretty enough to get fair treatment) which I could not prove." She was therefore feeling hostile about public standards of beauty. The conversation shifted to topics associated with beauty—makeup, clothes, bodies—and quickly became a free-for-all, with two gay women defending their decision to wear makeup, two of the men defending their approval of makeup "sometimes, when you want to feel good," and other women heaping disdain upon those who cared about such "superficial" things. The discussion moved from beauty to the rights of citizens to take the law into their own hands and deface public property for a principle when one of the gay women told how she had "removed" an offensive "ladies" symbol from a restroom door, a woman in a bustle.

Although I contributed to the discussion, I did not try to direct it, though maybe I should have, since it deteriorated into an acrimonious wrangle. Most of the students referred to it again with mixed or angry feelings, and several of them wrote follow-through "letters" to each other. Despite these tensions, debates created involvement not often found in a traditional classroom. The students did learn about rhetorical style; they were effectively engaged in discussing the assumptions behind the American portrayal of beauty in the two essays, and they presented their own arguments more effectively because they wanted to persuade other members of the class of their opinions. They read and listened; they felt the trial and error of confrontation; they tasted what can happen with effective and ineffective arguments.

The classes became progressively less agonistic. The Women Essayists class was so new that I was reluctant to assert much control at all, for fear of inhibiting the students' spirit. Or it may have been that I expected gender tensions to be volatile. However, there developed more tension between the gays and straights in the class than between men and women. Although the level of discomfort may have been high, the level of attention to rhetorical strategies was also high, removed from the abstract and comfortable in the experiential.

The Language Awareness class also showed discomfort, though here it was content-based rather than gender-based. The students expressed strong opinions about the assignments. For example, opinions clashed sharply over slang, profanity, rock lyrics, Black English, the language of AIDS, tabloid journalism, and advertising—topics chosen by the students. When they argued over these issues, they were aware that they were frequently speaking from their individual cultures and thus avoided acrimony. They were also collectively at approximately the same "level" of awareness (of language issues), whereas one of the salient complaints in the Women Essayists course was that some of the students knew all about the Women's Movement and its issues, and some knew next to nothing. The LA students, perhaps, felt more equal in their degrees of ignorance and knowledge. Most of the time their arguments would start over the issue of the day, i.e. the status of Black English, then they exchanged personal stories and information from reading material, and most of them found their minds had changed toward flexibility and provisional thinking. The arguments were more obviously (though perhaps not subliminally) constructive.

Advanced Argumentation was, oddly enough, the most ironic of the three courses. Although one might expect a course in argumentation to be, well, argumentative, the focus was on rhetorical strategies and techniques, not on explosive subjects like gender and language. The students paid intense attention to "audience awareness": they spoke and wrote of their awakening to a sense of audience, to learning how to be in another's shoes, to tailoring one's topic to the major premises of the audience. They were a polite group, too, with students who were unusually serious about assuming responsibility—I encountered less resistance to the unconventional pedagogy at the beginning of this class than the others, perhaps because two of the students had had one of the other two courses and were strong advocates.

Students Learning from Each Other

Students wrote that they enjoyed learning from each other and that their experience was significant. The *kinds* of learning fell into two general groups: the *content* of the presentations and attendant reading and writing assignments; and the *high interest* sustained when peers chose the topic and talked about it. The content of the students' choices is worth reporting. Here area few examples.

Jim (LA) illustrates how a common topic—diversity—can be personalized while referring to larger issues. He records his preparation: "I would talk about culture and the role it plays in the way we interpret, and generate, behavior; I would talk about the foundation of ethnocentrism and its expression in both segregation and assimilation; and I would discuss the experience of various minority groups in the United States, especially Native Americans and African Americans. My experiences in classes both for my major and my minor helped me in organizing this presentation." Jim "studied up" for weeks to build on his existing knowledge; when he made his writing assignment for the class, he dropped his specialized language and worded it to elicit a personal response: "Write a journal entry in which you reflect on some of the ways your attitudes, values and behavior have been shaped by your family, peers, ethnic community, church or by society in general. Guided by the 'Sounds of Silence' article [one of his reading assignments, by Edward T. Hall and Mildred Reed Hall], think of examples that are less obvious, that you are not normally aware of. How do you think they would affect the way you would relate to members of another culture?" Jim worried that he would "take over" the class because he liked to lecture and felt he had much to say; however, his writing assignment provoked students to assert themselves. Each student spoke of "hidden" experiences that had shaped their attitudes and beliefs. At one point the speaking competition was so great that Jim glanced at me with concern, then shrugged, grinned, and let them have the floor. The mesh of private revelation and public issue created a session of uncommon vitality. Jim was very pleased that "his" topic and assignment had been responsible for such a good class.

Ernesto (LA), a student from Bolivia accustomed to formal lectures, and somewhat disconcerted by the style of this class, first responded in his journal entries with a series of questions about my seriousness. But he changed his topic, shortly, to the readings and the other students' preparations, as well as to stories about life in Bolivia. For his own presentation, he distributed what was apparently an essay written by someone with an Hispanic name, "Eco." Ernesto had written it himself, then formatted it on his printer so it would look as though he had copied it from a book (he never did claim authorship). The essay was an unusual narrative, multivocal, multicultural, reminiscent of Gloria Anzaldua or Susan Howe, or, in its calmer moments,

Isabel Allende. It was fantasy, a fairy tale, a myth, a trip through the day of an old woman in a Latin American country. Written in a style that varied from paragraph to paragraph, sometimes from sentence to sentence, occasionally it was difficult to follow, amusing, poignant, and reflective of "a day in the life." Along with this essay, Ernesto assigned Orwell's "Politics and the English Language." In class, he pointed out how Orwell's strictures could be stifling; from a Latin American perspective, according to Ernesto, they were worse than stifling: they destroyed the natural movement of the mind, they squeezed vocabulary, they even prevented communication because they made language and expression too homogeneous. Ernesto got an argument from some of his classmates, but his perspective affected our class discussions from then on.

The initiatives the students brought to their assignments and presentations was perhaps the most salient feature of these courses. The students' proposals contrasted with many more conventional projects found in writing courses. Two collaborating African-American students (LA) assigned their classmates several articles on Black English, and then asked them to re-write the Gettysburg address into Black English. On that occasion I was the only person who was uncomfortable reading her rendition, and the students stood and stamped for one rendition by a normally silent black young man. Another assignment (WE) asked students to write an essay imitating the style of Zora Neale Hurston's "How It Feels to Be Colored Me," and in that class also the students competed to read their imitations. A rhetoric major (AA) showed clips of John F. Kennedy and Richard Nixon, then asked us to cover our heads with our jackets while listening to their debate (we all hoped no senior administrator would stroll by our classroom to see us watching television with hoods over our heads). We then wrote our impressions, *after* which she explained the image problems that TV had presented for Nixon. A student exploring sexism in language (AA) assigned the following: "Write a short essay about a first-year college student who wanted to be a doctor or a lawyer but for financial reasons dropped out of college to become a blue-collar worker." Only one student in the class caught on, realizing halfway through her essay that an incipient doctor or lawyer (or blue-collar worker) could be a woman—she then changed the student's gender. Every other student assumed a male, underscoring the student's point about gender assumptions. I now use this technique to introduce my classes to the CCCC's resolution on sexist language. One last example is the assignment by Tom and Lynda on women journalists. One reading was by Anka Radakovich, someone who had been unknown to me but not to the class. I was so unnerved by her essay ("Girl Talk, Part Deux") that I completely deconstructed it, probably to defuse it, as did the more self proclaimed feminists in the class. Although this text struck me as inflammatory, and I would not have included it myself, it elicited highly charged discussion about sexism in women, the nature of sexism, and the nature of female sexuality and female bonding.

One of the questions I have about my teaching experience is whether student-activated courses enable people from different cultural, economic, and ethnic backgrounds to be comfortable with exchanges that foster learning while at the same disclosing those backgrounds. It is difficult for me to tell whether there were particular patterns that distinguish these assignments and presentations along those lines. It is true that Ernesto's Latin American perspective broadened ours. Keran, from Haiti, though, took a traditional route, exploring the media from a useful but not culturally distinctive angle. The Black English collaborators were African-American: Carolyn was from an environment that included poverty and recovery from crack, and Cheryl was economically comfortable. What does seem to matter is that each student brought a perspective to a topic that was different from those I may have brought from professional experience. Rather than several weeks of my prism on the world, we had several prisms. Because of the makeup of the classes, these perspectives naturally reflected different cultural and economic contexts. The ways of knowing were indeed varied, sometimes because the student was from a different ethnic background from the majority in the class; sometimes because he or she reflected a contextual, non-hierarchical, web-making way of knowing that may be new to many students; sometimes simply because the freedom of the structure on one hand, and the demands the students put on themselves on the other, galvanized students to feats of creativity not ordinarily seen in the college classroom.

I did notice a shift in the kinds of exchanges that combined the personal with the public in the class discussions. In all three courses students enjoyed providing examples from their lives to make a point, further a discussion, or add an example. I am reminded in particular of Ernesto's response to Rose's presentation on profanity. In Ernesto's household, he told the class, his return from school was marked by his use of mild profanity and a "freer" use of language. His parents admonished him sharply to "respect the house" and were distressed over what they perceived as his "informality." Rick, from another culture, responded that his experience had been that age fifteen was the cut-off point: before fifteen, no profanity allowed; after fifteen, anything goes. Other students joined the discussion, and the links between profanity, maturity, and education became the topic of the day. The question of how education changes personal behavior and family relationships reappeared throughout the semester. Even though this class and others like it sometimes felt as though they were teetering on the edge of bull sessions, the students usually re-focused their discussion after exchanging their anecdotes. It seemed to me—and, I believe, to them—that these exchanges were fruitful, revealing, and substantive. They gave the issues personal resonance; they gave the stories academic pertinence.

One refrain I heard repeatedly, especially near the end of the semesters, was that the students felt empowered by the experience of these classes. As presenters, they enjoyed the responsibility and the success they had with teaching their classmates. They were excited and pleased by the high class interest and the response to their own topics and ideas. For example, Becky (WE) chose as her topic "mothers and daughters," and assigned a number of essays for reading. About her "class," she recalls that her writing assignment—one paragraph each on two different writers, exploring which one had more impact and why—was designed in part to guarantee that her "classmates would do the reading and would therefore contribute to the discussion." She adds that "my underlying strategy was to get my audience to really think about their experiences as a child and how those experiences led up to the present relationship they have with their mother. This way the written essays by the women authors have become more than just essays. They become a reminder of the past and then a reflection." Becky found the responses of the class "very interesting because of the diversity in terms each one used for description. Many themes were also pulled out of each essay and then were supported by the text. This was a great exercise. It really enabled us as a collective group to examine a piece of literary work in all different perspectives. I truly enjoyed the experience and learned a great deal."

Becky's assessment of her success is accurate, but also modest. I knew from watching her and I learned later from talking to her that this presentation for her was career-defining. She had always admired teachers and yet had thought her chances of being one were completely scuttled by her shyness, her tendency to blush, and her belief that everything went out of her head the minute she was the center of attention. Becky was also one of the most skeptical students; she liked structure and lectures and direction, and she was initially the most uneasy student in Women Essayists. But the day of her presentation, Becky went up to the front of the class, arranged her extensive notes on the podium, and became what she had hoped she could be but had not thought possible: a college professor. She subsequently decided to major in English, enrolled in a study abroad program in England to broaden her horizons, and now is applying to graduate school to get her Ph.D. She says her professional resolution began for her that day of her presentation.

In addition to feeling empowered by the teaching experience and learning from it, the students also felt empowered by learning from each other. Many commented in their final evaluations how surprised they were at the range of knowledge of their classmates. They praised the diversity of topics and pedagogical methods, and compared the course favorably with others. One student (AA) (nameless because the final evaluations were anonymous) wrote "It was a breath of fresh air. This promoted an immense amount of stimulation for me ... I felt a willingness to learn more than in any other area of study ever." Tom (WE) wrote in his self-evaluation, "I was also very surprised, at the end of the course, that the work actually began to *pile up;* had we actually *assigned* ourselves a heavy load of work? It may have been a heavy load, but I don't think it was in any way unfair or even 'too much'; I think it was perfect." Tom also wrote: "I also learned from my class-mates, some of whom I was already friends with, and didn't think they had it in them, and also, I think you learned from us." And another final evaluation (LA): "It really surprised me to see how much we as students, could do on our own to set up class structure, assign-ments, pee; review, etc. *AND* then actually do it and do it well."

I agree that the students were more actively engaged in their learn-ing. Simple things such as the posture of the students indicated their involvement; they sat up and forward when their classmates were pre-senting. They all spoke a great deal; one of the problems for presenters was to regain control of the class after relinquishing it to discussion. The students told me that they paid attention partly because they wanted attention paid to them. Several students used the presenta-tions of their classmates as springboards for their own topics; they would become intrigued by something said in class discussion, or by an assignment, and they would take that experience as their own starting point. For example, the class on profanity got Tim thinking about family culture, which led to his class on diversity. This cross-fertilization can happen in conventional classes when students use something the instructor said or assigned, but the results are not likely to be so varied. Students learned to exercise their freedom and chose topics that I may not have covered. I have little expertise in media studies or linguistics, for example, but several students chose topics concerned with television, advertising, slang, profanity, and ethics in media. Maddy (LA, AA) asked the class to assemble an "ethical newspaper"; her assignment had been urged by another student's presentation on ethics in advertising. She also drew on her experience in her journalism major.

In fact, many students started with material from other disciplines which made the content of the advanced composition courses interdisciplinary and wove disciplines together in unconventional configurations. Maddy combined her experience with the "ethical" newspaper and her education classes to write a research paper and make a presentation (in AA) on how to infuse ethical values into the elementary school system. Heather (LA) revisited *Play It As It Lays* because she had wanted to write about it without the "constrictions" of "literary criticism"; she explored its use of language in the Language Awareness course. As journalism majors, Tom and Lynda (WE) presented modern women in journalism. Linda (WE, AA) drew on her political science major and argued in favor of the electoral college. Nicki's experience with Media Studies helped her critique the televised debates of JFK and Nixon. I believe that the respect the students felt for each other stemmed in part from the knowledge they had built on from these other disciplines, as well as from their different cultures and their current research.

Spontaneous collaborative presentations were a feature of these courses. Several students teamed up in pairs, some in conventional ways and others more innovatively, and all but one of the collaborations provided satisfying work relationships. The satisfied students mentioned how much they had learned from their partner, how helpful it had been to plan and discuss together, and (usually) how surprised they were at how well their presentations went. Collaborative presentations were twice as long, and therefore sometimes more anxiety-producing despite the comfort of having a partner. These presentations were, with one exception, more relaxed yet just as productive.

Interestingly, in most cases the collaborators chose to stay seated in the classroom rather than present from the front of the class. They wrote of their satisfaction with the preparation as well as with the presentation itself. Lynda (WF) learned about women journalists from Tom, but she also learned how to budget time and do extra research. Nicki and Linda (AA) felt that their decision to join "the rhetoric of debate" and "the rhetoric of JFK" was perspicacious. The one unhappy pair (LA) experienced frustration because one partner worked much harder than the other, and was resentful that the other was lifted, so to speak, by her wings. However, it was clear to the class who had done the work, and the students pulled no punches in their critiques.

Colleagues have asked whether I intend to conduct all my classes this way. My answer is that, once you have made this leap, it is difficult to go back. However, I have not tried this approach—turning the whole class over—with first-year students because I think students respond better when they are somewhat acculturated to the academy. To some extent, all my classes, including those for first-year students, are decentered, and in the latter classes I require oral reports, negotiated grading contracts, and self-evaluations of their journals. They have choices for paper topics. Some entering students have little sense of the workload necessary for college level classes, and some (away from home for the first time, with unprecedented personal autonomy) are not in a frame of mind conducive to self-discipline.

A handful of my students did not work very hard on their presentations and fell flat as a result. They suffered the consequences in the critiques of their colleagues, and in their own self-evaluations, since they could not claim credit for a job poorly done. Two students in the Language Awareness course, which had more students and therefore fewer of my own presentations, wished for "more instruction"; although they did praise their classmates in their final evaluations, they wrote that they preferred the lecture format, where they could just listen and learn. Sometimes the classroom in all courses felt anarchic, though that isn't always bad. Students in all three classes had decided on a portfolio system, which was an unqualified success in terms of my own case because I did not need to grade (only respond to) papers and because grades lost their threatening effect. However, a few students evaluated themselves in ways I thought were inaccurate and I initiated a sometimes uncomfortable re-assessment. On the other hand, most students had done more work than I had expected. Those final evaluation sessions, in private in my office, were often simple chats that provided some closure to the course. On two occasions when I disagreed with a student's self-assessment, the students (LA) immediately acknowledged that they had asked for a half-grade higher than they thought they deserved, and they admitted that they had been goaded by students outside the class. They seemed uncomfortable with their decision to try for the higher grade and accepted my judgment. Two students in Women Essayists also gave themselves one-half grade higher than I would have. I had assumed that they had submitted work from another course because it was not in response to any assignment, but they convinced me (accurately, because I later checked) that they had chosen to do this work because of their freedom. These were the most uncomfortable assessments because the students were insulted by my assumption. Two students (WF) gave I themselves one full grade lower than I wanted to give them. They may have been modest, or they may have hoped I would raise the grade because they knew I had a high opinion of their writing from my written comments. Some students refused to grade themselves. They wrote the self evaluations, but left out the grade. "Deciding on a letter grade for my performance needs to be decided by both Dr. Warriner and myself. I feel that if I give my own grade it will be subjective. If the both of us decide I can accept it as being objective and appropriate" (Becky, WE). In those cases, we discussed the evaluations at length, considered each element being assessed, and the students responded to my request for a "verbal ballpark grade," which satisfied us. There were no grade differences in Advanced Argumentation.

I feel some discomfort with my assertion of final authority when I claim to have turned the class over to the students, but the students do not seem to mind. In the beginning, when they are discussing evaluation policy, a few have questioned the disparity between my assertion and my practice. By the end of the term they realize how much they have determined the direction of the course, and they trust the negotiation process. Those reluctant to give themselves grades are willing to write the evaluation, although they consider it difficult: "I've never had to evaluate myself academically. It's always been done for me, so this will be difficult" (Becky, WE). "O.K., now comes the hard part. Now I have to ask for a grade. I'm really no good at this" (Tom, WE). After finishing her evaluation, Kelly (WE) writes "I fully realized exactly how much time and effort each one of us must have put into this class." Grades aside, the final evaluation provides students with an overview of their work, and an occasion for reflection. It may not be fair to say the class belongs entirely to the students when I retain the right to final judgment, but I think the negotiating process allows teacher and student shared authority.

I expect to continue this pedagogy, for the pleasure the students take in it and for the pleasure I take in using it. I tried to do all the reading and writing assignments they devised. There were times when I could not keep up, and I would sacrifice the writing assignment, but I paid a price then because my interest level would dive. When I completed the work, I had something to offer, and I know the students felt encouraged, especially near the beginning of the term, when they realized I had done their assignments. Since we submitted our writing to the student in charge of the class, everyone saw what I produced under pressures similar to their own. There were occasions when the playing field seemed "too" level to me and I wondered if my authority would be diminished in their eyes. As far as I can tell, however, they only gained more respect for each other. We take a risk when we make knowledge accessible to anyone and everyone, not just ourselves. Hephzibah Roskelly, writing about group work, puts it this way:

> As teachers, we have to take on the risky business of looking at the academic house we live in, and the ways we invite students into it. We have to be willing to look at how we ourselves entered, how much we brought with us, how much we were forced to leave at the door. We have to make ourselves brave enough to risk the dissent that inevitably comes when democracy is in action. Once teachers do that, we'll see the work of the small groups in our classes become the real work in the class, with students negotiating their own ideas against and around the ideas they're offered. When students find a real voice, their own and not some mimicked institutional voice, both students and teachers acknowledge the possibility of the real change that might ensue. (146)

Not all of these students eschewed the institutional voice, though some did; what they did was make that bridge between their own personal voice and the institutional vehicle of teaching a class. And they were nothing if not democratic.

Is it possible to measure the depth and breadth of learning in these courses compared to others taught more traditionally? My impression is that the students had better classroom experiences because of the following: they consistently did *all* the reading, though the reading load was probably less than I would have assigned; they read more carefully because they *wanted* to be included in the discussions; they wrote more than other students I have taught (and they said themselves that they wrote more than ever before). The classes consistently sustained high interest; attendance was the best I've seen; and, finally, the richness and complexity of the classes are indicated by the varied subject matter, presentation styles, discussion content, and student-generated reading material that I have outlined here. In addition to my impressions are their own testimonies, some of which have been included here, that indicate the high degree of their classroom involvement. Their enjoyment is linked less to my influence than to their discoveries of their own knowledge and ability. They mention their control now; they feel they will always be learning. Tom sums it up: "This class has taught me that I will always be learning, even in the most unexpected places and from the most unexpected people. *That* is what I learned."

Sacred Heart University
Fairfield, Connecticut

Works Cited

Atkins, G. Douglas. "Envisioning the Stranger's Heart." *College English* 56 (1994): 629-41.

Belenky, Mary Field, et al. *Women's Ways of Knowing: The Development of Self, Voice, and Mind.* New York: HarperCollins Basic Books, 1986.

Bizzell, Patricia. "Beyond Anti-Foundationalism to Rhetorical Authority: Problems Defining Cultural Literacy." *College English* 52 (1990): 661-75.

Boardman, Kathleen. "Being Personal without Getting Personal in a Feminist Classroom." *ATAC Forum 5 (1993)*: 4-7.

Corder, Jim W. "Argument as Emergence, Rhetoric as Love." *Rhetoric Review* (1985): 16-32.

Freire, Paulo. *Pedagogy of the Oppressed.* Trans. Myra Bergman Ramos. New York: Continuum, 1968.

Gale, Fredric G. "Something Old, Something New, Something Borrowed." *Composition For All* 6 (1995): 31-34.

Gilligan, Carol. In *a Different Voice: Psychological Theory and Women's Development.* Cambridge: Harvard UP, 1982.

Institute for Writing and Thinking Summer Workshop. July 7-13, 1993. Bard College.

Lindemann, Erika. *A Rhetoric for Writing Teachers.* 2nd Edition. New York: Oxford University Press, 1987.

Nelson, Jennie. "The Research Paper: A 'Rhetoric of Doing' or a 'Rhetoric of the Finished Word'?" *Composition Studies* 22 (1994): 65-75.

"Nonsexist Language and CCCC Conventions." Resolution passed at the Denver CCCC Convention, 1987.

Radakovich, Anka. "Girl Talk, Part Deux." *Details* (1993): 82.

Roskelly, Hephzibah. "The Risky Business of Group Work." *ATAC Forum* 4 (Spring 1992): 1-5.

Tompkins, Jane. "Pedagogy of the Distressed." *College English* 52 (1990): 653-60.

Toulmin, Stephen. *The Uses of Argument.* Cambridge: Cambridge UP, 1958.

Williams, Joseph M. *Style: Ten Lessons in Clarity and Grace.* New York: HarperCollins, 1993.

Appendix

EN378 Women Essayists M-Th 1:40-2:55 Fall 1993
Course Agreement and Assignments

The students in this course have decided to use the portfolio system for collecting and evaluating their work, and have reached consensus that the following work will be completed by the given dates and included in their portfolio. They have also agreed that all items will be ungraded until the end of the semester, at which time the student and professor will decide in conference what grade the student should receive, based on attendance, oral presentation, journal and papers, as well as a final written self-evaluation by the student.

Portfolio Ingredients

Journal entries: a minimum of one per week, *preferably more*, of informal writing. Such writing will he composed of free writes (focused and unfocused), reader responses to texts, creative writing, letters to each other, to the professor, or to the authors of the texts, and other kinds of informal writing listed in the syllabus, such as "found poems," looping, metacognitive writing, dialectical notebooks, etc. Exercises from *Developing a Written Voice* could also be included.

Oral Presentation: Each student will present either a 20-30 minute presentation, or a 45 minute class on the author[s] or topic of choice. The student is responsible for distributing additional reading material in advance of the presentation (Alison will duplicate) and for designing the reading and/or writing assignments (Alison will duplicate them as well).

Responses to Oral Presentations: Each student will write a 1-2 page informal response to each oral presentation. Alison will make one copy of each of these so they can become part of the student's portfolio and also can be given to the presenter.

Papers: 3 formal papers with deadlines, and 3 revisions of these papers (without deadlines). The papers fall loosely into the following categories.

> Paper #1 On an author that you choose; could be a critique, a biographical sketch, an imitation of style, or all three.
>
> Paper #2: An essay on your own topic; could be on any of the topics on the "list," or prompted by class discussion, or anything of interest to the women essayists—perhaps a response to your reading.
>
> Paper #3 An argument. Could be taking a stand on an issue that is developed in the course or in your reading; could be an editorial or forum piece prompted by class discussion and additional reading on the topic.
>
> The formal papers are due for peer review on:
> Monday, October 25th; final due date Monday, November 1,
> Thursday, November 18; final due Monday, November 22
> Thursday, December 2; final due Thursday, December 9
>
> We have not yet decided which papers should be handed in on which dates; you may end up handing in whichever paper seems right to each student on that date.

Portfolio Evaluation: Each student will write up a formal portfolio self-evaluation at the end of the semester (and some students may want to write one at mid-semester). As mentioned above, the portfolio will be composed of journal entries, formal papers and revisions, classmates' responses to and one's own notes on the oral presentation, and anything else the student feels has bearing on his or her grade. This document will assess the ingredients in the portfolio and will take into consideration other matters such as class attendance and participation. Then in conference the student and professor will decide on a grade. No grades will be given until this conference unless the student makes a different agreement with the professor.

Therefore,

Minimum Portfolio Ingredients:

> 13 journal entries, oral presentation notes, and classmates' responses (approx 10)

> 10 1-2 page responses of your own to classmates' presentations, 3 formal papers, 3 revised papers, 1 self-evaluation

> This agreement can be revised at any time by mutual agreement between the professor and students.

Journeys in Journaling

Chris M. Anson and Richard Beach

Prologue: the Authors Explain Their Journey

When we first thought about writing a chapter on journal writing for this textbook, it was as if we were starting on a journey by choosing the most direct, boring route we could find. We talked about what we could tell you about journal writing, what sort of *information* we could impart about this useful and complicated genre. To us, the land-

---

Chris M. Anson directs the composition program at the University of Minnesota, where he teaches all sorts of courses in language, literacy, and writing. He has written several textbooks on writing, as well as scholarly books and articles exploring how people write and can learn to write. He has a special interest in informal writing used across the college curriculum as a way to help students learn. In his spare time he writes, remodels old houses, runs, and enjoys the outdoors with his wife Geanie and his two little boys, Ian and Graham.

Richard Beach, a former high school English teacher, is Professor of English Education at the University of Minnesota, where he teaches courses on literature, composition, and media methods. He is coauthor of *Teaching Literature in the Secondary School* and co-editor of *Developing Discourse Practices in Adolescence and Adulthood*. He doodles in his own journal for at least an hour a day. He has also found that student journals, particularly dialogue journals, improve the quality of talk in his own classes. He enjoys running (even in below-zero Minnesota winters), going to movies, and reading spy thrillers.

scape is familiar; we've traveled the journal road many times, both by keeping journals ourselves and by conducting research on how people, especially students, learn and write by journaling. We were planning to take you down a kind of textbook superhighway, telling you in a blur of ideas what you should think about journals and how you should use them.

But then we started wondering about the sort of journey we were mapping out for you. We would most certainly cover lots of ground and expose you to the "main ideas" about journal writing, even if at breakneck speed. Would you be interested? Possibly. Would you speculate much about journals? Maybe. Could we get across how varied and complex and interesting journal writing is? Doubtful. We could tell you all that, but you might not want to take our word for it.

Still undecided, we went home to do what we usually do when we're not sure how to begin a piece of writing: we journaled. And we kept journaling for many pages and many weeks, first writing to and for ourselves, in the form of "solo" journals and then, later, slipping into a kind of dialogue as we sent each other what we'd written.

Shortly before a draft of our (still unwritten) chapter was due, something curious happened. As we talked about all our journal writing, we began to realize that our own journey into this chapter was likely to be more interesting, with more (in)sights to see at a slower and more enjoyable pace, than the chapter we imagined producing for this book. Then it dawned on us that the best way we could tell you about journal writing would be to share with you what we did.

Our journey, then, begins early on in our journal writing, as we wrote loose, exploratory entries focusing on what we wanted to tell you. To help you to see us at work, we've inserted our initials in brackets to indicate who's writing [CMA] or [RB].

The Journey

November 10 [CMA]

Rick [RB] came up with a great idea: We simply journal our way into the essay for Wendy Bishop's book, and it could "show" us ideas that we'd otherwise have to conjure up academically. And even as I do this entry I feel that my usual journaling process is becoming different somehow, and I think it comes from knowing that maybe Rick will see this, not so much that it should be polished and formal but that someone is going to look into my thinking and my own learning as a way to understand this crazy genre. Because it *feels* more text-like. That may be a difference we want to explore in the piece because in most academic settings journals are, in fact, read by someone (a teacher? other students?), which doesn't necessarily change their informality but makes the sentences more complete, fewer personal abbreviations and short cuts, maybe. Something to do with the syntax. This project should be fun.

November 11 [RB]

Academic journals vs. personal journals. In discussing the journal, we're really talking about "academic journals" used in college courses to write about and reflect on the class readings, discussions, observations, related experiences, presentations, lectures, etc. This probably differs from a more private "personal diary" form of journal or a journal often used in therapy or as an observation log in creative writing. We need to make this clear. Also, I think journals have gotten bad press from seeming too "wishy washy" in some educational circles. Journals may be informal, but they *lead* to and *require* hard thinking. That's their point.

I think we should include at least the following information:

- What's an academic journal? How does it differ from the stereotypical diary?
- How do you keep one? This seems basic (who cares what sort of actual notebook you use?). But people do feel that the physical side of journals make a difference.
- Different sort of journals. Monologues vs. dialogues.
- How do we show journals at work? I like the idea of including examples from students' work in different courses. Maybe we could include some of our own?

November 12 [CMA]

Rick wondered whether we should include anything about our own personal uses of journals. I'm not sure what he means—focus overtly on how we use journals? Who wants to read all our professional musings? But it occurs to me that he might have meant how we ourselves started using journals, our personal histories. Makes journal writing seem close to writing autobiography. So here goes.

I guess I was about 11 or 12 years old when I started journaling. It was back when the (now common) American gerbil had just made its way into a few pet shops around the country as some sort of exotic new rodent (I don't think anyone knew at that point how prolific the little beasts were going to be!). I had a tank full of tropical fish and some of those little chameleons (I think they were just a common form of lizard from Mexico but they did turn from brown to green occasionally) and a guinea pig or two. And one day, clutching my 26 cents for a replacement carbon filter for my aquarium aerator, I went into our local pet shop. I remember how the door jingled when I opened it, and I went past the cages and tanks and barrels of bird food and cracked corn and there, right next to the charcoal filters, was a 25-gallon tank containing two gerbils.

I stood there for what seemed like a good half an hour, transfixed by these two strange little creatures, dashing around in their cedar chips, burrowing and nuzzling in their frenzied way. There was something jerky about their movements that I'd never seen in any other pet-store animal, and that fascinated me. I stood there, mezmerized by the way the gerbils would sit up with their little front paws dangling in front of them and then move a few inches to the left or right in one single, split-second twitch, stop, then twitch again. Stop, twitch. Stop, twitch. I wondered what that would be like, moving in that way. I was fascinated, and I just had to have one.

Then came the shock. As I stood there, the pet store owner had been preparing a little sign, his magic marker squeaking across a piece of white cardboard. Finally he brought it over and taped it on to the wall next to the gerbil tank. "Gerbils (South American rodent): $7.50 apiece."

Seven fifty! Two month's allowance, not including a cage!

Somehow, and I think it was probably my all-time greatest feat of parental persuasion, I managed, within the week, to get not just one gerbil but both. And a tank. And food. And a bag of cedar chips. And a little glass water bottle with a metal drinking spout. My father, who did amateur carpentry in the cellar in his spare time, then decided to build five gerbil cages for me, so that when my pair started to breed (which Dad, in all his wisdom, predicted they would do with a vengeance), I could start up a kind of cottage industry. Twenty dollars for two gerbils and a fully set up cage. Who could resist? After all, these were new, exotic animals. (I think that image, of our entire cellar turned into a profit-making breeding station for gerbils, was what finally got to Dad and got me my gerbils.)

One minor problem. After waiting for several months, with our five empty cages neatly lined up on a cellar shelf, we began wondering whether our pair of gerbils were capable of breeding. My father had never really looked too closely at them (he was still, I think, immersed in his dream of becoming the state's largest producer of exotic rodents). Finally, one Saturday, he took the gerbils out of the cage to conduct a close inspection. The verdict was instant and final: they were both males.

The following week, I managed to get another pair of gerbils (both female) by agreeing to wash the windows for a year and take out the garbage when asked and even clean up the sawdust in the cellar whenever Dad retreated there to build something. By that time, they were only $5 each (and falling). Before long, my five cages each sported two or more young gerbils. I twisted my best friend's arm to take one cage off my hands for ten dollars, but in spite of this first sale it didn't take long for the remaining four cages to grow in population, each housing a little kibbutz of five, eight, twelve gerbils. Dad frantically built cages. The price continued to drop. And soon, within the year, I was begging our friends, neighbors, distant acquaintances to take them, cage and all, for free.

Now, I had other pets. And when I needed advice about them, I'd turn to one of my little 50-cent pamphlets on "Caring for Tropical Fish" or "The Domestic Guinea Pig." But nothing, anywhere, on gerbils. I tried the library. Nothing. I combed the pet shops in three nearby towns. Nothing. Not a single word about domestic gerbils. This was it—my very first foray into Authorship. "Gerbils as Pets" by Christopher Anson.

So in the dim light of the dusty basement, amid the squealing of the gerbils' exercise wheels and the weep-weeping of my two guinea pigs and the bubbling of my aquarium aerators, I started my first, almost Darwinian journal, a little lined notepage of clinical observations about my rapidly proliferating pets.

My gerbil journal lasted for over six months, page after page of the most scholarly notes a 12-year old could conjure up about his pets' behavior. Once a gerbil got out of the cage and was lost in the cluttered basement for three weeks. When I finally did find him behind a box of wood, he'd killed a small field mouse (whose little dried up body lay nearby) and taken up residence in the mouse's winter home, a nest of tiny pieces of newspaper, thread, insulation material, part of an old sock from the laundry area, straw, and bits of cedar chips that had fallen from the gerbil cages. Now wild, the gerbil bit me so hard when I tried to pick him up that my finger bled for half an hour. Worse still, when I reintroduced the prodigal gerbil to his commune, the entire cage instantly became a battlefield, father turning on son, brother on sister, cousin on cousin, in a frenzy of indiscriminate attacks. When the dust and cedar chips settled, my renegade gerbil was dead, two others had lost substantial pieces of ear, and a fourth was missing the end of his tail.

After this incident (and a ritual burial of my first gerbil casualty), I remember sitting for a couple of hours in the dank cellar, writing and writing and writing about what it all meant. I figured an entire chapter in my pamphlet would have to be devoted to this problem of the escaped gerbil. And there was more: what could make such peaceful, adorable creatures so aggressive? Why did the gerbil turn on me—his caretaker and source of life—and then on his own kin? And how could they so ruthlessly kill him in his madness? As I wrote, my entries began slipping from rodent to animal kingdom, domestication, zoos, cages. And then to the idea of hostility and war, and humanity. And then to who I was and what I wanted to be.

And that's it, that's all to tell, I guess. I started journal writing that year, the year of the gerbils. I never did finish my pamphlet, but I found out that wasn't really the point.

I've never stopped journaling since.

November 17 [RB]

I want to look at characteristics of journal writing (informal, etc.), to contrast them with formal academic writing. What I noticed about Chris' gerbil story is how it's a blend of "polished" and informal writing. When he sent it over he said he was surprised at how well it turned out for something just done very quickly. So in a way he *aimed* to write informally and then ended up doing something that could pass as a formal narrative. The usual difference between journal writing and academic papers looks like this:

Formal Writing	Journal Writing
Organized	Unorganized
Formal language	Informal language
Definitive	Exploratory
Polished	Unpolished
Used to communicate	Used to learn, think, reflect

Most of the journal writing used to help students *learn* is informal, etc. But it may be possible to see the act of journal writing as a great way to write your way into a formal piece.

November 18 [CMA]

The most powerful thing about journal writing, for me, can be visualized as a sort of wheel, a snake with its tail in its mouth. At some point, the wheel is labeled "writing." Somewhere on the other side, it's labeled "thinking" or "learning." Writing, in other words, *leads* to thinking and learning. Thinking and learning lead, in turn, to more writing. And on and on, like a mantra. I think this concept works especially well with journal writing because it suggests the exploratory nature of journals and emphasizes their chief value: contemplation.

November 20 [RB]

One use of the journal is to extend or explore your thinking in order to construct your own knowledge. Rather than simply restate or rehearse ideas shared in a course, you're using the journal to reformulate and reflect on ideas *in your own words*. In that way, you're assimilating these ideas into what you already know and believe. For example, you might begin in a philosophy class by restating or rehearsing what the text, students or instructor has said about the idea of "free will." To extend or explore your own thinking about free will, you may then consider the following ways of extending and exploring (etc., finish this thought):

1. A loping freewrite: Peter Elbow suggests that one way to extend your thinking is to pick out a word, phrase or key term, and do a 5-or 10-minute freewrite about that word, phrase, or key term.
2. Reflecting on your own thinking. You may also use your entries to reflect—to stand back and interpret or evaluate the larger meaning of your thinking.
3. Using the journal as prewriting. You may also use your journal entries as prewriting to develop ideas for your papers. As you begin to define and clarify a possible paper topic, you could highlight or circle material and entitle that material in the margin according to its relevance to your overall topic, etc. *Chris—What do you think of this sort of listing/bulletin"?*

November 30 [CMA]

Rick: You notice that since we started exchanging journal entries we've slipped into a dialogue journal, and it's worth, I think, really making that distinction in the chapter for *The Subject is Writing*.

Because some classes may involve students in just plain journal writing, for and to themselves, while others might get students writing in dialogues like this. And frankly I'd rather just dialogue about our journal writing from now on, because I think we have to start getting more specific about what direction we want to take.

December 9 [RB]

Chris: We need to explore more of those functions I started working on the other day. Another one I want to add is something like mapping—in keeping a journal, you may want to use some mapping to explore your thoughts (or something like that). For example, in an economics class, you may be discussing the differences between socialism and capitalism. Using a circle and spoke map, put the key ideas—socialism and capitalism—in central circles. Then draw spokes out from the central circles and make smaller circles that represent the different characteristics of the central ideas. (And so on—each smaller circle can then suggest other circles so you begin to fill the page with concepts. Then draw lines and label them with "d" or "s" to represent differences and similarities.) We could actually show a map or maybe one of our own. You didn't do anything like that for the gerbil thing, did you?

December 15 [CMA]

Rick—I like the idea of adding something conceptual/visual to journal writing, because it always seems so "wordy," if you know what I mean—all language, in full and sometimes very elaborated sentences (like these, I guess). It would be wise to show how appropriate it is to carry on even the most highly conceptual doodling, mapping, diagrams, and so on in a journal. I also like the way you stuck in a reference to economics, to show the academic diversity of journals.

You asked if I used mapping with the gerbil piece, and no, I didn't. For some reason I find it less useful for narrative, but the main difference was that I didn't think I was actually writing anything formal. This is, for me, one of the most powerful aspects of journal writing: I *tricked myself* into writing something that with a lot of work might actually become a fairly decent, lighthearted piece, but when I was writing it I was just writing as fast as I could to tell you about when I started journaling, and somehow, maybe because I felt so relaxed and uninhibited, my words started coming out more descriptively. It's weird, but it never struck me as such a powerful way to start writing as it did then, and maybe it's precisely because I wasn't actually setting out to "start writing."

What do you want to do with the notion of dialogue journals? Since we started writing articles together (was it six years ago!?) I've noticed how much our stuff has really turned into dialogue journaling even when we're trying to do pretty formal chunks (notice, for example, how both of us, when we tire of writing a formal chunk, almost always do a kind of dialoguing at the moment we fizzle out, like "Rick, what else should we include here?" or (and you do this a lot) "Chris—fill in." It shows how dialoguing can become collaboration, and I like the idea of explaining that to students.

December 29 [RB]

Chris, here are some pieces on dialogue journals. Tell me what you think or just redo them.

Carrying on a written conversation. Keeping a dialogue journal differs from a solo journal in that you are sharing your thoughts with another person in a written conversation. You and your partner(s) can collaboratively explore your responses to readings, ideas, similar experiences, or difficulties. While you may do the same thing in an oral conversation, one advantage of using a written conversation is that you have time to reflect on each other's entries. There may be a gap of several days before you react. You can therefore mull over what your partner says in order to formulate a response.

Chris: How theoretical do you think we should get in this? I want to refer to Michael Halliday's finding that oral language portrays things more as unfolding processes, in a complex and dynamic way, while written language tends to describe products, turning those into a structure, so its complexity is static and dense. He notes that "writing creates a world of things; talking creates a world of happening." So that the dialogue journal, by combining the features of both oral and written language, encourages both an ongoing interactive exploration of ideas with the more structured exploration of written language. But that's a little too heavy, don't you think? Do you have any ideas for how to explain that?

January 6 [CMA]

Rick: I just looked back through the stuff we've been doing. I wondered whether instead of doing the same old boring *formal* kind of paper we could try to explore journals in a concrete and interesting way by actually *doing* what we're talking about. Do you think this could work? Because I'm worried that if we try too hard, we're going to end up doing a sort of "scholarly piece" disguising as a how-to chapter and maybe end up pandering too much or something.

I have one fear about this, and it's the conflict between the sort of journal writing we've been doing and the fact that if it's published in this form, then it sanctions sloppiness, random organization, etc. Let's face it, nothing is ever published unless it's formal and tidy and stylistically slick. We don't want to give the impression that a writer can be conceptually and linguistically messy and then just stop there. Do you think we'll be sending that message?

January 10 [RB]
Chris: The dialogue journal idea is tied up with the notion of building relationships, a kind of good conversation that leads to learning and thinking. So why not share the process we're going through?

January 15 [CMA]
Rick: Help! I don't know. I've read back through all this and I'm tempted to polish it up, especially my gerbil narrative (I was sort of amazed looking back at it to remember that it took me the lesser part of an hour to write, just blasting through.) But if we do that, we defeat the whole purpose of the chapter, which is to show journals in action, to go on a kind of journey in journaling. In other words, if the whole thing starts to look contrived and polished and slick, then it's not journal writing any more. And that's hard, because it takes a certain will power to resist "fixing it up."

We're putting ourselves on the line by going public with something so informal. But what I like about the idea is that we *had* to learn our way into and through this piece to begin with. We might have ended up with a polished article, but it wouldn't have shown *how* we learned our way into and through it.

And another thing I like about it in this form: We don't have all the answers about this sort of writing. It's too varied (I think we did five or six really different kinds of writing in the process of writing about it). I'd rather that people talk about journal writing and experiment with it than think that we have all the answers about just how and why it works. Again, that's a risk, don't you think? We're researchers, we have all sorts of data and expertise on journal writing. But I'd rather just be honest.

January 20 [RB]

Chris: I liked your phrase about a journey. Why don't we call it "Journeys in Journaling" and leave it at that?

Coda, the Authors Reflect on Their Travels

This is the first and probably the only time we will ever write about journaling by publishing our own journal writing. The advantage, for us, comes from the potential for our chapter to display some of the benefits of journaling: more and better thinking about a topic; less anxiety and procrastination because of the sense of having "started" a writing task; better planning for formal writing; and a more collaborative writing situation, especially when keeping a dialogue journal.

But, like the dramatic commercial in which someone flies over 10 piles of tires in a stock car or bungee-jumps 500 feet above a rocky river, we suggest that you don't try this at home. Turn in formal, polished writing. But by all means begin it by journaling. You'll find, as we do, that keeping a journal, alone or with someone else as a dialogue partner, really does work. Take our words for it.

Teaching Students to Revise: Theories and Practice

Richard C. Raymond

What can we do to help our students move beyond rewriting to revising?

In the prize-winning article, "Detection, Diagnosis, and the Strategies of Revision," Linda Flower and her colleagues at Carnegie Mellon define revision as "strategic action adapted to the necessities of the task" (19). As teachers of writing, we all strive with Professor Flower to make our students such strategists, able—at least by the end of our courses—to detect problems in text, diagnose those problems, then select a strategy of revision (21).

Inexperienced writers, however, sometimes cannot take that first step, unable to detect a problem in content or mechanics, much less to diagnose and solve it. Others can detect weaknesses but can manage only an "ill defined representation" of the problem (26). Therefore, when we ask—or require—such students to revise their work, we are asking the impossible. They can, however, "rewrite" their work, a "delightfully simple and efficient procedure," according to Flower, that begins in rereading for the "gist" of a flawed document, then moves forward with a fresh draft. As Flower puts it, "the rewrite process simply replicates the writer's original attempt to produce text" (43).

But what can we do to help our students move beyond rewriting to revising? Bleeding accusations in the margins of our students' papers is no solution, as study after study and C—after C—have shown us (Knoblauch 1) One action we can take is to keep up with and contribute to the research of Linda Flower; the more we know about the cognitive processes that underlie the acts of revision, the better teachers of writing we are likely to become. At the same time, we can insist that our students become skillful in situational analysis, having learned, as we have from Flower's work, that writers thoroughly acquainted with their readers' needs and the writers' "dynamic web of purpose" will be better revisers (531). Further, we can ensure that situational analysis carries through the recursive revision process by requiring and guiding sessions of peer evaluation of rough drafts, then making suggestions on second drafts that will assist students in diagnosing and solving problems (Brooke 686-89; Markel 510). Finally, we can publish a revision policy that rewards those students who learn to revise effectively.

Situational Analysis and Peer Evaluation

Revision begins with prevision, as the work of Stephen P. Witte on "Pre-Text and Composing" has shown. To help students form that pre-text, the "mental construction of 'text' prior to transcription" (397), we can provide writing projects rooted in students' interests, work experience, and/or reading-writing situations in which each student can readily identify a purpose and a reader.

To help English 101 students discover a sense of purpose and reader, we routinely spend a class period, either in one large group or in several small groups, generating ideas on assigned topics such as those in Figure 1.

They begin to realize that prewriting generates excitement for students who see themselves writing from experience to someone who wants to read or needs to know. Such class discussion also dispels the first impression that these topics call for tedious imitation on one rhetorical mode or another.

After such class discussion, I ask my students to move through and beyond pre-text by employing one or more of the pre-writing techniques we have studied—looping, branching, listing—then preparing a written statement of purpose and reader and a rough draft to be evaluated in class by a fellow student. As my students exchange rough drafts, I distribute guidelines for evaluation (see Figure 2).

In answering these evaluative questions, the student learns to detect errors in focus or development by holding up the draft to the other student's stated purpose, making it more likely that detection will be followed by diagnosis and suggested strategies for improve-

1. Focusing on two great athletes who play the same sport (tennis players Ivan Lendl and John McEnroe) or who play the same position in the same sport (two quarterbacks, two third basemen, etc.), contrast their styles for readers of *Sports Illustrated*.

2. You are a disgruntled (or pleased) citizen writing an editorial for the *Morning News* bewailing (or praising) the change in your community since the arrival or establishment of _____.

3. You are a free-lance writer who has decided to write an essay, perhaps a humorous piece, explaining why your favorite football team won or lost last weekend. Your publisher will be the *Savannah Morning News* or the *Atlanta Journal*, depending on which team you choose to discuss.

4. Contrast two ways of achieving the same objectives or two products designed to serve the same purpose. Which is better? Why? You plan to submit your piece to *Time*, *Changing Times*, or *Consumer Reports*, depending on your subject.

5. You are a free-lance writer wanting to break into the health-craze market. Write an article (feel free to be humorous) explaining how your health has changed (improved or worsened) since you started (or quit)_____ .

6. Devise your own topic (subject to my approval). The topic must employ comparison contrast, and/or causation as its pattern of organization; it must also be properly narrowed by consulting your *knowledge* and *experience*. Stick to what you know and what you care about.

Before you write the rough draft, follow up our class discussion with free writing and/or branching to sharpen your focus. Also, state your purpose, identify your reader(s), and explain your assumptions about your reader's attitudes toward and knowledge of your topic. Explain, too. how your assumptions about the reader will affect your content, arrangement, and diction. Bring your statements on purpose and reader with your rough draft to the peer evaluation session.

Figure 1 Generating Ideas

ment—"If McEnroe's serve is so great, give examples of major tournaments won by the power serve"—rather than by less well-defined detections of weakness—"Paragraph 2 is too short." Also, in writing their responses to rough drafts, students discover that reading, to use Flower's words, is "a constructive, cognitive process and a rhetorical event in which readers use their knowledge of human purposes to build a meaningful and coherent text" (549).

With evaluations written and signed, I encourage my students to talk peer to peer. Such one-on-one discussion helps students become reader centered, learning to detect the gap between the message intended and the message conveyed, a gap the student must fill to achieve the stated purpose and to serve the stated reader (Katz 366-67).

When the written and oral evaluations are complete, my students have one to two days (depending on the complexity of the assignment) to revise the rough draft. This second draft, done after the peer evaluation, receives a grade. To encourage my students to take seriously the process that led to this revision, I require that they turn in all prewritings, the statement of purpose and reader, the rough draft, and the signed evaluation with the second draft. Further, any student who does not participate in the peer evaluation forfeits the right to revise any further for a higher grade (as discussed below).

Introduction
- Is thesis preceded by sentences that identify the subject, narrow the focus, and reveal writer's purpose or motive in writing?
- Is thesis precise, identifying causes or stating points of contrast?

Body Paragraphs
- Does each topic sentence tie into thesis, stressing a cause, an effect, or stating a particular difference or similarity?
- Is each topic sentence followed by specific examples, precise figures? Are examples sufficiently varied?
- What suggestions for improvement would you offer?

Conclusion
- Are cause/effect relationships summarized? Does the point of doing the comparison/contrast emerge clearly?

Figure 2 Guidelines for Evaluation

This same three-part process—situational analysis, peer evaluation of rough draft, and revision—works effectively in higher level writing classes as well. Those teaching a literature-based 102 composition class may notice in the topics below that students can approach traditional literary analysis with a sense of reader beyond the teacher and a sense of purpose beyond completing the assignment. The topics are derived from our class discussion of Updike's "A&P," Wright's "The Man Who Was Almost a Man," and Hawthorne's "Young Goodman Brown":

1. You are Sammy five years later; you have turned to daily journal writing to help cope with your "hard" life. In your journal entry for today, explain why your quitting the A&P is now a source of embarrassment or of pride—or of both.
2. You are Dave, seven years later. After running away from home, you drifted for three years—Chicago, Detroit, LA, Atlanta—working in 7-11's, gas stations, and bars. Then you joined the Army and became an MP and an expert marksman. Now on leave, you are returning home for the first time, determined to reassert your claim to family. As you sit in your motel room, still one day's drive from home, you decide to write out your thoughts so that you can handle the reunion with a clear mind and a calm heart. Your primary concern is to understand why you had to jump on that train—not so much to assign blame but to allow understanding to heal the wounds. Your writing may be either a letter to your parents or a private diary entry.
3. In "Young Goodman Brown", Satan proclaims that "evil is the nature of mankind." Discuss the evidence the story provides that supports and/or contradicts the devil's thesis. Your reader is the 18-year-old grandson of Goodman Brown; your purpose is to prevent the youngest Goodman Brown from becoming a "sad, darkly meditative, distrustful" man.

Though the first topic sets up Sammy as his own reader, some would-be Sammys assert in small-group discussion of this topic that a still immature Sammy would likely be even more bitter toward Lengel for the hardness of his life; others argue that a more mature Sammy might be embarrassed by his heroic posturing for Queenie and sympathetic toward Lengel's challenge to Queenie. A highly motivated writer may seek self-justification, self-knowledge, and endurance in the details unearthed through journalistic digging.

Students discussing the second topic perceive a highly motivated writer, as do those examining topic three. The former see that Dave not only strives to clarity his motives in deserting his home but also longs to rebuild relationships with his once loving but unperceptive mother and his brutal father, both, no doubt, suffering from guilt. Clarifying motives, students realize, requires vividly remembered scenes, healing wounds, tact. The students exploring topic three come to realize that the youngest Goodman Brown's sanity depends on the writer's dexterity in contradicting Satan with convincing instances of goodness.

Like their 101 counterparts, these students leave the group discussions with pre-text forming in their brains. The next day they return with a rough draft to be submitted to much the same peer evaluation (see Figure 3).

Admittedly, some students refuse to take this evaluation seriously. Nevertheless, two students evaluating conscientiously do gain not only a thoughtful guide to revision but more experience in diagnosing strengths and weaknesses in writing. Note the helpfulness of the diagnostic comments offered by a student evaluating a rough draft on the implicit sources of happiness in "The Horse Dealer's Daughter":

> *Your greatest strength is telling why Mabel and Jack are so unhappy. You give good examples and quotes to convince the reader that they are unhappy. Your greatest weakness is that you don't have much on when they find each other, fall in love, and become afraid. You should really expand upon this because this is what your introduction is about. Explain why that quote in the first paragraph applies to the theme.*

These remarks stage the "rhetorical event" Flower has described (549), for the reader has done more than respond to the writer's stated purpose (to identify sources of happiness and unhappiness) and unstated purpose (to earn a high grade); the reader has also inferred (from the omission on the characters' fear) the writer's unconscious purpose: to avoid thinking about the ambiguity of the ending, the fearful recoiling of the happy lovers.

Those who teach technical writing classes or who direct composition assignments toward each student's field may notice in the assignment in Figure 4 the same emphasis on situational analysis as requisite to drafting and revising.

Having already practiced situational analysis in the letter-writing assignment and on the instructions assignment, my business and technical writing students are not surprised by the first objective listed here: "Practice situational analysis as a means of shaping content." You will note under the Prewriting heading that the students' articles

Introduction

Topic 1: Does Sammy reflect briefly on what has made the last five years "hard"? Does his thesis state his view of quitting and its effect on Lengel, on parents, on self?

Topic 2: Does Dave review the struggle of manhood over the last seven years? Does he express any longing for his parents as he sits in the lonely motel room? Does he express pride for his earned manhood? Does his thesis assess responsibility for the split?

Topic 3: Does the writer concede to young Goodman Brown that Satan was at least partly right? Does he/she assure Goodman Brown that his grandfather's grave stone is a monument to error rather than to willful "evil"? Does the thesis affirm goodness as well as evil?

Body Paragraphs

Topic 1 Does each topic sentence identify a source of embarrassment or pride?

Topic 2: Does each topic sentence identify a cause of running away?

Topic 3 Does each topic sentence identify a source of good or evil?

All Topics: Are support sentences and quotes persuasive? relevant? Are body paragraphs tightly knit one to the other and logically placed?

Conclusion

Does it review key points emphatically? Does it offer a thoughtful reflection on manhood?

Note

Read Statements on Purpose and Reader before evaluating drafts. After writing your comments on separate sheet of lined paper, sign your name, then discuss the evaluation with your peer. Written evaluations must be turned in with rough dreaft and revised version.

Figure 3 Questions for Peer Evaluation

follow a memo progress report that identifies topic related to major, situation, articles selected, and degree of progress. This same memo accompanies their rough drafts when they bring them to class for peer evaluation. In Figure 5 are the guidelines for evaluation they follow.

Notice that, once again, the statement of purpose and reader forms the foundation of evaluating the clarity, development, and arrangement of the piece and diagnosing solutions to problems.

Objectives

Practice situational analysis (audience and purpose) as a means of shaping content.

Devise precise headings to reveal organization of paper and to facilitate information retrieval. Develop a graphic that is integrated with text and reinforces a key point.

Become acquainted with journals in your field.

Learn more about a subject (related to your major or your profession) that interests you.

Task

Compose an article on a technical topic related to your major, generating ideas for your essay by reading journals in your field.

Your article should be 750-1500 words (typed or word processed) and should include references to at least two articles. See Markel, ch. 3, and the article discussed in class for models of quoting, paraphrasing, and documenting.

Prewriting

Before you write your paper, turn in a progress-report memo, addressed to me, providing the appropriate information under the following headings: Topic, Situation, Audience, and Purpose.

Articles Selected. Degree of Progress.

The Situation section should explain *how* your knowledge of the reader will affect arrangement (and headings), development (and graphic), and diction.

The Articles section should provide a 2-3 sentence abstract of each article you list.

The Progress section should state what you have done and what remains to be done to meet the October 23 deadline.

The memo report is due Wednesday, October 14. See ch. 12 to review memo format.

Figure 4 Research Article Assignment

Second Revision

Though I have claimed much for peer evaluations—and most students do improve as evaluators as the quarter progresses—such a system of

Introduction

Does introduction reflect writer's purpose and needs of reader (as stated in progress-report memo)?

Does it give background to problem or overview of subject before narrowing focus?

Does introduction set up organization of article?

Body Paragraphs

Does each paragraph state a point up front?

Does each topic sentence tie into thesis and make a smooth transition from the preceding paragraph?

Is each topic sentence supported by ample examples, statistics, quoted testimony, documentation? Do headings reveal organization and facilitate information-retrieval?

Is graphic integrated with text? Does it stress a key point?

Conclusion

Does it summarize key points and/or stress significance of findings?

Figure 5 Evaluation Guidelines

moving students from rough draft to essay is predictably fallible. Many errors in sentence structure, punctuation, and usage go undetected; many deficiencies in content go undiagnosed; alas, sometimes a poor student, as Markel says, "convinces the good student to change an excellent passage" (510). Consequently, I encourage my students to revise again: to solve errors in mechanics and content that I detect and, when necessary, diagnose. For example, a recent student wrote this sentence in her argumentative paper defending Union Camp as a vital, responsible industry in Savannah:

> There has been many different articles in the News-Press blaming Union Camp for the air pollution problems in Savannah.

Rather than correcting her subject-verb agreement error for her or telling her the name of the mistake, I simply placed an "X" in the margin next to the sentence, the symbol denoting a "major error." Having detected the error, I left it to her to diagnose the problem. When students cannot diagnose an "X" (or a problem in content), they have recourse to me and to our Writing Center, where faculty and student tutors are always on hand.

Similarly, the same student wrote the following sentence, neither she nor her peer detecting its lack of support in the paragraph:

> In the 1970's Union Camp's total expenditures on the air and water improvement program represented the largest environmental investment at any single manufacturing facility.

In my comment on her paper, I praised her thoroughness on Union Camp's economic and charitable contributions to Savannah, but I then suggested that her reader also needs to be persuaded that Union Camp is sensitive to the pollution problem, a need she might serve by providing examples, testimony, and statistical analysis. Here is the result in her revision:

> Union Camp is trying to clean up its act where water pollution and air pollution are concerned. The company's policy toward environmental improvement is summarized by Alexander Calder, President of Union Camp: "There is no reservation in our dedication to do our full share in solving environmental problems facing the country." This dedication was shown in the air quality program aimed at achieving massive reductions of particulates and odor-causing compounds in air emissions here in Savannah. The program went into effect in 1972 and expanded over three years at a cost of $34 million. The project involved the revamping of the mill's chemical recovery system and included building a new giant boiler and the updating of two other boilers to reduce air emissions from the pulp operation....
>
> Union Camp is also dedicated to water pollution control. In 1968 the company put into operation a $35 million clarifier that, according to Calder, "eliminated 90% of the plant's suspended solids." Then in 1972, a 200-acre, $17 million aeration lagoon was constructed to treat 33 million gallons a day of waste water.

Clearly, such ample revision has reinforced the student's understanding that persuasive argumentation must fuse varied examples with credible testimony. I detected the ailment and suggested a diagnosis; she proudly performed the cure.

My written comments, then, afford a chance to note the connection between incomplete situational analysis and poorly developed, writer-centered writing. Predictably, many first attempts at analyzing situation (audience and purpose) show that students cling stubbornly to their writer-centeredness, neglecting that last question asked on the first assignment sheet above: "How will your assumptions about your reader affect your content, arrangement, diction?" Nevertheless, tactfully worded diagnostic comments on the incomplete essay can direct the student through revision by helping her think about the reader.

Consider, for example, the case of Vivian, a mid-thirties student whose life as a physician's wife and medical office manager led to a paper contrasting the professional and familial lives of physicians with those of non-physicians. Though the points of contrast emerged clearly—medicine as a round-the-clock top priority, the resulting marital and parental pressures, interrupted vacations—Vivian held back too much of herself in the paper. In my comment I suggested that she "build [her] ethos by revealing how [she knew] all these conditions in the medical family." I asked her, too, if she could provide some specific cases of broken vacations, divorces, to enliven her case.

Granted, Vivian failed to detect the problem—or perhaps she was self-conscious about being so candid—but my diagnosis and suggestions led to a revision complete with sharply observed cases and, in the introduction, to this revelation of credentials:

> Being the wife of a physician for ten years has certainly given me first-hand information of the medical family. Holding several offices, including president, of the local medical auxiliary to the medical association gave me the opportunity to speak with hundreds of other medical spouses across the state of Georgia on the problems and solutions their families have experienced. Also, I have worked as medical office manager for the past three years in my husband's family practice office, thus giving me direct contact with patients. Sharing this understanding of the differences in the lifestyles of medical and non-medical families may help reduce the friction which silently exists between them.

This revision not only raised Vivian's grade but also bolstered her self-confidence.

Students "Writing Without Teachers"

Consider, too, that students recharged by such successful second revisions will eventually become skillful anticipators of problems, having learned to be reader-centered and independent of the instructor as detector and diagnoser. Regina and Elivia demonstrate this independence in the excerpts below. The students wrote these situational analyses on the last out-of-class paper, one which could not, as a solo flight, go through a second revision for a higher grade (see Revision Policy below).

Regina

Purpose
I am a new car consumer. I am interested in this subject because I need to make a wise decision in purchasing a car. I want my audience to understand why I decided to purchase the Mazda 626 instead of the Honda Accord. I would like my audience to purchase a Mazda 626, but I am not contemplating changing my major to peddle cars on Abercorn.

Audience
My audience would be married couples with no more than three children. The family would be on a budget and need to understand the facts concerning the Honda and the Accord. The family would not be able to understand mechanical jargon, so I will discuss things that really matter, such as hip room, leg room, and trunk space. I must also overcome the readers' indifference by citing examples in which the Mazda is superior to the Honda: gas consumption, warranty, price. I will use testimony from *Consumer's Report,* combining stats and quotes with a case history from my experience with the Mazda. I will also use parallel structure in the conclusion to urge the readers to take the Mazda "challenge."

Elivia

Purpose
I am a clerical worker who wants to persuade my Congressional Representatives and Senators to vote for S.1885, the act for better child care. I am interested in this issue since I am a working parent and well aware of the high cost of day care as well as the inadequacies of day care. I will try to influence them by showing them how day care is inadequate: personal examples, survey of fellow workers, national examples. I will point out to them how the ABC bill will correct and improve day care.

Audience
Senator Sam Nunn, Senator Wyche Fowler, Congressman Lindsay Thomas. I am not sure how familiar my audience is with the ABC bill, so I will point out how it would benefit their constituents. Elected representatives are concerned about voters' viewpoints, so they are a receptive audience.

Regina's analysis shows not only her sense of humor ("changing my major to peddle cars") but also her careful consideration of the defined reader's needs: space, affordability, economy. Equally thoughtful, Elivia's analysis reflects her excitement over addressing Congressmen in terms of serving their constituents.

Revision Policy: Motivation

To motivate students to go to the trouble of a second revision, I begin the course by distributing and illustrating my grading standards and emphasizing the Revision Policy:

> Because revision creates clarity, emphasis, and correctness, each student is required to revise the first assignment, making mechanical corrections and expanding (or deleting) content where necessary. The grade on the assignment will be an average of the original mark and the grade on the revision. For example a student who receives a "D" on the first writing, then a "B" on the revision, will receive a "C" for the assignment.
>
> Revision is optional on subsequent assignments. However, having discovered the power of revision to clarify information and to sharpen persuasion, most students will want to revise other writings, not just to improve marks but also to overcome problems in communication.
>
> Exceptions: Because the last writing assignment is a solo flight, a chance to show what one has learned about writing, revisions should be done before the student first submits the paper. There will be no revision for a higher grade. Also, for obvious reasons, there will be no revision of the final exam essay.

Before beginning this revision-for-a-higher-grade policy, I received approximately 10 percent revisions, with only the most conscientious and the most desperate students revising in hopes that such work would hasten improvement. Now, 70-90 percent of my students (the percentage varies assignment to assignment, class to class) choose to do this second revision, knowing that through averaging they can raise the grade on the assignment slightly or considerably, depending on the quality of the revision. With such immediate rewards, students are much more receptive to my argument that revising will—eventually if not immediately—improve one's capacity to detect problems and to diagnose solutions.

Regrettably, some students who revise faithfully do not, in one or even two quarters, become better detectors, diagnosers, or writers, a fact painfully reflected in their C-, D, or F on the last out-of-class paper and on the final exam essay. (Neither writing, collectively determining 30 percent of the course grade, can be revised for a higher grade. See Revision Policy above.) Though we teachers grieve over such lack of progress, we can take comfort knowing that—to put it negatively—this revision policy encourages improvement *without* creating grade inflation; or—to put it positively—this policy duly rewards those students who have achieved independence and proficiency in moving from pre-text to text.

Works Cited

Brooke, Robert. "Lacan, Transference, and Writing Instruction." *College English* 49 (1987): 679-91.

Carter, Michael. "Problem Solving Reconsidered: A Pluralistic Theory of Problems." *College English* 50 (1988): 551-65.

Flower, Linda. "The Construction of Purpose in Writing and Reading." *College English* 50 (1988): 528-50.

Flower, Linda, *et al.* "Detection, Diagnosis, and the Strategies of Revision." *College English* 48 (1986): 10-55.

Katz, Steven B. "The Epistemic Trend in Rhetorical Theory: A Four-Dimensional Review." *The Technical Writing Teacher* 14 (1987): 355-71.

Knoblauch, C. H., and Lil Brannon. "Teacher Commentary on Student Writing: The State of the Art." *Freshman English News* 10 (1981): 1-3.

Markel, Michael. "Teaching the Writing Process: Revising." *College English* 50 (1988): 509-10.

Witte, Stephen P. "Pre-Text and Composing." *College Composition and Communication* 38 (1987): 397-425.

Constructing Taxonomies for Error (or Can Stray Dogs Be Mermaids?)[1]

Glynda Hull

According to Jorge Luis Borges, some unknown or apocryphal compiler of an old Chinese encyclopedia once saw fit to divide the world's animals into categories which must now seem to us strange and fanciful. This remote taxonomy had as its divisions animals "(a) . . . that belong to the Emperor, (b) embalmed ones, (c) those that are trained, (d) suckling pigs, (e) mermaids, (f) fabulous ones, (g) stray dogs, (h) those that are included in this classification, (i) those that tremble as if they were mad, (j) innumerable ones, (k) those drawn with a very fine camel's hair brush, (l) others, (m) those that have just broken a flower vase, [and] (n) those that resemble flies from a distance" (103). It is tempting to smile at this encyclopedist's apparent naiveté, at his quaintly inaccurate notions of similitude and difference, but, as Borges reminds us, "obviously there is no classification of the universe that is not arbitrary and conjectural" (104).

My purpose in this essay is twofold: I want, like the ancient Chinese encyclopedist, to offer a taxonomy, and I want, like Borges, to keep my readers' sights on what such a taxonomy cannot do. My taxonomy isn't so grand as one which encompasses all of the world's animals, nor does it deal with "real" objects like stray dogs or real "imagined" objects like mermaids. It cannot even be said to deal strictly with the linguistic representation and ordering of such objects or the point at which, in Foucault's words, "language has intersected space" (xvii). Rather, it treats and orders a set of phenomena which exists only as a by-product of written language representation and which generates attention only by its presence, not (except in unnatural situations) by its absence. I refer to "sentence-level" error in writing—commonly known as mistakes in grammar, punctuation, spelling, usage, and syntax.

It has not been customary in composition research to invent taxonomies for the analysis of "sentence-level" error. Instead, an existing taxonomy is appropriated, and typically, it consists of categories with which we are familiar from grammar and usage handbooks—categories like punctuation, agreement, spelling, and so on. To take some early examples, R. L. Lyman published in 1929 a *Summary of Investigations Relating to Grammar, Language, and Composition,* his review of some 400 research articles, including studies on the "more mechanical elements of writing and speaking, known as 'usage'" (2). One of these articles reported an analysis of a random sampling of over 300 letters to the editor of the *Chicago Daily Tribune* to determine the kinds of errors these writers made. To sort the errors, the following taxonomy had been devised: *errors in punctuation, errors in expression, errors in capitalization, errors in abbreviation, errors in spelling, errors in grammar, improper margins, errors in writing numbers,* and *errors in word-compounding* (96). Lyman describes another article that reported counting the errors in over 3,000 essays by high school students; these errors were classified as *mistakes in case; other misuse of pronouns; misuse of verbs, adjectives and adverbs, prepositions and conjunctions; ungrammatical sentence structure; lack of clearness; mistakes in punctuation; misuse of the apostrophe; mistakes in capitalization; omission and repetition; misspelling; quotation mark;* and *miscellaneous* (103).

In more recent research, Lillian Bridwell analyzed the revision changes, including the corrections, that twelfth-graders made as they composed an in-class essay. By examining the changes students made in the process of writing several drafts of the essay, Bridwell could determine the stage at which her writers chose to attend to error correction and revision, and thereby she created for her study a more sophisticated design that had been customary for product analyses. Yet her choice of a taxonomy for sentence-level error was not innovative, for it is, in fact, similar to those taxonomies reported in Lyman's review. Bridwell lists *spelling; punctuation; capitalization; verb form; abbreviations, symbols and contractions vs. full form; singular vs. plural;* and *morphological conditioning* (203).[2]

The fact that, for most of this century, we have relied upon similar taxonomies for representing "sentence-level" error may seem to suggest for those categories a kind of psychological reality. The argument would be that these categories have persisted because they represent a true representation and ordering of error. What else is there to say about an error in punctuation except that it is an error in punctuation? About an error in spelling except that it is an error in spelling? In fact, so accustomed have we become to thinking of sentence-level error in terms of particular labels that we are apt to describe our knowledge of such errors in a much more confident manner than we assume in speaking about other aspects of writing. In his evaluation of the First National Assessment of Educational Progress in Writing, Reading, and Literature, John Mellon warns that we ought not award the data collected on "writing mechanics" more attention than their due simply because the "categories can be defined, the data easily obtained." He goes on to comment that "sometimes the ease of getting the information leads people to overstate its value" (33). And so goes the usual attitude toward sentence-level error in writing: We know how to count it and how to categorize it; it's the one part of written language upon whose nature we can all agree.[3]

If, however, we think of categories of error as comprising taxonomies, we might be more skeptical about their reality. We might, for example, in the preceding taxonomies, wonder whether "omission and repetition" could not overlap with "ungrammatical sentence structure." We might argue that "quotation marks" are certainly "mistakes in punctuation." We might think "prepositions" and "conjunctions" sufficiently different to deserve separate categories. We might ponder the classification of the errors in a sentence like the following *The two of us worked together on our hike, we lead each other and complimented at the same time.* Error in expression? Error in grammar? And we might believe "lack of clearness" to be a category almost as discreet as these containing all those animals "which resemble flies from a distance."

I am arguing, then, that the "act" of imposing a system of categories on any set of phenomena—even sentence-level error—is a matter or some judgment and choice. I do not mean to imply, however, that since taxonomies are arbitrary, it doesn't matter which one we choose, or that since taxonomies are conjectural, we might as well not try to construe any. How we divide things up circumscribes how we view things. There are ways of organizing errors that can yield different views about what happens, and what is important about what happens when a writer makes an error and when he turns to the task or correcting it. It's extremely important that we try to imagine taxonomies that, though still provisional, allow us to view the phenomena of sentence-level error in helpful and interesting ways. A few such taxonomies have been proposed.[4]

In *Errors and Expectations* Shaughnessy grouped errors in broad categories: her chapter headings were "Handwriting and Punctuation," "Syntax," "Common Errors," "Spelling," and "Vocabulary." By *common errors* she meant errors in verb and noun inflection, pronoun usage, and subject-verb agreement. Her category *vocabulary* included many errors often designated "diction," or "word choice" or mistakes in "register." She classified *syntax errors* as accidental errors, blurred patterns, consolidation errors, and inversions—labels that are Shaughnessy's own coinages for syntactic problems not normally treated in handbooks of grammar and usage.

On the face of this summary, Shaughnessy's categories don't seem very different from those found in traditional taxonomies (except for her syntax categories). But simply listing her category types obscures what is most important in her method of analysis. Once she has called our attention to the usual error category, Shaughnessy proceeds to discuss the category in terms of its source or the possible reasons writers might have made errors of a particular variety. Instead of just offering us the category "spelling errors," she provides examples of misspellings that may have been caused by a writer's failure to see or to remember words: the splitting or joining of common words in unconventional ways, such as *in stead* or *suchas*, and letter or word reversals, such as *about* for *out* or *farther* for *father*. This activity of speculating about possible sources of error loads traditional error labels with new meaning, for it gives a teacher a new way of representing (for herself and her student) the mistakes in a paper. A misspelling no longer need suggest that a student is careless or neglectful or just a poor speller; it might instead suggest a general inexperience with reading and writing which manifests itself in a specific pattern of error which in turn informs a particular pedagogy.[5]

The assumption behind causal analyses is, of course, that knowing the source of an error can guide how one teaches to that error. If a teacher appreciates the context in which errors are produced, then she will be in a better position to teach a student not to make those errors or to detect and correct them. There is, however, a great deal that we do

not understand about the relationship between causality and remedi-
ation. Even after a student knows a rule for subject-verb agreement
and is on the lookout for his own speech interference in third person
singular, he can still fail to see (or hear) an error on the page.[6]

While I do not want to discount the contribution that attention to
sources has made in the study of error—the contribution has been
enormous even if we consider only the changes in attitude brought
about by the recognition that errors, in most cases, are evidence of
purposive behavior—I do want to suggest that attending to source of
error isn't sufficient, for teachers or researchers. In fact, I want to argue
for an analysis that is independent of any assumption about the
source of an error in the production of texts and that instead focuses
on the phenomenology of error in the rereading of texts. I'll do this by
proposing a new way to organize sentence-level errors.[7]

The taxonomy that I want to offer turns upon the editing process,
upon the process of error recognition and error correction. I want to
sort errors according to what happens when a writer, acting as an editor, perceives an error in a text. Let us take, as an example, the errors in
the text printed below. (To make the best use of this example, readers
should themselves edit the essay, making any changes necessary for
the text to be correct.)

1   "Very bad" is too mild a rating for the man who was my
2 senior organic chemistry teacher, Dr. Lesgold. I would
3 guess his age to be about sixty, but his theories had to have
4 been much older than his age. In fact, he might have gone
5 to school in the Dark Ages.

6   Although Dr. Lesgold considered himself a scientist, he
7 seemed to me to have tunnel vision. Our chemistry book,
8 for example, said that insulin consisted of fifty-one amino acids.
9 Lesgold said there were only forty-eight. The omniscient
10 one had spoken, and our class grudgingly accepted
11 this geniuses words.

12   Dr. Lesgold's class was a study in confusion. He would start
13 at the back of a chapter, skip to the middle, and then to the front
14 (Chronological order must be too easy for powerful minds.) I think
15 that by adding to the confusion was the fact that Dr. Lesgold had an
16 inferiority complex. He claimed that he could solve everything that

17 ailed the world if he had the right equipment. But for some
18 unknown reason, he never used his new electronic balance
19 the school had bought for him a year before.
20 Dr. Lesgold was able to devise a way to deprive our senior
21 class of the highlight of senior year. However, every year the biology
22 class had gone to an anatomy lab to see the medical
23 students work on cadavers. My senior year would have been no
24 exception, but Dr. Lesgold scheduled the trip on Senior skip Day,
25 knowing all too well that none of the senior class would attend.

26   To be fair, I have to admit that Dr. Lesgold always thought
27 he was doing the right thing Although most of me thoroughly
28 dislikes the guy, a small portion of me has to admire the man
29 for his dedication in teaching at a place where he apparently
30 was not appreciated by anyone.

31 I believe that good teaching involves developing a student's
32 ideas, not force-feeding a teacher's ideas to a student. In the
33 "Lesgoldian" method of teaching, there was no willingness to
34 compromise or to listen to the blasphemous students who dared to
35 challenge him. Teachers should try to expand the horizons
36 of their students. Instead, Lesgold only narrowed ours.

Several things are possible at the intersection of editor and error in a text. An editor can, for one, *consult* her knowledge or the conventions of written language. When an editor comes to line 11 in the essay above and sees *this geniuses words,* she might recall a rule for forming the possessive in order to correct the mistake. And to detect and correct many sentence-level errors, a writer does begin by drawing upon a set or available definitions or rules like "i before e except after c" or "quotation marks go outside commas" or "everyone takes a singular verb." These rules then serve as a frame within which to test individual cases. Thus one category in my taxonomy turns upon a writer's being able to call up a rule, and in it I include all those errors that writers would recognize and correct because they violate agreed-upon conventions for written language. I call this category *consulting*

A second strategy an editor might adopt on encountering an error is to rely on a general sense that something is wrong with the text that it doesn't seem right. An editor might, for example, read lines 14-16 of the essay printed above, *I think that by adding to the confusion was the fact that Dr. Lesgold had an inferiority complex,* and hear that it sounds wrong and experiment until he can make the wording sound better. Instead of beginning with a verbal representation of a particular rule, then, an editor would begin with a dissatisfaction that something is out of synch based on his knowledge of the structure of the language. What Shaughnessy calls "blurred patterns" and other problems within syntax often fit in this category, as do missing words or extra words, mistakes in word order, some missing morphemes, and for many editors, nonparallel like the following: *She did this by going to Rebecca's home and looked at the furnishings to find her tastes.* When an editor has a sense that something is wrong that he cannot name, but nonetheless alters the text based on this intuition, I call the error *intuiting.*

A third strategy that is possible at the intersection of editor and error is that an editor can notice that something is wrong with the meaning of the text; he can, that is, attend to semantics. In line 21, an editor might notice that the *however* doesn't make sense in the context of that paragraph. When writers use what I call a *comprehending* strategy, they don't call up a rule or experiment based on a general sense that something is wrong; they pay attention to what the text means or what it fails to mean. Errors that require editors to attend to meaning include ambiguous pronouns, missing or wrong connective words, diction mistakes, and sentence boundary errors like the following: *Things started to get rough after a day or so we were tired.*[8]

I want to shift attention, then, from the production of an error to the perception of it. I propose that instead of categorizing errors according to traditional handbook types like spelling or according to a source like speech interference, we categorize them according to the kind of strategy we would *expect* to see an editor use in the process of recognizing and correcting errors—*intuiting, comprehending, consulting.*

If these categories do represent different correction strategies, one would expect a difference in how writers respond to errors that represent these categories in written texts. To test this expectation, I asked some college writers to correct any errors they saw in an essay they wrote for me, as well as in some essays that I provided, which I called "standard passages"—one of which is the essay printed above. I categorized the errors the writers made and corrected as *consulting, intuiting, comprehending.* Some of the writers, whom I called *experts,* were competent editors; that is, they had written essays that contained no errors from the three categories. Each of the experts was enrolled in an upper-division writing course. Other students, whom I called *novices*, were less competent editors; their essays contained errors from each of the three categories. Each of the novices was enrolled in a basic writing class.[9]

When I looked to see what proportion of the errors in each category the two groups of writers could correct, I found that novices were poorest proportionately at correcting errors in the *consulting* category, and experts were much better here (their correction rate was 49% as compared with 23% for the novices). We might expect novices to have the most trouble with the *consulting* category, for it turns on knowing written language conventions, and novices would presumably have had the least familiarity with such conventions. Experts were poorest proportionately at correcting errors in the *comprehending* category, but novices were somewhat better here (35% as opposed to 31%). One would expect experts to detect and correct mistakes that have to do with meaning more readily than novices, who are often characterized as being too concerned with the surface features of texts. This is a puzzling result that I will return to later. Both groups were best at correcting errors in the *intuiting* category (38% and 56% for novices and experts, respectively). And it stands to reason that novices and experts alike would be best at correcting errors that have to do with noticing that something sounds wrong in a sentence. When tasks were considered, the editors were much better at correcting both consulting and comprehending errors in someone else's writing than in their own (47% as opposed to 24% for consulting and 52% as opposed to 14% for comprehending). However, they could correct intuiting errors about equally well in both tasks (48% and 47%).

These proportions illustrate differences in the percentage of errors writers corrected from the three categories. Such numerical differences suggest that these errors require writers to use different correction strategies, and in fact, the conversations I recorded with the writers as they attempted to correct the errors provide some evidence concerning these different strategies. The language used by writers to describe the errors and to propose corrections for them was often distinct for each error category. When *consulting* rules, writers talked in terms of *need* and *requirement*. Here are excerpts from several protocols in which expert editors corrected a possessive error, in the essay printed earlier and in a similar essay, with my comments in parentheses.

- Okay, line 11. Geniuses—that would just cross out the e and that should be an apostrophe.
- Uh, and then, in line 20, ladies has to have an apostrophe.
- I don't know, on line 11, this geniuses word. There should be a—punctuation. (Supplies apostrophe.)
- I don't know if geniuses is right? It's—since it's him, it should have like, an apostrophe. Because, well it was his genius, his word. So, it was, it should be an apostrophe.
- Strike that e—apostrophe. (You did that very quickly.) My freshman high school teacher was a woman who made Captain Bly seem like Florence Nightingale, and he would have hanged anyone who handed in something like that.

In contrast, when correcting *intuiting errors*, writers almost, never tried to state a rule and seldom appeared so certain that a particular thing must be changed. Instead, they often mentioned that a sentence sounded wrong and then went on to experiment, attempting to find the wording they wanted. In the following examples, expert editors attempted to correct the blurred pattern in lines 14-16 above and also in one of the following two sentences (each from a different essay): "I think by breaking the stereotypical mold of the woman in the kitchen demonstrates one way women can at home and in the kitchen achieve equality" and "I realized that by a deli operating at peak efficiency during lunch hour is a lot like the performance of a well oiled machine."

- That by? Well, I could simply just delete that." (How did you know to make the correction?) It just, I saw it immediately. Ummm—that by sort of sets up, ummmm, this is funny. I know automatically it should not be there. But telling you why is going to be difficult. . . . It's going to take the reason some time to surface.
- That last sentence doesn't sound right for some reason. Uh—it's the part of—the woman at home and in the kitchen. Demonstrates one way women can achieve equality. I think one way which might sound a little bit better. I think I would put, uh—I would change the whole sentence around, put, uh, I think women can achieve equality by breaking the stereotypical mold of the woman at home and in the kitchen.
- Uh, line 8. That sentence, there's something wrong there. I realized that by a deli operating at peak efficiency. That by, I don't—I don't think it should be in there.

- I don't know how you explain this, but line 8 and 9, lot of extras in there. It seems like it doesn't make sense. Change that by. Take it out? I don't know, it just—looked really funny to me.
- Uh, maybe 17—line 17. (Reads.) I think by breaking the stereotypical mold. Well, I think—that by. Yeah, put in a that. That's not really a major thing. Umm, maybe I'm not familiar with the word. I didn't know, uh, I never use stereotypical. I use stereotypic. I think I'd like to go without the al. (Reads sentence again.) Let's get rid of the by. (Reads again.) That was very tricky.

When editing began with an act of comprehension, editors talked not about how the text sounded or what rules to apply, but about what the text meant or didn't mean. Here several expert editors respond to a misplaced *however* in one of two essays:

- This however, it doesn't really fit. Because—however should say something else. She doesn't say however like it contradicts and there's nothing else there.
- She—whoever wrote this—was saying she will win? How do they know that? Hey, that doesn't make sense. Because it says, she has the best qualifications of the twelve candidates. Then it says, however, she will win. They're like on the same thing and however makes it seem like they're not. Subsequently would be much better.
- I'm not sure, on line 21. I don't understand why there would be however. Something is wrong. I'd just lay it aside for now. I don't know what else I'd. . . . Uh, well, it says he was able to devise a way to deprive our senior class of the highlight of senior year. And then, however. Okay, so it sounds like he's gonna deprive the class, but, then something is gonna happen almost save them, so I wasn't expecting to hear that.
- This seems really bad. Line 20, with the however. You know, it doesn't make sense. I think I would put Dr. Lesgold was able to devise a way of depriving our senior class of the highlight of the year, I guess. This however, you just don't need it.
- However is unnecessary in line 21. What does it have to do with the first sentence? It doesn't make any sense to have it there.

There are several ways that the taxonomy I have proposed might be used in research on sentence-level error. Most research on error consists simply of counting the errors left in texts, classifying them, and drawing conclusions about the kinds of errors writers make and don't correct—in much the same way as those studies reported by Lyman in 1929. The National Assessment, for example, has tallied the errors in thousands of student essays, using a taxonomy that divides error into *sentence constructions that contain punctuation errors, faulty sentence construction, punctuation,* and *word level errors,* and has concluded that the number or errors in students' writing does not decrease, but remains more or less constant across ages 9, 13, and 17.[10] One might similarly use the taxonomy I have proposed to classify the errors in students' texts *ex post facto* as *consulting, intuiting,* and *comprehending.* Perhaps the new taxonomy would reveal that there are, after all, differences in the kinds of errors that students of various ages can correct.

This is not to say, however, that the categories I have proposed are free of the problems associated with other taxonomies of error and taxonomies in general. There is the same difficulty, for example, in deciding which elements belong to which category. In textual analyses that attempt to discover the source of an error, there is always the complication that one error can arise from several different causes.[11] Similarly, while it is easy to categorize some errors as *consulting, intuiting,* or *comprehending,* in other cases, the decisions will seem arbitrary. An additional complication is that the taxonomy I propose here is context-dependent. Though it is possible to say that most spelling errors are consulting errors and many syntax errors fall into the intuiting category, some errors will cross category boundaries, depending on their context.

I believe, however, that there is a more insightful way to use the taxonomy, a way, in fact, that skirts much of what is problematic about taxonomies. The whole notion behind the system is that there are certain *strategies* that we have available to us when we edit, strategies for locating and altering errors in texts. Assigning a particular error to a particular strategy or category *ex post facto* tells us something about our own notions of editing, the notions that experienced readers and writers have, but gives us little hint of what actually happens at the intersection of another editor and that error. Yet what happens can be interesting and important if we are teachers and our students need to learn to edit. Consider, for example, these excerpts from protocols with novice editors as they responded to the errors they saw in the preceding essay.

- (Line 1) NOVICE: It would look like—there should be—a comma after very bad. Inside the quotes. It looks, it looks silly within quotes without a comma. Usually when you have quotes, you have a comma too, especially at the beginning of a sentence.
- (Line 10) NOVICE: I don't, I don't know ... what it means. I don't like this geniuses words—because I don't know what it means. What the heck is this word. I don't know what I'm missing. I sorta get an idea of what I'm missing. If I was writing it, I would change it. I would have to know him, but I would change that.
- INTERVIEWER: I know you don't know the person who wrote this essay, but try making the change you want anyway.
- NOVICE: How 'bout changing his, maybe his godlike words.
- (Line 11) NOVICE: I don't know if I'd say, Dr. Lesgold's class was a study in confusion. I'd say which was confusing maybe. He's act—the writer here is acting like that's what they studied. I'm not really sure how I'd word that. Maybe, Dr. Lesgold's class was quite confusing.
- (Line 21) NOVICE: Cross out however. I don't need it, I guess. I heard you're not supposed to start a sentence out with words like that.
- (Line 22) NOVICE: Maybe line 22. Had gone? I don't know if that sounds right or not? But I think maybe, uh, However, every year the biology class went to the anatomy lab. I don't—you know, it sounds better.
- (Line 28) NOVICE: Okay, right here in 28, after guy. Is that a comma splice?
- INTERVIEWER: You tell me. What's a comma splice?
- NOVICE: There's gonna be two independent clauses. Now wait. There's gonna be two—completed—let's make two sentences that could be separated, but you just—put them together with a comma. Be like a—two independent clauses—and a comma inside. See, I think that the first one, even though most of me thoroughly dislikes the guy, that would be a sentence. Period. Then start, A small portion of me has to admire the man as a new sentence.
- INTERVIEWER: How do you tell when a sentence is a sentence?
- NOVICE: When it belongs, like, back here—well, they have to have a complete thought. Right?
- INTERVIEWER: Yeah.
- NOVICE: It has to have a—subject and verb.
- INTERVIEWER: Yeah.
- NOVICE: That's all the ones I know.

What is remarkable about these examples is how they force us to consider the activity of editing from a different vantage. In each instance, the novice editors used one of three editing strategies—consulting, intuiting, or comprehending—but used them in ways we would not likely predict. In the first example, we would expect an editor to consult a rule for forming the possessive in order to correct *geniuses words*. Instead, the student attended to meaning since he wasn't familiar with the word *geniuses*, yet he managed a correction that got rid of the error. In the second example, a novice editor again attended to meaning, but in so doing he misinterpreted the text and introduced correction where none was needed. In line 21, where we would expect an editor to notice that *however* doesn't fit in the context of the paragraph, the student used a consulting strategy to apply an erroneous rule—don't use *however* at the beginning of a sentence—and made a correction nonetheless. (The rule restricting the use of *however* was common among the students in this study. In fact, their use of the rule accounts in part for their good showing on the comprehending category in the data reported earlier.) In the fourth example, line 22, an editor relied on his sense of what a sentence should sound like—what I have called the intuiting strategy—in order to introduce a change that wasn't mandatory. And in the last example, an editor again introduced an unnecessary change, but this time the change was an error, the creation of a fragment. Interestingly, in making the change, the student consulted rules about complete sentences and comma splices, and the rules he consulted were not idiosyncratic ones, but familiar formulas learned most likely in grammar class.

We can think of editing, I have suggested, as three operations—*comprehending, consulting,* and *intuiting.* Sometimes editing begins with an act of comprehension as a writer attends to the meaning of a text. Sometimes it begins with a verbal representation of a rule. And sometimes it begins with a writer's sense that something is amiss, although he cannot specifically name what it is. We can also locate the difficulty students have with learning to edit in the context of these three operations. Sometimes the difficulty has to do with applying one strategy where another (or none) is required. Sometimes it centers on a student's inability to operationalize a strategy. And sometimes the problem is that the student's particular application of a particular strategy is erroneous. The taxonomy thus provides teachers and researcher with a conceptual schema for thinking about the acquisition of editing skills.

For a long time we've made the mistake of thinking about editing as a skill which is easy for everyone—because we've already acquired it, because for us it is often an activity that is internalized and automatic. We've thought of editing as a kind of simple pattern-matching: an error on the page triggers the remembrance of a general rule; we see an error and we access its correct form, card-catalog fashion. Thinking of error this way hasn't allowed us to be very imaginative or helpful in our attempts to teach students to edit. Thinking of error this way, we could only send students to workbooks to learn that subjects and verbs agree in number and to apply this knowledge in drill and practice exercises.

As an alternative to this traditional pedagogy, I suggest that we represent editing to our students as a procedure, as an activity with several facets. We all want to demonstrate that there are rules that writers muse know in order to correct their texts—rules about possessive markers and commas and semicolons—but we'll want to demonstrate that editing can begin with an act of comprehension or with a general dissatisfaction that something is amiss in a text as well. We'll also want to make it possible for students to practice the procedure of editing by attempting themselves to locate and detect errors in whole texts (not isolated workbook sentences). Those texts of course must be their own; but essays written by other students, essays containing different kinds of errors that require different correction strategies, can be used with a class to model the editing process or with individual students to diagnose idiosyncratic rule systems or procedures.

A taxonomy, says Foucault, "enables thought to operate upon the entities of our world" (xvii). Or, to use the language of science, taxonomies provide a means of discovering and defining the variables we want to test. In the end, then, it matters little that the taxonomies we create are of necessity provisional—except to the extent that this fact serves to remind us that our schemes are but our schemes and thus can be refined. To construct a new taxonomy is to see an old phenomenon in a new way, to impose a new template upon an old order. The great challenge for research on error has been first to recognize that traditional category schemes are only one way, and an arbitrary way, to represent error, and then to go on to discover and define variables that help make errors interesting and available to teachers, writers, and researchers. The taxonomy I propose here is one such attempt.

Notes

1. The preparation of this manuscript was supported by the Learning

Research and Development Center, which is supported in part by the National Institute of Education. The research I report here is based on my doctoral thesis, "The Editing Process in Writing: A Performance Study of Experts and Novices." I wish especially to thank William L. Smith, who directed my thesis, and David Bartholomae, who influenced my thinking about error.

2. I should make clear here that I have excerpted only a part of Bridwell's taxonomy; she goes on to offer categories for textual changes other than sentence-level error.

3. A few researchers have acknowledged the difficulties involved in categorizing error. Braddock, Lloyd-Jones, and Schoer note the limitations of frequency counts and suggest some ways to improve them (15; 1). Charles Cooper and colleagues note that the "greatest obstacles to error analysis are the sheer variety of errors and the fuzzy boundaries of some error categories" (24), and, to improve error analyses, they advise limiting the number of errors studied and providing readers sufficient examples of particular error types. David Bartholomae has discussed how determining the nature of an error is an interpretive act, writing that "for any idiosyncratic sentence ... there are often a variety of possible reconstructions, depending on the reader's sense of the larger meaning of which this individual sentence is only a part, but also depending upon the reader's ability to predict how this writer puts sentences together" (265). For additional evidence that to identify an error a reader must interpret a writer's intentions, see Glynda Hull, "Assessing Errors in Writing." If different readers can be expected to "reconstruct" a writer's text in different ways, one might expect a rather low agreement among readers attempting to categorize errors. However, interrater reliability for the identification of sentence-level error is rarely reported, Lillian Bridwell's aforementioned research being a notable exception.

4. In the following discussion, I treat only Mina Shaughnessy's taxonomy. Other taxonomies that depart from traditional category systems have been proposed by Sondra Perl ("The Composing Processes of Unskilled College Writers"), David Bartholomae, and Joseph Williams.

5. The procedure of analyzing error patterns in order to infer error sources originated, as Barry Kroll and John Schafer explain, in research on English as a second language. In addition to Shaughnessy's work on the error patterns of young adults, a number of related articles have appeared, some of which do not associate themselves with the error analysis procedure, but nevertheless do concern themselves with explaining why writers make sentence-level errors. I am thinking here, in particular, of Colette

Daiute's study, "Psycholinguistic Foundations of the Writing Process."

6. For an account of the difficulty basic writers have in seeing error on the page, see Sondra Perl ("A Look at Basic Writers in the Process of Composing") and Patricia Laurence ("Error's Endless Train").

7. My approach is analogous to Joseph M. Williams' in "The Phenomenology of Error" where he suggests categories of error based on whether or not a rule is violated, whether or not a reader responds to the violation, and whether or not the response is favorable. See also Elsa Bartlett, who has provided empirical evidence that one kind of error draws on different correction strategies than does another. The errors she investigated were pronoun reference mistakes and left-out words, which would appear to fit, respectively, into my comprehending and intuiting categories.

8. These findings are discussed in more detail in Hull, "The Editing Process in Writing."

9. For comparison's sake, each example comes from a session in which an editor was working with a text he or she had nor written. However, this should not be taken to suggest that editing someone else's writing is the same as editing one's own. In fact, research shows that the former is usually easier than the latter: see my dissertation and the research by Bartlett, both cited earlier.

10. These categories are further subdivided so that there are at least three levels in the taxonomy, sometimes four. For the complete taxonomy, see Mullis. For another recent example of error and tabulation research, see Freedman and Pringle.

11. For discussions of the complexities involved in causal analyses of error, see Bartholomae, Epes, and Schachter and Celce-Murcia.

Works Cited

Bartholomae, David. "The Study of Error." *CCC* 31 (1980): 253-69.

Bartlett, Elsa Jaffe. "Learning to Revise: Some Component Processes." *What Writers Know: The Language, Process, and Structure of Written Discourse.* Ed. Martin Nystrand. New York: Academic, 1982, 345-63.

Borges, Jorge Luis. "The Analytical Language of John Wilkins." *Other Inquisitions.* University of Texas Press, 1964.

Braddock, Richard. Richard Lloyd-Jones, and Lowell Schoer. *Research in Written Composition.* Champaign, IL: NCTE, 1963.

Bridwell, Lillian S. "Revising Strategies in Twelfth Grade Students' Transactional Writing." *RTE* 14 (1980): 197-222.

Cooper, Charles R. Roger Cherry, Barbara Copley, Stefan Fleischscher, Rita Pollard, and Michael Sartisky. "Studying the Writing Abilities of a

University Freshman Class: Strategies from a Case Study." Ed. Richard
Beach and Lillian S. Bridwell. New York: Guilford, 1984. 19-52.

Daiute, Colette. "Psycholinguistic Foundations of the Writing Process." *RTE* 15
(1981): 5-22.

Epes, Mary. "Tracing Errors to Their Sources: A Study of the Encoding Processes
of Adult Basic Writers." *Journal of Basic Writing* 4 (1985): 4-33.

Foucault, Michel. *The Order of Things: An Archaeology of the Human Sciences.*
Translation of *Les Mots et les Choses.* Vintage Books Edition. New York:
Random House, 1973.

Freedman, Aviva, and Ian Pringle. "The Writing Abilities of a Representative
Sample of Grade 5, 8, and 12 Students: The Carleton Writing Project, Part
II, Final Report." ERIC, 1980. ED 217 413.

Hull, Glynda "Assessing Errors in Writing." American Educational Research
Association's Annual Meeting., New Orleans, 1984.

———. "The Editing Process in Writing: A Performance Study of Experts and
Novices." Diss. University of Pittsburgh, 1983.

Kroll, Barry, and John Schafer. "Error Analysis and the Teaching of
Composition." *CCC* 29 (1978): 243 48.

Laurence, Patricia. "Error's Endless Train: Why Students Don't Perceive Errors."
Journal of Basic Writing 1 (1975): 23-13

Lyman, R. L. *Summary Investigations Relating to Grammar, Language, and
Composition.* Chicago: University of Chicago Press, 1929.

Mellon, John C. *National Assessment and the Teaching of English.* Urbana, IL:
NCTE, 1975.

Mullis, Ina. *Guidelines for Describing Three Aspects of Writing: Syntax,
Cohesion, and Mechanics.* Report No. 10-W-50. Denver: NAEP, 1980.

Perl, Sondra. "The Composing Processes of Unskilled College Writers." *RTE* 13
(1979): 317-36.

———. "A Look at Basic Writers in the Process of Composing." *Basic Writing:
Essays for Teachers, Researchers, and Administrators.* Ed. Lawrence N.
Kasden and Daniel R. Hoeber. Urbana, IL: NCTE, 1980. 26-30.

Schachter, Jacquelyn, and Marianne Celce-Murcia. "Some Reservations
Concerning Error Analysis." *TESOL Quarterly* 11 (1977): 441-51.

Shaughnessy, Mina. *Errors and Expectations: A Guide for the Teacher of Basic
Writing.* New York: Oxford U P, 1977.

Williams, Joseph M. "The Phenomenology of Error." *CCC* 32 (1981): 152-68.

Teaching Punctuation as a Rhetorical Tool

John Dawkins

Punctuation—just one of the "mechanics" of writing, after all—is perhaps not the first thing you turn to after checking the *CCC* table of contents, but you are here now, so let me try to keep you here by announcing, quickly, the not unimportant claims to be made. First, manuals of style and college handbooks have it all wrong when it comes to punctuation (good writers don't punctuate that way); there is, I propose, a system underlying what good writers, in fact, do; it is a surprisingly simple system; it is a system that enables writers to achieve important—even subtle—rhetorical effects; it is, even, a system that teachers can teach far more easily than they can teach the poorly systematized rules in our handbooks and style manuals.

It takes only a little study of the selections in our college readers to realize that the punctuation rules in handbooks and style manuals are not sacred texts for a great many good writers. Fragments and comma splices, violations of the coordinate clause and elliptical coordinate

John Dawkins, an instructor in the Language and Literature Department at Bucks County Community College (Pennsylvania) and English Department at Manor Junior College, has been an editor and author of elementary and high school instructional materials. He began thinking about punctuation because graduate-level courses in linguistics at the University of Chicago encouraged him to ask questions about language performance.

clause rules for commas, and inconsistencies in use of the comma with introductory word, phrase, and clause—these and other failures to follow the rules are frequent enough to raise questions about the rules themselves. Quirk et al. have examined statistical data on the use of the comma to mark coordination and concluded: "These results show we are dealing with tendencies which, while clear enough, are by no means rules. In such cases, it is probable that the general truth that punctuation conforms to grammatical rather than rhetorical considerations is in fact overridden" (1060).

Moreover, handbook rules provide no instruction for use of the comma in the following:

(1) Slowly, he walked to the store.
(2) He walked, slowly, to the store.
(3) He walked to the store slowly.

And when we produce a sequence of three or more independent clauses, punctuation questions often cross sentence (or independent clause) boundaries, and handbooks do not offer help for such interdependent problems. Consider a sequence of three simple independent clauses:

(4) It caught my eye—I swiveled around—and the next instant, inexplicably, I was looking down at a weasel—

There weren't any handbook rules to tell Annie Dillard to use a semicolon rather than a period or a dash or a colon or a comma splice between the first two clauses; or to follow that with a dash rather than a comma or a period or, yes, a colon between the last two.

And what do handbooks tell students about Orwell's punctuation of the following sentences from "Marrakech"?

(5) It was very hot and the men had marched a long way. They slumped under the weight of their packs and the curiously sensitive black faces were glistening with sweat.
(6) When a family is travelling it is quite usual to see a father and a grown-up son riding ahead on a donkey, and an old woman following on foot carrying the baggage.

According to the handbooks, Orwell is wrong, for their rules are essentially a right-or-wrong approach, providing little—if any—basis for considering options according to rhetorical intentions. Such instruction is negative in that it tells students what not to do and how not to do it; better instruction—in any skill, I assume—is going to tell students what to do and how to do it; it is going to encourage the "good" behaviors, not discourage the bad.

Sentences and Independent Clauses

Conventional punctuation is grammar based—marks are prescribed in terms of grammatical structure—but what "good writers" do, writers like Orwell, is punctuate according to their intended meaning, their intended emphasis.[1] It is an approach to use of the functional punctuation marks that follows "principles" rather than "rules."[2] To understand the principles, however, one grammatical element must be recognized—the independent clause. And the reason for this requirement is clear enough: all prose, written or spoken, consists of concatenations of independent clauses, and punctuation is a matter of showing appropriate relationships between them (some get punctuated as sentences, some do not). It is a mistake to assume that the sentence is the basic element in prose; it is also confusing, for it is the wrong basis for analyzing written language.[3]

To repeat: all discourse, written or spoken, consists of independent clauses or underlying independent clauses. The principle for "underlying" structures is well known: in spite of the missing element(s) in the surface structure, a clause is independent if the missing element(s) can be readily provided by a native speaker:

(7) Where are you going? Home.
(8) Mary read the book. John too.
(9) We went to the beach. Enjoyed the sun.

Sentences, therefore, are but one way of punctuating independent clauses:

(10) First it was rain. Then it was snow.
(11) First it was rain; then it was snow.
(12) First it was rain, then it was snow.

And so on—there are a number of other options for marking this boundary between independent clauses.

Mark	Degree of Separation
sentence final (. ? !)	maximum
semicolon (;)	medium
colon (:)	medium (anticipatory)
dash (—)	medium (emphatic)
comma (,)	minimum
zero (0)	none (that is, connection)

Table 1 Hierarchy of Functional Punctuation Marks

Sentences like (10-12) suggest a hierarchy of functional punctuation marks. The complete hierarchy is shown in Table 1 with the marks and their different degrees of separation (or connection, if you prefer) within independent clauses as well as between independent clauses.

As this table suggests, the colon and dash have functions in addition to the hierarchical (to be explained later). The differences in the marks are made still more clear by categorizing them according to basic function, which reveals a top two, middle two, and bottom two:

TOP (. ;)	separate independent clauses
MIDDLE (: —)	separate independent clauses, or separate non-independent clause element(s) from the independent clause.
BOTTOM (, 0)	separate non-independent clause elements from the independent clauses

Table 2 Basic Functions

The functions in Table 2 are general and basic; in addition, they are used by writers—as my discussion of raising and lowering will explain—to gain separation (emphasis) by using an appropriate higher mark, a mark not limited to the next one up; and writers gain connectedness (under-emphasis) by using an appropriate lower mark, a mark not limited to the next one down.

Punctuating Single Independent Clauses

Sentences can be analyzed as single independent clauses with or without attachments or as multiple independent clauses with or without attachments. With a single independent clause, possible attachments create three patterns: pre-clausal, post-clausal, and medial. In each case, the writer must decide: *Do I punctuate or don't I?*

I   (word/phrase/clause) + *pct?* + John laughed aloud.
II John laughed aloud + *pct?* + (word/phrase/clause).
III John + *pct?* + (word/phrase/clause) + *pct?* + laughed aloud.

Table 3 Patterns

In Pattern III the interruption may of course occur elsewhere within the independent clause.

Three of the four "rules" required by this principle-based approach to punctuation are needed to punctuate these patterns (rules that literate students will know or quickly learn without instruction):

Rule 1 (for Pattern I)	Only zero, comma, dash, or colon are permissible.
Rule 2 (for Pattern II)	All functional marks are permisible.
Rule 3 (for Pattern III)	Only paired marks (commas, dashes, zeros, and parentheses) are permissible.

Table 4 Rules

As these tables indicate the writer has choices, so there arises the question of how one goes about making these choices. The answer, theoretically, is simple, for it is found in anyone's principle of good writing; that is, it is found in the effort to get sentences to say what one means with the kind of emphasis one intends. The principle is general. All writers, evidently, want a sentence to say what they intend it to say. It is, of course, the same principle that guides choices among word and syntactic options; one chooses among the options the best one can. A little imaginative effort will suggest how, in the following examples, choices might be made according to "meaning and intended emphasis" (Summey 4):

(13) Surely (zero, comma, dash) the kid will come clean.
(14) The kid will come clean (any functional mark) and go home for a good night's sleep.
(15) The kid (zero, comma, dash, parenthesis) who has a guilty conscience (zero, comma, dash, parenthesis—each paired with the first) will come clean.

In ordinary contexts, one would expect the following:

(16) Today John went to school.

But one can easily create a context (John having been hospitalized for a year) which suggests

(17) Today, John went to school.

The non-independent clause element in Pattern I might, of course, be really expanded:

(18) When Mary sat at her desk and gave careful attention to it and decided, finally, that John wasn't as foolish as he had acted, she ...

But the principle is the same: meaning and emphasis.

For pattern II the problem is the same—does one want to mark a separation at the boundary or not? And the principle that guides the decision maker is, again, the same:

(19) John wanted the money (*pct?*) which he was owed.
(20) John wanted the money (*pct?*) which was right for him.
(21) John wanted the money (*pct?*) thinking he'd take Mary to dinner.
(22) John wanted the money (*pct?*) even though he hadn't earned it.

For pattern III, the problem is different only in that the choice is "two marks or none":

(23) The student (*pct?*) who was too sick to play (*pct?*) watched on TV.
(24) The candidate (*pct?*) deemed unfit for public office (*pct?*) won 70% of the vote.

Insertions in Pattern III can, of course occur elsewhere: The candidate won 70% (*pct?*) according to his figures (*pct?*) of the vote.

Raising and Lowering

Within a sentence having a single independent clause, the basic marks are zero and comma:

(25) John asked for a date when he got the nerve.
(26) John asked for a date, when he got the nerve.

The comma gains some emphasis for the attachment. And because of the nature of the hierarchy, the higher the mark the greater the emphasis:

(27) John asked for a date—when he got the nerve.
(28) John asked for a date. When he got the nerve.

Thus, justification for the sentence fragment.

Pressure to use a mark higher in the hierarchy I call *raising*. It develops naturally when commas within a sentence boundary mark different degrees of separation; thus meaning can be made more clear by using a higher mark at the major boundary. In the following sentence by James Baldwin, pressure for raising will be felt where Baldwin used the semicolons:

(29) I don't think the Negro problem in America can be even discussed coherently without bearing in mind its context; its context being the history traditions, customs, the moral assumptions and preoccupations of the country; in short, the general social fabric.

Some writers might have resisted the pressure for the first semicolon and stayed with a comma; most, I think, would have used a dash instead of the second semicolon. In either case, the sentence illustrates conditions for raising.

Raising, obviously, calls attention to itself, and thus gains emphasis. And it is this that Frost evidently felt a need for in the next example.

(30) I once heard of a minister who turned his daughter—his poetry-writing daughter—out on the street to earn a living, because he said there should be no more books written ...

Raising is thus a device for gaining rhetorical effect. In (31) Alice Walker uses a comma instead of zero to gain emphasis; and in (32) Ellen Goodman chooses an even higher mark to gain even more emphasis:

(31) White men and women continued to run things, badly.
(32) Date rape, after all, occurs in a context, a culture that—still—expects men to be assertive and women to be resistant.

And why does Dillard want commas in the next example?

(33) I think it would be well, and proper, and obedient, and pure, to grasp your one necessity and not let it go.

Pressure for raising accounts for two rules in our handbooks—a semicolon rule and a dash rule. If one or more of the items in a series has internal commas or if the individual items are lengthy, a semicolon at the major boundaries is needed for clarity, as in a sentence by Forster:

(34) We read that the Franks built it in the thirteenth century and called it Misithras or Mistia; that it became the chief fortress in the Peloponnese during an uninteresting period; that it was taken from the Franks by the Byzantines, and from the Byzantines by the Turks; that it was governed by a long succession of tyrants whose lives were short and brutal.

If the interrupting material contains commas, there is need for a higher mark at the major boundaries, and the dash is appropriate because, unlike the semicolon, it can be used in pairs, as in a Lewis Thomas sentence.

(35) Although we are by all odds the most social of all social animals—more interdependent, more attached to each other, more inseparable in our behavior than bees—we do not often feel our conjoined intelligence.

I propose that the hierarchy and raising account for these rules systematically—if you know the system, you know how to do it—and more effectively than the disconnected, essentially unsystematized rules in handbooks.

Notice, finally, that *lowering*—the opposite of raising—is also a natural consequence of understanding the hierarchical system. The semicolon in most of its uses, the comma splice, and the avoidance of a comma with a coordinator between independent clauses are common examples of lowering. Raising seems to be required, in certain contexts, to satisfy the need for clarity—as in (29), (34), (35). Lowering, on the other hand, does not seem to be required by a contextual need for clarity, except in a more subtle sense of this need, as in a good comma splice.

Multiple Independent Clauses

Discourse consists of multiple independent clauses, and the good writer marks the junctures between them according to an intended meaning and emphasis. Punctuating between independent clauses is different from punctuating within the clause, but the answer is based on the same principle (meaning and emphasis) and on the same knowledge (recognition of the independent clauses).

There are but two devices for marking the juncture between independent clauses: the hierarchy of punctuation marks (Table 1) and a set of coordinate conjunctions (*and, but, or, nor, for, so, yet, then*). Let me emphasize that these are the only devices for marking the juncture between independent clauses—in spite of what handbooks and style manuals and workbook exercises tell us, or seem to tell us.[4] Writers use these devices to convey semantic intent, and as they use them, they use the differences inherent in each group as well as combinations among them (more numerous than the brief list suggests) to produce their intended semantic effects.

Punctuation Alone

Table 5 is a further representation of the hierarchy as indicated in Tables 1 and 2:

MAXIMUM:	I gravitated to the random. I swung with the nonsequential. —JOAN DIDION
	I gravitated to the random; I swung with the nonsequential.
MEDIUM:	The fire is dying, the sparks scattering over the sand and stone: there is nothing to do but go.
	The fire is dying, the sparks scattering over the sand and stone—there is nothing to do but go. —EDWARD ABBEY
MINIMUM:	And it is true that all of us write within traditions, we all have a history and a context. —DONALD MURRAY
	And it is true that all of us write within traditions we all have a history and a context.

Table 5 Degrees of Separation Between Clauses

The "meaning" of these markings ranges from maximum separation to no separation (or connection)—but see the remarks on the dash and colon below. And since we use punctuation to clarify our meaning and gain appropriate emphasis, it is reasonable that, for ease of reading, the two marks or minimum separation between independent clauses are not as effective as the marks of medium or maximum separation. Zero, of course, is even confusing (and found only in experimental writing or certain kinds of poetry where, however, it is used for the very reasons indicated by the hierarchy—to show connection where, normally, separation would be shown). The comma splice, however, is an intentional mark in the writing of most "good" writers and, as indicated by the hierarchy, shows less of a separation than the higher marks—thus the purpose, an absolutely legitimate purpose, of the comma splice, as illustrated in another sentence by E. M. Forster (a fearless comma splicer):

(36) He could not stand the insecurities that are customary between officials, he refused to make use of the face-saving apparatus that they so liberally provide and employ.

There is a similar difference between the period and semicolon—the significance of the hierarchy, after all, is pretty straightforward. Look at the following ways of punctuating some words by E. B. White:

(37) The great days have faded. The end is in sight.
(38) The great days have faded; the end is in sight.

White actually used a comma splice here—forgive the deception, a way to make two points at once.

The dash and the colon are similar in function and, sometimes, even in meaning (see Tables 2 and 5). For example, which one would you choose for E. M. Forster's well known sentence:

(39) So Two Cheers for Democracy (pct?) one because it admits variety and two because it permits criticism.

Forster used a colon, but I suppose that many of us would choose a dash (and if your background is British, you'd be tempted by a semicolon).

Coordination Alone

According to our handbooks, marking the boundary between independent clauses with a coordinator alone is not done—unless the clauses are short and clear:

(40) The hare slept and it lost the race.

But we note that sentences like the following are not infrequently found in the nonfiction prose of good contemporary writers:

(41) Well—the sun will be up in a few minutes and I haven't even begun to make coffee.   —EDWARD ABBEY
(42) He told them very badly but you could see there was something there if he could get it out.   —ERNEST HEMINGWAY
(43) I could write a syndicated column for teenagers under the name "Debbie Lynn" or I could smuggle gold into India or I could become a $100 call girl, and none of it would matter.   —JOAN DIDION

What, then, is the meaning signaled by coordinator alone? The answer lies in the hierarchical function of punctuation marks—to mark a separation (or degree of connection, if you will). Thus, in the absence of a separating mark, as in (41)-(43), the signal is just that: as close a connection as the system allows.

Punctuation with Coordinator

What happens when we combine a mark with a coordinator is what the hierarchy predicts: more of a separation. A long sentence by Didion illustrates both coordinator alone and coordinator with punctuation:

(44) But after a while the signs thin out on Carnelian Avenue, and the houses are no longer the bright pastels of the Springtime Home owners but the faded bungalows of the people who grow a few grapes and keep a few chickens out here, and still the hill gets steeper and the road climbs and even the bungalows are few, and here—desolate, roughly surfaced, lined with eucalyptus and lemon groves—is Banyan Street.

One can see clearly, in that sentence, the difference between the two possibilities with independent clauses: coordinator plus comma creates greater separation, greater emphasis, than coordinator alone; the options provided by these devices are needed—and used by good writers. To oversimplify and suggest that one should use a comma whenever a coordinator is used between independent clauses—or not use one when the second clause is ellipted—is to falsify the description of written English and to misinform the student. As a matter of fact, we commonly enough find coordinators between independent clauses with any of the punctuation marks:

(45) I wish good fortune to both sides, good will to all. Or conversely, depending on my mood of the moment, damn both houses and *pox vobiscum*
—EDWARD ABBEY

(46) Find them, and clone them. But there is no end to the protocol.
—E. B. WHITE

(47) Whether or not our old drainboard was a guardian of our health I will never know; but neither my wife nor I have enjoyed as good health since the back kitchen got renovated.   —E. B. WHITE

(48) Since then I have walked, and prefer walking to horseback riding—but I had forgotten the depth of feeling one could see in horses' eyes.
—ALICE WALKER

(49) . . . the job in Burma had given me some understanding of the nature of imperialism: but these experiences were not enough to give me an accurate political orientation.   —GEORGE ORWELL

Even more options are available with ellipsis in the second or third clause, the most common form of which is the ellipted subject; the "rule" tells us to punctuate as follow:

(50) This is called "anchoring the mall" and represents seminal work in shopping-center theory.

But the system here allows the writer some options:

(51) This is called "anchoring the mall," and represents seminal work in shopping-center theory.
(52) This is called "anchoring the mall"—and represents seminal work in shopping-center theory.
(53) This is called "anchoring the mall": and represents seminal work in shopping-center theory.

Didion chose (50), but the other choices must be considered as "correct," and perhaps as reasonable as well. Sometimes a writer will even choose maximum separation:

(54) But all I could do was to try to rein him out of it. Or hug his back.
—ALICE WALKER
(55) It is made; not described.   —ERNEST HEMINGWAY

The ellipted independent clause in the following example by Updike could be punctuated with any mark but zero, making five options:

(56) [Doris Day's] third picture, strange to say, ended with her make-believe marriage to Errol Flynn. A heavenly match, in the realm where both are lovable.

Yet five more options were available for Updike if he considered the deleted *It was*. And with coordinator plus *It was* there are—considering just *and*—probably four more. A total of fourteen options for a writer to consider.

Notice that (51)-(56) are in fact examples of raising and represent options that good writers know how to exploit. Notice also that teaching a "rule" actually denies these options, for a rule indicates—at least for students—only one way of doing something, the "right" way; the rule thus denies students the opportunity to learn an important writing strategy. which raises the question of pedagogy.

Pedagogy

Because the choices are limited (rules 1, 2, and 3) and the knowledge base specific (tables 1, 2, 3, and awareness of the independent clause), the punctuation system here is not difficult to learn. It is to be learned by doing—the way all language skills are learned, which means a lot of doing, of course. So instruction consists of enough examples for discussion (numerous in college readers) and enough opportunities in writing to develop the experience needed for making good choices. In providing these opportunities the teacher will realize one of the strengths of the approach: it encourages students to analyze their semantic and rhetorical intentions. The student doesn't try to match his or her sentence with a rule in a handbook, then respond in a behavioral sense; instead, the student reads and considers her or his intentions and the reader's needs, then decides according to an intended meaning and emphasis. We like to say, in our discussions of the writing process, that writing is thinking. Indeed! In contrast to the rule-matching process required by a handbook, this approach to punctuating is an expression of the writing-is-thinking premise, for it provides the occasion and the tools for thinking.

To teach the system one needs a few handouts (like tables 1, 2, 3, and 4) and a feeling for student needs in sequencing the material along with reading and writing assignments. For example, with basic writers one might want to present the hierarchy but limit initial practice to the period, comma, and zero (one can write a flawless paper with just these marks). Good instruction will still sequence the introduction of writing problems according to student needs. Of course, learning a system well takes lots of practice. Good writers get lots of practice; students should too.

As should be clear by now, learning to punctuate effectively requires only a little knowledge of grammar, much less than most English teachers will grant. One needs to recognize an independent clause in one's writing, which requires bringing to a conscious level what one knows intuitively. All native speakers have what linguists call a "competence" that includes the ability to speak and comprehend independent clauses; so students who are native speakers quickly enough master the consciousness-raising task of identifying subject and finite verb (irregular syntax obviously requires additional work).

An appealing aspect of this meaning-based approach to punctuation is that it allows for individual differences in its application. (The fifth-grader, for example, should use his or her knowledge of the hierarchy—which may be incomplete, of course—according to his or her intentions.) A good writer chooses to *do* something (to choose a work, to begin a sentence adverbially, to punctuate). In choosing to do there is a positive, a constructive, a meaning-creating approach to writing: in contrast, in obeying a negatively worded rule, there comes a negative attitude, a negative approach to the process, for the student is punctuating to avoid error rather than to create meaning. Learning theory, as I understand it, suggests that learning to use a systematic procedure is far easier than learning to use a list of poorly ordered rules defined by a technical terminology with exceptions and footnotes and meager examples—all made more difficult because a behavioristic response is expected from very uncertain stimuli (the student's own sentences).

Let me illustrate these general remarks on pedagogy with some examples of raising and lowering, punctuation practices that can and should be analyzed and practiced during reading and writing assignments. Reading how a good writer punctuates helps anyone grasp more surely some small yet significant point as well as, on occasion, a major point; and such study will thus help anyone punctuate more tellingly. So, consider what some good writers have done.

The following is raising to a comma (the fourth one) where a handbook asks for zero because the compounding is not of independent clauses:

(57) The business of being out for a walk, coming across something of fascinating interest and then dragged away from it by a yell from the master,

> like a dog jerked onwards by the leash, is an important feature of school
> life, and helps to build up the conviction, so strong in many children, that
> the things you most want to do are always unattainable.—GEORGE ORWELL

This sentence, with its long independent clause with three commas, would become confusing if zero were used at the major point of separation within the sentence, even though zero would follow the handbook rule. Raising thus is important for clarity of meaning.

Raising from zero to a comma is common because it produces a simple yet clear emphasis, as in this:

(58) I was driving down the Thruway in Vermont to consult a doctor in New York, and hit a deer.   —EDWARD HOAGLAND

The following illustrates raising from commas to periods:

(59) They float on the landscape like pyramids to the boom years, all those Plazas and Malls and Esplanades. All those Squares and Fairs. All those Towns and Dales.   —JOAN DIDION

Didion clearly uses raising here to gain emphasis.

The effective sentence fragment also gains emphasis when an expected colon is raised to a period:

(60) I call recall that I hated [Southern black country life] generally. The hard work in the fields, the shabby houses ...   —ALICE WALKER

When the fragment shows raising from an expected comma, there is—as the system predicts—even more emphasis:

(61) The very name hallucinates. Man's country. Out where the West begins.
                    —JOAN DIDION

The first fragment is raised from a colon the second from a comma.

Teaching the punctuation of fragments and when to use them teaches students how to write—quite different from the usual textbook instruction in how not to write. Teaching how teaches judgment—sensitivity to context—important in the development of taste. How else do we learn that some fragments work and others don't?

Consider an example of lowering, first punctuated as it might have been a hundred years ago and next punctuated as it typically is today:

(62) He searches for the lamppost with his cane, like a tennis player swinging backhand, and, if he loses his bearings and bumps against something, he jerks abruptly back, like a cavalier insulted, looking gaunt and fierce.
(63) He searches for the lamppost with his cane like a tennis player swinging backhand, and if he loses his bearings and bumps against something, he jerks abruptly back like a cavalier insulted, looking gaunt and fierce.
　　　　　　　　　　　　　　　　　　　　　　　　—EDWARD HOAGLAND

The modern style (comma lowered to zero) better reflects the meaning, better reinforces the meaning, by more clearly reflecting what goes together and what does not. He "searches … like a tennis player swinging backhand"—a comma between those words separates what meaningfully goes together. And the same can be said for "he jerks abruptly back like a cavalier insulted." One may be in the habit of marking off such similes with commas—and one has that option, of course—yet it is clear, I think, that the relationship is better expressed without the commas. Moreover if *and* is separated from *if* with a comma the suggestion is that *and* relates to "he jerks abruptly back" (the independent clause); however *and* is more meaningfully understood as relating all that follows it with all that goes before—the two halves of the sentence.
　　Lowering is a device that reveals more connection between words, phrases, or clauses than the expected punctuation would; it is most commonly illustrated by lowering from a period to semicolon:

(64) The term "scientific literacy" has become almost a cliché in educational circles. Graduate schools blame the colleges; colleges blame the secondary schools; the high schools blame …　　　　　　—LEWIS THOMAS

A frequent example of lowering is the common violation of the handbook rule that tells us, unless the clauses are short to use a comma between independent clauses:

(65) They are brimming with good humor and the more daring swell with pride when I stop to speak with them.　　　　　　—JAMES BALDWIN

And what effect is achieved in the following by lowering commas to zero?

(66) They asked it in New York and Los Angeles and they asked it in Boston and Washington and they asked it in Dallas and Houston and Chicago and San Francisco.　　　　　　—JOAN DIDION

Lowering justifies the effective comma splice (and of course suggests that teachers teach it). A couple of examples:

(67) But even so [Harvey] had his consolations, he cherished his dream.
　　　　　　　　　　　　　　　　　　　　　　　—VIRGINIA WOOLF
(68) I did not know that the British empire is dying, still less did I know that it is a great deal better than the younger empires that are going to supplant it.　　　　　　　　　　　　　　　　　　　—GEORGE ORWELL

Handbooks I have seen do not discuss the problem of punctuating three or more independent clauses as a single sentence but according to the rule for "punctuating compound sentences" one should use two commas in the following

(69) The debate might well have been little more than a healthy internal difference of opinion, but the press loves the sensational and it could not allow the issue to remain within the private domain of the movement.
　　　　　　　　　　　　　　　　　　—MARTIN LUTHER KING, JR.

King, however, was clearly sensitive to the major and minor boundaries and followed the hierarchical principle by lowering (comma to zero) at the minor boundary—accurately reflecting his semantic intent.

A long while ago, in a long-neglected book, George Summey told us what was wrong with style manuals and handbooks: "The notion that there is only one correct way of punctuating a given word pattern is true only in limited degree. Skillful writers have learned that they must make alert and successful choices between periods and semicolons, semicolons and commas, and commas and dashes, dashes and parentheses, according to meaning and intended emphasis" (4). By teaching raising and lowering, we will be adding to our students' repertoire of skills; we will be encouraging students to clarify the meaning of sentences and to gain intended emphasis. Such instruction illustrates what in our composition classes we like to proclaim but don't always demonstrate: writing is thinking.

Acknowledgments

I want to thank Pat Belanoff and Joseph Williams for many valuable comments on the drafts of this manuscript; and I want especially to thank Jim Sledd for his original comments and ongoing support.

Notes

1. "Good" writers is in reference to nonfiction by writers of recognized stature, whose work can be found in college readers. If fiction were included, the evidence would be only more evident. For more on this topic, see my *Rethinking Punctuation*.

2. Functional marks are those marks regularly and typically used to mark syntactic functions. I neglect parentheses, perhaps too arbitrarily, but unlike the other marks, parentheses are limited to pairs, giving them a unique and typically non-rhetorical function, suggesting that the primary use of parentheses is for "non-text" information.

3. For plentiful and convincing diachronic evidence for the claim that the basic unit in prose is the independent clause and that the sentence is simply one way to mark this clause, the reader should see Levinson's dissertation (1985) and derived article (1989).

4. Subordinate conjunctions are not used to join independent clauses; they form "dependent" elements (phrases or clauses), elements which function as the attachments in patterns I, II, and III—and are punctuated accordingly. Similarly, conjunctive adverbs are simply dependent words and phrasal words ("on the other hand") that function as the same kinds of attachments: "However, they played the next day" (pattern I). "They played the next day, however" (pattern II). "They played, however, the next day" (pattern III).

Works Cited

Dawkins, John. *Rethinking Punctuation*. ERIC ED 340 048. 1992.

Levinson, Joan Persily. *Punctuation and the Orthographic Sentence*. Diss. City University of New York, 1985.

———. "The Linguistic Status of the Orthographic (Text) Sentence." *CUNY Forum* 14 (1989): 113-17.

Quirk, Randolph, Sidney Greenbaum, Geoffrey Leech, and Jan Svartje. *A Comprehensive Grammar of the English Language*. London: Longman, 1985.

Summey, George. *American Punctuation*. New York: Ronald, 1949.

Talking in the Middle: Why Writers Need Writing Tutors

Muriel Harris

The work of a writing center is as varied as the students who stream
in and out the doors. A writing center encourages and facilitates writing emphasis in courses in addition to those in an English department's composition program; it serves as a resource room for writ-
ing-related materials; it offers opportunities for faculty development
through workshops and consultations; and it develops tutors' own
writing, interpersonal skills, and teaching abilities. Moreover, writing
centers, by offering a haven for students where individual needs are
met, are also integral to retention efforts, are good recruiting tools, provide a setting for computer facilities that integrate word processing
with tutoring, are rich sites for research, and by their flexibility and
ability to work outside of institutionalized programs are free to spawn
new services and explore new writing environments. But these
aspects of the work of a writing center do not define its core, its primary responsibility—to work one-to-one with writers. In doing so,
writing centers do not duplicate, usurp, or supplement writing or

Muriel Harris is Professor of English and Director of the Writing Lab at Purdue
University. She edits the *Writing Lab Newsletter* and has written several books,
including *Teaching One-to-One: The Writing Conference* (NCTE, 1986) and *The
Prentice-Hall Reference Guide to Grammar and Usage* (2d ed. 1994), as well as
articles on writing center theory, administration, and pedagogy.

writing-across-the-curriculum classrooms. Writing centers do not and should not repeat the classroom experience and are not there to compensate for poor teaching, over-crowded classrooms, or lack of time for overburdened instructors to confer adequately with their students. Instead, writing centers provide another, very crucial aspect of what writers need—tutorial interaction. When meeting with tutors, writers gain kinds of knowledge about their writing and about themselves that are not possible in other institutionalized settings, and it is this uniqueness of the tutorial setting that I will focus on here.

Tutorial instruction is very different from traditional classroom learning because it introduces into the educational setting a middle person, the tutor, who inhabits a world somewhere between student and teacher. Because the tutor sits below the teacher on the academic ladder, the tutor can work effectively with students in ways that teachers can not. Tutors don't need to take attendance, make assignments, set deadlines, deliver negative comments, give tests, or issue grades. Students readily view a tutor as someone to help them surmount the hurdles others have set up for them, and as a result students respond differently to tutors than to teachers, a phenomenon readily noticed by tutors who end a stint of writing center tutoring and then go off to teach their own classes. Dave Healy, who both tutors and teaches, aptly describes this scenario:

> In the center, writers may try to invest me with authority, but I can resist their efforts. In the classroom, I can try to resist, but as long as I'm going to be assigning my students grades, my nonauthoritative pose is simply that—a pose. In the classroom, I can't get away from making assignments, and as long as I make them, no matter how enlightened or open-ended they may be, they're still mine. I can never adopt the kind of stance in relation to one of my assignments that I can in relation to an assignment that a writer brings to the center. And increasingly that stance feels crucial to the kind of work I want to do with writers.

Most students come to writing centers because they are required to (Bishop, Clark), but even so, students leave feeling that the tutorial has been a beneficial experience. Why is this so? The relationship with a tutor is likely to begin with questions like "How can I help you" or "What would you like to work on today?" A truly reluctant student knows that she doesn't have to do anything, won't be graded, and in a worst-case scenario, can silently count the cracks in the ceiling while the tutor talks. But the vast majority of students start on a more positive note. Here's someone who might just help them, maybe even show them what's wrong, what to fix, or what the writing assignment is about. As the conversation progresses, they begin to talk more freely and more honestly because they are not in the confines of a teacher/student relationship where there are penalties for asking what they perceive as "dumb" questions (the penalty being that the teacher will find out how little they know or how inept they are in formulating their questions). Moreover, students realize that they don't have to listen passively and accept what is "told" to them by an authoritative speaker.

In addition to student attitudes toward tutors, another powerful component of the tutorial has to do with how tutors acquire needed information. Whereas teachers get information about students from conferences and from students' contributions to classroom interaction, much of what's needed comes from the written products students turn in. And those products are often analyzed when teachers are sitting alone at their desks, away from the students. By contrast, in the interaction between tutor and student, the tutor picks up clues from watching and listening to the student. Tutors' questions can lead students to offer information they didn't know was needed and to clarify their answers through further questioning. Students can also offer other useful information they would be less willing to give teachers. Sitting with a student for a half-hour or an hour, a tutor is able to work primarily with the writer as a person, even when the paper is there on the table between them. Tutors use talk and questioning and all the cues they can pick up in the face-to-face interaction. The conversation is free to roam in whatever direction the student and tutor see as useful. That is, the tutor can ask about writing habits and processes, can listen to the student's responses to various questions, and can use them as cues for further questions; and the student can express concerns not visible in the product. Moreover, either one is free to bring up some potentially relevant concern that takes them off in a different, more fruitful direction. The flexibility and interaction of a tutorial permits a close look at the individual student, something that Jim, a peer tutor in our Writing Lab, has noted. Jim spends one day a week in the classroom and then works with those students every week in tutorials. He notes that in the classroom his students are a sea of "hands, faces, and comments," but when these same students come to the Writing Lab, they become very different individuals with distinct personalities, needs, and ways of learning. Linda Flower views teachers' "product-based inferences" as a limitation that may radically underestimate students' knowledge, problem-solving efforts, and unresolved dilemmas. When that happens, notes Flower, teachers "may be trying to diagnose and teach a thinking process in the dark" ("Studying Cognition" 21). The face-to-face interaction of tutor and student permits some light to enter.

The power of the tutor's position outside the evaluative setting is also apparent in student evaluations that acknowledge tutors' expertise. There are always impressively high ratings, positive comments, and effusive notes of appreciation, far beyond what any of us who also teach in classrooms will get when we switch to wearing our grade-giving-instructor hats. As tutors we are there to help reduce the stress, to overcome the hurdles set up by others, and to know more about writing than a roommate or friend, maybe even as much as their teachers. Students may not have come willingly and may (as is often the case) have come with inappropriate expectations that the tutor will fix the paper or show them what to do. Accordingly, they may initially be irritated or unhappy that the tutor's role is not to proofread the paper for them or tell them how to get a higher grade. But given a few minutes of tutorial conversation, students begin to see that the tutor can help them learn how to proofread or how to fix their papers. Every tutor has tales of students who turn sullen, morose, or even hostile when they learn that the tutor isn't a free editor, but who eventually calm down and join in the conversation about strategies they can use. At the end of such a tutorial, as they are packing up, such students are apt to offer a "Hey, thanks a lot. That helped." Just as frequently, students who come in nervous, apprehensive, defeated, or eager to get any help they can emerge from their sessions feeling more positive, more in control of their own writing. The enormous power of these positive responses to tutors cannot be overemphasized. Students may ignore the existence of the Center until required to come in, they may come with all the wrong expectations, and their attitudes toward writing may vary from anger to anxiety about grades to eagerness to produce the best paper they are capable of, but the vast majority emerge feeling that the experience was positive. A number of useful consequences account for how tutors and students can work together and why tutorial collaboration is different in kind from the way students interact with their teachers.

To illustrate this collaboration as well as to shine some light on what goes on in a tutorial, I will use not only language we are familiar with as teachers and scholars but also the language of students—who constitute a different though not entirely separate discourse community. The student comments are typical of the hundreds made each semester on evaluation forms that students attending our Writing Lab are asked to fill out anonymously.

Encouraging Independence in Collaborative Talk

- I felt very comfortable with Pam. She helped me by making me do the work. She let me think my problems through instead of telling me what to do to correct my problems.
- Richard is a great tutor. He helps you understand more what you're doing, by having you do it yourself.
- He let me decide everything instead of telling me what to change or do.
- He made me think and realize more than in our class without telling me exactly how to write.
- These people know their stuff. But she didn't just give me answers. She got me thinking.
- Colleen's tutorial style challenges you to think and re-think your material.
- He made me teach myself. He didn't tell me anything.
- She knows how to help without giving answers. She makes me think.
- The help at the Writing Lab allows you to think on your own. He did not critique my paper, but he asked me questions that made me see how to critique and think about my own paper.
- I like how she wanted answers from me. She didn't just tell me what to do to make something right.

A number of common threads tie these comments together. Students insist that they prefer to do their own work, come to their own conclusions, write what was in their own heads; these students do not want to be told what to do. Cynics and new tutors-in-training may assume that most writers, when faced with turning in a paper, would probably be happiest if given directions for action. But this is not the case, as studies by Allen and by Walker and Elias have shown. Students were asked to rate how satisfied they were with tutorials in which the tutor either assumed control and explained what had to be done or used questioning that permitted the student to think through the process and reach her own conclusions. From the students' perspectives, the more highly satisfactory tutorials were those in which the students were active participants in finding their own criteria and solutions. Among the hundreds of completed forms that I read every semester, I can remember only one student complaint about this approach: "All she did was ask me questions." Given the student perception of a tutor as other than a teacher, we can see why students feel free from the classroom constraint of having to listen to the teacher and to do as they are told. Even non-directive, student centered teachers who see their advice and suggestions as open-ended possibilities their students can freely reject should recognize that such suggestions are often not taken precisely as they are intended. Students feel freer to develop their own ideas in settings other than teacher/student conversations (and, of course, teacher comments on papers) and welcome the opportunity to have someone help them sort through and formulate conceptual frameworks for drafts of their papers. Peer response groups may help, but a tutor who is trained to ask probing questions and who focuses her attention on the writer offers a more effective environment for the writer during the generative stages of writing (Harris, "Collaboration"). It appears that writers both need and want discussion that engages them actively with their ideas through talk and permits them to stay in control.

A second strand in these comments, the reiteration of the word "think," indicates that tutorial conversation differs from classroom discussion. As Douglas Barnes explains, tutorial or "exploratory" talk encourages thinking and discovery:

> Exploratory talk often occurs when peers collaborate in a task, when they wish to talk it over in a tentative manner, considering and rearranging their ideas. The talk is often but not always hesitant, containing uncompleted or inexplicit utterances as the students try to formulate new understandings; exploratory talk enables students to represent to themselves what they currently understand and then if necessary to criticize and change it. . . . Presentational talk performs a different and more public role When students are called on in class, when they feel to be under *evaluation*, they seldom risk exploration, but prefer to provide an acceptable performance, a "right" answer. (50)

I have italicized the word "evaluation" because it highlights the limitations of classroom discussion and teacher-student conferences. When talking with a teacher, most students will feel pressure to perform, to look as if they're knowledgeable—in other words, to use presentational talk. Tossing around ideas to see how they play out is more easily accomplished in a tutorial than in a teacher's conference, and as Cynthia Onore points out, exploratory language, though less controlled and controlling, has more power to generate confident assertions and make connections than does presentational language. Tutors adept at the kind of collaboration that encourages useful exploratory talk may guide the conversation, but they do not inhibit the student. In students' perceptions, the person sitting next to them is merely a tutor, someone to "help you bring out your ideas." In light of current theories of collaboration and social construction of knowledge—that, as Kenneth Bruffee states, "knowledge is an artifact created by a community of knowledgeable peers and that learning is a social process not an individual one" (11)—we are less inclined to see the resulting paper as containing only the student's ideas, but that is not the issue here. Getting the student engaged—truly and actively engaged—is. Long before "empowerment" became a coin of the composition realm, tutors basked in the glow of hearing students leave a tutorial saying, "OK, so now I know what I want to write. It was there in my head, but I just couldn't get it out."

Assisting With Acquisition of Strategic Knowledge

- She made me think, didn't tell me what to do, just how to do it.
- She helped me look at my paper from a different point of view. That helped a lot, and I know how to do that now.
- I learned how to bring out ideas by asking questions and what to do to develop them.
- The Writing Lab helped me see how to solve a problem instead of just telling me what's wrong.
- I learned how to organize my paper. It was hard to see how to do that with all the notes I collected from my library searching.
- I learned to discuss what I want to say and how to go about doing that.
- I explained my organizational problems, and she was able to help me revise my paper without doing it for me, giving me skills to connect with other papers I may write.
- This makes me focus on how I write.

- I wanted to structure my paper but I didn't get exactly how I could do this. She helped me see how, and now I know I can write the paper I am capable of writing.
- I didn't see how I was causing myself problems with my writing. She really helped me see how to do it better for the way that I write.

Writers need several types of knowledge, some more easily gained in the classroom and others more appropriately acquired in the one-to-one setting of a tutorial. If Barnes shows us *why* tutorial talk encourages knowing, Louise Phelps tells us *what* kinds of knowledge are needed: propositional and procedural. One kind of knowledge, that which she identifies as propositional knowledge, is theoretical. It consists of knowing about a set of possibilities for action but does not help us know *how* to act, for as Phelps says, "theory can never tell people directly what to do" because theoretical knowledge does not embed within itself rules for how to apply it (863). Such knowledge is general and not tied to the individual. Phelps explains that much of what is given in textbooks and lectures is formal knowledge in which knowing is learning to name concepts and to articulate their relationships (870). By contrast, practical knowing—the knowledge of the practitioner—arises out of the individual's recognition of a set of possibilities for actions, internalized images, descriptions, and prescriptions. Textbooks and classroom discussions can build this kind of practical knowledge but not the second kind of practical knowledge that Phelps identifies. This second kind of practical knowledge is knowing from personal experience *how* to act, in the sense of possessing a habit or skill for performing an activity. For example, students may think they know how to brainstorm an idea or argument, but only when sitting with a student can a tutor help the student see *how* it feels to turn off that internal editor, which rejects avenues of thought before they are fully explored, or *how* to take brainstorming notes before an idea evaporates from memory, or *how* to let threads of an argument or analogy continue to play themselves out in various directions. A student who began a tutorial complaining that he doesn't know what else to add to a paper that's too short is likely to progress from answering a tutor's questions to offering some suggestions to grabbing a sheet of paper and forgetting that there is a tutor sitting next to him as he works through a more extended reason for supporting (or rejecting) election campaign reform. The student begins to learn "how it feels" to do this. An even more concrete example is the student who learns how to proofread for spelling, missing words, or typos. Such a student may have come to the writing center knowing in some general sense what proofreading is but not knowing what it feels like to pace oneself very slowly or to focus on words one by one.

Helping students get the "feel" of some aspects of writing is part of what a tutor can do as she sits next to the student, talking, modeling, and offering suggestions, even though writing is a more sophisticated activity than any of these. Tutors can help students learn *how* to proofread, *how* to let go and brainstorm, *how* to capture a flood of ideas in the planning stage, *how* to take all those scraps of paper and note cards and organize them, *how* to insert revisions into a text, *how* to draw back and figure out if the organizational structure is appropriate, or *how* to check on paragraph development. If needed, a tutor can model a process or can watch the student as she goes through a process herself (Harris, "Modeling"), looking for what is working appropriately and what might be done more effectively in a different way. Or a tutor can suggest a few possible strategies, any one of which might be more appropriate for this particular writer who writes in his or her particular way. This may seem obvious because it is what tutors often do in a tutorial, but it can startle a student as he suddenly "sees" what he's supposed to do in order to achieve whatever it was he was trying to achieve.

This recognition of possible strategies is part of what Linda Flower includes in the kinds of knowledge writers need. Such knowledge, she explains, "involves reading a situation and setting appropriate *goals,* having the *knowledge* and *strategies* to meet one's own goals, and finally, having the metaknowledge of *awareness* to reflect on both goals and strategies. Strategic knowledge is a contextualized form of knowing; it develops over time and out of experience" ("Studying Cognition" 23). Similarly, Alred and Thelen recognize the need for strategic knowledge: "We know intuitively that teaching students to write requires much more than teaching a canon of rules; it requires that we enable students to rehearse a variety of strategies" (471). The rehearsal by some students may go well on their own, but it may not for others. That rehearsal enacted with a tutor watching and offering feedback and advice is a particularly effective tutorial practice. Strategies are easy to learn in an environment where the person next to the writer can answer questions as the writer proceeds and can offer some midstream correction or encouragement when something is not going well. Flower's strategic knowledge is that form of procedural knowledge, or knowing *how*, that Phelps describes, and Flower also notes that writers should have optional strategies in their repertoire for different tasks and different purposes ("Negotiating Academic Discourse" 245). When knowing-in-action, as Phelps calls it (873), bogs down and doesn't work, the writer needs what Phelps calls "reflection-in-action" and what Flower points to when she insists on the writer's need for metacognitive awareness of the acts of setting goals and invoking strategies ("Negotiating Academic Discourse" 222). Learning how to view what has been done, gaining the high ground, is yet another task the tutor can assist with. In the tutorial conversation the tutor helps the student recognize what's going on and how to talk about it as well as how to act. Although tutors often help with propositional knowledge—for example, knowledge of various academic genres of writing, knowledge of rhetorical structures, or knowledge of cultural variations in rhetorical values that perplex international students—the art of the tutor is to collaborate with students as they acquire the practical knowledge they need.

Assisting with Affective Concerns

- I learned my paper wasn't as bad as I thought it was. It's easier to do a good job when you don't think your writing's terrible.
- I like the atmosphere. I can ask my questions here, and I learned some techniques to overcome writing anxiety.
- They treat you as equals. It is not like teachers helping students. This makes the student feel more at ease.
- If you have a block, as I did on how to write a paper, the tutor will help you remember what you have learned in the past.
- She talked to me with an accepting attitude even though my paper was shaky. She worked with me, and not like she was over me.
- I'm trying to overcome my fear of writing, and this is the place to be.
- He helped me sort through my lack of confidence.
- I am less stressed about my paper because I actually know what I am trying to say now.
- She was easy to talk to. I could ask questions without feeling stupid.
- She was patient and gave me confidence. I needed to be convinced that I was approaching my paper correctly.

No one doubts that student writers too often lack confidence in their skills or that they find writing to he an anxiety-producing task, but the classroom teacher cannot attend to the variety of worries that inhibit some student writers. Those fears range from evaluation anxiety to long-standing reluctance to have a teacher "bleed all over" their papers, from writing blocks of various levels of intensity to defeatist convictions that they are not good writers. In tutorials students often unburden themselves and find a sympathetic ear as well as some suggestions for getting past their affective concerns. As I read evaluations every semester, it appears that tutorial assistance gives students confidence about themselves and their writing. The word "confidence" repeats itself so often that I have asked students to talk about why they feel more confident after talking with a tutor. Typically the response is that a student initially feels unsure that a paper meets an assignment or is well written. When a tutor helps the writer set up criteria to use for her own assessment, the writer gains confidence in deciding whether the paper is ready to be turned in. Or the tutor can give the writer some reader response that helps her see what needs more clarification. Tutors can also help when students worry that their mental representation of what they wanted to write does not sufficiently overlap the product that actually appears on paper. Helping writers match intention or plan with the written result is often a useful exercise, particularly since tutors often find that the writer's mental representation is far richer than the less impressive draft. Asking the writer some questions or requesting more details often results in the writer's seeing what else he should have included or where (or how) the paper drifted away from the intended goal. After such sessions, students talk about "feeling better" about their papers or knowing what else they want to do when they revise. It appears from some evaluations that their newly found confidence also results in stronger motivation. While the role of motivation in language learning has not been a major topic of composition research, tutors recognize that dealing with affective concerns and offering encouragement result in increased motivation to continue expending effort on a paper.

Another affective concern reflected in student comments is that it is stressful for them to talk about their writing with someone whom they perceive as having some institutional authority over them. Such students view themselves as being treated as inferiors, talked down to, demeaned in some way when talking with teachers, but not with tutors. The collaborative atmosphere of the tutorial, the sense of being with someone who does not assume any authoritative posture, seems to relieve that strain or eliminate the fear. It is undoubtedly true that some teachers do reinforce the stereotypical authoritarian stance or aren't as adept as they might be in using language that their students understand. But it would be worth investigating whether students' perceptions of teachers' roles in some way create in some students the belief that they have been reduced to an inferior stance or treated as a lower form of life. Though teachers may well seek the same collegial tone as tutors, some students cannot see the similarity because they expect their teachers to perceive them as inferiors. The power structure of academia may remain intact in part because some students perpetuate it in their own minds. There may also be a language issue here, the issue of different discourse communities, as discussed below.

Interpreting the Meaning of Academic Language

- He helped me understand my prof's meaning.
- She explained what needed to be done in a language that I understood.
- I got in-depth explanations of handouts given in class. I didn't understand in class with just the teacher's explanations.
- You do a fantastic job with helping students understand what to do with an assignment. I had interpreted it in a way that was not correct.
- Now I know how to write an expressive paper. I was off course before. I was having a problem seeing what continuity was.
- We worked on what is a letter to an editor. This is not something I learned to do in my country.
- Thanks. You helped me see what my teacher wants me to do when I revise.
- She answered all my questions about what response writing is. I got the help I needed.
- The prof couldn't explain what I needed to know, but thanks to Linda, I understand now.

A cursory reading of these student comments would be that they are praising tutors for being able to explain better than teachers, but a more appropriate analysis might be that these students are reporting that the tutor interpreted teacher language by translating it into their language, that is, gave meaning to terms they had heard and read and not understood. Just as Phelps points out that practitioner teachers cannot easily translate their problems into the critical discourse of theory (863), student writers cannot easily translate their problems into the discourse of composition or make meaning of the language about writing. When students recognize problems, they normally do not have the metaknowledge that Flower says is needed or the necessary metalanguage to locate the appropriate section of a textbook, ask a teacher, or tell a tutor. Students coming to a writing center do not—most often cannot—say they want to work on invention strategies or sharpen their focus or improve the coherence of a paper. They come in saying that they "need help" or that the paper "doesn't flow." It is even more likely that they give the paper to the tutor, hoping the tutor can give names to their internal sense that something is needed. Student language is not the language we use. Mary Louise Pratt observes that students and teachers inhabit separate communities, though she acknowledges that there is hardly total homogeneity in either the teacher community or student community. Pratt's interest is in getting us to move away from viewing groups as existing separately, a view that gives rise to a linguistics that seeks to capture the identity but not the relationality of social differentiation. But, she explains, dominant and dominated groups are not comprehensible apart from each other, for their speech practices are organized to enact these differences and their hierarchy. Any dominated group is required simultaneously to identify with and disassociate itself from the dominant group.

Students' discourse consequently is both distinct from and permeated by that of teachers, the dominant group. Pratt offers the interesting suggestion that there be a "linguistics of contact" (60), which studies the operation of language across lines of differentiation, focusing on the nodes and zones of contact between groups. Since tutors live in this contact zone somewhere between teachers and students, tutorial talk may be a particularly fruitful area in which to research what those nodes and zones are.

That teachers view themselves as set apart and different from their students is apparent from Cheryl Towns' study of how members of the composition profession refer to students when writing articles in the pages of *College Composition and Communication*. In the nineteen articles she analyzed, Towns found that students were referred to often, over 345 times, with the highest frequency characterizing them as "mere fledglings," new and inexperienced, novices, learners. Much of the language was about relationships between teachers and students, and the most prevalent category was "teacher as teacher" and "student as student," despite comments in the same articles which deplored this traditional relationship. The metaphors used were often of seeing, getting students "to see," "to observe," and teachers were perceived as givers with students as receivers or teachers as leaders and students as followers. Towns concluded that "though we may be beginning to see the need to move beyond the traditional power structure of the classroom, we are still deeply entrenched in it" (97).

Tutors are thus other than teachers in that they inhabit a middle ground where their role is that of translator or interpreter, turning teacher language into student language. "Focus," "coherence," and "development" are not terms as readily understood by students as teachers think. As a result, a common tutorial task is helping the student understand the comments a teacher has made on a paper, thus confirming the results of a study by Mary Hayes and Donald Daiker which vividly demonstrates how little of what teachers write in the margins of papers is understood in any useful way. Similarly, Jill Burkland and Nancy Grimm note: "Through our experiences as tutors in our university's Writing Center and through years in the composition classroom, we were aware that teachers' intentions are often unrealized, that written communication on papers is often misunderstood or misinterpreted by students" (937-38). Other studies report similar conclusions in tones of defeat and discouragement. As Knoblauch and Brannon note, "The depressing trouble is, we have scarcely a shred of empirical evidence to show that students typically even comprehend our responses to their writing, let alone use them purposefully to modify their practice" (1). Similarly, in a large-scale study that looked at teacher comments, Robert Connors and Andrea Lunsford found a portrait of teachers having little time and less faith that their comments would be understood

Students' difficulties in understanding teacher comments are partly this difference in vocabulary, but there is also the problem of students' perception of teacher intent behind the comments. When a paper is returned with numerous teacher responses, some students may read the marginalia and end comments; most don't. They skip down to the grade and wander into the writing center assuming that the teacher didn't like their writing. For too many students, the intent of a teacher's comments is "to rip my writing," "to bleed all over my paper," or "to cut me to shreds " Suggestions, notes of encouragement, and even praise are not always noted by student writers. A large number of comments "means" (from the student's perception) that the teacher didn't like the paper, and so another tutorial task is to help students read and interpret teacher response in a different light, not entirely as criticism but as including well-meaning suggestions. For example, a student who came to our Writing Lab had a paper with the following comment: "What is the thread of connection here to your explanation on page 7—that such cultural practices provoke inter-family rivalry?" While the teacher was suggesting some potentially interesting connections for the writer to explore, the writer read that as a comment on her failure to see the connection herself. She needed a tutor to help interpret the intent of that message just as other students need tutors to help them understand the meaning of other kinds of teacher language. It is certainly not the case that all written response fails or that all students draw a complete blank when seeking to comprehend the import of those comments. Some response gets through, but instead of beating our breasts and assuming guilt by failure or taking such findings as indictments of teachers, we need to recognize the reality of language users in different groups straining across chasms to hear each other. If we accept differences in language communities as realities, then we can view the writing center as the institutionalized mechanism to facilitate the flow of otherwise impeded communication.

It follows from this problem of different languages that students often don't understand their assignments (which are, after all, written by teachers, not students). Misunderstanding the assignment happens with such astonishing regularity that we ought more properly to view it as part of the educational process—learning the language of academic communities, learning how to understand that language, and learning how to act on that understanding. John Ackerman, using restraint in reporting on the findings of an extensive research project, notes that "in many cases the assignment given by an instructor and the assignment taken by a student are not a reciprocal fit" (96). Because students often need help in learning how to interpret these writing assignments, it is a frequent topic of tutorial collaboration. An assignment to "interpret" a passage in a literary work is as confusing to some students as an assignment to "interpret" readings in current health care economics is to other students. Other students are overwhelmed by "analyze and compare" assignments or unable to figure out how to respond to what Louise Z. Smith calls a "bewildering array of heuristics" in complex assignments with multiple prompts (465). In composition courses as well as writing-across-the-curriculum courses, students may be unable to plunge in, stymied by an inability to figure out what the assignment is asking for. "We worked on improving his understanding of the assignment" is perhaps one of the most common summaries of tutorial sessions in writing centers. Some students recognize their difficulties with this and come to the center asking that the tutor read the paper to see if it meets the assignment; others come with a draft asking, "Am I on the right track?" Such students are neither stupid nor lazy—they are being honest in acknowledging that they don't have a clear idea of what the assignment is or whether they have managed to write a paper that lands somewhere in the right ballpark. The tutor's task is to help the student see how her long, impassioned narrative of the emotional stresses and strains on her family during a divorce does not meet the assignment to "take a stance on a current societal issue and defend it." Flower sees the frequent tendency to misunderstand or misinterpret assignments in terms of the individual differences students bring to the classroom:

> Students hold some significantly different, tacit representations of supposedly common academic tasks. Because these multifaceted mental representations are constructed from prior experience, from inferences about the social and rhetorical context, and from writers' own values and desires, students may approach a common reading-to-write assignment with meaningfully different sets of goals, strategies, and criteria. These differences can cause problems. Because these representations are often tacit, students and teachers may be in unspoken disagreement about what constitutes an "appropriate" representation. ("Studying Cognition" 21)

Yet despite these differences, says Flower, classroom syllabi assume a homogeneity that doesn't exist, a "one size fits all" situation ("Studying Cognition" 22). Individual differences as well as language confusions must have an appropriate setting in which they can be tended to when the need arises, and the writing center is that place.

To compound the problem of the need for individualized attention to differences in student representations of task assignments, we have to be aware that students are also not always well versed in the shifting conventions in various kinds of academic discourse. An engineering student may need help in understanding why his nuclear engineering report was graded down ("lacks conciseness") for having the kind of extended introductory paragraph that earned A's in his freshman composition course. The student who wrote objective problem statements in her research reports for computer science classes doesn't understand the need for some subjectivity in writing the problem identification section of a research report on a controversial environmental policy in which she has to defend or refute an issue. One instructor may view a nursing student's clinical knowledge as acceptable support; another may require the writer to support that the writer articulate what the problem is. The tutor may assist in identifying which conventions and rules the writer is working with and when the writer has to return to the content teacher for clarification. Occasionally students appear with personal sets of half-understood suggestions that have become rigid and inappropriate rules (Harris, "Contradictory Perceptions"; Rose); at other times, as Terese Thonus has shown us, students learning English as a second language need particular help threading their way through the multiple messages, different criteria, and different standards they encounter in academia.

When Gerald Alred and Erik Thelen note that writing "is bound up with creativity, cognition, language formation, personality, and social interaction" (471), their list nicely captures the sense of a mix of internal variations among writers as well as the outside forces that play upon writers and their texts. Situated as they are to work one-to-one with each writer and his or her needs, tutors can attend to individual differences. Equally important, as students repeatedly tell us in their evaluation comments, tutors work with them in ways that enable and encourage independent thinking and that help them see how to put their theoretical knowledge into practice as they write. Moreover, tutorial interaction helps writers gain confidence in themselves as writers by attending to their affective concerns and assists them in learning what academic language about writing means. Writing centers may still have to contend with a diminishing minority who view them as unnecessary frills, sucking up funds, space, and personnel to duplicate what goes on in the classroom or to coddle remedial students who shouldn't have been admitted in the first place, but as we turn our attention to the work of the tutor, we become increasingly aware that writing instruction without a writing center is only a partial program, lacking essential activities students need in order to grow and mature as writers.

Works Cited

Ackerman, John. "Students' Self-Analysis and Judges' Perceptions: Where Do They Agree?" In *Reading-to-Write: Exploring a Cognitive and Social Process.* Ed. Linda Flower et al. 96-111.

Allen, Nancy. "Developing an Effective Tutorial Style." *Writing Lab Newsletter* 15.3 (November 1990): 1-4.

Alred, Gerald, and Erik Thelen. "Are Textbooks Contributions to Scholarship?" *College Composition and Communication* 44.4 (December 1993): 466-77.

Barnes, Douglas. "Oral Language and Learning." In *Perspectives on Talk and Learning.* Ed. Susan Hynds and Donald Rubin. 41-54.

Bishop, Wendy. "Bringing Writers to the Center: Some Survey Results, Surmises, and Suggestions." *Writing Center Journal* 10.2 (Spring/Summer 1990): 31-44.

Bruffee, Kenneth. "Peer Tutoring and the 'Conversation of Mankind.'" In *Writing Centers: Theory and Administration.* Ed. Gary Olson. Urbana: NCTE, 1984: 3-15.

Burkland, Jill, and Nancy Grimm. "Motivating through Responding." *Journal of Teaching Writing* 5 (1986): 237-47.

Clark, Irene. "Leading the Horse: The Writing Center and Required Visits." *Writing Center Journal* 5.2/6.1 (Spring/Summer 1985; Fall/Winter 1985): 31-34.

Connors, Robert, and Andrea Lunsford. "Teachers' Rhetorical Comments on Student Papers." *College Composition and Communication* 44.2 (May 1993): 200-23.

Flower, Linda. "Negotiating Academic Discourse." In *Reading-to-Write: Exploring a Cognitive and Social Process.* Ed. Linda Flower et al. 221-52.

———. "Studying Cognition in Context." In *Reading-To-Write: Exploring a Cognitive and Social Process.* Ed. Linda Flower et al. 3-32.

Flower, Linda, et al. *Reading-to-Write: Exploring a Cognitive and Social Process.* New York: Oxford UP, 1990.

Harris, Muriel. "Collaboration Is Not Collaboration Is *Not* Collaboration" *College Composition and Communication* 43.1 (February 1992): 369-83.

———. "Contradictory Perceptions of Rules of Writing "*College Composition and Communication* 30.2 (May 1979): 218-20.

———. "Modeling: A Process Method of Teaching." *College English* 45. 1 (January 1983): 74-84.

Hayes, Mary H. and Donald Daiker. "Using Protocol Analysis in Evaluating Responses to Student Writing." *Freshman English News* 13.2 (Fall 1984): 1-4, 10.

Healy, Dave. "late night talk." Posting to the WCenter electronic bulletin board, 13 May 1993.

Hynds, Susan, and Donald Rubin, eds. *Perspectives on Talk and Learning.* Urbana: NCTE, 1990.

Knoblauch, C. H. and Lil Brannon. "Teacher Commentary on Student Writing."

Freshman English News 10 (1981): 1-4.

Onore, Cynthia. "Negotiation, Language, and Inquiry: Building Knowledge Collaboratively in the Classroom." In *Perspectives on Talk and Learning*. Ed. Susan Hynds and Donald Rubin. 57-72.

Phelps, Louise "Practical Wisdom and the Geography of Knowledge in Composition." *College English* 53.8 (December 1991): 863-85.

Pratt, Mary Louise. "Linguistic Utopias." In *Linguistics of Writing: Arguments between Language and Literature*. Ed. Nigel Fabb. New York: Methuen, 1987. 48-66.

Rose, Mike. "Rigid Rules, Inflexible Plans, and the Stifling of Language: A Cognitivist Analysis of Writer's Block." *College Composition and Communication* 31.4 (December 1980): 389-401.

Smith, Louise Z. "Composing Composition Courses." *College English* 46.5 (September 1984): 460-69.

Thonus, Terese. "Tutors as Teachers: Assisting ESL/EFL Students in the Writing Center." Writing *Center Journal* 13.2 (Spring 1993): 13-26.

Towns, Cheryl Hofstetter. "Dumbo or Colleague: Our Professional Perceptions of Students." *Composition Studies/Freshman English News* 21.1 (Spring 1993): 94-103.

Walker, Carolyn, and David Elias. "Writing Conference Talk: Factors Associated for High- and Low-Rated Writing Conferences." *Research in the Teaching of English* 21.3 (1987): 226-85.

Bibliography

In this edition, I've made an attempt to broaden the range of journals consulted and the variety of approaches represented. In particular, articles on basic writing, teaching to non-traditional students, gender, reading, and computers in writing instruction have been beefed up. The multiplicity of approaches in rhetoric and composition scholarship means that many of these works could easily be listed in several sections. Therefore, please review any relevant sections to make sure you find all the works you're looking for.

Abbreviations

CCC	College Composition and Communication
CE	College English
CEA	College English Association
EE	English Education
EJ	English Journal
JAC	Journal of Advanced Composition
RR	Rhetoric Review
RTE	Research in the Teaching of English
TETYC	Teaching English in the Two-Year College

Theory: Literary and Rhetorical

Atkins, G. Douglas. *Reading Deconstruction/Deconstructive Reading.* Lexington: U P of Kentucky, 1983.

Bakhtin, Mikhail. *Marxism and the Philosophy of Language.* NY: Pantheon, 1972.

Barthes, Roland. *Image—Music—Text.* NY: Hill and Wang, 1977.

Berlin, James. "Rhetoric and Ideology in the Writing Class." *CE* 50 (1988): 477-494.

Berlin, James A., and Michael J. Vivion, eds. *Cultural Studies in the English Classroom.* Portsmouth: Boynton/Cook Heinemann, 1993.

Berthoff, Ann. *The Making of Meaning: Metaphors, Models, and Maxims for Writing Teachers.* NJ: Boynton/Cook, 1981.

———. *Reclaiming the Imagination: Philosophical Perspectives for Writers and Teachers of Writing.* NJ: Boynton/Cook, 1984.

Bitzer, Lloyd F. "The Rhetorical Situation." *Philosophy and Rhetoric* 1.1 (1968): 1-14.

Bizzell, Patricia. "Arguing about Literacy." *CE* 50 (1988): 141-153.

———. "Beyond Anti-Foundationalism to Rhetorical Authority: Problems Defining 'Cultural Literacy'." *CE* 52 (1990): 661-675.

Bizzell, Patricia, and Bruce Herzberg, eds. *The Rhetorical Tradition: Readings From Classical Times to the Present.* Boston: Bedford Books of St. Martin's, 1990.

Blum, Jack. "Postructural Theories and the Postmodern Attitude in Contemporary Composition." In W. Ross Winterowd, *Composition in the Rhetorical Tradition.* Urbana: NCTE, 1994. 92-111.

Booth, Wayne C. "The Rhetorical Stance." *CCC* 14 (1963): 139-145.

Burhans, Clinton S., Jr. "The Teaching of Writing and the Knowledge Gap." *CE* 45 (1983): 639-656.

Burke, Kenneth. *A Grammar of Motives.* Englewood Cliffs, NJ: Prentice Hall, 1945.

Chase, Geoffrey. "Accommodation, Resistance, and the Politics of Student Writing." *CCC* 39 (1988): 13-22.

Christensen, Francis. *Notes Toward a New Rhetoric.* NY: Harper, 1967.

Clifford, John. "The Neopragmatic Scene of Theory and Practice in Composition." *RR* 10 (1991): 100-107.

Clifford, John, and John Schilb, eds. *Writing Theory and Critical Theory.* NY: MLA, 1994.

Coles, William E., Jr. *Composing: Writing as a Self-Creating Process.* Rochelle Park, NJ: Hayden, 1974.

Corbett, Edward P. J. "Literature and Composition: Allies or Rivals in the Classroom?" In *Composition and Literature: Bridging the Gap,* ed. Winifred Bryan Horner. Chicago: U Chicago P, 1983. 168-184.

Corder, Jim W. "On the Way, Perhaps, to a New Rhetoric, but Not There Yet, and If We Do Get There, There Won't Be There Anymore." *CE* 47 (1985):162-170.

Craige, Betty Jean, ed. *Literature, Language, and Politics.* Athens: U Georgia P, 1988.

Crusius, Timothy W. *Discourse: A Critique and Synthesis of Major Theories.* NY: MLA, 1989.

D'Angelo, Frank. *A Conceptual Theory of Rhetoric.* Cambridge, MA: Winthrop, 1975.

de Beaugrande, Robert. "Writer, Reader, Critic: Comparing Critical Theories as Discourse." *CE* 46 (1984): 533-559.

Derrida, Jacques. *Of Grammatology.* 1967; Baltimore: Johns Hopkins U P, 1976.

Dillon, George L. *Constructing Texts: Elements of a Theory of Composition and Style*. Bloomington: U Indiana P, 1981.

———. *Rhetoric as Social Imagination*. Bloomington: U Indiana P, 1986.

Eagleton, Terry. *Literary Theory: An Introduction*. Minneapolis: U Minnesota P, 1983.

Eco, Umberto. *The Role of the Reader*. Bloomington: Indiana U P, 1979.

Eddins, Dwight. "Yellow Wood, Diverging Pedagogies; Or, The Joy of Text." *CE* 51 (1989): 571-576.

Fish, Stanley. *Is There a Text in This Class?* Cambridge: Harvard U P, 1980.

Fishman, Stephen M., and Lucille McCarthy. "Community in the Expressivist Classroom: Juggling Liberal and Communitarian Visions." *CE* 57.1 (1995): 62-81.

Fleishman, Avrom. "Changing the Subject: Origins and Outcomes in English." *South Atlantic Review* 61.2 (1996): 69-105.

Foucault, Michel. *The Archaeology of Knowledge*. 1969; NY: Pantheon, 1972.

Freedman, Aviva, and Ian Pringle. *Reinventing the Rhetorical Tradition*. Conway, AK: L&S Books for the Canadian Council of Teachers of English, 1980.

Freire, Paolo. *Pedagogy of the Oppressed*. NY: Seabury, 1968.

Freund, Elizabeth. *The Return of the Reader: Reader-Response Criticism*. London: Methuen, 1987.

Fulkerson, Richard. "Composition Theory in the Eighties: Axiological Consensus and Paradigmatic Diversity." *CCC* 41 (1990): 409-429.

Gould, Christopher, and Kathleen Gould. "College Anthologies of Readings and Assumptions about Literacy." *CCC* 37 (1986): 204-211.

Graff, Gerald. "Debate the Canon in Class." *Harper's* (April 1991): 31 ff.

Greene, Stuart. "Toward a Dialectal Theory of Composing." *RR* 9 (1990): 149-172.

Hatlen, Burton. "Michel Foucault and the Discourse[s] of English." *CE* 50 (1988): 786-801.

Holzman, Michael. "The Social Context of Literacy Education." *CE* 48 (1986): 27-33.

Horgan, Paul. *Approaches to Writing*. 2nd ed. Middletown, CT: Wesleyan, 1973.

Hymes, Dell. "The Ethnography of Speaking." *Readings in the Sociology of Language*. Ed. Joshua A. Fishmann. The Hague: Mouton, 1968. 99-138.

Iser, Wolfgang. *The Implied Reader*. 1972; Baltimore: Johns Hopkins U P, 1974.

Kelly, George A. *A Theory of Personality: The Psychology of Personal Constructs*. NY: Norton, 1963.

Kennedy, George A. *Classical Rhetoric and Its Christian and Secular Tradition from Ancient to Modern Times*. Chapel Hill: UNC P, 1980.

Kent, Thomas. "On the Very Idea of a Discourse Community." *CCC* 42 (1991): 425-445.

Kinneavy, James. "A Pluralistic Synthesis of Four Models for Teaching Composition." In *Reinventing the Rhetorical Tradition*, ed. Aviva Freedman and Ian Pringle. Conway, AK: L&S Books for the Canadian Council of Teachers of English, 1980. 37-52.

Kinneavy, James. *A Theory of Discourse*. 1971; NY: Norton, 1980.

Knoblauch, C. H., and Lil Brannon. *Rhetorical Traditions and the Teaching of Writing*. NJ: Boynton/Cook, 1984.

Kostelnick, Charles. "Process Paradigms in Design and Composition: Affinities and Directions." *CCC* 40 (1989): 267-281.

Kraft, Quentin G. "Toward a Critical Re-renewal: At the Corner of Camus and Bloom Streets." *CE* 54 (1992): 46-62.

Kuhn, Thomas S. *The Structure of Scientific Revolutions*. 2nd. ed., enlarged. Chicago: U Chicago P, 1970.

Leitch, Vincent B. "The Lateral Dance: The Deconstructive Criticism of J. Hillis Miller." Critical Inquiry 6 (1980): 593-607.

Lynn, Stephen. "A Passage into Critical Theory." *CE* 52 (1990): 258-271.

———. "Reading the Writing Process: Toward a Theory of Current Pedagogies." *CE* 49 (1987): 902-910.

McEwan, Hunter. "Five Metaphors for English." *EE* 24 (1992): 101-128.

Moffett, James. *Teaching the Universe of Discourse*. Boston: Houghton, 1968.

Murphy, James J., ed. *A Short History of Writing Instruction from Ancient Greece to Twentieth-Century America*. Davis, CA: Hermagoras, 1990.

———. *The Rhetorical Tradition and Modern Writing*. NY: MLA, 1982.

Newkirk, Thomas, ed. *Only Connect: Uniting Reading and Writing*. NJ: Boynton/Cook, 1986.

North, Stephen M. *The Making of Knowledge in Composition: Portrait of an Emerging Field*. NJ: Boynton/Cook, 1987.

Parker, Robert P. "Theories of Writing Instruction: Having Them, Using Them, Changing Them." *EE* 20 (1988): 18-40.

Parker, Robert P., and Vera Goodkin. *The Consequences of Writing*. NJ: Boynton/Cook, 1987.

Pattison, Robert. *On Literacy: The Politics of the Word from Homer to the Age of Rock*. NY: Oxford, 1982.

Perelman, Les. "The Context of Classroom Writing." *CE* 48 (1986): 471-479.

Phelps, Louise Weatherbee. *Composition as a Human Science: Contributions to the Self-Understanding of a Discipline*. NY: Oxford, 1988.

———. "Practical Wisdom and the Geography of Knowledge in Composition." *CE* 53 (1991): 863-885.

Polyani, Michael. *Personal Knowledge: Towards a Post-Critical Philosophy.* Chicago: U Chicago P, 1969.

Poovey, Mary. "Cultural Criticism: Past and Present." *CE* 52 (1990): 615-625.

Purdy, Dwight. "A Polemical History of Freshman Composition in Our Time." *CE* 48 (1986): 791-796.

Raymond, James C. "What Good Is All This Heady, Esoteric Theory?" *TETYC* 17 (1990): 11-17.

Richter, David H., ed. *The Critical Tradition: Classic Texts and Contemporary Trends.* NY: St. Martin's, 1989.

Rosenblatt, Louise. *Literature as Exploration.* 1938; NY: MLA, 1983.

———. *The Reader, the Text, the Poem: The Transactional Theory of the Literary Text.* Carbondale: S. Illinois U P, 1978.

Saussure, Ferdinand. *Course in General Linguistics.* 1916; NY: Philosophical Library, 1959.

Schilb, John. "What's at Stake in the Conflict between 'Theory' and 'Practice' in Composition?" *RR* 10 (1991): 91-97.

Scholes, Robert. *Textual Power: Literary Theory and the Teaching of English.* Yale, 1985.

Sledd, James. "Product in Process: From Ambiguities of Standard English to Issues That Divide Us." *CE* 50 (1988): 168-176.

Sledd, Andrew. "'Readin' not Riotin': The Politics of Literacy." *CE* 50 (1988): 495-508.

Smith, Robert E., III. "Hymes, Rorty, and the Social Construction of Meaning." *CE* 54 (1992): 138-158.

Tate, Gary, and Edward P. J. Corbett, eds. *The Writing Teacher's Sourcebook.* NY: Oxford, 1981.

Tompkins, Jane. "Pedagogy of the Distressed." *CE* 52.6 (1990): 653-660.

———. "A Short Course in Post-Structuralism." *CE* 50 (1988): 733-747.

Tuman, Myron C. *A Preface to Literacy: An Inquiry into Pedagogy, Practice, and Progress.* University, AL: U Alabama P, 1987.

White, Edward M. "Post-Structural Literary Criticism and the Response to Student Writing." *CCC* 35 (1984): 186-195.

Winterowd, W. Ross. *Composition in the Rhetorical Tradition.* Urbana: NCTE, 1994.

———. "The Purification of Language and Rhetoric." *CE* 49 (1987): 257-273.

Overviews of and Perspectives on Pedagogy and Composition Theory

Adler, Mortimer J. "Beyond Indoctrination: The Quest for Genuine Learning." *What Teachers Need to Know: The Knowledge, Skills, and Values Essential to Good Teaching.* Ed. David D. Dill and associates. San Francisco: Jossey-Bass, 1990. 157-165.

Albritton, Tom. "Honest Questions and the Teaching of English." *EE* 24 (1992): 91-100.

Anson, Chris M. "A Computerized List of Journals Publishing Articles in Composition." *CCC* 37 (1986): 154-166.

Anson, Chris M., Joan Graham, David A. Jolliffe, Nancy S. Shapiro, and Carolyn Smith. *Scenarios for Teaching Writing: Contexts for Discussion and Reflective Practice.* Urbana: NCTE, 1993.

Anson, Chris M., and Hildy Miller. "Journals in Composition: An Update." *CCC* 39 (1988): 198-216.

Applebee, Arthur M. *Writing in the Secondary School: English and the Content Areas.* NCTE Research Report No. 21. Urbana IL: NCTE, 1981.

Atchity, Kenneth. *A Writer's Time: A Guide to the Creative Process, from Vision through Revision.* Norton, 1986.

Bartholmae, David, and Anthony Petrosky. *Facts, Counterfacts, Artifacts: Theory and Method for a Reading and Writing Course.* Boynton/Cook, 1986.

Bassett, John E. "Confronting Change: English As A Social Science?" *CE* 57.3 (1995): 319-333.

Bazerman, Charles. *Constructing Experience.* Carbondale: Southern Illinois UP, 1994.

Beard, Ruth M. *An Outline of Piaget's Developmental Psychology for Students and Teachers.* NY: New American Library, 1969.

Bishop, Wendy, ed. *The Subject Is Writing: Essays by Teachers and Students.* Portsmouth: Boynton/Cook Heinemann, 1993.

Bizzell, Patricia, and Bruce Herzberg. *The Bedford Bibliography for Teachers of Writing.* 4th ed. Boston: Bedford, 1996.

Booth, Wayne C. *The Vocation of a Teacher: Rhetorical Occasions, 1967-1988.* Chicago: U Chicago P, 1988.

Britton, James, et al. *The Development of Writing Abilities (11-18).* London: Macmillan, 1975.

Calkins, Lucy McCormick. *The Art of Teaching Writing.* Portsmouth, NH: Heinemann, 1986.

Christensen, Norman F. "Avoidance Pedagogy in Freshman English." *TETYC* 18 (1991): 133-136.

Cooper, Marilyn, and Michael Holzman. "Talking about Protocols." *CCC* 34 (1983): 284-293.

Daniel, Beth, and Art Young. "Resisting Writing/Resisting Writing Teachers." In *The Subject is Writing.* Ed. Wendy Bishop. Portsmouth: Boynton/Cook Heinemann, 1993. 223-234.

David, Denise, Barbara Gordon, and Rita Pollard. "Seeking Common Ground: Guiding Assumptions for Writing Courses." *CCC* 46.4 (1995): 522-532.

Devine, Thomas G. "Caveat Emptor: The Writing Process Approach to College Writing." *Journal of Developmental Education* 14.1 (1990): 2-4.

Dobrin, David N. "Protocols Once More." *CE* 48 (1986): 713-25.

Dunstan, Angus, Judy Kirscht, John Reiff, Marjorie Roemer, and Nick Tingle. "Grounding Theory in Practice in the Composition Class." *Journal of Teaching Writing* 9.2 (1990): 159-174.

Eble, Kenneth E. *The Craft of Teaching: A Guide to Mastering the Professor's Art.* 2nd ed. San Francisco: Jossey-Bass, 1988.

Elbow, Peter. "Embracing Contraries in the Teaching Process." *CE* 45 (1983): 327-339.

Emig, Janet. *The Composing Processes of Twelfth Graders.* Urbana, IL: NCTE, 1971.

———. *The Web of Meaning.* Boynton/Cook, 1983.

Faigley, Lester. "Competing Theories of Process: A Critique and a Proposal." *CE* 48 (1986): 527-542.

Farber, Jerry. "Learning to Teach: A Progress Report." *CE* 52 (1990): 135-141.

Flower, Linda. *The Construction of Negotiated Meaning: A Social Cognitive Theory of Meaning.* Carbondale: Southern Illinois UP, 1994.

———. "The Construction of Purpose in Writing and Reading." *CE* 50 (1988): 528-550.

Flower, Linda, and John R. Hayes. "A Cognitive Process Theory of Writing." *CCC* 32 (1981): 365-387.

Foster, David. *A Primer for Writing Teachers: Theories, Theorists, Issues, Problems.* NJ: Boynton/Cook, 1983.

Gebhardt, Richard C. "Unifying Diversity in the Training of Writing Teachers." In *Training the New Teacher of College Composition,* ed. Charles W. Bridges. Urbana, IL: NCTE, 1986. 1-12.

George, Diana. "Who Teaches the Teacher? A Note on the Craft of Teaching College Composition." *CE* 51 (1989): 418-423.

Graves, Richard L., ed. *Rhetoric and Composition: A Sourcebook for Teachers and Writers.* Boynton/Cook, first edition 1976; second edition, 1983; third edition, 1990.

Haefner, Joel. "Democracy, Pedagogy, and the Personal Essay." *CE* 54 (1992): 127-137.

Hairston, Maxine. "Different Products, Different Processes: A Theory about Writing." *CCC* 37 (1986): 442-452.

———. "The Winds of Change: Thomas Kuhn and the Revolution in the Teaching of Writing," *CCC* 33 (1982): 76-88.

Harris, Muriel. "Don't Believe Everything You're Taught: Matching Writing

Processes and Personal Preferences." In *The Subject is Writing*, ed. Wendy Bishop. Portsmouth: Boynton/Cook Heinemann, 1993. 189-201.

Harste, Jerome C., Virginia A. Woodward, and Carolyn L. Burke. *Language Stories and Literacy Lessons.* Portsmouth, NH: Heinemann, 1984.

Hashimoto, Irvin Y. *Thirteen Weeks: A Guide to Teaching College Writing.* Portsmouth, NH: Boynton Cook/Heinemann, 1991.

Hatch, Gary Layne. "Reviving the Rodential Model for Composition: Robert Zoellner's Alternative to Flower and Hayes." *RR* 10 (1992): 244-249.

Hayes, John R., and Linda S. Flower. "Writing Research and the Writer." *American Psychologist* 41.10 (1986): 1106-1113.

Heilker, Paul. "Public Products/Public Processes: Zoellner's Praxis and the Contemporary Composition Classroom." *RR* 10 (1992): 232-238.

Hilbert, Betsy S. "It Was a Dark and Nasty Night It Was a Dark and You Would Not Believe How Dark It Was a Hard Beginning." *CCC* 43 (1992): 75-80.

Hoffman, Eleanor M., and John P. Schifsky. "Designing Writing Assignments." *EJ* 66 (1977): 41-45.

Irmscher, William. *Teaching Expository Writing.* NY: Holt, 1979.

Jacoby, Jay. "Authority in English 102: Whose Text Is It Anyway?" *CEA Critic* 52 (1989/1990): 2-12.

Lindemann, Erika, ed. *The Longman Bibliography of Composition and Rhetoric.* (1984–, continued as *The College Composition and Communication Bibliography of Composition and Rhetoric*).

———. *A Rhetoric for Writing Teachers*, 3rd edition. NY: Oxford, 1995.

———. "Teaching as a Rhetorical Art," *CEA Forum* 15.2 (1985): 9-12.

Lindemann, Erika, and Gary Tate, eds. *An Introduction to Composition Studies.* Oxford, 1991.

McAndrew, Donald A. "That Isn't What We Did in High School: Big Changes in the Teaching of Writing." In *The Subject is Writing*, ed. Wendy Bishop. Portsmouth: Boynton/Cook Heinemann, 1993. 31-38.

O'Donnell, Thomas. "Politics and Ordinary Language: A Defense of Expressivist Rhetorics." *CE* 58.4 (1996): 423-439.

Passmore, John. *The Philosophy of Teaching.* London: Duckworth, 1980.

Ponsot, Marie, and Rosemary Deen. *Beat Not the Poor Desk! Writing: What to Teach, How to Teach It, and Why.* NJ: Boynton/Cook, 1982.

Reither, James A. "Writing and Knowing: Toward Redefining the Writing Process." *CE* 47 (1985): 620-628.

Ruskiewicz, John J. "Training Teachers is a Process, Too." *CCC* 38 (1987): 462-463.

Scott, Patrick, and Bruce Castner. "Reference Sources for Composition Research: A Practical Survey." *CE* 45 (1983): 756-768.

Shaughnessy, Mina. *Errors and Expectations: A Guide for the Teacher of Basic Writing*. NY: Oxford, 1977.

Stevens, Scott. "Serious Work: Students Learning from Students." *JAC* 16.2 (1996): 313-324.

Stewart, Donald. "Collaborative Learning and Composition: Boon or Bane?" *RR* 7 (1988): 58-85.

Stice, James E., ed. *Developing Critical Thinking and Problem-Solving Abilities*. San Francisco: Jossey-Bass, 1987.

Sullivan, Patricia A. "Social Constructionism and Literacy Studies." *CE* 57.8 (1995): 950-959.

Summerfield, Judith, and Geoffrey Summerfield. *Texts and Contexts: A Contribution to the Theory and Practice of Teaching Composition*. NY: Random House, 1986.

Swales, John. "Dicourse Communities, Genres, and English as an International Language." *World Englishes* 7 (1988): 211-220.

Tate, Gary, ed. *Teaching Composition: Twelve Bibliographical Essays*. Revised and enlarged edition. Fort Worth: TCU Press, 1987.

Tibbetts, Arn, and Charlene Tibbetts. "Can Composition Textbooks Use Composition Research?" *CE* 44 (1982): 855-858.

Tobin, Lad. "Reading Students, Reading Ourselves: Revising the Teacher's Role in the Writing Class." *CE* 53 (1991): 333-348.

Tremmel, Robert. "A Habit of Mind." *EE* 24 (1992): 20-33.

Walters, Margaret Bennett. "Robert Zoellner's 'Talk-Write Pedagogy': Instrumental Concept for Composition Today." *RR* 10 (1992): 239-243.

Weimer, Maryellen. "Scholarship of Teaching." *Journal of the Freshman Year Experience* 3 (1992): 41-58.

Welch, Kathleen E. "Ideology and Freshman Textbook Production: The Place of Theory in Writing Pedagogy." *CCC* 38 (1987): 269-282.

Winterowd, W. Ross. "A Philosophy of Composition." *RR* 9 (1991): 340-347.

Young, Richard E., Alton L. Becker, and Kenneth L. Pike. *Rhetoric: Discovery and Change*. NY: Harcourt, 1970.

Zoellner, Robert. "Talk-Write: A Behavioral Pedagogy for Composition." *CE* 30 (1969): 267-320.

Praxis: Intervening in the Writing Process

Teaching about Prewriting and Audience

Boley, Thomas J. "A Heuristic for Persuasion." *CCC* 30 (1979): 187-191.

Coles, William E., Jr. *The Plural I: The Teaching of Writing*. NY: Holt, 1978.

Corbett, Edward P. J. *Classical Rhetoric for the Modern Student*. NY: Oxford, 1989.

———. *The Little English Handbook.* 5th ed. Glenview, IL: Scott, Foresman, 1986.

Ede, Lisa, and Andrea Lunsford. "Audience Addressed/Audience Invoked: The Role of Audience in Composition Theory and Pedagogy." *CCC* 35 (1984): 155-171.

———. "Representing Audience: 'Successful' Discourse and Disciplinary Critique." *CCC* 47.2 (1996): 167-179.

Elbow, Peter. *Writing with Power.* NY: Oxford, 1981.

———. *Writing without Teachers.* Oxford, 1973.

Fleckstein, Kristie S. "Progress Logs: Teaching Writing Process Awareness." *TETYC* 16 (1989): 106-112.

Flower, Linda. "Cognition, Context, and Theory Building." *CCC* 40 (1989): 282-311.

———. "Writer-Based Prose: A Cognitive Basis for Problems in Writing." *CE* 41 (1979): 19-37.

Fulwiler, Toby. *The Journal Book.* NJ: Boynton/Cook, 1987.

Kneupper, Charles W. "Revising the Tagmemic Heuristic: Theoretical and Pedagogical Considerations." *CCC* 31 (1980): 160-168.

Larson, Richard L. "Discovery through Questioning." *CE* 30 (1968): 126-134.

Lauer, Janice M., Gene Montague, Andrea Lunsford, and Janet Emig. *Four Worlds of Writing.* NY: Harper, 1981.

Macrorie, Ken. *Searching Writing.* NJ: Boynton/Cook, 1980.

———. *Writing to be Read.* Rev. 3rd ed. NJ: Boynton/Cook, 1984.

———. *Uptaught!* NJ: Boynton/Cook, 1980.

Memering, Dean, and Frank O'Hare. *The Writer's Work.* Englewood Cliffs, NJ: Prentice, 1980.

Moffett, James. *Active Voices.* NJ: Boynton/Cook, 1986.

Moffett, James, and Betty Jane Wagner. *Student-Centered Language Arts and Reading, K-12.* 4th ed. Portsmouth, NH: Boynton/Cook/Heinemann, 1991.

Murray, Donald. *Colleague in the Classroom.* NY: Houghton, 1986.

———. *A Writer Teaches Writing.* 2nd ed. Boston: Houghton, 1985.

Neeld, Elizabeth Cowan. *Writing.* 2nd. ed. Glenview, IL: Scott Foresman, 1986.

Ong, Walter S., S. J. "The Writer's Audience is Always a Fiction." *PMLA* 90 (1975): 9-21.

Park, Douglas B. "Analyzing Audiences," *CCC* 37 (1986): 478-488.

Rider, Janine. "Must Imitation Be the Mother of Invention?" *Journal of Teaching Writing* 9.2 (1990): 175-185.

Rohman, D. Gordon, and Albert O. Wlecke. *Pre-Writing: The Construction and Application of Models for Concept-Formation in Writing.* USOE Cooperative Research Project No. 2174. East Lansing, MI: Michigan State U, 1964.

Stotsky, Sandra. "On Planning and Writing Plans—Or Beware of Borrowed Theories." *CCC* 41 (1990): 37-57.

Wallace, Karl. "Topoi and the Problem of Invention." *Quarterly Journal of Speech* 58 (1972): 387-395.

Winterowd, W. Ross. *Contemporary Rhetoric.* Boston: Houghton, 1979.

Witte, Stephen P. "Pre-Text and Composing." *CCC* 38 (1987): 397-425.

Teaching about Drafting, Organization, and Structure

Bain, Alexander. *English Composition and Rhetoric: A Manual.* American Edition (revised) 1866; NY: Appleton, 1980.

D'Angelo, Frank. "Tropics of Arrangement: A Theory of *Dispositio.*" *JAC* 10(1990): 101-109.

Fahnestock, Jeanne, and Marie Secor. "Teaching Argument: A Theory of Types." *CCC* 34 (1983): 20-30.

Harris, Muriel. "Composing Behaviors of One- and Multi-Draft Writers." *CE* 51 (1989): 174-191.

Irmscher, William. *The Holt Guide to English.* 3rd ed. NY: Holt, 1981.

Kostelnick, Charles. "Process Paradigms in Design and Composition: Affinities and Directions." *CCC* 40 (1989): 267-281.

Krest, Margie. "Monitoring Student Writing: How Not to Avoid the Draft." *Journal of Teaching Writing* 7 (1988): 27-39.

Witte, Stephen, and Lester Faigley. "Coherence, Cohesion, and Writing Quality." *CCC* 32 (May 1981): 189-204.

Teaching about Revision: Paragraphs, Sentences, Words

Braddock, Richard. "The Frequency and Placement of Topic Sentences in Expository Prose." *RTE* 8 (1974): 287-302.

Christensen, Francis. "A Generative Rhetoric of the Sentence." *CCC* 14 (1963): 155-161.

Daiker, Donald, Andrew Kerek, Max Morenberg, eds. *Sentence Combining and the Teaching of Writing.* Conway, AK: L&S Books, 1979.

Faigley, Lester, and Stephen Witte. "Analyzing Revision." *CCC* 32 (1981): 527-542.

Flower, Linda, John R. Hayes, Linda Carey, Karen Schriver, and James Stratman. "Detection, Diagnosis, and the Strategies of Revision." *CCC* 37 (1986): 16-55.

Haswell, Richard H. "Textual Research and Coherence: Findings, Intuition, Application." *CE* 51 (1989): 305-319.

Huff, Roland K. "Teaching Revision: A Model of the Drafting Process." *CE* 45 (1983): 800-816.

Lutz, William. *Doublespeak: From "Revenue Enhancement" to "Terminal Living," How Government, Business, Advertisers, and Others Use Language to Deceive You*. NY: Harper, 1989.

Mohr, Marian M. *Revision: The Rhythm of Meaning*. NJ: Boynton/Cook, 1982.

O'Hare, Frank. *Sentence Combining: Improving Student Writing Without Formal Grammar Instruction*. Urbana, IL: NCTE, 1973.

Sommers, Nancy. "Revision Strategies of Student Writers and Experienced Writers." *CCC* 31 (1980): 378-388.

Wall, Susan V. "The Languages of the Text: What Even Good Students Need to Know about Re-Writing." *Journal of Advanced Composition* 7 (1987): 31-40.

Williams, Joseph. *Style: Toward Clarity and Grace*. 4th ed. NY: Harper, 1991.

Willis, Meredith Sue. *Deep Revision: A Guide for Teachers, Students, and Other Writers*. NY: Teachers and Writers Collaborative, 1993.

Witte, Stephen. Review of *Sentence Combining and the Teaching of Writing*, ed. Donald Daiker et al. *CCC* 31 (1980): 433-437.

Teaching about Editing

Harris, Jeannette. "Proofreading: A Reading/Writing Skill." *CCC* 38 (1987): 464-465.

Hartwell, Patrick. "Grammar, Grammars, and the Teaching of Grammar." CE 47 (1985): 105-127.

Hunt, Kellogg. *Grammatical Structures Written at Three Grade Levels*. Urbana, IL: NCTE, 1965.

Hunter, Susan, and Ray Wallace, eds. *The Place of Grammar in Writing Instruction: Past, Present, Future*. Portsmouth: Boynton/Cook Heinemann, 1994.

Kutz, Eleanor. "'Must I Watch My Language?' Linguistic Knowledge and the Writer." In *The Subject is Writing*, ed. Wendy Bishop. Portsmouth: Boynton/Cook Heinemann, 1993. 40-52.

Meyer, Charles F. "Teaching Punctuation to Advanced Writers." *JAC* 6 (1985 - 1986): 117-129.

Noguchi, Rei I. *Grammar and the Teaching of Writing: Limits and Possibilities*. Urbana, IL: NCTE, 1991.

Weaver, Constance. *Grammar for Teachers: Perspectives and Definitions*. NCTE, 1979.

———. *Teaching Grammar in Context*. Portsmouth: Boynton/Cook Heinemann, 1996.

Evaluation of Students and Teachers

Allen, Jo. "Approaches to Teaching: A Machiavellian Approach to Grading Writing Assignments." *Technical Writing Teacher* 15 (1988): 158-160.

Anson, Chris M., ed. *Writing and Response: Theory, Practice, and Research.* Urbana: NCTE, 1989.

Auten, Janet Gebhart. "A Rhetoric of Teacher Commentary: The Complexity of Response to Student Writing." *Focuses* 4 (1991): 3-18.

Bain, Robert. "A Framework for Judging." *CCC* 25 (1974): 307-309.

Bartholomae, David. "The Study of Error." *CCC* 31 (1980): 253-269.

Belanoff, Pat. "What Is A Grade?" In *The Subject Is Writing*, ed. Wendy Bishop. Portsmouth, NH: Boynton/Cook Heinemann, 1993. 179-187.

Belanoff, Pat, and Marcia Dickson, eds. *Portfolios: Process and Product.* Portsmouth, NH: Boynton/Cook/Heinemann, 1991.

Black, Laurel, Donald A. Daiker, Jeffrey Sommers, and Gail Stygall, eds. *New Directions in Portfolio Assessment: Reflective Practice, Critical Theory, and Large-Scale Scoring.* Portsmouth: Boynton/Cook Heinemann, 1994.

Connors, Robert J., and Andrea A. Lunsford. "Frequency of Formal Errors in Current College Writing, or Ma and Pa Kettle Do Research." *CCC* 39 (1988): 395-409.

———. "Teachers' Rhetorical Comments on Student Papers." *CCC* 44 (1993): 200-23.

Cooper, Charles R., and Lee Odell, eds. *Evaluating Writing: Describing, Measuring, Judging.* NCTE, 1977.

Dragga, Sam. "The Effects of Praiseworthy Grading on Students and Teachers." *Journal of Teaching Writing* 7 (1988): 41-50.

Elbow, Peter. "Ranking, Evaluating, and Liking: Sorting Out Three Forms of Judgment." *CE* 55.2 (1993): 187-206.

"Evaluating Instruction in Writing: Approaches and Instruments." *CCC* 33 (1982): 213-229.

Faigley, Lester. "Judging Writing, Judging Selves." *CCC* 40 (1989): 395-412.

Fuller, David. "A Curious Case of Our Responding Habits: What Do We Respond to and Why?" *JAC* 8 (1988): 88-96.

Greenburg, Karen L. "Assessing Writing: Theory and Practice." *New Directions for Teaching and Learning* 34 (Summer 1988): 47-58.

Hairston, Maxine. "Not All Errors Are Created Equal: Nonacademic Readers in the Professions Respond to Lapses in Usage." *CE* 41 (1982): 794-806.

Haswell, Richard H. "Minimal Marking," *CE* 45 (1983): 600-604.

Herter, Roberta J. "Writing Portfolios: Alternatives to Testing." *EJ* 80.1 (1991): 90-91.

Hunt, Alan J. "Taped Comments and Student Writing." *TETYC* 16 (1989): 269-273.

Huot, Brian. "Reliability, Validity, and Holistic Scoring: What We Know and What We Need to Know." *CCC* 41 (1990): 201-213.

Lawson, Bruce, Susan Sterr Ryan, and W. Ross Winterowd, eds. *Encountering Student Texts: Interpretative Issues in Reading Student Writing.* Urbana, IL: NCTE, 1989.

Machina, Kenton. "Evaluating Student Evaluations." *Academe* (May-June1987): 19-22.

Marting, Janet. "Writers on Writing: Self-Assessment Strategies for Student Essays." *TETYC* 18 (1991): 128-132.

Rule, Rebecca. "Conferences and Workshops: Conversations on Writing in Progress." In *Nuts and Bolts: A Practical Guide to Teaching College Composition.* Ed. Thomas Newkirk. Portsmouth: Boynton/Cook Heinemann, 1993. 43-66.

Sommers, Nancy. "Responding to Student Writing," *CCC* 33 (1982): 148-156.

Stanford, Gene, ed. *Classroom Practices in Teaching English 1979 -1980: How to Handle the Paper Load.* Urbana, IL: NCTE, 1979.

Straub, Richard. "The Concept of Control in Teacher Response: Defining the Varieties of 'Directive' and 'Facilitative' Commentary." *CCC* 47.2 (1996): 223-251.

———. "Teacher Response as Conversation: More than Casual Talk, an Exploration." *RR* 14.2 (1996): 374-399.

White, Edward. *Assigning, Responding, Evaluating: A Writing Teacher's Guide.* NY: St. Martin's, 1995.

———. *Teaching and Assessing Writing.* San Francisco: Jossey-Bass, 1985.

Wiener, Harvey S. "Collaborative Learning in the Classroom: A Guide to Evaluation." *CE* 48 (1986): 52-61.

Witte, Stephen, and Lester Faigley. *Evaluating College Writing Programs.* Carbondale: S. Illinois U P, 1983.

Computers in Writing Instruction

Hawisher, Gail E., and Cynthia L. Selfe. "The Rhetoric of Technology and the Electronic Writing Class." *CCC* 42 (1991): 55-65.

Moran, Charles. "Computers and English: What Do We Make of Each Other?" Review. *CE* 54 (1992): 193-198.

Rice, H. William. "Computers in Freshman English." *TETYC* 16 (1989): 29-34.

Sadler, Lynn Veach. "The Computer-and-Effective Writing Movement: Computer-Assisted Instruction." *ADE Bulletin* 87 (Fall 1987): 28-33.

Schwartz, Helen J. "Computer Perspectives: Mapping New Territories." Review. *CE* 54 (1992): 207-212.

Selfe, Cynthia L. and Susan Hilligloss, eds. *Literacy and Computers: The Complications of Teaching and Learning with Technology.* NY: MLA, 1994.

Valeri-Gold, Maria, and Mary P. Deming. "Computers and Basic Writing: A Research Update." *Journal of Developmental Education* 14.3 (1991): 10-12, 14.

Vockell, Edward L., and Eileen Schwartz. "Microcomputers to Teaching English Composition." *Collegiate Microcomputer* 6 (1988): 148-154.

Wepner, Shelley B. "Reading, Writing, and Word Processing." *Reading Psychology* 8 (1984): 295-309.

Williamson, Michael, and Penny Pence. "Computers in the Basic Writing Classroom Part II: Word Processing." *Research and Teaching in Developmental Education* 7.2 (1991): 101-110.

Developmental and Basic Writing

Bartholomae, David. "Inventing the University." In *When a Writer Can't Write*, ed. Mike Rose. NY: Guilford, 1985. 134-165.

Bizzell, Patricia. "College Composition: Initiation into the Academic Discourse Community." *Curriculum Inquiry* 12 (1982): 191-207.

Davis, Judith Rae. "Basic Writing in the Academy: A Taxonomy of Scholarship." *Research & Teaching in Developmental Education* 7.2 (1991): 11-25.

Enos, Theresa, ed. *A Sourcebook for Basic Writing Teachers.* NY: Random House, 1987.

House, Elizabeth B., William M. Dodd, and John W. Presley. "Problem Solving: A Link between Developmental Writing and Reading." *TETYC* 15 (1988): 81-87.

Hull, Glynda, and Mike Rose. "'This Wooden Shack Place': The Logic of an Unconventional Reading." *CCC* 41 (1990): 287-298.

Marting, Janet. "The Disenfranchisement of Composition Students." *TETYC* 15 (1988): 157-164.

Regan, Sally Barr. "Warning: Basic Writers at Risk—The Case of Javier." *Journal of Basic Writing* 10.2 (1991): 99-115.

Rose, Mike. "Remedial Writing Courses: A Critique and a Proposal." *CE* 45 (1983): 109-128.

Adult, Returning, and Other Non-Traditional Students

Brookfield, Stephen D. *Understanding and Facilitating Adult Learning.* San Francisco: Jossey-Bass, 1988.

Connors, Patricia. "Some Attitudes of Returning or Older Students of Composition." *CCC* 33 (1982): 263-266.

Gillam, Alice M. "Returning Students' Ways of Writing: Implications for First-Year College Composition." *Journal of Teaching Writing* 10.1 (1991): 1-21.

Holzman, Michael. "A Post-Freirean Model for Adult Literacy Education." *CE* 50 (1988): 177-183.

Martin, Judy L. "Removing the Stumbling Blocks: 25 Ways to Help Our Learning Disabled College Writers." *TETYC* 18 (1991): 283-289.

O'Hearn, Carolyn. "Recognizing the Learning Disabled College Writer." *CE* 51 (1989): 294-304.

Rose, Mike, ed. *When a Writer Can't Write: Studies in Writer's Block and Other Composing Process Problems.* NY: Guildford, 1985.

Sommer, Robert F. *Teaching Writing to Adults: Strategies and Concepts for Improving Learner Performance.* Jossey-Bass, 1989.

Gender and Composition

Bauer, Dale M. "The Other 'F': The Feminist in the Classroom." *CE* 52 (1990): 385-396.

Belenky, Mary Field, et al. "Toward an Education for Women." *Women's Ways of Knowing: The Development of Self, Voice, and Mind.* NY: Basic, 1986. 190-213.

Bleich, David. "Genders of Writing." *JAC* 9 (1989): 10-25.

Gabriel, Susan L., and Isaiah Smithson, eds. *Gender in the Classroom: Power and Pedagogy.* Chicago: U of Illinois P, 1990.

Gannett, Cinthia. *Gender and the Journal: Diaries and Academic Discourse.* Albany: SUNY P, 1992.

Greenwood, Claudia M. "'It's Scary at First': Reentry Women in College Composition Classes." *TETYC* 17 (1990): 133-142.

Hunter, Susan. "A Woman's Place *Is* in the Composition Classroom." *RR* 9 (1991): 230-245.

Lassner, Phyllis. "Bridging Composition and Women's Studies: The Work of Ann E. Berthoff and Susanne K. Langer." *Journal of Teaching Writing* 10.1 (1991): 60-66.

Lunsford, Andrea, and Lisa Ede. "Rhetoric in a New Key: Women and Collaboration." *RR* 8 (1990): 234-241.

Osborn, Susan. "'Revision/Re-Vision': A Feminist Writing Class." *RR* 9 (1991): 258-273.

Reichert, Pegeen. "A Contributing Listener and Other Composition Wives: Reading and Writing the Feminine Metaphors in Composition Studies." *JAC* 16.1 (1996): 141-157.

Tedesco, Janis. "Women's Ways of Knowing/Women's Ways of Composing." *RR* 9 (1991): 246-257.

Reading Critically

Bauso, Jean Arrington. "Incorporating Reading Logs into a Literature Course." *TETYC* 15 (1988): 255-261.

Cooper, Jan, Rick Evans, and Elizabeth Robertson. *Teaching College Students to Read Analytically: An Individualized Approach.* Urbana: NCTE, 1985.

Gilbert, Pam. "From Voice to Text: Reconsidering Writing and Reading in the English Classroom." *EE* 23 (1991): 195-211.

Haas, Christina, and Linda Flower. "Rhetorical Reading Strategies and the Construction of Meaning." *CCC* 39 (1988): 167-184.

Sheridan, Daniel. "Changing Business as Usual: Reader Response in the Classroom." *CE* 53 (1991): 804-814.

Community, Collaboration, Conferencing

Arkin, Marian, and Barbara Shollar. *The Writing Tutor.* NY: Longman, 1982.

Bishop, Wendy. "Helping Peer Writing Groups Succeed." *Teaching English in the Two-Year College* 15 (1988): 120-125.

Bizzaro, Patrick, and Stuart Werner. "Collaboration of Teacher and Counselor in Basic Writing." *CCC* 38 (1987): 397-425.

Bruffee, Kenneth A. "Collaborative Learning and 'The Conversation of Mankind'." *CE* 46 (1984): 635-652.

———. "Social Construction, Language, and the Authority of Language: A Bibliographical Essay." *CE* 48 (1986): 773-790.

Fontaine, Sheryl L. "The Unfinished Story of the Interpretative Community." *RR* 7 (1988): 86-96.

Garrison, Roger. *One-to-One: Making Writing Instruction Effective.* Instructor's Manual to accompany Garrison's *How a Writer Works.* NY: Harper, 1981.

———. "One-to-One: Tutorial Instruction in Freshman Composition." *New Directions for Community Colleges* 2 (Spring 1974): 55-84.

Golub, Jeff, et al., ed. *Focus on Collaborative Learning: Classroom Practices in Teaching English,* 1988. Urbana, IL: NCTE, 1988.

Harris, Joseph. "The Idea of Community in the Study of Writing." *CCC* 40 (1989): 11-22.

Harris, Muriel. "Peer Tutoring: How Tutors Learn." *TETYC* 15 (1988): 28-33.

Lyon, Arabella. "Re-presenting Communities: Teaching Turbulence." *RR* 10 (1992): 279-290.

Madden-Simpson, Janet. "A Collaborative Approach to the Research Paper." *TETYC* 16 (1989): 113-115.

Reither, James A., and Douglas Vipond. "Writing as Collaboration." *CE* 51 (1989): 855-867.

Shollar, Barbara. *Tutoring Reading and Academic Survival Skills.* NY: Longman, 1982.

Simmons, Jo An McGuire. "The One-to-One Method of Teaching Composition." *CCC* 35 (1984): 227-229.

Trimbur, John. "Consensus and Difference in Collaborative Learning." *CE* 51 (1989): 602-616.

Willey, R. J. "Fostering Audience Awareness through Interpretative Communities." *TETYC* 19 (1992): 148-155.

Writing Across the Curriculum

Dick, John A. R., and Robert M. Esch. "Dialogues Across Disciplines: A Plan for Faculty Discussions of Writing Across the Curriculum." *CCC* 36 (1985): 178-182.

Fulwiler, Toby, and Art Young, eds. *Language Connections: Writing and Reading Across the Curriculum.* Urbana, IL: NCTE, 1978.

O'Dell, Lee, and Dixie Goswami. "Writing in a Non-Academic Setting." In *New Directions in Composition Research*, ed. Richard Beach and Lillian S. Bridwell. NY: Guilford, 1984.

Parker, Robert. "The 'Language Across the Curriculum' Movement: A Brief Overview and Bibliography." *CCC* 36 (1985): 173-178.

Russell, David R. "Writing Across the Curriculum in Historical Perspective: Toward a Social Interpretation." *CE* 52 (1990): 52-73.

Siegel, Muffy E. A., and Toby Olson, eds. *Writing Talks: Views on Teaching Writing from across the Professions.* NJ: Boynton/Cook, 1983.

Writing Centers and Other Support Services

Besser, Pam. "Bridging the Gap: The Theoretically and Pedagogically Efficient Writing Center." *Writing Lab Newsletter* 16 (Nov. 1991): 6-8.

Calabrese, Marylyn E. "'Will You Proofread My Paper?': Responding to Student Writing in the Writing Center." *Writing Lab Newsletter* 15 (Jan. 1991): 12-15.

Cosgrove, Cornelius. "Explaining and Justifying Writing Centers: An Example." *Bridging Learning Communities.* Ed. Benneth Rafoth & Lea Masiello. Terre Haute, IN: East Central Writing Centers Assoc., 1991. 175-79.

Davis, Kevin. "Notes from the Inside." *TETYC* 18 (1991): 18-21.

Harris, Muriel. "Talking in the Middle: Why Writers Need Writing Tutors." *CE* 57.1 (1995): 27-42.

Healy, Dave. "Specialists vs. Generalists: Managing the Writing Center— Learning Center Connection. *Writing Lab Newsletter* 15 (May 1991): 11-16.

Hubbuch, Susan M. "Some Thoughts on Collaboration from a Veteran Tutor."

Writing Lab Newsletter 16 (Sept. 1991): 1-3, 8.

Joyner, Michael A. "The Writing Center Conference and the Textuality of Power." *Writing Center Journal* 12 (1991): 80-89.

Maimon, Elaine P. "Tourists, Travellers, and Citizens: Teaching Writing in the Twenty-First Century." *Focuses* 4 (1991): 109-115.

North, Stephen M. "The Idea of a Writing Center." *CE* 46 (1984): 433-446.

Perdue, Virginia. "Writing Center Faculty in Academia: Another Look at Our Institutional Status." *WPA: Writing Program Administration* 15 (Fall/ Winter 1991): 13-23.

Powers, Suzanne. "What Composition Teachers Need to Know about Writing Centers." *Freshman English News* 19.2 (Spring 1991): 15-21.

Wolff, William C., ed. "Annotated Bibliography of Scholarship on Writing Centers and Related Topics." Published annually in *Focuses*.

Culturally and Linguistically Diverse Students

Daniels, Harvey A., ed. *Not Only English: Affirming America's Multilingual Heritage.* Urbana, IL: NCTE, 1990.

Dean, Terry. "Multicultural Classrooms, Monocultural Teachers." *CCC* 40 (1989): 23-37.

DiPardo, Anne. "Narrative Discourse in the Basic Writing Class: Meeting the Challenge of Cultural Pluralism." *TETYC* 17 (1990): 45-53.

Heath, Shirley Brice. *Beyond Language: Social and Cultural Factors in Schooling Language Minority Students.* Los Angeles: Evaluation, Dissemination, and Assessment Center, California State University, Los Angeles, 1986.

———. *Ways with Words: Language, Life, and Work in Communities and Classrooms.* Cambridge: Cambridge U P, 1983.

Kaplan, R. B. "Cultural Thought Patterns in Intercultural Education." *Language Learning* 16 (1966): 1-20.

Krashen, Stephen D. *Second Language Acquisition and Second Language Learning.* Oxford: Pergamon, 1980.

Labov, William. *The Study of Non-Standard English.* Urbana, IL: NCTE, 1970.

NCTE 1986 Task Force on Racism and Bias in the Teaching of English. "Expanding Opportunities: Academic Success for Culturally and Linguistically Diverse Students." *CE* 49 (1987): 550-552.

Peitzmann, Faye, and George Gadda, eds. *With Different Eyes: Insights into Teaching Language Minority Students Across the Disciplines.* Los Angeles: California Academic Partnership Program [UCLA Center for Academic Inter-institutional Programs], 1991.

Purves, A.C., ed. *Writing Across Languages and Cultures: Issues in Contrastive Rhetoric.* Beverly Hills, CA: Sage, 1988.

Rigg, Pat, and Virginia C. Allen, eds. *When They Don't All Speak English: Integrating the ESL Student into the Regular Classroom.* Urbana, IL: NCTE, 1989.

Sarris, Greg. "Storytelling in the Classroom: Crossing Vexed Chasms." *CE* 52 (1990): 169-185.

Shuy, Roger. *Discovering American Dialects.* Urbana, IL: NCTE, 1967.

Smitherman, Geneva. *Talkin' and Testifyin'.* Boston: Houghton, 1977.

Strickland, Judy. "Working with International Students." *Writing Lab Newsletter* 16 (November 1991): 9-10.

Surviving as a Writing Teacher

Booth, Wayne C. "The Common Aims that Divide Us: or Is There a 'Profession 81'?" *Profession 81* (1981): 13-17.

Deen, Rosemary. "Notes to Stella." *CE* 52 (1992): 573-584.

Dunn, Richard J. "Teaching Assistance, Not Teaching Assistants." *ADE Bulletin* 97 (1990): 47-50.

"Essentials of English." *CE* 45 (1983): 184-189.

Goswami, Dixie, and Peter R. Stillman, eds. *Reclaiming the Classroom: Teacher Research as an Agency for Change.* Portsmouth, NH: Boynton Cook/Heinemann, 1988.

Hairston, Maxine. "Breaking Our Bonds and Reaffirming Our Connections." *CCC* 36 (1985): 272-282.

Holbrook, Sue Ellen. "Women's Work: The Feminizing of Composition." *RR* 9 (1991): 201-229.

Kroll, Keith. "Building Communities: Joining the Community of Professional Writing Teachers." *TETYC* 17 (1990): 103-108.

Lunsford, Andrea A. "Composing Ourselves: Politics, Commitment, and the Teaching of Writing." *CCC* 41 (1990): 71-82.

NCTE College Section, "Guidelines for the Workload of the College English Teacher." *CE* 49 (1987): 560A-560D.

Ohmann, Richard. "Graduate Students, Professionals, Intellectuals." *CE* 52 (1990): 247-257.

O'Reilley, Mary Rose. "'Exterminate. . . the Brutes'—And Other Things That Go Wrong in Student-Centered Teaching." *CE* 51 (1989): 142-146.

Peterson, Jane E. "Valuing Teaching: Assumptions, Problems, and Possibilities." *CCC* 42 (1991): 25-35.

"Position Statement on the Preparation and Professional Development of Teachers of Writing." *CCC* 33 (1982): 446-449.

Robertson, Linda R., Sharon Crowley, and Frank Lentricchia. "The Wyoming Conference Resolution Opposing Unfair Salaries and Working

Conditions for Post-Secondary Teachers of Writing." *CE* 49 (1987): 274-280.

Robinson, Jay L. "Literacy in the Department of English," *CE* 47 (1985): 482-498.

Winterowd, W. Ross. *The Culture and Politics of Literacy*. NY: Oxford, 1989.

Acknowledgments

Anson, Chris. "Portfolios for Teachers: Writing Our Way to Reflective Practice" reprinted by permission of Chris M. Anson. In *New Directions in Portfolio Assessment: Reflective Practice, Critical Theory, and Large-scale Scoring* edited by Laurel Black, Donald A. Daiker, Jeffrey Sommers, and Gail Stygall (Boynton/Cook Publishers, a subsidiary of Reed Elsevier Inc., Portsmouth, NH, 1994).

Anson, Chris, and Richard Beach. "Journeys in Journaling" reprinted by permission of Chris M. Anson and Richard Beach. In *The Subject is Writing: Essays by Teachers and Students* edited by Wendy Bishop (Boynton/Cook Publishers, a subsidiary of Reed Elsevier Inc., Portsmouth, NH, 1993).

Bartholomae, David. "Inventing the University." *When A Writer Can't Write*, edited by Mike Rose. Reprinted by permission of Guilford Press: New York, 1985.

Bruffee, Kenneth A. "Social Construction Language and the Authority of Knowledge," Kenneth A. Bruffee, *College English* 48.8. Copyright 1986 by the National Council of Teachers of English. Reprinted with permission. Readers may find a more recent exploration of issues discussed in this article in Kenneth Bruffee's *Collaborative Learning: Higher Education, Interdependence, and the Authority of Knowledge*, Baltimore, MD: Johns Hopkins University Press, 1993.

Dawkins, John. "Teaching Punctuation as a Rhetorical Tool," John Dawkins, *CCC* 46.4. Copyright 1995 by the National Council of Teachers of English. Reprinted with permission.

George Gadda in *With Different Eyes*, edited by Faye Pietzman and George Gadda. Copyright © 1994 by The Regents of the University of California. Reprinted by permission of Addison Wesley Longman.

Harris, Muriel. "Talking in the Middle: Why Writers Need Writing Tutors." Muriel Harris, *College English*, 57.1. Copyright 1995 by the National Council of Teachers of English. Reprinted with permission.

Hull, Glynda. Reprinted by permission: Glynda Hull, "Constructing Taxonomies of Error (or Can Stray Dogs be Mermaids?)" from *A Sourcebook for Basic Writing Teachers*, edited by Theresa Enos, McGraw-Hill, New York (1987): 231–44.

Lunsford, Andrea, and Lisa Ede. "Representing Audience," Andrea Lunsford and Lisa Ede, *CCC* 47.2. Copyright 1996 by the National Council of Teachers of English. Reprinted with permission.

Raymond, Richard C. "Teaching Students to Revise: Theories and Practices," Richard C. Raymond, *TETYC* 16.1. Copyright 1989 by the National Council of Teachers of English. Reprinted with permission.

Schwegler, Robert. "The Politics of Reading Student Papers" reprinted by permission of Robert A. Schwegler. In *The Politics of Writing Instruction: Postsecondary* edited by Richard Bullock and John Trimbur and Charles Schuster (Boynton/Cook Publishers, a subsidiary of Reed Elsevier Inc., Portsmouth, NH, 1991).

Sommers, Jeffrey. "Bringing Practice into Line with Theory: Using Portfolio Grading in the Composition Classroom" reprinted by permission of Jeffrey Sommers. In *Portfolios: Process and Product* edited by Pat Belanoff and Marcia Dickson (Boynton/Cook Publishers, a subsidiary of Reed Elsevier Inc., Portsmouth, NH, 1991).

Straub, Richard. Reprinted by permission: Straub, Richard. "Teacher Response as Conversation: More than Casual Talk, an Exploration." *Rhetoric Review* 14.2 (1996): 374–98.

Warriner, Alison. Reprinted by permission: Warriner, Alison. "'I Didn't Think They Had it In Them': Students Learning From Students." *JAC: A Journal of Composition Theory* 16 (1996) 325–40.